OLD GODS FALLING

OLD GODS FALLING

MALCOLM ELWIN

Essay Index Reprint Series

 BOOKS FOR LIBRARIES PRESS
FREEPORT, NEW YORK

First Published 1939
Reprinted 1971

INTERNATIONAL STANDARD BOOK NUMBER:
0-8369-2045-7

LIBRARY OF CONGRESS CATALOG CARD NUMBER:
73-142622

PRINTED IN THE UNITED STATES OF AMERICA

TO THE MEMORY
OF MY FATHER
*Who founded his business in
the Jubilee Year of 1887
and died soon after this
book was finished,*
and
TO MY MOTHER
*Who married in the Year of
"Tess of the D'Urbervilles"*

CONTENTS

9

CHAPTER ONE

Jubilee England of 1887

§1

EIGHTEEN eighty-seven! Jubilee year, when the British Empire celebrated the completion of half a century with Queen Victoria on the throne. June 21st was the day of celebration, and George Gissing declared the scene 'amazing'. "At night all the great streets were packed from side to side with a clearly divided double current of people, all vehicles being forbidden. You walked at the rate of a funeral horse from top of Bond Street to the Bank, by way of Pall Mall, Strand, etc. Such a concourse of people I never saw. The effect of illuminated London from the top of our house here was strange. Of course, I didn't try to see the daylight proceedings."

So a casual observer might have written after the Jubilee of George V. in 1935. And they had much the same motive for celebration in 1887; in the words of Sir Richard Holmes, Librarian at Windsor Castle under Edward VII, "the Jubilee was a great rally of the people round the Throne; it was the apotheosis of constitutional monarchy, it was the triumph of that unique system which had been built up through the centuries." It was an occasion for hearty self-congratulation by the respectable, self-respecting body of the public which formed the backbone of the British Empire and the bulwark of its security—the men of property who comprised the great new middle-class created by the Industrial Revolution.

These people had more obvious cause for self-congratulation than their grandchildren forty-eight years later, for theirs was the golden age of prosperous complacence. During the half-century since Victoria came to the throne, the discontent prevailing at her accession had vanished from memory; the "hungry forties", when men like Thackeray were republicans, Peel took his life in his hands to repeal the Corn Laws and replenish the the national exchequer with an income tax of sevenpence in the 'pound, and industrial centres were terrorised by Chartism, were a nightmare recollection of the elderly from their childhood. Except for a twopenny war or two on the Empire's far-off frontiers affecting nobody save the wives and mothers of professional soldiers, whose job was the winning of honour and glory, unbroken peace had reigned for thirty years since the Indian Mutiny. Through thirty years the new middle-class had pleasured in the feather-bed of prosperity. When Palmerston, the last of England's aristocratic rulers, died in 1865, the middle-class acquired the reins of government; henceforth the suggestion of the existence of a governing class was an indiscretion to be deprecated as an aspersion upon a benevolent democracy, in which Tom was as good as Dick, and if neither was as good as Harry, nobody must say so.

This artificial attitude was the naïve device of the Victorian parvenu to impose his authority upon the working-class as a substitute for the old system of tradition. Formerly you were either born in the purple or you were not; the gentle-born expected and received allegiance as a matter of course, in return for which they cared for their workpeople as dependents to whom they owed a trust, while the working folk gave service and fidelity as their fathers had given it before them. But the Napoleonic wars and the lean years which followed reduced the landed gentry to penury, while the innovation of machinery deprived the landworkers in the villages of their secondary livelihood. The new generation of the labouring class found itself robbed of its birthright; the owners of the land on which they were born could not afford to employ them and there was no market for the products of the handicrafts practised by their parents. Gradually they were driven to seek a living in the growing industrial centres, where they found in the self-made masters of industry a type of employer utterly unlike their former landlords.

The early factory-owners made their fortunes from sweated labour. They were ruthless pioneers, who had raised themselves from the bottom by hard work, shrewd bargaining, and personal sacrifice, which left them callous megalomaniacs in pursuit of their ambition. Treated like galley-slaves, the factory-workers rubbed the salt of resentment into the wounds of their grievances;

the seeds of class hatred were sown, and eight years after Victoria's accession, there were plenty of agitators, like Stephen Morley in Disraeli's *Sybil*, to point out that she reigned over "two nations; between whom there is no intercourse and no sympathy; who are as ignorant of each other's habits, thoughts, and feelings, as if they were dwellers in different zones, or inhabitants of different planets; who are formed by a different breeding, are fed by a different food, are ordered by different manners, and are not governed by the same laws."

Trade unions were formed to exact justice from the employers. In their origin, they were the inevitable corrective of a national evil. Disraeli was guilty of no exaggeration when he told of families which existed on seven or eight shillings a week, though working for twelve, "sometimes for sixteen hours a day"; boys and girls went to work in the pits at the age of five, women and boys worked naked to the waist side by side in the sweltering atmosphere of spinning mills, and as late as 1869 Charles Reade agitated for simple remedies to preserve workers in the file-cutting trade from disease and early death by lead-poisoning. In the history of trade unions there are many cases where they have abused their power; the seventh Lord Shaftesbury, who secured many reforms in factory conditions, declared that "all the single despots and all the aristocracies that ever were or ever will be, are puffs of wind compared with those tornadoes, the trade unions," and Reade called them a "dirty oligarchy" when collecting cases of their terrorist methods for the writing of his novel about Sheffield, *Put Yourself in His Place*.

Like all democratic organisations, the trade unions mingled evil with good in their achievements, but, good and evil, their activities drew attention to the working-classes as a formidable force in the community. The classes which made a comfortable living in the light of commercial convention looked askance at the less fortunate, who defied law and order to better themselves. They had no tradition, privilege, or pride of birth to give them confidence in their capacity to control their inferiors, whose tendencies to turbulence they dreaded, lest the even tenor of their own comfort might be disturbed. So they took refuge in a religious adherence to the forces of law and order. The blue uniform of the law became sacrosanct; the police, who had been irreverently called "peelers" and "bobbies" by the early Victorian bucks, found themselves addressed with pompous politeness as "officers". Likewise the parsons, accustomed to being condescended to by the nobility and gentry as little better than menials, to paying lick-spittle service for their livings, sometimes even to countenancing the vices of wealthy patrons, now found themselves objects of reverence and importance, for it became an essential of respectabilty to attend Sunday church once, twice, and even three times a day.

Respectability was the bulwark erected by the middle-class to preserve its prestige against revolutionary irregularity. A man might keep a mistress, but he must install her respectably at Richmond while he himself lived with his lawful wife at High-gate; there must be no scandalous divorce or "open living in sin". They appropriated all the virtues, in order to be respected for their possession and seem like a community of Cæsar's wives, above suspicion and beyond reproach. Compelled by the trade unions to make concessions to the working-class, they paraded such concesssions as concrete evidence of their charity and humanity. They gave them Factory Acts, education, and sanitation, recognised the Co-operative Movement, introduced local government, and reformed the poor laws; when they extended the franchise to the working-class, they said in effect, "Now you can have nothing against us—you have as much say in the government of this great nation as we have—you are as good as we are." The era of benevolent democracy had arrived.

"Respectability," wrote George Moore in the Jubilee summer of 1887, "is sweeping the picturesque out of life; national customs are disappearing . . . even the Japanese are becoming Christian and respectable; in another quarter of a century silk hats and pianos will be found in every house in Yeddo. . . . The duke, the jockey-boy and the artist are exactly alike; they are dressed by the same tailor, they dine at the same club, they swear the same oaths, they speak equally bad English, they love the same women." Whoever instituted the fashion of plain black as the conventional formal dress was a diplomat of genius. The eighteenth-century finery which had distinguished the gentleman from the plebeian had vanished; ostentation was decreed "bad form". Plain black, with the stiff white collar, was alike the fitting garb of respectability and democracy. Any counting-house clerk could appear in the same dress as Mr. Gladstone himself! It was the most cunning move of the middle-class, for it bereft the working-class of a great block of its numbers—the "black-coated workers", who came to be grouped, with the small tradesmen and all dwellers in suburban villas, within the inter-mediate category of the "lower middle-class".

To the upper middle-class an artificial convention, respect-ability became the religion of the lower middle-class. The former set an example of impeccable respectability, which the latter followed with the fanaticism of easily gullible ignorance. Thousands of awkward youths commenced a life of respectability like Galsworthy's Gradman, to whom James Forsyte said on engaging him: "Now, Gradman, you're only a shaver—you pay attention, and you'll make your five hundred a year before you've done." And Gradman did—he paid attention, "and feared God, and served the Forsytes, and kept a vegetable diet at night . . . and after fifty-four years in the Law he was getting a round eight hundred a year." And if occasionally a little worry occurred, he habitually consoled himself with the reflection that "the good God made us all."

Gradman was a type. Pandering to the petty ambition alive in every human, the upper middle-class addressed the lower in the same terms as James Forsyte to Gradman: "At present you are nobody, but—if you serve us faithfully, remember your manners, fear God, observe moderation in all things, keep honest, sober, and, above all, respectable—then you may some day be somebody—you may, indeed, if you are lucky and have very exceptional talents, become men like us." There lay the obvious advantage of benevolent democracy; the meanest might be apprenticed to respectability, and having successfully served his articles, Tom might reckon himself as good as Dick and at least feel no conscious inferiority by comparison with Harry. Five hundred a year and a suburban villa qualified for the hall-mark of respectability, enabling the Gradmans to vie among themselves in aping the manners of the Forsytes. Being no mere device, but the creed directing their daily conduct, respectability with the Gradmans was a mania; they were not content with going to church as often as possible on a Sunday, but set aside their best clothes for wear, hid away all newspapers and light literature in the house, forbade all amusements and useful occupations, and allowed nothing but hymns on their daughter's pianos. Ironically the housewives had to do extra work on Sundays, for the ritual included a hot mid-day meal, enabling everybody to assist the unusual tax upon their digestive organs by walking or sleeping in the afternoon, and so mercifully to kill a little of the tedium of every seventh day of their lives.

The Gradmans were not yet in being when Thackeray wrote his *Book of Snobs*, the first classic satire on Forsytes and Forsyteism; hence he omitted the suburban snob, the meanest, cruellest, most inveterate of snobs. This sort of snob hardened its heart against any sense of charity in pursuit of respectability. Fingers of indictment were levelled in malignant triumph at every hole in the armour of a neighbour's respectability to emphasise the impregnability of their own. From not only the adulterer, the thief, the drunkard, and the vagabond, but from their family connections, were the skirts of respectability withdrawn; the sins of a father were visited upon his children, wife, brothers, sisters, and parents. If a neighbour's daughter "got herself talked about", her levity of conduct was never allowed to be forgotten, for it emphasised by contrast the maidenly modesty of her compeers. No Gradman—or Forsyte—employed a domestic servant without a "character"; respectability could run no risk of contamination, and the housemaid found guilty of petty theft, or immodesty with the milkman, had finished her career in domestic service. If she could find neither a husband nor other employment, and was driven by necessity to theft or prostitution, it was the better tribute to the judgment of respectability—the respectable could say in triumph, "I told you so."

The literal Christian might ask if misery must not be the just lot of those daily guilty of malice, mischief-making, and uncharitableness, but the Gradmans were happy in their respectability—or rather they were pleasurably complacent. For happiness was an ideal, and ideals were questionably respectable.

Passion was definitely the antithesis of respectability; it was generally associated with Byron, whose works were too indecent to be allowed in any Forsyte household, and whom Andrew Lang, presumably to discourage youth's taste for the forbidden, described as a poet "without sense or grammar" and "a frost". Marriage followed a courtship approved by the parents on either side; there was usually mutual attraction, with curious anticipation on the bride's side, which she cherished in secret shame before the event, and blushed for inwardly if ever she remembered her feelings afterwards. After the honeymoon, sex for the woman was one of the private natural functions of the body, over which respectability drew such a veil as to suggest their non-existence; she performed her duty, which the husband exacted as he expected his Sunday dinner. A Forsyte might seek secret recreation with a mistress at Richmond, but the Gradmans had no relief from respectable thraldom. For one thing, they could not afford it, but anyhow they valued their respectability too highly to risk it.

Bigotry inevitably springs from the suppression of natural instincts; the evils of the Spanish Inquisition and seventeenth century Puritanism alike arose from unnatural asceticism. As if to insure the security of their respectability against temptation, the Victorian middle-class waged war against everything and everybody suggestive of fleshly pleasures. The Gradmans had no such outlet for the satyric instinct in every male as have their grandchildren; there were no cinemas or sex novels with which to procure a few hours oblivion to posture in the imagination as a Casanova, no fox-trotting to afford close bodily contact with otherwise untouchable women, no low blouses or short skirts to offer fleeting sensations on train or bus, over a counter or up a staircase. Women were beguiled into dressing themselves in a style calculated to reduce fleshly allurement to a minimum. In the whole history of feminine fashion, there have been no such monstrosities as the bonnet, bustle, and red flannel petticoat; only a woman of Queen Alexandra's beauty could have looked attractive in the striped "military" tunic, high collar and stock, bunched-up caged shirt, and miniature Hessian boots, with a silly little straw boater tilted over her nose, which she wore as

Princess of Wales in 1870. Beauty, since it appealed to the passions, was immoral, and ugliness therefore became a compliment to the religion of respectability.

Thus born of Respectability was a greater god—or goddess, since Mrs. Grundy wore petticoats—the great Victorian idol of Humbug. "Respectability," said George Moore, "has wound itself about society, a sort of octopus; and nowhere are you quite free from one of its suckers. The power of the villa residence is great; art, science, politics, religion, it has transformed to suit its requirements. The villa goes to the Academy, the villa goes to the theatre, and therefore the art of to-day is mildly realistic; not the great realism of idea, but the puny reality of materialism; not the deep poetry of a Pieter de Hooch, but the meanness of a Frith—not the winged realism of Balzac, but the degrading naturalism of a coloured photograph." The middle-classes required realism because they lacked the imagination to escape from the material facts of everyday life, because fantasy or romance were only fitted for feather-headed misses, savoured of the old days of aristocratic privilege, and were beneath the level of a respectable adult intelligence. But the realism had to be only superficial; it must not penetrate below the surface to remind the respectable of the existence of things not respectable. There were such people as prostitutes, such places as brothels, such nameless vices as sodomy and lesbianism, but these were not things to be written about. Everybody knew that their time was not entirely devoted to sleep when a man and woman went to bed together—in fact, large families were an asset to respectability as evidence of marital virtue and duty well and truly performed— but the young were expected to believe that doctors brought babies in Gladstone bags till they reached the age to procreate themselves. A man might daily wonder what his neighbour's wife looked like without her hideous clothes on, but no such thoughts must be attributed to a character of fiction. Respectability, like an ostrich, buried its head in the sands of illusion.

Every man of imagination was conscious of the voluminous petticoats of Humbug concealing the nether limbs of truth in Victorian art. Dickens was reproved for the unnecessarily Hogarthian realism of *Oliver Twist*, and Thackeray was uncomfortably outspoken in his early Titmarsh tales and in *Vanity Fair*. Both conformed with practical commercial sense and abjured anything likely to offend as soon as their popularity was established, and when Dickens was asked by Wilkie Collins to say something in defence of Charles Reade against the charges of indecency levelled at *Griffith Gaunt*, he acknowledged that the offending book was the work of "a writer with a brilliant fancy and a graceful and tender imagination," but confessed that, as "the editor of periodical of large circulation," he would not have passed certain passages for publication in his magazine. The first quality of a novel was that it should be suitable for "family reading", an epithet discovered by publishers during the eighteen forties, when the Forsytes were yet young and the Gradmans barely born. Hence the vogue of Mrs. Henry Wood and her sedate magazine, *The Argosy*, during the 'sixties and 'seventies, while the theatre echoed polite plaudits at the genteel comedies of that "genius of the commonplace", the respectable predecessor of Pinero, Tom Robertson.

The truly begotten daughter of Respectability, Humbug was duly deified, and her rites religiously observed by her idolators. The habit of consciously setting an example to inferiors became instinctive; nobody was natural, everybody acting a part—the part of a devout disciple of respectability. In the old days of class distinction, everybody recognised superiors from equals, equals from inferiors, and knew how to address them. Now, with no class barriers, everybody was on their guard, looked with suspicion, and spoke with aggressive self-assertion. After an acquaintance of years, a Gradman was still "Mr. Gradman" to his neighbour —never plain "Gradman"—and a Gradman's wife spoke never of "my husband", but always of "Mr. Gradman". The mask of formality became so habitually worn that, like the mask of Lord George Hell in *The Happy Hypocrite*, it became the natural physiognomy. A woman took off her clothes to go to bed with her husband, and he possessed her body, but formality forbade that either should know the other's thoughts. The cynicism that all women are alike in the dark had more than a physical significance; though a wife showed her body naked, her mind remained clothed in the bonnet, fichu, bustle and petticoats of formality.

Men treated their wives as inferiors because they acted a part before them as before their servants; men set the standard of respectability and women followed it. Once married, a woman ceased to have a personality of her own; unless she wished to risk the reputation of being reckoned "not quite nice", or worse, she resigned all ideas of sex attraction and dressed like a grand-mother; she conceived children as often as she could in lawful wedlock, facing with placid fortitude the repeated agonies of childbirth and, though only less proud of breathing the same air as Dr. Huxley than as Mr. Gladstone, never dreamed of recourse to science for a healthy respite; she devoted her waking hours to domestic duties and regulated her household according to the demands of "the master". The Victorian wife was a mere squaw, at night a concubine, and by day an upper servant.

And just as Forsytes and Gradmans feared the possibilities of self-assertion by the working-class, so they feared the same possibilities on the part of women. With one as with the other, every device of Humbug was invoked to consolidate their security. The most affected fine lady in all Restoration comedy never con-ceived such an extravagance of prudery as fashion demanded for Victorian respectability. Women's underclothes were nameless; she wore neither bodice nor corsets, but had a corsage; her numerous petticoats were skirts; drawers were not supposed to exist, and one looked hastily the other way when seeing a pair billowing obscenely in the wind on a working-class washing line. Nobody used a lavatory; they went to a cloakroom.

"' Naked '" wrote George Moore in *Vale*, "is using a word that nobody of taste would think of using—' unclothed ' or ' undraped '; no reasonable man or woman would object to meeting this sentence in a novel: ' I would give all my worldly wealth to see Venus walk undraped from her bath '; the novelist might even write: ' I would give all my worldly wealth to see Elizabeth Hawkins walk undraped from her bath '; but if you were to write: ' I would give all my worldly wealth to see Elizabeth Hawkins walk naked from her bath ' he would be dubbed a very gross writer by the newspapers."

Even the definite designation of men and women was depre-cated; lavatories were designed for the use of Gentlemen and

Ladies, with the same deference to democracy's susceptibilities as lodgers becoming paying guests.

In the eighteenth century it had been a great lady's privilege to vent her displeasure in a volley of oaths, but Victorian women not only eschewed the mildest expletives, but worked themselves into a sate of hysteria if they overheard a " damn" from a man. Manners and customs worthy of a harem exaggerated their femininity, and man's masculinity was intensified to emphasise his dominion over the weaker sex. Beards and moustaches were the fashion, because they were emblems of man's physical superiority, and the heroes of fiction were no longer engaging young men in the Tom Jones tradition, like Pendennis or David Copperfield, but hirsute he-men, bred in the Kingsley school of muscular Christianity, like Ouida's guardsmen, Rider Haggard's Viking-like adventurers, and the long line of strong and silent from Mrs. Henry Wood to Miss Ethel M. Dell. The club became respectability's device for man's escape from the hothouse artificiality of the drawing-room; though he there indulged in nothing more vicious than a game of cards, or a whisky or two, and the gleaning of tit-bits of scandal and stock-exchange or racing tips, he was pleased to strike an attitude of condescension, twirl his moustache, and look knowing when the announcement of an engagement at the club was greeted by a tittering chorus of " Oh, you men!" Man's eager anxiety to preserve the illusion of the dominant male in defiance of advancing enlightenment, is illustrated in the ever-increasing stridency of masculine attire through the 'seventies and 'eighties till, in the 'nineties, he appeared in the Sherlock Holmes cap, Norfolk jacket, and check knicker-bockers of the bicycling age.

Respectability and Humbug were the middle-class substitutes for the old aristocracy's tradition and privilege. They were fathered by fear—the fear of the middle-classes that others might rise, as they had risen, to displace them from their status in the community and to deprive them of their newly-acquired property. The prevailing emotion of the middle-classes was that of any one of their number invited to dine for the first time with a rich man —wondering if he was correctly dressed for the occasion, if he was saying the right things to his hostess, if he was remembering his *h*'s and drawling his *a*'s, and all the time covertly watching his neighbour to see that he used the right knife and fork for each course. They were never quite sure of themselves, and their uneasiness increased, instead of lessening, with the years.

For all the time fear was driving them into further concessions. Perpetually pandering to the notion of benevolent democracy, they caused the Reform Acts of 1867 and 1884 to colour the pettiest transactions of daily life. Everything was run on democratic lines. Clubs, which had formerly been autocracies under the private commercial enterprise of an individual, like White's and Crockford's, now solemnly elected committees, though these did little but employ a paid secretary to do the work formerly undertaken by the proprietor. Companies had boards of directors annually elected by the shareholders; here again the work was mostly done by a paid secretary, and the election itself was a farce of formality, since the directors inevitably retired by rotation and as inevitably "offered themselves for re-election." It was the same with all the county councils, city corporations, urban and rural district councils and parish councils, introduced to do the work of the old squires and landlords; a salaried clerk did the work, but a number of pompous apostles of respectability had to be elected as councillors to flatter their own self-importance, and to satisfy Tom that he had the same say in everything as Dick or Harry. As for the parsons, they at last found a week-day occupation; they revelled in the organisation of committees and sub-committees for the promotion of the welfare of this and that, on which the charwoman sat side by side with the lady of the manor, and though she never spoke unless spoken to, felt that she was somebody, and at any rate a good deal better than less fortunate charwomen not yet elected to a committee. Church-going being part of the paraphernalia of respectability, the average parson was a high-priest of Humbug; there is no shrewder comment on the parson's power in Victorian suburbia than Wilkie Collins's description in *The Woman in White* of Mrs. Catherick's defence of her character.

" ' I came here a wronged woman—I came here robbed of

my character and determined to claim it back. I've been years and years about it—and I have claimed it back. I have matched the respectable people fairly and openly on their own ground. If they say anything against me now, they must say it in secret; they can't say it, they daren't say it, openly. I stand high enough in this town to be out of your reach. The clergyman bows to me. Aha! you didn't bargain for that when you came here. Go to the church and inquire about me; you will find Mrs. Catherick has her sitting like the rest of them, and pays the rent on the day it's due. Go to the town hall. There's a petition lying there—a petition of the respectable inhabitants against allowing a circus to come and perform here and corrupt our morals—yes, our morals! I signed that petition this morning. Go to the bookseller's shop. The clergyman's Wednesday evening lectures on Justification by Faith are publishing there by subscription—I'm down on the list. The doctor's wife only put a shilling in the plate at our last charity sermon; I put half a crown. Mr. Churchwarden Soward held the plate and bowed to me. Ten years ago he told Pigrum the chemist I ought to be whipped out of the town at the cart's tail. Is your mother alive? Has she got a better Bible on her table than I have got on mine? Does she stand better with her tradespeople than I do with mine? Has she always lived within her income? I have always lived within mine. Ah, there is the clergyman coming along the square. Look Mr. What's-your-name—look, if you please!'

"She started up with the activity of a young woman, went to the window, waited till the clergyman passed, and bowed to him solemnly. The clergyman ceremoniously raised his hat and walked on. Mrs. Catherick returned to her chair, and looked at me with a grimmer sarcasm than ever.

"'There!' she said. 'What do you think of that for a woman with a lost character?'"

Such was the potency of Humbug fostered by Forsytes and Gradmans for self-preservation, and woe betide all who offended against the code of respectability. If they so offended, none was too high for an example to be made of him as a warning to others; Bradlaugh the demagogue, Dilke the statesman, Parnell the leader of a nation, and Wilde the pet of Mayfair, all in turn were sacrificed on the altar of respectability.

By 1887 the goddess of Humbug was in the heyday of its worship, and the middle-classes at the height of their complacency. Nobody knew yet what results would be forthcoming from the universal franchise, but at present there was nothing to worry about; there were eighty thousand unemployed in London, and the police were occasionally called upon to disperse Socialist meetings, but the apostles of progress could triumphantly point out that these turbulent elements were as nothing to the days of Chartism. The Married Women's Property Acts had given all Forsytes a nasty jar, and fashion tended to display the feminine figure more disturbingly, but rabid feminists were few and mostly wholesomely unattractive, and the wives of Forsytes and Gradmans showed no revolt against the yoke of respectability. In spite of respectability's inhibitions, some writers were contriving to be uncomfortably outspoken, but they counted for little, since democracy had taken the precaution to set the artistic outside the pale of respectability. There was much talk of a fellow named Zola, but he was a Frenchman, and everything French was not quite the thing.

Nevertheless, the fortifications of Humbug must needs be carefully strengthened, and the Jubilee was a good opportunity. As Sir Richard Holmes records, though by 1887 "revolutionary sentiments had practically vanished, the fact that they had existed demonstrated the importance of an appeal to the loyalty and good sense of the people. The Jubilee was that appeal . . ." And so the almost mythical Queen was disinterred from the moth-balls of Windsor and, that uncomfortable fellow Randolph Churchill having been lately jockeyed out of the job as Leader of the House of Commons, his successor, Mr. W. H. Smith, an impeccable ornament of middle-class respectability, moved on May 17th that "in celebration of the fiftieth year of Queen Victoria's reign the House should attend at St. Margaret's Church, Westminster, on the following Sunday." The great day of celebration followed on June 21st, and if Soames Forsyte witnessed the same scenes as Gissing, he might have reflected as he afterwards did on Mafeking night: "After all, we're the backbone of the country. They won't upset us easily. Possession's nine points of the law."

§ 2

Even the writing fellows were exceptionally docile in 1887. On the death of Dickens in 1870, Charles Reade was generally conceded to be the greatest living English novelist. His supremacy was especially recognised in America, where he had been frequently reckoned not merely the closest rival but even the equal of Dickens during the latter's lifetime. In his little known but able book on *Modern Men of Letters Honestly Criticised*, published in 1870, Hain Friswell went so far as to ask his readers to "compare Charles Dickens and his pantomime touch with Charles Reade, and you will see how infinitely superior the latter is as an artist." At the time of writing, Friswell spoke with reason, for Reade had published in 1866 a novel in *Griffith Gaunt* far exceeding anything ever achieved by Dickens in loftiness of artistic design and unflagging dramatic fervour. But, as Friswell remarked, Reade was "in his aspirations far in advance of the ruck and vulgar herd of humanity." Men like Dickens, who never more freely revealed the purely commercial nature of his artistic ethics, stood by while the humbugs of the press slandered *Griffith Gaunt* with charges that it was indecent, immoral, and that "the modesty and purity of women cannot survive its perusal." A few enlightened and honest souls, like Wilkie Collins and Edwin Arnold, raised their voices in protest, but the appalling realisation was that a novelist of genius had for the first time unmasked the battery of truth against the forces of Humbug, and middle-class respectability was alarmed into massed reprisals to punish his temerity. The success of respectability is reflected in Reade's reputation to-day; he is known as the author of a great mediaeval romance, *The Cloister and the Hearth*, while *Griffith Gaunt*, one of the most important novels of its generation, in spite of plaudits from time to time by critics like Swinburne and W. L. Courtney, is obtainable only with difficulty.

From the time Friswell wrote, Reade's art declined. He felt the insult to his art as Congreve felt it when Collier attacked the stage—as Hardy was later to feel it when *Jude the Obscure* was traduced—but unlike Congreve and Hardy, Reade did not retire from the lists in disgust. All his life Reade was a crusader. He

was an eccentric, and his vision was often distorted by the spectacles of exuberant enthusiasm and obstinate bias, but he sought
sincerely after truth in his own headlong fashion. He became
rabid in his hatred of Humbug, fought it in every form, and by
introducing polemical truculence into his art, gradually sacrificed
his reputation as a novelist to become the ageing, battered
champion of the movement, peopled by those young enough to
be his grandchildren, for realism in art. His enthusiasm overwhelmed taste and reason; truly Friswell declared that "his
reality is beyond realism." He collected more detail of fact for
the writing of fiction than Lytton Strachey ever dreamed of
collecting for the writing of a biography; if any foolhardy
reviewer ventured to suggest that any character or incident in
one of his books was overdrawn in striving after realism, Reade
immediately dived into his carefully indexed catalogues of
press cuttings and produced black and white evidence that his
fiction was founded on fact.

Reade was an irritant thorn in the hide of respectability,
but the forces were too strong against him. His very sincerity
and courage were handicaps, for he was so far in advance of his
time that it was easy to dress him in ridicule. He was a fine old
boy who had survived his best period, with bees buzzing where
his brains had been, who became so balmy that he developed
religious mania in his last years. So respectability affected to
scoff at him, and when he died in 1884, the press organs of respectability played loud pedal about the greatness of *The Cloister
and the Hearth*, discretely ignored his other books, and encouraged
the readily forgetful public to forget about them.

In 1887 Reade had been three years dead, and there seemed
none to sustain the banner he had borne. Wilkie Collins, who had
given up writing best-selling thrillers for novels of purpose in
Reade's manner but without his inspiration, had two years to
live, but he was long since a back number; he was regarded, as
he is to-day, as the author of *The Woman in White*, which had
appeared a quarter of a century before, and nobody bothered
about his more recent books much more than since. Most of his
contemporaries had predeceased Reade; of the writers sufficiently
eminent for admission to Friswell's book in 1870, Carlyle

Trollope, Bulwer, Lever, Ainsworth, and Charles Kingsley were all gone. Browning, like Collins, had only two years to live, and Tennyson five—Tennyson, who at the age of seventy-seven had just published *Locksley Hall Sixty Years After*, which "disquieted" Mr. Gladstone as "a serious indictment of representative institutions." Of the old brigade there remained only Ruskin, who was old enough to have been taken to respectability's bosom and given honorary degrees by university authorities who deplored his doctrines, and Swinburne, who was happily secured from indiscretion, like a caged canary, in the suburban home of Mr. Theodore Watts-Dunton.

Altogether, the Jubilee was fortunately designed to celebrate the glories of the past fifty years, for there was little to brag about in the present as far as literature was concerned. There were two novelists of genius, one of whom had been writing for thirty, the other for nearly twenty years—George Meredith and Thomas Hardy. Both had been treated by the reviewers with a scurviness sufficient to sour a cherub, and Hardy was soon to turn his back forever on the novel-reading public. Meredith, on the other hand, persevered in "giving the world, not what it wanted, but what he thought was good for it", and as his seniors and contemporaries died off, the public began to recognise his existence. Many tried to read him, failed to understand him, and decided, like Dr. Johnson with Congreve's *Incognita*, that they would rather praise him than read him. Meredith was growing old, and old age was both respectable and to be respected; there was nobody like Dickens or Thackeray, who had obvious genius and yet was readable, so Meredith was duly deified when he was made president of the Society of Authors on Tennyson's death in 1892, and *The Ordeal of Richard Feverel* was reckoned a great book, not because any subscriber to Mudie's Library had ever succeeded in getting through it, but because they hadn't, and because it had been written over thirty years ago.

For the Victorians had a reverence for antiquity characteristic of everybody lacking tradition, like the modern Americans and all democracies in the world's history. The Elizabethans had been lately rediscovered by Adolphus William Ward, who subsequently received a knighthood for it; Shakespeare stood next to the

Bible in every middle-class household; and somebody restarted the hare that Bacon, or somebody who was anybody but Shakespeare himself, wrote Shakespeare—a harmless amusement which has employed the literary leisure of university dons from that time till the invention of crossword puzzles. A new branch of literary journalism was therefore created; popular magazines and newspapers, catering for the demands of intellectual improvement fostered by cheap education, employed men with impeccable university degrees, like George Saintsbury, Edmund Gosse and Andrew Lang, who could digress as easily about Icelandic sagas as they could quote Aristotle or Cicero, to write chatty articles about the classics. Nothing new, therefore, could be great; thanks to cheap education, everybody now knew something, but very little, and they were uncomfortably aware that either Shakespeare or the Bible said a little knowledge was a dangerous thing. Therefore, the great dodge was to appear knowing—that is, you pumped somebody else for their views and built your own about them, so acquiring what Arnold Bennett called "the invaluable, despicable, disingenuous journalistic faculty of seeming to know much more than one does know." If somebody asked your views about Meredith and you had once tried vainly to negotiate *Richard Feverel* or *Evan Harrington*, you said, "I don't quite know. Of course, I've read most of his stuff, but I can never quite get on with him." Eagerly the other fellow said, "I know what you mean. That's the beauty of Meredith—you've got to read him carefully to get what he's driving at. But he's marvellous stuff—a treat after all the rubbish written up for the libraries." And at once you agreed, and got upon safe ground by instancing some of the rubbish turned out by your library, which you had read with real enjoyment, but, of course, would never have dreamed of saying so. The Saintsburys and Gosses were obviously as useful as the Sixpenny Bazaar or Harrod's; you picked up all sorts of scraps of learning from them and trotted them out as your own.

Thackeray was recognised as a master at thirty-seven, and Dickens before he was thirty, but universal education had not yet been hought of, and the educated minority had the courage of their opinions. The Victorians had no standards of taste except respectability, and they were uncomfortably conscious that genius was not to be measured by respectability. After all, neither Shakespeare nor the Bible was respectable, unless you had Charles and Mary Cowden-Clarke's "Family" Shakespeare, or a Bible castrated by one of Mr. Bowdler's disciples. But Shakespeare and the Bible had stood the test of time; hence, the test of time was the only safe standard for the timidity of Victorian ignorance. Tennyson was so old that he was already a classic: Meredith and Ruskin were soon old enough to qualify. And the Victorian fashion subsists to-day, for though the Victorian era is happily dead and decently buried, cheap education is even more intrusively with us. When Meredith died in 1909, Hardy was suddenly hailed as the greatest living novelist, though he had written no novel for thirteen years to remind anybody that he had even been a novelist; when Hardy died in 1928, many people thought Galsworthy hardly old enough to take his place, and preferred Barrie, whose claims on the notice of posterity will probably rest on a single children's play, while the critics belatedly discovered genius in the late Poet Laureate, Robert Bridges, when he published his *Testament of Beauty* at an age when most of the minority who reach it have resumed juvenility and dribble down a bib. And now Barrie is dead, the most convincing evidence that old age is a safe conduct to respectability appears in the unwilling recognition of Mr. Bernard Shaw's genius after a long life spent in making the too comfortable uncomfortable. Unless he lives past sixty-five, genius is recognised only by dying young, like Beardsley, Stevenson, Rupert Brooke and D. H. Lawrence.

According to their standards, therefore, the celebrations of the Jubilee in 1887 could be proud of few living men of letters, apart from the unsatisfactory Swinburne, Meredith, and Ruskin, for nobody else was old enough. It was, in fact, an epoch of transition: Queen Victoria had still fourteen years to reign, but the Victorian era was petering out, and those remaining years, usually called *fin-de-siécle* because they were "the Beardsley period", were really the beginnings of a new era, when a new generation of writers and thinkers was struggling to break down the conventional barriers created by its parents, and make it possible to introduce reasonably intelligent conversation into the

atmosphere, fetid with formality, of the drawing-room. Charles
Reade, after all, had not sacrificed his reputation in vain; there
were many ready to take up the banner fallen from his hand,
though none afterwards remembered to mention that he had
carried it before them.

§ 3

WHO were these valorous young men blossoming, or about to
blossom, in 1887? The answer is some way to seek in available
literary histories, for our critics still follow the pattern of Gosse
and Saintsbury by keeping to the safe well-trodden paths. Week
in, week out, the learned anonymous pundits of the *Times Literary
Supplement* monopolise their editor's valuable space in making
mountains out of molehills from the exhausted stories of the
seventeenth and eighteenth centuries; they will devote a leading
article to an obscure divine who once had dinner with Dr. Johnson,
discuss at length whether Shakespeare cribbed Malvolio's name
from Montaigne, or whether his sonnets are richer "in context
and more pleasing than ever as poetry", if "we are justified in
seeing veiled references" to Lord Southampton in some of them,
and speculate about Congreve's reasons for forsaking the stage
after *The Way of the World* as if the subject was as unexplored
as Shiva's Temple.[1] They know the precise dimensions of the
wart on Cromwell's nose and how many pimples Hazlitt had when
he sued *Blackwood's Magazine* for libel, but appear serenely innocent that anybody ever wrote anything between the death of
Dickens and the declaration of war in 1914, except the few whose
names are household words.

Reference to "the naughty 'nineties" recalls for most people
only Oscar Wilde, Beardsley, the *Yellow Book*, women with beautiful bosoms, bicycles, and Mr. Max Beerbohm. Most of the literary
histories used in schools and universities, after dealing with "the
Great Victorians", conclude with a chapter on "The novel from
1850", treating Reade, Trollope, George Eliot, the Kingsleys, and
finishing with R. L. Stevenson, while a few add a list of names
and titles under the heading of "Writers Still Living", explaining

[1]In issues between July and October, 1937. During 1938 appeared signs of change
in editorial policy.

that "it is beyond the limits of this work to enter upon controversy and discuss" so on and so on. Few text-books are ever
admitted to an official syllabus unless from the pen of university
dons—usually compilers of a syllabus prescribe their own work—
and since university dons as a class are only less remarkable for lack
of originality than ecclesiastics, they must wait for the Gosses and
Saintsburys to give them a lead, which the Gosses and Saintsburys
refrain from doing till they have received a guide in their turn.

There have been only three considerable attempts to deal with
English literature after 1887—*The Eighteen Nineties*, by Holbrook
Jackson, published, not by a university press, but by that enterprising bookman, Grant Richards, as long ago as 1913: *The
Beardsley Period*, by an unjustly under-rated critic, Osbert Burdett
in 1925; and *Modern English Writers* by Harold Williams, first
issued in 1918 and revised in 1935. Each of these has obvious
limitations. Holbrook Jackson's has the blundering uncertainty
of the early pioneer: he is painfully obviously in unexplored
country. Long lists of names are grouped together every few
pages in generalisations; there is little effort at selection and an
oppressive consciousness of groping in the dark. And its very
limitations indicate the huge burden of a task pluckily undertaken;
as Burdett acknowledged, it is "a monument of industrious
research", and all subsequent critics must owe it some measure of
indebtedness, if only as a catalogue. Mr. Williams's book makes
even less effort at selection, nor has it the same value of universality as a catalogue, for it follows the plan of the traditional
text-book; it is divided into the four bleak categories of Poetry,
Irish poets and playwrights, Literary and Intellectual Drama,
and The Novel, and under each head the critic treats one writer
after another as they occur to him, marshalling them together
into groups which serve his convenience, but are little indicative
of comparative merit, motive, or importance. Burdett's book,
on the other hand, is selective; for him the 'nineties "is not a
period but a point of view", and his business is confined to that
intellectual minority which Lane the publisher collected to equip
the staff of *The Yellow Book*. Within the limited range of its
subject, it is likely to remain a standard work when it is old enough
to be dignified into the respectability of a "classic", for Burdett

was a critic of shrewd judgment and sophisticated taste, with a decisive vein of originality and an uncommercial courage of his convictions.

But Wilde, Beardsley, and the *Yellow Book* circle were no more representative of the 'nineties than the Pre-Raphaelite brotherhood of the fifties and 'sixties or the Bloomsbury sisterhood of the nineteen-twenties. It is an irony of democracy that the shrill pipe of the minority echoes long after the majority's reverberations have died away, and the *Yellow Book* coterie has received homage which, if not excessive, is disproportionate by comparison with that accorded to many of its contemporaries. The dice have been heavily loaded in its favour. Against the drab respectability of late Victorian suburbia, the *Yellow Book* writers presented a splash of vivid colour, which was sufficiently tainted with the unhealthy to appeal irresistibly to the respectable. If Wilde and Beardsley had not both died young and both evinced vicious tendencies excusable to respectability only in genius, Wilde being sent to prison for unpleasant habits while Beardsley had the sex mania common to tubercular subjects, it is a safe bet that their fame for posterity would have been much less pronounced. For those whose natural animal instincts are imprisoned and suppressed by the conventions of respectability, the obscene, perverted, or bizarre offer a fascinating allurement; the present vogue for Van Gogh derives largely from his having cut off his ear as a present to a prostitute. Wilde was a witty talker, but his reputation as such was no greater than Theodore Hook's, who is forgotten; he wrote in *Intentions* some brilliant and entertaining criticism, but much less than that by Lockhart, Wilson, and Maginn, which lies hidden in dusty magazines; he produced one brilliantly clever farcical comedy of manners, three comedies which time has proved to have dated beyond redemption, some indifferent poetry, and *The Picture of Dorian Gray*. Many have done much more who now lie forgotten on the shelves, but the criminal trial which ruined Wilde in his life has made his reputation since death. Similarly the names of such *Yellow Book* associates as Hubert Crackanthorpe and Ernest Dowson are remembered, not because either achieved half as much work of merit, as for instance, a writer so neglected as Grant Allen, but because each found a premature death in circumstances outside the pale of respectability, the one by suicide, the other by alcohol.

The Yellow Book was a glorious experiment, a bold and brilliant effort to champion the freedom of artistic expression in the teeth of suburban philistinism, to represent "the mentality which commerce was unable to understand", containing "the kind of product with which commerce was unable to compete", but even so regarded, it was less remarkable than Sir John Squire's effort a quarter of a century later with the *London Mercury*, which endured so much longer, achieved so much more, and so nearly succeeded in effecting a permanent influence on national taste. Nor was it the purple patch of splendid isolation, "the final eddy of an ebbing tide", which Burdett describes; it was only one manifestation of the swelling movement for freedom of expression in art from the rusted shackles of Humbug, just as the Vedrenne-Barker management of the Court Theatre in 1905-6 was another. Each of these manifestations is flung into relief against the background of contemporary art, because each represented the work of an organisation, but the forces against which they directed their energies were the same which oppressed every creative artist of their day.

The literary history, not only of the 'nineties, but of the whole era between 1887 and 1914 is the story of art's struggle against Humbug. Since the relations between the sexes intrude private problems into everybody's lives, democracy's insatiable appetite for instruction demanded that sex relationship should be written about. But democracy also demanded that its respectability must be preserved inviolate; the susceptibilities of its wives and daughters must not be shocked. The two demands were incompatible for the conscientious artist. Novelists had to live, so most of them compromised with conscience, as their predecessors had done, by obscuring or side-tracking the natural course of a story to avoid giving offence. A few, like Stevenson, avoided sex altogether rather than commit artistic dishonesty; a few more took the bit between their teeth, sailed under the wind, and suffered for their pains.

In the theatre, democracy's susceptibilities were guarded by that curious survival from the days of privilege, the Lord

Chamberlain, whose job it was not only to ban entirely the performance of "advanced" plays like Shaw's *Mrs. Warren's Profession*, but to pounce upon any naughty words or suggestions in the same way as policemen kept a watchful eye for street venders of dirty postcards. Novelists suffered under no official censorship and against their bugbear there was no appeal, for a circulating library was a commercial enterprise controlled by a private individual, who was within his rights to decide whether a book would excite complaints from his subscribers. And the circulating library was a power in the land, with whom every publisher strove to curry favour and without whose benediction no novelist could live.

The circulating library was a characteristic product of the Victorian era. When Dickens and Thackeray began to write, the new middle-class obtained its fiction only in serial form, by instalments in shilling monthly numbers or in monthly magazines. The majority could not, or would not, afford to buy three-volume novels issued at half-a-guinea a volume, and though H. G. Bohn soon showed it was possible to produce classics at a price within reach of the masses, current publishing conditions would not allow a cheaper format for copyright fiction. But in 1842 Charles Edward Mudie revolutionised the book trade and adminstered a rude shock to booksellers by starting his circulating library. For an annual subscription amounting to little more than the price of one three-volume novel, Mudie's customer could read all the novels which Mudie chose to keep on his shelves— "nice large handsome books that none but the élite could obtain," as George Moore said, "and with them a sense of being put on a footing of equality with my Lady This and Lady That," which was a pleasing thought for benevolent democracy, in which Tom was supposedly as good as Dick or Harry. And soon from Mudie accrued an additional advantage. At some time soon after his beginning in business, Mudie must have been approached one day by a lady of the new rich bent on her daughter's improvement, who, having explained that the dear child had exhausted Miss Austen, asked for the work of some other recognised novelist. Was there not a certain Mr. Fielding, for instance? No doubt Mudie supplied a copy of *Tom Jones*, which he received back between the drawing-room tongs, and lost a subscriber in consequence. And since Mudie could not afford to lose subscribers, he was careful for the future to exclude from his shelves anything likely to have the same offending nature as Mr. Fielding.

Mudie naturally had his imitators and rivals, the most formidable of whom was W. H. Smith, who extended the system to the provinces by means of his bookstalls on railway stations all over the country. The circulating libraries soon monopolised the market for novels, for who would buy when they might borrow, and consequently no publisher dared to issue a book which might run the risk of refusal at the hands of these autocratic arbiters of the public taste. No better evidence of how Humbug Humbugged itself can appear than by comparison between the books and newspapers of the time. Not till the nineteen-twenties did a British Government deem it advisable in the interests of public decency to forbid the detailed reports of divorce cases, and still the most sordid records of rape and murder may be read alongside the football results and the discreet doings of the British Broadcasting Corporation for the price of a penny. Respectability required that the lecheries and miseries of those, either incapable of suppressing their natural instincts or indiscreet enough to have been discovered in their gratification, should be exposed as a warning to others; Humbug permitted the penny press to make free with the misfortunes of living persons, while it prohibited creative artists from illustrating the problems of such misfortunes in relation to fictitious characters.

The situation paralleled the wildest absurdity in the Gilbert and Sullivan operas, at the inanities of which the Victorians loved to writhe in laughter. It was so absurd that few of the rising generation of writers in 1887 could have foreseen that it would so long endure against all arguments of reason, culture, and common-sense. They had the innocent confidence of youth, and writing on "Reticence in Literature" in the *Yellow Book* for July 1894, Hubert Crackanthorpe said:

"The position of the literary artist towards Nature, his great inspirer, has become more definite, more secure. A sound, organised opinion of men of letters is being acquired; and in the little bouts with the *bourgeois*—if I may be pardoned the use of that wearisome word—no one has to fight single-handed. Heroism is at a discount; Mrs. Grundy is becoming mythological; a crowd of unsuspected supporters collect from all sides, and the deadly conflict of which we had been warned becomes but an interesting skirmish. Books are published, stories are printed, in old-established reviews, which would never have been tolerated a few years ago. On all sides, deference to the tendency of the time is spreading. The truth must be admitted: the roar of unthinking prejudice is dying away."

But the gods of Victorianism were not so easily shaken. Within six months of the date when Crackanthorpe, a young man under thirty, blew this truculent note, the publisher of the *Yellow Book* had jettisoned Aubrey Beardsley in deference to the demands of six of his authors, who feared the contamination of being associated with one whose name was habitually linked with Oscar Wilde's. The same year George Moore published *Esther Waters*, which was followed within another two years by Hardy's *Jude the Obscure*. Both works created a sensation by their outspoken realism. But, in spite of Crackanthorpe, Mrs. Grundy was far from mythological, and the gods of the middle-class could still rise in wrath. The suffragan Bishop of Bradford, the Rev. W. W. How, wrote to the papers to say he had put *Jude the Obscure* on the fire, and then exerted himself to induce W. H. Smith and Sons to withdraw the book from their libraries and bookstalls. Such was still the awe inspired by gaiters that the firm complied, with the servile assurance that "any other books by the same author would be carefully examined before they were allowed to be circulated". They did not have to take that trouble, for, sickened at "the censorship of prudery", Hardy, at the height of his powers, renounced novel-writing in disgust, while George Moore, standing on the brink of popular success, feared to face his destiny by leaping the threatening chasm of disapproval and changed the course of his career.

A year after Crackanthorpe's article, Mr. Grant Richards found that unthinking prejudice was still in excellent voice. Having the job of editing a Christmas annual, he secured a ballad from John Davidson and an article from Grant Allen, on hearing which the annual's publisher demanded to read both contributions in proof before he paid for them, because he wanted nothing from Grant Allen on the lines of *The Woman who Did*, and nothing from Davidson " on the lines of a recent contribution of his to the *Yellow Book*." "Writing of that character," declared this apostle of repectability, " may be Literature, but it is not decency." And when in 1898 Mr. Richards, youthfully venturing where older rivals hesitated, undertook the publication of Mr. Shaw's *Plays Pleasant and Unpleasant* and tried to dispose of the American rights, the head of the Lippincott firm wrote urging him "from the wealth of his experience, from a sense of expediency, and from . . . the prompting of his sense of decency, to have nothing to do with the issue of the ' Unpleasant ' plays," however much he might believe in the "literary value of the ' Pleasant! ' " adding his surprise that Mr. Richards should have thought the book a suitable one to offer to a firm of their standing. As late as 1910 the *Times* Book Club, in the teeth of protests from Arnold Bennett, the Authors' Society, and the Publishers' Association, banned John Trevena's *Bracken* and Mary Gaunt's *The Uncounted Cost* with the same autocratic aloofness as Mudie had refused in 1856 to circulate a volume of Charles Reade's short stories, and Mr. Wells recalls that when he published *Ann Veronica* in 1909, "if I had been a D. H. Lawrence, with every fig leaf pinned aside, I could not have been considered more improper than I was." In spite of all the striving and struggling of everybody with the smallest pretensions to creative art, the great Victorian gods of Respectability, Prudery, and Humbug still maintained the power of their idolatry in 1914. They had sustained some nasty shocks, sometimes their pedestals had seemed momentarily to topple, but they had never been utterly overthrown.

It was the war which tolled the knell of their doom. Respectability was no longer a religion when fathers, brothers, and sons were being hourly blown to eternity. The spirit of service and the bond of common suffering smashed down like cobwebs the conventions which had seemed like barriers of steel through the generations. Men returning on leave, scarred in body and soul from the battlefield, were welcomed home in a wild extravagance of hysterical joy, and every consideration went by the board in the determination to "give the boys a good time." On accepting a declaration of love, young women did not blushingly require their lovers to "ask papa"; they either rushed off to a registry office or went to bed without waiting for the parson to say grace. With a troop train waiting in the station, special constables turned their backs on copulating couples in the waiting-rooms or on seats in the dim lights of platforms. Such excesses were necessarily limited to the duration of war's nightmare, but the cheeks of respectability were bound to burn at the thought that they had ever been allowed to happen, and Humbug could no longer confront the rising generation with the same impregnable prudery. In *All Our Yesterdays*, Mr. H. M. Tomlinson summarises this work of the war:

> "In France we had grown used to opinions which, had they been exposed carelessly in daylight to civilians at home, might have caused alarms from police whistles . . . It no longer shocked us to see Law and Religion derelict, as were other honoured things, on the flood which had left traditional bearings below the horizon of 1914. The talk at most mess-tables in France wandered freely and with slight deference even to the presence of august military rank. Generals were generals, with the privileges due to their degree, even yet they shared the common lot of a day, wherein the wreckage of Society's moral safeguards was like the policeman's battered helmet in the gutter the morning after the joy of Mafeking night. We were looking for clues to a new order, if there were any, because a new order might not be easy to find since most of Europe's younger men had a duty, as good soldiers, to deride and destroy all that priest and schoolmaster had once advised them was of divine ordination. Our elders, in the desperation of their fears, had allowed youth to see how much society had ever deserved its respect and fidelity. That peep, as into the interior of a hitherto revered and terrible family sarcophagus, made even the enemy's machine-guns the less terrible to face. Before the last shot was fired, ancient thrones and altars would be tottering through the work of worms unsuspected."

The old gods fell, and the Victorian era appeared in retrospect from 1920 very like the mausoleum which Soames Forsyte recognised in his Uncle Timothy's house. The change was swift and sudden; Lawrence's *The Rainbow*, suppressed in 1915, could be marketed in a cheap edition in the nineteen-twenties, and a satirical comedy like *Our Betters* was the success of its year in the West End. As Soames reflected, seated beside the Forsyte family vault at the end of *To Let*:

> "The waters of change were foaming in, carrying the promise of new forms only when their destructive flood should have passed its full. He sat there, subconscious of them, but with his thoughts resolutely set on the past—as a man might ride into a wild night with his face to the tail of his galloping horse. Athwart the Victorian dykes the waters were rolling on property, manners, and morals, on melody and the old forms of art—waters bringing to his mouth a salt taste as of blood, lapping to the foot of Highgate Hill where Victorianism lay buried."

By the unruly waters the images of the Victorian gods were swept away. But at the time of writing, in 1937, the flood has assuaged or been temporarily dammed, and time alone will show whether a pipe-smoking survival of the pre-war generation, with the unemployed herd of mitred hogs hanging hopefully to his coat-tails, has succeeded in resurrecting the images and resuscitating the old rites of idolatrous worship.

§ 4

THE business of this book is not to examine social and political evolution, except in so far as it affected the more popular writers of the years between 1887 and 1914. The whole story of Victorian civilisation—how its outwardly splendid structure was erected, like Beckford's mansion of Fonthill, without foundations, how its cracks appeared and alarmingly increased, and how it finally crashed—is told in one of the most brilliant historical studies since the war, Dr. Esme Wingfield-Stratford's trilogy, *The Victorian Tragedy*, *The Victorian Sunset*, and *The Victorian Aftermath*. *Old Gods Falling* owes its title to the household gods of Victorianism, Respectability, Prudery, and Humbug, which were firmly seated in public worship in 1887 and were on the eve of destruction in

1914; the worship of these gods affected every writer of popular appeal during the period, and since a survey of the period's popular literature is here attempted, the title is aptly descriptive.

There can therefore be no suggestion that the writers whose names appear at the heads of the following chapters are the "old gods falling". Which is a comforting reflection, for when the names of nine writers figured as chapter-headings in my *Victorian Wallflowers*, some people conceived it to be a book of essays. It was not; as stated on the first page of the book, *Victorian Wallflowers* was "a panoramic survey of popular Victorian literature, more especially the literary periodical or magazine," against which background were planted nine "wallflowers"— writers of distinction in their time who had fallen into un-deserved neglect. The period embraced was roughly 1817 to 1880; the first wallflower was "Christopher North" and the last "Ouida"; the history of the literary periodical as a literary force, from the early greatness of *Blackwood* and *Fraser* to its decline and fall before the influx of popular education, the new middle-class public, and the penny weekly, was comprehensively attempted for the first time.

Old Gods Falling is in some sense a sequel to *Victorian Wallflowers*, for it begins more or less where the latter left off in the 'eighties and extends the survey of popular literature through thirty years to 1914. But its scheme is necessarily different. The periodical magazine had ceased to function as a literary force in the 'eighties. Many magazines continued to rely for their principal attraction upon the serial story, but nobody took in the *Strand* or *Pearson's* as their parents had taken *All the Year Round* for Dickens or *Cornhill* for Thackeray, though it is true that the *Strand* owed much of its early success to Conan Doyle's *Sherlock Holmes* stories, as it has latterly derived much attraction from featuring Mr. P. G. Wodehouse. But the decline in the magazine's importance was reflected in novelists no longer writing their novels primarily as serials, devising sensational situations for the conclusion of every instalment, as Wilkie Collins always did; they wrote their novels simply as complete books for the obvious reason that magazine serialisation was merely a tributary source of income, the principal market being the circulating library. Novelists had to conform with the demands of their principal market or starve, and since the circulating library was the faithful hand-maid to Humbug and its kindred gods, Respectability and Prudery, the decrees of those gods dictated the nature of the novelist's output.

Nor are the principal subjects of criticism in the following subjects selected on the same grounds as those in *Victorian Wallflowers*. Perhaps some of them might be fairly described as "wallflowers", but none of them could be fairly described as "unjustly neglected", except, perhaps, Andrew Lang as a writer of fairy stories, and ironically, R. L. Stevenson. At a superficial glance, they are an odd assortment—George Moore, first a high priest of realism, finally the god of a coterie as a writer of epi-curean romance, and always a garrulous egotist; Stevenson, a recognised "classic" ever since his early death; Lang the scholar who loved he-men heroes, blood and thunder, his old school tie, and elegance, and contrived to be the most influential critical personality of his age; Rider Haggard, the beloved of schoolboys; Hall Caine, the compiler of the largest fortune ever left by a professional man of letters; Mrs. Humphry Ward, the problem novelist of moral purpose; Locke, the charming story-teller; Arnold Bennett, novelist of the five towns, critic, commercial caterer to popular fancy, a "card"; Galsworthy, social historian of the Forsytes, dramatist, gentleman, and genius. Nobody but a lunatic would attempt to gather separate essays on these subjects into a volume under a generic title.

But their dissimilarity is a cogent reason for their selection, since their work mirrors the entire tendencies of fiction in their time and a survey of their lives and writings unfolds the landscape of the period. If the aim was to select the greatest novelists working during the period, only Galsworthy, Bennett, and Stevenson of these here treated at length could command places, and they would bear company with Meredith, Hardy, Henry James, Gissing, Conrad, and possibly Wells. But neither a book of essays nor an academic text-book is attempted; there is no effort to take refuge in either the specialised detachment of the one or the pretentious superficiality of the other. It is attempted to reveal in panorama the fields of popular fiction in the three decades preceding 1914, to present a general impression as seen from a promontory at a distance. As the casual observer thus glancing over a landscape will not at once recognise its most remarkable features, so the reader of this book will not find his attention called to several great literary figures who have received specialised individual attention from previous scrutinisers.

Obviously this sketching of a vast landscape presents greater difficulties than specialised concentration on a single selected figure. A prodigious universality of reading is required. There may be many who devoured Rider Haggard in their youth, some few of whom have likewise greedily enjoyed Stanley Weyman and Anthony Hope, but how many of these are equally conversant with George Moore or Arnold Bennett? Those who intimately know their George Moore may be equally familiar with Bennett and Galsworthy, but it is long odds against their having much appreciation of Haggard or William J. Locke, and they have doubtless never dreamed of stooping to Marie Corelli or Hall Caine! But even when armed with an enormous consumption of all sorts of fiction, the critic of a period possesses only half of his equipment; to assess the motives inspiring the writing of the fiction he has read, he must absorb the pith of innumerable biographies, critical studies, and contemporary magazines. The fullest achievement of his task is beyond the powers of human accomplishment, for knowledge of no subject of research can be exhaustive; the constructive critic of a period, who has conscientiously tackled his task, can only aspire to the humble hope that he has contributed to the better appreciation of his subject.

No very close critical inspection will be required to detect an apparent inequality of design in this book. George Moore, an inconsiderable writer in the terms of consideration applicable to Bennett and Galsworthy, occupies more than twice the space allotted to either; Stevenson receives an almost equal tribute in length, while Haggard enjoys alone an equal space to that which Seton Merriman, Weyman, and Anthony Hope share with several others. But a continuous narrative, unlike a set of separate studies, requires the creation of atmosphere, and the earlier receive lengthier treatment than the later subjects because the story and analysis of their careers reveals the conditions in which their successors began. The story of George Moore embraces the entire period under review, and for that platitudinous reason, as well as because he early played the part of an anarchial revolutionary against the supreme dominion of Humbug—and in this Jubilee summer of 1887 was busily writing the epitome of his creed in *Confessions of a Young Man*—he is the subject of the next two chapters.

CHAPTER TWO

George Moore: The Comedy of a Card

§ 1

NOBODY in English literature since De Quincey has written so much about himself as George Moore. Differing degrees of doubt have been cast upon all candid autobiographers from Benvenuto Cellini to Frank Harris, so no sensational originality can be claimed for suspecting George Moore's strict fidelity to fact. In some aspects—in his habit of critical speculation, his discursive mingling of anecdote and reflective introspection, his inevitable digressions in pursuit of hares starting from the covers of his imagination—Moore resembles De Quincey. But he lacked De Quincey's intellectual integrity. In spite of abundant evidence that his statements and opinions were tainted by a bias merely human, and savour more strongly of sincerity than those of contemporaries usually exalted at his expense, De Quincey is still periodically accused of malice and the warped outlook of an unsuccessful man. But nobody can accuse him of posturing before a mirror; he had no physical vanity, and his intellectual pose was the guiding principle of his life, which he not only believed in, but sedulously sustained at the sacrifice of all practical considerations of personal comfort.

Moore had the egregious physical vanity of an undersized and insignificant-looking man. One could imagine that he kept a full-length mirror in his bathroom for beginning the day well by smirking in satisfaction at the reflection of his naked charms! Of his physical imperfections, his chinlessness, his spindly legs, sloping shoulders, and womanish hands, his conceit verges on the sadistic and in *Vale* he describes how, as he noticed his mistress looking "pleased and happy" under his caresses, "the thought came into my mind that if Lewis Marshall were to see us lying together he would be astonished by it, for it had always been his conviction that no woman could ever love me." It is characteristic that he felt no gratitude or humility for the passion

46

and affection lavished upon him by a beautiful woman, but sensual triumph at the tribute to his vanity, and self-congratulation that he, with his ugliness, could enjoy a woman as completely as the most handsome and charming libertine of his acquaintance.

"Recollection," he said, "is the resource of the middle-aged," and living daily amongst his memories after fifty, he allowed his imagination to flatter his vanity so that his memoirs, as Messrs. William Gerhardi and Hugh Kingsmill have said of Casanova's, "are not misleading through failing to reveal what he did, but through the addition of imaginary embellishments." In Moore's imagination the cocottes he had paid for their favours became *grandes amoureuses*, betraying their keepers to lavish voluptuousness upon him for nothing; he endowed with romance that least romantic, most mercenary and business-like body of women, the artists' models of Montemartre and Montparnasse; the memory of a woman who had smiled at him behind her escort's back, of a shapely leg in a white stocking, of a glimpse through a half-open door of white shoulders with a plait of yellow hair falling over them, conjured up the tale of an amour that might have been Moore's, was somebody's, and after so many years, in the seclusion of his study, might just as well be Moore's. According to himself, he was an insatiable amorist, but his copious writings about them alone suggest that his amours were not what happened, but what he would like to have happened. He was no Casanova or Frank Harris, whose conduct had forfeited the respect of their fellows, and whose only resource was to seem contemptuous of convention by scandalising; he was a very respectable old gentleman, who very much valued the admiration of his lady friends. That women invariably liked him belied his character of himself as an amorist; with the amorist, women are instinctively on their guard, but they found in Moore a charming and amusing companion, whose graceful compliments they could enjoy because they never took him seriously. Which success with the sex piqued his vanity, and because he could not be a cave man in fact, he posed as a cave man on paper. As a witty Dublin lady is reported to have said, "some men kiss and tell, Mr. Moore tells but doesn't kiss."

"My thoughts run upon women," he confessed in *Memoirs of my Dead Life*, "and why not? . . . Woman is the legitimate subject of all men's thoughts. We pretend to be interested in other things . . . We forget women for a while when we are thinking about art, but only for a while. The legitimate occupation of man's mind is women, and listening to my friend who is playing music—music I do not care to hear, Brahms—I fall to thinking which of the women I have known in years past would interest me most to visit." As he thought of them, licking his lips over the memory of a seductive or compromising attitude his sensuality incited him to enjoy their favours in imagination, and he eagerly wrote down the tale of these imaginary amours for the delectation of the woman of his present acquaintance. This posturing as "a mock satyr" and "a nasty little schoolboy", which his mercilessly shrewd female critic, Miss Susan Mitchell, regarded contemptuously as one of his less amiable eccentricities, was suppressed sexual desire, aggravated by wounded vanity. The elderly *roué* inevitably dresses his reminiscences with sentiment, but Daniel Halévy acutely observed that "*Memoirs of my Dead Life* is not a book of love", and Moore's salacious appetite in his study reflected a man of limited physical experience in sex, who now realised that he was past the age for augmenting it. And so to soothe his vanity he posed, proclaiming himself a shameless sensualist, and as he chattered archly to an amused female companion, occasionally remembering to leer knowingly at her, implying that if years had not mitigated his erstwhile virility, she herself would have been the heroine of one of his fancied orgies.

Though he posed principally for women, and his imaginary success as a seducer was his favourite boast, his insatiable vanity demanded appeasement in everything. All his life his haunting dread was failure, the most crushing possible blow to his vanity. In *Ave* occurs one of the most sincere passages of self-revelation in all the endless farrago of his reminiscences.

"I have told in *My Confessions* how I found myself obliged to give up painting, having no natural aptitude for it; but I do not know if I tell in that book, or lay sufficient stress on the fact that the agony of mind caused by my failure was enhanced by remembrances of the opinion that my father formed of me and my inability to learn at school. I think I am right in saying that I tell in *My Confessions* of terrible insomnias and of a demon who whispered in my ear that it would be no use my turning to literature; my failure would be as great there as it had been in painting."

He not only failed in painting; he failed as a seducer of women, failed as a dramatist, and so feared failure as a novelist that, having attained to a measure of success, he gave it up and devoted himself to what he tried to deceive people into thinking a new form of literary expression.

Frank Harris relates how, in the early 'eighties, Oscar Wilde convinced him that " to write about himself whenever he got the opportunity was the successful line to adopt, at any rate in a democracy." Possibly Moore got the idea from Harris, whom he met some time before writing *Confessions of a Young Man*; in any case, they all had the publicity methods of Charles Reade as an example. Like Reade, Moore laid hold of every available handle of controversy on publishing a novel, and successfully forced himself upon public notice, and when he gave up novel-writing, he devoted himself to writing interminably about himself, partly because his vanity was his most absorbing occupation, partly because he hoped to inveigle his readers into assessing him at his own valuation. For while no man is so remarkable as persistent flattery can delude him into regarding himself, it is equally true that the masses are so gullible that they conceive greatness in anybody who, in his littleness, shouts loudly enough that he is great. Thus, by sheer perseverance in his vanity, Moore came, from being tolerated as an amusing and rather absurd eccentric, to be acclaimed as a genius; the last thirty years of his life were devoted to the elaboration of a legend about himself, constructed with the bricks and mortar of his vanity, and his supreme achievement lay in his inducing admirers to accept the legend.

§ 2

George Moore came of an old Irish family, whose ancient history was probably much the same as any of the country gentry. The Moores of Ashbrook professed descent from Sir Thomas More, but had certainly been settled in Co. Mayo from Stuart times. In the mid-eighteenth century, one, George Moore, migrated to Alicante in Spain and there made a fortune by manufacturing iodine from kelp imported from Galway and by exporting wine, so that he was enabled to return to the land of his fathers about 1790 and build Moore Hall on the slope of Muckloon about Lough Carra. Another George, his son, who married a cousin of the first Marquess of Sligo, was a student and a scholar, who wrote Whiggish history and such tales as appeared in *The Keepsake* of Lady Blessington and Heath's *Book of Beauty*. His eldest son and heir, George Henry, went up to Cambridge from the Roman Catholic college of Oscott about the same time as Thackeray and Tennyson, and sowed a crop of wild oats, including an amour with a married woman and an illegitimate child. He dissipated much of the family fortune in hunting and racing before entering Parliament in 1847 and marrying in 1851, at the age of forty-three, Mary Blake of Ballinafad—possibly a niece or cousin of the beautiful Miss Blake who captivated young De Quincey on the canal boat from Tullamore to Dublin. The eldest offspring of the marriage, born on February 24th 1852, was George Augustus Moore, who dropped the Augustus, if for no other reason than that it was bestowed upon the second of his three younger brothers.

His boyhood was spent among grooms and stables, and though he never excelled at games and was always remarkable for the nerveless clumsiness of his hands, he learned to ride and shoot well. Sent to school at Oscott, near Birmingham, he proved an appallingly backward boy, and when he was fourteen he was ordered by his father to write home a three-page letter daily to improve his spelling. About a year later, according to himself in *Salve*, he had an intrigue with a maid-servant and expressed reluctance about going to confession, but his inference in *Salve* that he was expelled from the school was denied by his brother,

Colonel Maurice Moore, in a letter to his biographer, Mr. Joseph Hone. Soon afterwards his father, who had reverted to racing from Parliament some ten years before, reverted again to Parliament and moved to London, taking his family with him.

"Youth," says Moore sententiously in *Vale*, "is a very unhappy time. Art and Sex driving us mad, and our parents looking upon us with stupid unconscious eyes." But there is little evidence that he was much troubled by considerations of art in his adolescence. "At Moore Hall," he admits, "there was no life except the life of the stable-yard," and his ambition on leaving Oscott was to ride in a steeplechase at Aintree. On his arrival in London, he certainly evinced some preoccupation with sex, for after running wild for a year, the discovery about the house of photographs of chorus girls, in tights and short skirts, decided his father to prepare him for "that very sympathetic asylum for booby sons", the Army, and he went to an army tutor's in the Marylebone Road "to read the *Sportsman* under the table" and back horses with his shillings at the tobacconist's round the corner.

His inclination to art was inspired by an acquaintance with a distant cousin, Jim Browne, "a great blond man, who talked incessantly about beautiful women, and painted them sometimes larger than life, in somnolent attitudes, and luxurious tints." According to *Vale*, Browne's influence and his own wish to learn painting occasioned his attending evening classes at the South Kensington Museum before going to the army tutor's, but the *Confessions* relate that his determination to be a painter "encouraged me to tell my father that I would go to the military tutor no more, and he allowed me to enter the Kensington Museum as an Art student." However, his father's death in the spring of 1870 "gave me power to create myself", and having attended the funeral and informed his mother that he could not spend all his life at Moore Hall going to the cemetery with flowers, he was allowed to return to London to study art, though his guardian, Lord Sligo, vetoed his going to Paris where Browne declared he must go, if he meant to be a painter.

He admits in *Vale* that "it was my sense of the voluptuous and romantic that drew me to Jim and his pictures," and it was the hope of gratifying that sense rather than any real artistic urge, which decided him on painting as a career. He approached art licking his lips like a sex-obsessed adolescent of the respectable middle-class, like Miss Mitchell's "nasty little schoolboy", a studio of his own spelled adventure, "tapestries, models, and preparations for France." He longed to be like Jim Browne and have a mistress, big, blonde, and beautiful, who would meet him in a nook of the Fulham Road behind the back of her keeper, who paid for what he received for love. He aspired high, which was one reason why he enjoyed no serious amours. At Moore Hall after his father's funeral, he had the opportunity of enjoying his *droit de seigneur* with a peasant's daughter; "she was not an ugly girl, but I had been to Lodge Road and had seen Jim Browne's pictures." And

"there was a pretty, tall, fair woman, whom I ran across in Covent Garden on her way to the theatre, and whom I took to lunch. She would have loved me if my heart had not been engaged elsewhere, but, as usual, I abandoned the prey for the shadow. And the shadow was the stately Annie Temple, who dared to listen to my courtship for dread of the rage of her fierce cavalry officer, a stupid fellow who snarled at me once so threateningly at the stage door that Annie must fain refuse me her photograph."

So he had to buy one of her photographs and content himself by painting her portrait from it; most likely he painted her facial likeness above the body of the most voluptuous of Browne's models.

Partly because he invariably "abandoned the prey for the shadow" and partly because of his instinctive *bourgeois* caution, being "naturally endowed with a very clear sense of self-preservation", he neglected those opportunities which were to be the subject of salacious regret in after years of elderly reminiscence. Then, as afterwards, he boasted of dissipations; he haunted the mid-Victorian scenes of iniquity, Cremorne Gardens and the Argyle Rooms, and courted the acquaintance of all the famous demi-mondaines, whose price was beyond his pocket even if they could look without laughing at the singularly unprepossessing, absurdly dandified youth, who must have seemed a scented effigy of Mr. Wells's *Kipps*. His *Confessions* aver that he "neither betted nor drank, nor contracted debts", but the statement is true on only one of the three counts. He never drank, and had so little appreciation of wine that a maid-servant offered a jug of water to his guests when their glasses were filled. But he retained his love of racing, and his biographer tells how he negotiated a secret loan with one of his tenants and escaped from "a serious financial scrape . . . on the plea that he was under age". This scrape apparently was when he put money into the management of the Lyceum production of the light opera *Chilperic*, which E. L. Blanchard described as "the most abominable rubbish", and was produced by the Mansell brothers, the Maitlands of *Vale*, one of whom, Richard Mansell, is supposed to have sat for Dick Lennox in *A Mummer's Wife*.

At the art school he met Whistler, whom he naturally disliked, since Whistler affected such a pose as he himself afterwards adopted. He "despised and hated him when he capped my some-what foolish enthusiasm for the pre-Raphaelite painters with a comic anecdote", and to annoy Whistler, he attached himself to the rival celebrity of the class, Oliver Madox Brown, the son of the pre-Raphaelite painter, Ford Madox Brown, who was hailed as a genius in his teens, but whose untimely death left no evidence of his gifts to the world beyond the two now rare volumes of tales and fragments called *The Dwale Bluth*. Young Oliver's physical ugliness appealed to Moore, "for he seemed to me even more unfortunate than myself, less likely to win a woman's love."

As soon as he came of age, Moore set off for Paris with an Irish valet, and found in place of Browne another mentor in Lewis Weldon Hawkins, the Henry or Lewis Ponsonby Marshall of the reminiscences, who supplied the character of Lewis Seymour in *A Modern Lover*. Like Browne, Hawkins had a mistress, big, blonde, and beautiful, whose name also was Alice, but otherwise he bore scant resemblance to Browne, the leonine, muscular, splendidly healthy animal. He was "a tall, thin young man and yet powerful", lithe, alert, square of shoulder; "the head small and covered with dark brown curls"; a small face saved from girlishness by a broken nose, which "gave character to the face, going well with the soft violet eyes". He had a dissipated look, a fine contemptuous air, and "his manners were winning and easy"; in company he shone, "delighting everybody", men and women alike, and he fascinated Moore as even more an antithesis of himself than Jim Browne.

For a year Moore led in Paris much the same life as in London, revelling at cafés and dance-halls and working casually at the Academie Julian, invariably in the company of Hawkins and his mistress. Early in 1874 he returned to London, renting a studio in Cromwell Mews, where Millais sometimes visited him. Jim Browne came and talked as of old, but Moore had grown *blasé* and no longer admired this apostle of the fleshly:

> "For in London, Lewis was always by me in spirit controlling me, exciting me in a desire to be loved for myself, prompting the conviction that for a young man to go to Cremorne Gardens or the Argyle Rooms, armed with a couple of sovereigns, was merely to procure for himself a sensual gratification hardly on a higher level than that which schoolboys indulge in."

He had, in fact, emerged from the chrysalis state of the undergraduate, and aspired to be a butterfly with wings like Hawkins's.

To Paris he returned after another year, "a sort of minor Lewis," affecting Hawkins's airs and graces as well as his ideas. "The society I frequent is the most viceous (*sic*) and the most splendid in Paris," he told his mother exultantly. But Hawkins broke with his splendid prostitute, and when he found her successors unable to keep him, he had to work for his living by painting china. Concerned at this loss to art, Moore invited him to share an *appartement* with him, while M. Julian, who, according to *Vale*, had an interest in Hawkins unconnected with his art, allowed him to work at his studio without charge. At first, he worked enthusiastically beside his friend and wrote to his mother:

> "I have only one bit of news—I am completely changed. When I think of the follies I have made I can scarcely believe it was myself. I work ten hours a day. If I fail in painting it won't be my fault. The pen is so bad I really can't go on I have rooms of my own hoping all are well . . ."

But soon he saw the poverty of his ability beside Hawkins's, and grew jealous of him. Hawkins won the monthly prize offered by Julian for the best drawing; a party was given in celebration for which Moore paid, and as he listened to Julian's singing of his friend's praises, he envisaged the future with himself "humble and obscure", Hawkins "great and glorious, looking down upon me somewhat kindly, as the lion looks upon the mouse that has gnawed the cords that bound him."

"And one day, horrified at the black thing in front of me, I laid down my pencil saying to myself, 'I will never take up pencil or brush again,' and slunk away out of the studio home . . . to my bed . . . and on that bed under its green curtains I lay all night weeping, saying to myself: 'My life is ended and done. There is no hope for me. All I wanted was Art, and Art has been taken from me.'"

To Moore in his self-pity it seemed that Hawkins "flaunted his superiority relentlessly in my face—his good looks, his talents, his popularity." And unable to bear his society any longer, he packed his bag and fled to Boulogne, without a thought of how his unlucky friend would pay his way without him.

He spent the months at Boulogne in pursuit of a young heiress, recommended to him as an eligible wife by his mother. Confindently he thought he had "the race in hand" with the girl, but it came to nothing; though he professed to have abandoned the chase on finding she had a smaller income than he had thought, it was generally believed that he proposed and was rejected. Returning to Paris, he found Hawkins, to his indignation, still occupying his rooms, and after waiting vainly for his departure, he gave notice of leaving. But Hawkins thereupon found him a fresh *appartement*, and so busied himself over the decorating and furnishing that Moore could do nothing but ask him to stay with him till he had painted a picture and sold it. So they went on living together, Moore forever longing to be rid of the needy friend who wore his hats and neckties and borrowed money he never repaid, no longer under his influence, and seeking new friends of his own.

Having renounced art, he now looked to literature for a

career, a seemingly more absurd ambition than his painting, for the letters published by Mr. Hone reveal that his spelling and punctuation had little improved since Oscott. Nor is it likely that he read even as much as he suggests in the *Confessions*. After reading *Lady Audley's Secret* as a boy, he read everything that came out of Miss Braddon's; at school, he got hold of Shelley, but used his agnosticism and passion for beauty to suit his own pose; on first coming to London, he had devoured Dickens. But how he "would read a chapter of Kant . . . while waiting for my coach to take a party of *tarts* and *mashers* to the Derby" smells a Moorish pose; probably he kept a volume of Kant for that purpose, and it remained forgotten in his baggage till he decided, having abandoned art, to try writing.

According to the *Confessions* he had already made his first literary effort in a comedy called *Worldliness* based on Hawkins's "attempt to marry his mistress to one of his friends" and inspired by reading the works of Wycherley, Congreve, and Farquhar (in Leigh Hunt's edition, for Victorian prudery did not relax sufficiently to permit their reprinting in the *Mermaid Series* till the late 'eighties), which he failed to persuade Henry Neville to produce during his London residence in 1874. But now he read Victor Hugo and Alfred de Musset, and stumbling on Gautier's *Mademoiselle de Maupin*, he found the supplement to Shelley he longed for. "For a long time the reconstruction of all my theories of life on a purely pagan basis occupied my attention", Gautier's book was his Bible, and he always presented a copy to his inamoratas. Under the influence of Maupin, he wrote *Flowers of Passion*, a volume of verse published in London in 1878, with a skull, cross-bones and a lyre embossed in gold on the cover, of which Edmund Yates wrote in *The World* an article on "A Bestial Bard", beginning, "The author of these poems should be whipped at the cart's tail, while the book was being burnt in the market-place by the common hangman." Full of Gautier and Baudelaire and Catulle Mendès, Moore was delighted to be "abused for immorality but not for bad writing", and felt he had achieved "quite a little success" because "none could make out that I write badly although very indecently". Though he had outlived the naïve undergraduate's fascination for the lewdness of a Jim

Browne, he had still to reach that stage in regard to literature; he was only a little guttersnipe shocking respectability by pulling out his shirt.

His first literary friend, into whose hands he gave his first copy of *Flowers of Passion*, was a Parisian journalist named Lopez, who set him off with the notion of a tragedy about Martin Luther because it would be a good part for Irving, and introduced him to Villiers de l'Isle Adam at the "Rat Mort". Villiers introduced him in his turn to Mallarmé, who gained him the *entrée* to the Nouvelles Athènes in Montmartre, where the Impressionists gathered nightly around Manet and Degas. How intimate he was with the intelligentsia of the Place Pigalle is difficult to tell, but he was certainly not so much as he makes out in the vast body of writing he has left about them. Few of them survived long enough for Moore to be of sufficient importance for anybody to ask them about their memories of him, but Mr. Hone tells that Daniel Halévy could find nothing about him in the family papers and Léon Hennique remembered having met him only "four times in all my life". Theodore Duret remembered him as "a golden-haired fop, an aesthetic before the days of Wilde", who "tried to shock and astonish people" and whose "manners were amusing and his French very funny". Even when he wrote *Vale*, Moore had no suspicion that Manet intended a *double entendre* when he told him that "there is no Frenchman in England who occupies the position you do in Paris"; his vanity was incapable of realising that he was just *le petit anglais amusant*, and that Degas must have laughed much more at his snobbery about art than at Hawkins's outspoken *gaffe*. For Degas was the means of his getting rid of Hawkins at last. He took him one night to the Nouvelles Athènes, and thought he would have died of shame when Hawkins expressed to Degas admiration of the art of Jules Lefebvre! In snobbish embarrassment he sought to apologise for his friend's *gaucherie*, until he feared Degas might be thinking him stupid, and then went home to implore Hawkins at white heat to leave him. And Hawkins did leave, perhaps because he recognised that his pigeon had few more feathers for plucking, and his final characteristic gesture was to borrow from Moore's especial lady friend. Hawkins wounded Moore's vanity more than any

man, and Moore took his revenge, tentatively in the *Confessions*
and *A Modern Lover*, completely and cruelly in *Vale* after
Hawkins's death in 1910.

His life in Paris was not long after Hawkins left him. Clouds
had appeared on his financial horizon on his London visit of 1874,
when his mother's brother, Joe Blake (Dan of *Ave*), grumbled at
having to manage his affairs, and suggested that he should "get
sense and come home and collect his own rents". Collecting rents
became a hopeless and dangerous task in the famine-stricken
Ireland of 1878, and Blake wrote to Moore in the tone of an
ultimatum. Not only was his income no longer forthcoming,
but he was in debt to his uncle for "a few thousands". In
the *Confessions* he uses the reflection that "some wretched farmers
and miners should refuse to starve, that I may not be deprived
of my *demi-tasse* at Tortoni's", to introduce a theatrical statement
of his belief in paganism, and affects a fine contempt for financial
considerations. Regarding himself as a brilliant young genius
torn in the bud from the refined artistic setting where he would
naturally have blossomed, he posed as bearing his misfortune
with gaily cynical fortitude, condescendingly deprecating the
lamentations of his admirers over his sad lot. With her actual
letters at his elbow as a model, he concocted an epistle supposed
to come from a lady friend whom he infers to have been his
mistress, though she seems to have confided in him her temptations
to sin with others because she was never so tempted to sin with
him—who attended the sale of his effects at his Paris *appartement*
in a mood of such sentimental sadness as Thackeray recorded at
the sale of Gore House after Lady Blessington and D'Orsay were
ruined. It nearly broke her heart "to see those horrid men tramp-
ing over the delicate carpets"; she sentimentalises over his bygone
luncheon parties and how she read Browning to him on the
balcony; she sorrows that "that pretty little retreat . . . is
ended for ever for you and me", and sighs suggestively of how
"men never appreciate the risks women run for them": She
indulges in sundry recollections flattering to Moore's amorous
powers, and begs him to return to his old haunts. And with a
cynical smirk, the noble exile tosses the letter aside, and shrugs
his shoulders free of Parisian memories, as he would of the lady's

supposed embraces, ere he bravely faces his new distasteful lot.

Such was the Moorish garnishing of much more prosaic facts. On receiving his uncle's "odious epistle", he replied with a plaintive epistle unearthed by his biographer, expressing alarm at his tenants' refusal to pay rent, asking if it meant Communism, admitting his inattention to business matters, but pleading that he never "committed any follies" and never spent more than five hundred a year, though he had been told on coming into the property that he "had ever so much". In spite of his talk of his Parisian splendours, he had most likely kept within the limits of what he conceived to be his allowance, for though he affected disdain for money matters, he valued his personal security and comfort, and his "very clear sense of self-preservation" not only rejected any tendency to reckless magnificence but guided his subsequent conduct. Hurrying to England, he was advised by a solicitor to contest his uncle's accounts, but having alienated family sympathy by unjustified reflections on his uncle's conduct, he raised money on a mortgage to pay his debts instead of instituting an action, theatrically proclaiming that he preferred losing money to having his mind distracted from literature. Discreetly he drew a veil over his doings immediately following this crisis in his affairs; all Paris knew was that the little *dilettante* had vanished from the boulevards, and that his effects had been sold up, including his Japanese dressing-gown and the tame python which he had fed on guinea-pigs.

Apparently he settled down for a year or two to a life approved by his mother and her advisers, going between Moore Hall and and her London house in Merrion Square, and appearing in Dublin society with his sister. He dallied with the idea of settling at Moore Hall as a country squire, but besides a town-dweller's repugnance to a rustic life, he felt a genuine fear of failing at estate-management as he had failed in art, and when his uncle adamantly refused to continue as his agent, he engaged the services of a young man named Ruttledge, selecting him probably because owing to youth and inexperience he was cheap. His tragedy of *Martin Luther* was published but not performed, and though a novel begun in the winter of 1880 was abandoned, he still hankered after a literary career, and for some time in 1880 had a journalistic job at two guineas a week on the *Examiner* under Heinrich Felbermann, who pronounced his services "dear at the price". He had one or two poems accepted by the *Spectator*, which led to his obtaining some occasional book-reviewing, but this soon ceased, because he "was handicapped with dangerous ideas, and an impossible style". The latter defect he blamed upon his long residence in France; admitting that "even ordinary newspaper prose was beyond my reach", he declared that, during his last two years in Paris, "I began to lose my English". But it seems that he had never had any to lose; the letters published in Mr. Hone's biography display the construction, punctuation, and orthography of a junior schoolboy. Most successful writers have revealed some sort of talent for composition even in childhood, but George Moore is a remarkable, possibly a unique, instance of a comparatively illiterate young man who lived to acquire a mastery of fluent prose. His early novels are marred by their crude and clumsy style, and at the age of thirty he might have derived a moneysworth from an "earning while learning" correspondence course of how to become an author; as Mr. Humbert Wolfe has put it, "he started like the stammering Demosthenes, walking on the seashore with pebbles in his mouth to cure his impediment", and as Demosthenes came to be likened by Aeschines to a syren for eloquence, so it is claimed for Moore that "the English language has been brought to a new exercise" in the prose of *The Brook Kerith*.

Like an infant learning to articulate by watching its mother's lips, Moore sought the faculty of expression by abundant reading. Arnold Bennett was yet an urchin under the smoke of the Five Towns, so there was no such manual as *Literary Taste and How to Form It*, and Moore had to select his own books. He started his course of contemporary fiction with Henry James's *Portrait of a Lady*, probably because, being published in 1881, his mother or sister had it on their list at Mudie's. His criticism in the *Confessions* is more understandable than its repetition, tainted with personal antipathy, thirty years later in *Avowals*, for the youthful illiterate might well have thought, with Andrew Lang, that too little happens to justify such a flux of words, whereas the author of *The Brook Kerith* should have remembered the decent dignity

of literary judgment before the petty malice inspired by long
ago impressions. He next turned to W. D. Howells, because his
name was often coupled with James's; Howells has never had
much appreciation in England, and Moore set him down as a
mere imitator of James, recognising in him no kinship as a
disciple of Balzac. He stumbled on Meredith when his landlady
lent him *The Tragic Comedians*—he professed· to have wondered
how she came to be possessed of it, but probably it wore Mudie's
label, being published in 1881, like *The Portrait of a Lady*, but if
there could be a more intangible proposition for the illiterate
than Henry James, it is Meredith, and after tackling three of his
novels, Moore appeased his vexation at feeling himself out of his
depth with the fatuous paradox that Meredith was "primarily
a poet". Forgetting that it was no more commonplace than
George Moore, he was prejudiced against Thomas Hardy because
"a name so trivial . . . cannot . . . . foreshadow a great
talent", and after reading *Far From the Madding Crowd*, decided
that he "was but one of George Eliot's miscarriages". He found
Lorna Doone "childishly garrulous", but though he spoke contemptuously of Robert Buchanan, Rider Haggard, and David
Christie Murray, he seems to have dipped more easily into them
than Meredith or James. Of Stevenson, whom he read with
pleasure, he showed shrewd insight in his criticism, but he
evidently read him later, after the publication of *Dr. Jekyll and
Mr. Hyde* in 1886, and it was not till the spring of 1885 that he
read Pater's *Marius the Epicurean*, "the book to which I owe the
last temple in my soul."

His contributions to the *Spectator*, scanty as they were, served
as an excuse to escape from Moore Hall and escorting his sister
into the Dublin society of *A Drama in Muslin*, and he established
himself at a cheap lodging-house in Cecil Street, Strand, to play
the apprentice to literature as he had to painting.

"I wrote a play or two, I translated a French opera, which had
a run of six nights. I dramatised a novel, I wrote short stories,
and I read a good deal of contemporary fiction."

The French opera was *Les Cloches de Corneville*, in an English
libretto of which Moore collaborated with his younger brother

Augustus, who started his career as a journalist about this time and acted as press agent to Wilson Barrett. He also wrote an article on Zola, which he sent to the French novelist with the suggestion that he should translate *L'Assommoir* into English. In *Impressions and Opinions* and all subsequent re-hashings, Moore suggests that he was on familiar terms with Zola during his butterfly days in Paris, but it appears that he had met him only once—when Manet presented him at a fancy-dress ball. In a letter printed by Mr. Hone, he seeks humbly to recall himself to the great man's memory—perhaps "you have heard my great and intimate friend Alexis speak of me, perhaps also my friend Hennique"—Hennique himself said that he met Moore only four times in his life. He talked so volubly of Zola in after years, as if he had discovered him, that his gullible admirers believed that he really was the first Englishman to advertise Zola and his Naturalism. Yet Charles Reade had been practising the rudiments of "naturalism" when Moore was a boy at Oscott, before he had ever heard of Zola or even *Thérèse Raquin* had been written. In 1879 Reade adapted and produced a version of *L'Assommoir* as *Drink*, a play which roused a storm of comment and enjoyed enormous success. As Moore first met Zola through Manet in 1877 or 1878 and yet failed to follow up the acquaintance till 1881 or 1882, it is more than likely that his infatuation for naturalism was inspired, not of his imbibings at the Nouvelles Athènes, but by seeing *Drink* at the Princess's Theatre late in 1879. As Reade had made a success with a stage adaption of *L'Assommoir*, what more natural than that the literary aspirant, more at home with the French language than his own, should seek to catch the public created by Reade with a translation of the novel?

Moore did not translate *L'Assommoir*, but the project served as a pretext to engage Zola's interest in him, and he called on him at Médan when he visited Paris in 1882, writing up the interview in the society reporter's style initiated by Edmund Yates. "There was never any real intimacy between my husband and Mr. Moore", said Zola's widow. "They had merely agreed to make each other's work known, the one in England, the other in France". The advantage of this agreement between a national celebrity and an unknown novice was manifestly all on Moore's side, and he made use of Zola until he found in Edouard Dujardin, the young editor of two influential reviews, an agent more willing and active in advertising his work, because he had little to lose and the possibility of gain by puffing a writer as much in the making as himself. So Moore could afford to disparage Zola in the *Confessions*, after having sat at his feet and written *A Mummer's Wife* in avowed devotion to the Naturalistic creed; when Zola showed no resentment but calmly explained his inability to write an introduction for the French edition of *A Mummer's Wife*, remarking that it was merely "the eternal law —children devour their fathers", Moore confessed that tears came into his eyes, and "never did I feel so distinct a sensation of my inferiority". But the contrition was momentary, and did not prevent him from gibing eternally at Zola for the rest of his life; he told how he and Huysmans used to "lie on the floor and kick up our heels when we think of him", and he sneered at Zola's "thoroughness" in seeking "local colour" for his novels, forgetting how he himself went on tour with an opera company and lodged for some time in one of Arnold Bennett's Five Towns in search of atmosphere for *A Mummer's Wife*.

Neither gratitude nor generosity was in George Moore. He had few words praise for contemporary writers, and none for any whose work might be called into comparison with his own, especially if he borrowed ideas from them; there is no record of his ever having gone out of his way to do anybody a good turn, unless in his old age he gave advice or an introduction to one of his youthful admirers, and then he would have had the motive of flattery to his vanity.

§ 3

Characteristically, Moore harboured no gratitude for the publisher of his first novel. When he took his lodgings in Cecil Street, he looked about him for some such Bohemian resort of men of art and letters as the Nouvelles Athènes, and the best he could find was the Gaiety bar. Here he met William Tinsley, the Catherine Street publisher, David Christie Murray, Byron Webber, and Richard Dowling. He found them "poor substitutes" for Manet, Degas, and the rest, but probably he knew them better, and familiarity bred contempt. At least they were of use to him and merited kinder treatment than they received in the *Confessions*, where Tinsley is described as "a dear kind soul, quite witless and quite *h*-less", who "conducted his business as he dressed himself, sloppily"—Dowling, one of the Irish legion in Fleet Street inevitable since Captain Shandon of *Pendennis*, as possessing a "flabby face and hands, without distinctive feature except, perhaps, weak eyes"—Webber as "a thick-set man", who "waddled", and had "a red flush in the small portion of his face that was not covered with a black beard."

Webber was editor of a weekly paper called *Life*, and probably Moore met him first when employed by Felbermann, and was first taken by him to the Gaiety. That he was "the chief advocate" for Moore's first novel, *A Modern Lover*, is testified by Edmund Downey, whom Moore caricatured as O'Flanagan, the Irishman employed by Tinsley, who "for three pounds a week, edited the magazine, read the MSS, looked after the printer and binder, kept the accounts and entertained the visitors." Moore's first short story, called *Under the Fan*, appeared in *Tinsley's Magazine*, and he was glad enough "to straddle on the counter" of Tinsley's office and "play with a black cat"—which he affirmed was "the way to be published by Mr. Tinsley"—until Webber had persuaded the publisher to accept *A Modern Lover*, which he had written out "in copybooks from daylight till dark" in his Cecil Street lodgings.

To the despised Mr. Tinsley, who in twenty years had published all sorts of novels, from Miss Braddon to Thomas Hardy, Wilkie Collins to Mrs. Hungerford, *A Modern Lover* was merely the usual gamble with a first novel, but Moore felt even greater anxiety than the average author over a first book. "Am I going to fail again as I failed before," he recalled asking himself. "Will my novel prove as abortive as my paintings, my poetry, my journalism?" The old fear gripped him, and in the relief following publication he was able to write in spontaneous honesty to Zola: "I owe you everything. My book alas is not good. I know it well, but it has succeeded."

A Modern Lover could hardly be called a real success, but it succeeded sufficiently to encourage and banish the bogey of failure. The reviewers were generally kind, but the libraries put the book on their black list. W. H. Smith took only fifty copies and declined to circulate them, except when a subscriber specially asked for the novel, as two country ladies objected to the scene where Gwynnie poses in the nude for the artist hero. Moore at once plunged into press correspondence to air his grievance, as Charles Reade had done so often before him, and he must secretly have exulted in the libraries' attitude, for he tasted the salt of notoriety for the first time. He honestly admitted his craving for "notoriety", citing as an instance how, being invited to a Mayfair reception, he picked a quarrel with Lord Rossmore over a difference in views on Gladstone's Land Act of 1881 and challenged him to a duel. He fetched Hawkins, whom Rossmore described as "an offensive, dictatorial individual", over from Paris to act as his second, but Rossmore refused to treat the affair seriously and it petered out in a mutual apology.

Longing to be the hero of a sensation, he would have liked Tinsley to join him in a fighting protest against the libraries' interdict, and when the publisher declined to offend the arbiters of his bread and butter, he turned from him in disgust and took the idea of his next novel to Henry Vizetelly, that extraordinary adventurer in publishing and journalism, who forty years before had given the needy Thackeray a job on one of his papers, and soon, in his old age, was to suffer imprisonment for publishing translations of Zola. He relates how Vizetelly's suggestion inspired him to seek local colour for *A Mummer's Wife* by visiting Hanley and other industrial towns, whither he went in 1883 with the touring company of *Les Cloches de Corneville*, collecting anecdotes of the touring actor's life. The winter of 1883-84 he spent in Ireland, at Moore Hall, staying with his friend Edward Martyn, and finally at Dublin for the season, again collecting local colour in Zola's manner, this time in preparation for a third novel, *A Drama in Muslin*.

In *Ave* he declares: "I've forgotten how long I lived in the Strand lodging described in *My Confessions*—two years, I think; I was five or six in Dane's Inn, and seven in the Temple—about twelve years in all". He went to Dane's Inn, in Wych Street—the vanishing of which some years later, in building alterations on that side of the Strand, suggested one of Stacy Aumonier's best short stories—on returning to London from Ireland in the spring of 1884, and his pockets were no longer so lean that he needed to live on two pounds a week, as he says he did in Cecil Street. Evidently Ruttledge had contrived a brighter complexion on the estate ; ccounts; anyhow, he did not want for money, as he arranged with Vizetelly the publication of *A Mummer's Wife* on a profit-sharing basis. This novel he finished at Dane's Inn before paying a visit to Paris, where he fraternised with Manet and commenced his life-long friendship with M. Jacques-Emile Blanche, the painter and critic, who, with his father, the doctor of "Spent Love" in *Memoirs of My Dead Life*, gave him "year after year the same affectionate welcome."

He was back in Ireland, writing *A Drama in Muslin*, when *A Mummer's Wife* was published in December, 1884. Wishing to be invited to a state banquet at Dublin Castle to garner local colour for *A Drama in Muslin*, he contrived useful publicity out of the State Steward's reply that the invitation lists were closed, writing to the Nationalist press to vent his spleen. As an important landowner, he was entitled to an invitation; why then was he refused? The reason was obvious; Moore's deliberately calculated eccentricity, his little top-hat, baggy trousers, and high-heeled boots, making him look like the cartooned "Froggy" of a comic paper, his parade of paganism, and his delight in shocking ladies by talking of women with the freedom of the boulevards, were the worst of recommendations to the correct, old school tie atmosphere of the Lord Lieutenant and his staff. But Moore acutely suggested the reason to be that he was a man of letters seeking, not mere amusement, but subjects for study, and the Castle dignitaries were afraid of his publishing their nefarious practices. "It would be presumptuous on my part to hope to unearth any fresh crime," he wrote, "the lists of shame are already filled." And shrewdly self-advertising, he announced that his "writing table is covered with human documents", which would serve to illustrate his opinions of the Castle in his next novel. The Nationalists, eager for any excuse to attack English authority, readily backed him up, and one M.P., hailing him as "our best ally against that stronghold of shame", assured him that he merited comparison with Swift or Junius in his gibe that, after death, the State Steward's "claim to be remembered will be that he refused to invite me to dinner at the Castle."

This publicity came opportunely for the publication of *A Mummer's Wife*, which achieved a success far beyond anything Moore could have hoped for, if he had really considered *A Modern Lover* a success. Few of his friends and acquaintance had thought the preposterous little *dilettante* capable of such a striking novel; the general view is reflected in Mr. Charles Morgan's amusing anecdote of how Mr. Bernard Shaw, informed by William Archer of the book's merit, exclaimed, "Nonsense! But I know George Moore." In *Avowals* the book is said to have been "helped by an enthusiastic Press", but the adjective was hardly apt, for few went further in praise than that "the novel deserves recognition as a serious attempt in something better than ordinary fictional frivolities of the day". It had an attentive press, being noticed in nearly all the important journals, but the majority lacked the courage to be favourable, and while praising the power and reality of the story, deplored its sordidness.

The libraries refused to circulate *A Mummer's Wife*, but Moore —or, more likely, Vizetelly—had foreseen this and published the novel in a single volume at the popular price of six shillings. This was a revolutionary measure in 1885. As Moore said in *Avowals*, "Fiction was issued in the eighties only in the three volume form, which allowed the libraries to dictate what might or might not be written"; with novels published in three volumes at thirty-one shillings and sixpence, few, if any, copies could be sold to private purchasers, and the libraries therefore had a monopoly. In the following year, a writer in the *Fortnightly Review* compared the system of publishing fiction in England with that prevailing in France, where novels appeared in a single volume at a little over half a crown, and best-sellers consequently ran to eighty or a hundred thousand copies, and advocated that publishers should get together and fix upon an agreed popular price for novels. But publishers would not get together or agree, and feared to offend the omnipotent libraries. Vizetelly's six shilling novels, advertised as "Crown 8vo, good readable type, and attractive binding", were a pioneer enterprise, eventually to be universally imitated, though long frowned upon, and even ridiculed, as a recklessly unprofitable innovation.

Nevertheless, Moore secured the rights of *A Modern Lover* from Tinsley, and enabled Vizetelly to bring out a second edition at three shillings and sixpence, while he wrote an introduction for the first of Zola's books to be translated into English, *Pot-Bouille*, published at six shillings by Vizetelly as *Piping Hot!* One reviewer of *A Mummer's Wife*, praising as "intensely pathetic and weirdly sad" the description of "the death of an infant which wears out its little life in convulsions while its mother is in a drunken sleep by its side", had remarked that, "if all the book were as powerful as this, Mr. Moore might fairly claim the title of the English Zola." Moore desired nothing better, and thus openly championing Zola, sought to identify himself with the French novelist. As Zola was stigmatised as a filthy pornographer, his disciple was therefore presumed to wallow in the same dung, and Moore thus obtained the notoriety of a shocker, whose books had a vogue amongst young ladies, to be read in the inviolable privacy of the bedroom, locked up in jewel boxes, and furtively popped under pillows when mothers came with good-night kisses. Thus Moore was able to write to Zola that "all doors are shut, and yet *A Mummer's Wife* continues nevertheless to sell."

As in the case of *A Modern Lover*, he prosecuted publicity by plunging into controversy over the libraries' attitude. His pamphlet, *Literature at Nurse, or Circulating Morals*, was an outspoken attack on the libraries as the handmaids of Humbug. The libraries selected as the basis of their charge of immorality against *A Mummer's Wife* the passage where Kate Ede goes downstairs, risen from bed and scantily clad, to let her seducer into the house, and is kissed in the dark by him. Moore selected three novels then in circulation at the libraries—Mrs. Campbell Praed's *Nadine*, Robert Buchanan's *Foxglove Manor*, and *A Romance of the Nineteenth Century*, by W. H. Mallock—summarised their plots, and quoted scenes from each as suggestive as anything in *A Mummer's Wife*. The argument was elaborated in *Avowals*, where the Bible, Shakespeare and Plato were cited as containing passages exceeding in licence anything in Zola. But these were "classics", and Mrs. Praed, Buchanan, and Mallock had all written unexceptionable books before, whereas Moore had drawn suspicion upon himself with *A Modern Lover*, the title-page description of *A Mummer's Wife* as "A Realistic Novel" was itself a challenge, and the book was issued in a cheap single volume to reach the public in defiance of a possible ban by the libraries. Moreover, he proclaimed himself a disciple of Zola, whose very name stood for obscenity, and he did not pretend to be writing with a moral purpose.

Fourteen years before, the formidable Reade had defended his novel, *A Terrible Temptation*, by pointing out that he had drawn a vicious character in Rhoda Somerset, deliberately making her reprehensible and not whitewashing her into "a well-bred, delicate-minded woman, as your refined and immoral writers would", and therefore the story had a moral purpose. Ever since, Humbug had made a fashion of excusing outspokenness if it served a moral purpose, and significantly those reviewers who praised *A Mummer's Wife* excused themselves with some such saving clause as that of the *Spectator:* "Mr. Moore has not gone out of his way to invest with adventitious attractiveness the sin with which he deals". But Moore disdained to shelter under Humbug's hypocritical device for salving its conscience. Rightly he took the stand that art should be free to deal with life's problems, as was allowed to almost everybody else except imaginative writers. As long before as 1871, Reade had taken the same stand. He pointed out that the newspapers had liberty to report as they pleased criminal cases and divorce court proceedings, demanding the right for imaginative artists to treat the same subjects, and in reply to the humbugging reply of *The Times* that "ours are public duties; his are private", retorted that his English circulation was larger than that of *The Times*, while the sales of one of his novels in America was "about thirty times the circulation of *The Times* in the United States, and nearly six times its English circulation." Moore echoed this argument in his *Confessions*, remarking how, from the volcano of the law courts "the terrible lava rolled unceasingly" through the columns of the newspapers, and "the burning cinders of fornication and the blinding and suffocating smoke of adultery were poured upon and hung over the land." But in his pamphlet he was content to concentrate upon ridiculing the libraries, attacking only one of its institutions instead of the entire citadel of Humbug, and so avoiding the alienation of another even more powerful institution, the press. Consequently, he enlisted some support from the popular press, ever ready for sensational controversy, and his old critic, Edmund Yates, made the pamphlet the subject of a leading article in *The World*, which criticised the libraries in its character of fostering "the wants and interests of every section of the English community."

Published by Vizetelly in 1886, after being serialised in *The Court and Society Review*, *A Drama in Muslin* sustained Moore's reputation for shocking. The satire on convent schools in the opening chapter brought the threat of a libel action, which was averted by the deletion of the offending passages in subsequent editions. The book created sensation and indignation in Ireland. Many of the characters were thinly veiled caricatures of personalities encountered by the author in Dublin society, easily recognisable by all their acquaintance, and Moore would have been venturing into a den of ravenous wolves, athirst for blood, if he had returned to Ireland while the memory of the novel lasted.

But he was quite content to discontinue spending part of each year at Moore Hall and at Dublin. He was eager to enjoy his notoriety in London, and he found another rural retreat on renewing an old friendship of his Jim Browne days with Colvill Bridger, the Colville of *Vale*, whose family lived at Southwick, near Brighton. There he spent the summer of 1886, writing his fourth novel, *A Mere Accident*, the scene of which is laid in these surroundings, while the ascetic hero, who escapes marriage by the "mere accident" of his fiancée's being deflowered by a tramp, was modelled on his Irish friend Martyn, with whom he had lately visited Paris. By this time he had read *Marius the Epicurean* and flung himself into an ecstasy of enthusiasm for Pater; he had also read Huysmans and felt his influence conflicting with Zola's. The result was that *A Mere Accident* fell between the stools of cynical Symbolist decadence and the crudity of realism. None of the reviewers could stomach the casual sordidness of the "mere accident": the *Times* expressed the general view in thinking that the power and pathos of the treatment "only serve to enhance the painfulness of the affair." A more crushing blow came from the admired Pater himself, who, when Moore asked him to review the book, gracefully declined to do so, politely excusing himself as "he was no proper critic of the story" and "the recording of violent acts was not clear to him."

A Mere Accident appeared in 1887, and Moore kept himself in the public eye by issuing in the same year a pamphlet reviewing his own novels, *Defensio pro Scriptis Meis*, and a collection of Irish sketches, *Parnell and His Island*. Deciding that, rather than assume the part of valour by returning to Ireland to face the fury excited by *A Drama in Muslin*, he would abide with discretion in exile, he put his thumb to his nose, with fingers outspread, from a safe distance, by vilifying Irish manners, institutions, and personalities in a swashbuckling imitation of Thackeray's *Irish Sketch Book*. The book was published as a political pamphlet, and illustrates the power of sensational journalism in the unsavoury warfare of party politics. No atrocity ascribed to the Black and Tans some thirty years later exceeded the savagery with which Moore scourged the hide of his own countrymen. Miss Susan Mitchell found more indecency in this book than the novels which were accused of that characteristic, because "it is indecent in the revolting display of his country's hurt". In *Salve*, he pretended that he would not consent to the book's re-issue because it was "mere gabble", but by then he had tired of being an Englishman, and having reverted to his Irish nationality, felt discomfort at the consciousness of this skeleton in the cupboard of his past. In 1887, however, mindful of the Nationalist M.P.'s praise of his taunts at the Dublin Castle authorities, he probably saw himself as another Swift or Junius.

Dividing his time between London and Sussex, with occasional visits to Paris, he was working hard to secure success. He confessed that he found it "very hard to make an income out of literature"—"this year I only made a trifle over four hundred pounds, and this is very little when you consider my reputation for I am well-known not only in England but in Europe. This makes me feel often very anxious." Mistaking notoriety for celebrity, he had not the reputation to which he pretended; in England, as Mrs. Atherton remarks, he was "a mere notoriety", and by being known in Europe, he meant only France, where his friendships with men like Dujardin and Blanche secured the translation of his books, and found him a market for magazine articles. His confession of anxiety can be well understood, for the failure of *A Mere Accident* must have revived the old fears of his complete failure as a writer.

In 1888 his notoriety increased, but in a manner unfavourable to his reputation, by means of the publication of *Confessions of a Young Man* and his association with the prosecution of Vizetelly for publishing Zola in English. Pater was proving an unfortunate influence. He and Huysmans were jointly responsible for the abortion of *A Mere Accident*, and he was now indirectly responsible for the *Confessions*. For Moore declared that "having saturated myself with Pater, the passage to De Quincey was easy", and it is clear that the notion of writing his own confessions was inspired by reading those of the Opium-Eater. To Moore, for whom vice maintained a puerile fascination, and freshly drugged as he was by the unhealthiness of Huysmans, De Quincey's revelations must have presented an absorbing orgy, and his vanity at once showed himself the hero of a similar saga. He neither drugged nor drank, but he suffered instead from sex obsession; he was self-educated like De Quincey, had likewise spent the years of his nonage in haunting theatres and courting the society of genius yet unrecognised, and adopted the pose of art for art's sake which De Quincey had followed faithfully as a creed; if De Quincey had been intimate with Wordsworth and Coleridge, he could profess intimacy with Degas, Manet, Zola, Mallarmé, and many more; probably he even noted that he was almost exactly the same age as the Opium-Eater at the time of writing his *Confessions*. Seeking to claim for the *Confessions* the quality of originality, the aged, ever-revising Moore asserted that he "wrote without a model", as if oblivious that the idea of autobiography had ever occurred to anybody else, but though he usually contrived to avoid mentioning De Quincey, except to link him with Landor and Pater as "our great prose writers", he committed the indiscretion of confessing that he was led to

De Quincey by Pater, and as he first read *Marius* in 1885, the Opium-Eater was fresh in his mind when he wrote his *Confessions* in Sussex during the Jubilee summer of 1887.

The *Confessions* had originality in being the self-revelation of an unusual young man, unafraid of registering his comments however immature and wrong-headed, on what he saw and read and what he experienced of life and people. The book is incomplete, as he admitted, but the obvious suppressions, insincerities, and perversions of the truth reflect the more vividly the personality of the writer and intensify the character of the book itself. If George Moore ever achieved a considerable work of art, it was in the *Confessions*, just as he was never more false to art's integrity than when his vanity forbade the admission of fallibility, and he reiterated defiantly in old age his continued belief in such dictums as Meredith "was no novelist, and will be remembered by his verses" and Hardy was "one of George Eliot's miscarriages". In the sensation-seeking young poseur, such posturings for cheap effect were amusing; in the mature author of *Hail and Farewell*, even in the garrulous old crony of the pundit Gosse in *Avowals*, they were merely contemptible.

Moore took sundry opportunities of reprinting Pater's letter on receiving a copy of the *Confessions*, and not until he came to write *Avowals* thirty-two years later, did he suspect that Pater was poking fun at him under ambiguous phrases of praise. Pater said he read it with great interest and "admiration for your originality—your delightful criticisms—your Aristophanic joy, or at least enjoyment, in life—your unfailing liveliness . . . Thou com'st in such a questionable shape! . . . shape morally, I mean; not in reference to style. You speak of my own work very pleasantly; but my enjoyment has been independent of that." The subtlety was lost on Moore, who had no humour where his vanity was concerned. He was delighted with the letter: "Pater wrote to me," he told one of his brothers, "well, just as he did not write about *A Mere Accident*."

"The book is much admired," he said, "more admired than anything I have done." It was widely noticed, rarely with praise but in that sort of acid criticism which provokes remark, and was consequently widely read. But it cost him the good will of many friends. Besides losing the confidence of Zola, Catulle Mendés and Edmond de Goncourt naturally knew him no more, and de Goncourt got some of his own back by describing in his *Journal* how Moore used to dine at his friends' tables and took notes on his cuff. Degas was amused, but arguing that an artist should have no private life, declined to see him again.

In England, he was a notoriety no longer amusing, but rather to be avoided. Nobody liked to feel they might be sitting for caricature at their own dinner table; ever since Edmund Yates was expelled from the Garrick Club for writing gossip paragraphs about Thackeray, personal journalism had been barred in polite society—formal interviews with recognised reporters were in another category. Moore wrote little of his life at this time, but he must have received a meagre supply of invitation cards for an author so well advertised. But his social ostracism was due perhaps less to the *Confessions* than his association with Vizetelly and Zola. Soon after the *Confessions* were published, Vizetelly was charged at the instance of the Vigilance Society, another of respectability's institutions, for publishing obscene literature in the shape of three of Zola's novels. Though it was found that the books were obscene and had been published for profit, Vizetelly, on account of his old age, was bound over on a surety of £200 and the understanding that the books would be withdrawn from circulation. This was done, but the following year Vizetelly reprinted the books and was again prosecuted. It does not appear whether Moore had a hand or not in urging the publisher to defy authority in the interests of art by reprinting, for Vizetelly pleaded guilty and no witnesses were called. He certainly did not counsel this course of surrender; according to *Avowals*, the counsel employed by Vizetelly "took the fees, but Counsel was very pious and said that he could not go on with the case because to do so, he would have to read the books". So poor Vizetelly pleaded guilty and went to prison, a martyr to the inquisition of Humbug. Four years later, in September, 1893, Zola was the honoured guest of the Institute of Journalists, with a late attorney-general, Sir Charles Russell, among his hosts, and the *Standard* had the decency to remark, "No man ever received a more courteous and respectful greeting than he, in Lincoln's

Inn to-day—yet it is only a few years ago since his English publisher, an old man with a name respected in English journalism, was haled to prison for publishing what at most was but a bowdlerised edition of one of the Sage of Médan's most harrowing dissections of the moral cancer. How changed to-day!"

Moore undoubtedly suffered socially from the stigma attaching to association with the convicted publisher. The American novelist, Mrs. Gertrude Atherton, relates how her sister-in-law and hostess in Paris, on hearing that she had met and talked with Moore, exclaimed in horror that she had spoken to "a man who was arrested in London for writing obscene literature", and how the lady was but "little placated" by the assurance that "it was his publisher, not he, who was arrested." Mrs. Atherton evinces the distaste for dates frequent in feminine autobiographies, but she seems to have met Moore in Paris in 1889 at a dull party, where they amused each other as man and woman do when both are intelligent and one attractive. Moore promptly called on her, and she had much anxiety in getting him out of the house without inflicting upon her sister-in-law "the indignity of meeting him." Finding his calls were unwelcome at the sister-in-law's, he suggested that Mrs. Atherton should meet him at her dress-maker's, but she explained that she "was not permitted to go out alone." When she let fall that she was going to a Boulogne convent to write a book, Moore said: "Good! I'll see you there. I know those convents. There are no restrictions placed upon boarders. We'll walk on the ramparts and I know a charming little restaurant." But the lady "shuddered at the vision of George Moore's face on one side of the wicket and a nun on the other," and headed him off from a Boulogne meeting with a promise that he should see her when she visited London. There she received a note inviting her to tea with him at his chambers—he had recently moved from Dane's Inn to rooms in King's Bench Walk—but she "thought it wise to decline!" Moore, she says, took offence; doubtless cursed me as a hopeless Grundy-ridden Californian, and unworthy of pursuit." Mrs. Atherton was young, and ingenuous even for an American; she saw his "long colourless face that looked like a codfish crossed by a satyr," and a little excited by his notoriety, her imagination conceived him as Adah Isaacs Menken expected to find the poet of Swinburne's impassioned verse. Had she gone to his rooms, her surprise might have been like Menken's! So far from taking offence, Moore's vanity must have exulted at the knowledge of a charming woman's flight from the possibilities of his masculinity, and it is wonderful that Mrs. Atherton did not find herself a heroine of fiction in *Memoirs of My Dead Life*.

The Confessions brought Moore one curious friendship flattering to his vanity. The Marquise Clara Lanza chanced upon the book, was so impressed that she persuaded Brentano's to issue an American edition, and wrote to Moore telling him of her admiration for his work and of her being the means of the book's American publication. She was not only a novelist herself, but a celebrated beauty in New York Society, and naturally Moore was highly intrigued. Apparently they never met, as Moore did not visit America and the Marquise did not come to England, but an intimate correspondence subsisted for twenty years, Moore confiding freely the details of his work, while she advised, criticised, and negotiated the American publication of some of his books. The correspondence ended when he reproached her for conversion to Roman Catholicism; this was soon after the publication of *Memoirs of My Dead Life* in 1906, and the speculation arises that Moore, reflecting upon this long intimacy with a woman endowed with all the gifts of romance, beauty, intellect, wealth, title, whom he had never had the fortune to meet in the flesh, allowed his imagination to play upon the possibilities of a personal encounter with such a woman, and evolved that ludicrous obeisance to his vanity, *Euphorion in Texas*.

CHAPTER THREE

George Moore : Tragedy or Farce?

§ 1

OF the six years between the *Confessions* and *Esther Waters*, Moore wrote few tangible reminiscences. He liked to infer that his art advanced from strength to strength without vicissitudes, and the memories of these years disturbed the serenity of his vanity. Besides the social disadvantages accruing from the *Confessions* and Vizetelly's prosecution, his work was not going well. Almost simultaneously with the publication of the *Confessions*, his fifth novel, *Spring Days*, began to appear serially in the *Evening News*. Though newspapers had serialised novels ever since Harrison Ainsworth's *Old St. Paul's* appeared in the *Sunday Times*, serials were not a regular feature in the leading papers and were usually only taken from novelists of standing. Publication in the *Evening News* was therefore a scoop for Moore, who must have felt that he was well on the way to making big money and an established reputation.

But *Spring Days* proved a complete flop. "Everybody is abusing *Spring Days*," Moore told Madame Lanza ; "the papers say it is the worst book I have ever written." There were hundreds of novels equally worthless in the circulating libraries at the time, but these have long since found their way to the paper mills for pulp or to the sixpenny lumber of second-hand bookshops, whereas Moore saw fit to exhume the corpse of *Spring Days* from its legitimate grave. He excused himself for revising and reprinting the book by professing to find in it a certain "zest", but zest was one of the qualities most painfully lacking. The trouble was that he was not sure of what he was trying to do. In the preface to the novel, which was dedicated "to my friend Frank Harris", he referred readers to the preface of *A Drama in Muslin*, where he "promised a companion book, dealing with a group of young men, in which the women will be blotted out, or rather in their turn constitute the decorative background." *Spring Days*, he said, was the "prelude" to this book, which would be called *Don Juan*. "If I ever write a great novel," he announced to Madame Lanza, "it will be *Don Juan*," and he had some notion of portraying this traditional character as a complex psychological study, instead of "only a pretty boy with whom numerous women fell in love". Yet, after the book appeared, he wrote to Madame Lanza:

> "I am a great admirer of Jane Austen and I said to myself, 'I will recreate Jane Austen's method in *Spring Days*.' It was an attempt not to continue but to recreate *Pride and Prejudice*, *Emma*, etc. Apparently I have failed horribly."

He had indeed! That a writer already the author of four novels should have so little appraisement of his own powers, even allowing for his vanity and his unbalanced critical outlook, seems beyond belief. But in *Avowals*, he asserts his view that Jane Austen "described the society of which she was part and parcel", and invented "the formula whereby domestic life may be described." What seems to have happened, therefore, was that, starting out with his Don Juan notion, he placed it against the background of country society, which he saw in Sussex, and which he intended to treat as he had treated Dublin in *A Drama in Muslin*, then read Jane Austen on remembering that she had written of county society, and finally floundered in a morass of confusion, with Zola pulling on one hand, Jane Austen on the other, and Flaubert and Huysmans in turn hanging on to the hair of his head.

The sales of *Spring Days* were so slight that the surplus copies continued to be re-issued for a long time in a variety of bindings. But in spite of its utter failure, Moore went on to write the promised sequel, which appeared in 1889 as *Mike Fletcher*, and failed only less completely than its predecessor. Moore thought he was writing a masterpiece in this tale of a raffish, unprincipled egotistical bounder and his amours; he told Madame Lanza that his publishers and the friends "who have seen fragments" thought it his best book. Frank Harris was among the friends and ardent in his encouragement, but on reading the completed book, he first decided that it was not so good as *A Mummer's Wife* and then became "loud in his abuse of it". Moore was so shocked that he thought Harris must be mistaken; "it is impossible," he said, "that a man who writes as well as I have done, and am still writing, should be the author of three hundred pages of twaddle." But when he found Harris's to be the general opinion, he came to realise that "*Mike Fletcher* is not good," adding bitterly, "I wish I had known how bad it was and I wouldn't have published it." Few writers, even when just critics, can accurately assess the merits of their own work, and Moore was not a just critic, but he derived no comfort from any such reflection. The humiliation of finding himself to have written rubbish, when he thought he was creating a masterpiece, rankled for the rest of his life; *Mike Fletcher* failed less abjectly than *Spring Days* and is rather more readable, but not only was it the only novel which he never thought of revising and reprinting, but the merest reference to its existence aroused his annoyance.

Mike Fletcher was dedicated "to my brother Augustus, in memory of many years of mutual aspiration and labour", and Gus Moore, mingled with something of George himself, seems to have been the model of the hero, just as the other two principal characters, Frank Escott and John Norton, were drawn respectively from Colvill Bridger and Edward Martyn. The absence of any but the barest reference to his brother Augustus in his manifold memoirs reveals a vein of ungenerous harshness in Moore. When George Moore about 1880 settled in London to try making a living from journalism, his brother Gus was setting out on the same enterprise, and they seem to have shared the rooms in Dane's Inn where Moore lived for four or five years. Apparently an ebullient Bohemian, consorting mainly with the rank and file of the theatrical profession and the working journalists of Fleet Street, Gus Moore was notorious throughout the 'eighties and early 'nineties as editor of *The Hawk*, a somewhat "yellow" specimen of sensational journalism, making a speciality of scandalous gossip which accumulated a sequence of libel actions, quarrels and enemies. Mr. Francis Gribble, who worked for the paper for several years, first met him about 1888—"a tall blond man of rather dissipated appearance—editing his paper in his pyjamas at four o'clock in the afternoon". George Moore contributed to *The Hawk* throughout the 'eighties, and the dedication of *Mike Fletcher* shows that he was still intimate with his brother in 1889. But soon afterwards they quarrelled, on what score does not appear. Gus declared caustically, "If you wish to be friends with George see him once a year," while Moore rejoined, quite unconscious that he was inviting a comparison of pot with kettle, that his brother "must cease to think the whole world is in the wrong." He professed his willingness to continue friendly with Gus and his innocence of the causes of their estrangement, but the omission from his reminiscences of any details relating to the brother who was his daily companion, close ally, and in some sense his colleague, for nearly a decade, suggests a sore which he shrank from disclosing. In decency he could not deride and caricature his brother as he treated others of his friends, so he ignored him as if he had never existed. Perhaps Moore's distaste for *Mike Fletcher* in after years was enhanced by the dedication, a poignant reminder of the differing fortunes attending those "years of mutual aspiration and labour", with his dead brother merely a fading impression on the memories of a few ageing actors and journalists, while he sat in the cosy comfort of Ebury Street, perennially posing about himself for his little public of enthusiastic idolators.

He had obvious reasons for cutting adrift from Gus and *The Hawk*. He had awakened to the realisation that notoriety was not celebrity and an unstable stepping-stone to established reputation. Perhaps he attributed the failure of *Spring Days* and *Mike Fletcher* not a little to the notoriety accruing from the *Confessions* and the Vizetelly case. His tail was down, the old spectre of possible failure hovered at his shoulder, and he had enough of notoriety for the present—at least, the sort of notoriety he had hitherto courted, and associated with Gus and *The Hawk*. He had no further use for Bohemians, either; he longed to be lionised in polite circles, in such society as Madame Lanza would move if she came to London. He had changed his pose, and was modelling his manners on Oscar Wilde and the elegant decadents; it is recorded of him how, on entering a crowded drawing-room, he remarked, looking round him, "I like this room," adding with the traditional æsthete's theatricality, "the wallpaper sets off my yellow hair." And Mr. Gribble remembers how about this time, "he objected to being spoken of as ' the English Zola,'" and would have liked to be called the English Flaubert.

He started another novel. The idea of a story about servants he declared long afterwards to have occurred to him soon after the publication of *A Drama in Muslin*, and he was working on the book which became *Esther Waters* during the summer of 1890. But he worked on it only fitfully; the old fears of failure haunted him, and turned his attention to other branches of literature in the hope that he might there secure the success which he had begun to despair of achieving as a novelist. His old enthusiasm for the theatre inspired him to write a play, *The Strike at Arlingford*, and when it was finished and dispatched for the consideration of John Hare, his spirits were again raised by Frank Harris's rash verdict that it was "the biggest thing" he had done, and he reflected that "it will be so pleasant to have a great deal of money", and how he would visit Italy, and when the play, after its English success, was staged in America, he would go there and meet Madame Lanza. But his castles in the air came toppling down when Hare refused the play, and when Wilson Barrett announced the production of a play about strikes, he bitterly supposed it would be plagiarised from his and swore he would never again write for the stage.

He joined J. T. Grein's Independent Theatre, however, and started a newspaper controversy on the state of the stage with an article for the *Fortnightly*, then edited by Harris, on *Our Dramatists and their Literature*, in which he set up the playwrights of the day like so many ninepins and knocked them down one by one— Gilbert, Burnand, George R. Sims, W. G. Wills, Sydney Grundy, Robert Buchanan, Pinero, Henry Arthur Jones. He described Sims's melodramas as "realism in its naïvest form", whereupon that popular playwright offered the Independent Theatre a hundred pounds if it would dare to produce a play of Moore's composition. In *Ave*, Moore relates how he took up the challenge, after arguing about conditions, but with characteristic consideration for his vanity, implies that he wrote *The Strike at Arlingford* specially for the occasion, suppressing the fact that it had been previously rejected by both Hare and Herbert Tree.

Sims paid up his money, and *The Strike at Arlingford* was performed in February of 1893. "It was not a failure," said Moore—William Archer preferred it to Bernard Shaw's *Widowers' Houses*—but it was no triumph. "A real success under such circumstances was impossible," argued Moore, and grumbled because he "could not get proper actors."

By this time he had made himself a more secure reputation as a critic than as a novelist. His views were unusual and provocative, and when in 1891 he collected the best of his articles for the *Fortnightly* and the *Universal Review* in a volume called *Impressions and Opinions*, issued under the reputable imprint of David Nutt, it was well received. In the preface to a new edition of the book in 1913, Moore fairly stated its value to his career: "The author was sinking in a flood of public disfavour caused by *Spring Days*, and the book that followed *Spring Days* (its name we fear to pronounce), when *Impressions and Opinions*, like a big Newfoundland dog, dived after him and brought him to shore." Read with regard for the time of their writing, many of these papers have lasting interest, and better represent Moore's claims to consideration as a critic than such books as *Avowals* or *Conversations in Ebury Street*, where the rescue of good sense from a farrago of theatrical garrulity is like rooting for truffles in a rubbish-heap. Besides the *Fortnightly* article on *Our Dramatists*, the book includes papers on Balzac, Turgeniev, Verlaine, and Rimbaud, Ibsen's *Ghosts*, Meissonier and the Salon Julian, Degas, and the important essay on "Mummer-Worship."

The last is important as a contemporary comment on Respectability's influence upon the theatrical profession. It is marred by such characteristic over-statement as "the stage was once a profession for the restless, the frankly vicious—for those who sought any escape from the platitude of their personality; the stage is now a means of enabling the refuse of society to satisfy the flesh, and air much miserable vanity." But it bluntly demonstrates how Victorian actors and actresses degraded the dignity of their art by courting cheap publicity—how they emphasised their respectability to remove the middle-class prejudice against the theatre's traditional immorality, advertising their domestic bliss, the actresses posing as prudes or devoted mothers, while actors insisted on their gentility, how they wheedled their way into fashionable society, and how they caressed the cheapest sort of journalism for "interviews". Their evil has survived to flourish tenfold in the twentieth century; in the old days Garrick was a cultured man of letters and Edmund Kean a drunkard, but both received recognition of their genius at their job without regard for their private characters; to-day an actor's stature is measured by his appearance in the illustrated papers and his popularity with fashionable hostesses, and film actresses play a divorce court game of musical chairs on the knees of their husbands to stimulate "human interest" in their professional perform-ances.

The *Athenæum*, which, as Moore proudly reminded his mother, was "the first literary journal in the English language," reviewed *Impressions and Opinions* on its front page, and the book's success gained him the post of regular art critic on another respectable "highbrow" journal, the *Speaker*. His novel about servants and betting was laid aside, probably not unregretfully, for he had no wish for a recurrence of his old notoriety to detract from his newly-found repute as a literary pundit, and such was his new consideration for respectability that he accepted a commission to write a serial story, under the editorial stipulation that it should contain nothing "offensive", for such an unrevolutionary organ as the *Lady's Pictorial*. To Madame Lanza he denied that *Vain Fortune* was a "potboiler", professing to be writing to "please myself", but it is a thin, unconvincing tale of a playwright, whose play fails, and a neurotic girl to whom he is engaged, who commits suicide when he elopes with her friend. As a serial, the story appeared under the pseudonym of "Lady Rhone", but it was published under Moore's own name by Henry and Co., with illustrations by Maurice Greiffenhagen. *Vain Fortune* is remark-able only for the hero's moody meditations at the end of the final chapter:

> "He did not think that he would live long. Disappointed men—those who have failed in their ambition—do not live to make old bones. There were men like him in every pro-fession—the arts are crowded with them . . . One hears of their deaths—failure of the heart's action, paralysis of the

brain, a hundred other medical causes—but the real cause is, lack of appreciation."

The passage has a dual biographical significance; it reveals Moore as aping the conventional æsthete's pose of theatrical fatalism, just beginning to be called *fin-de-siécle*, and it reflects his own bitterness of spirit at the failure of *Spring Days* and *Mike Fletcher*.

If he had not utterly despaired of success as a novelist, he obviously decided to concentrate on the bird in the hand—his growing reputation as a critic. He was art critic to the *Speaker* for rather more than four years between 1891 and 1895, during which time he made those friendships with Wilson Steer, Professor Henry Tonks, Walter Sickert, and D. S. MacColl, which supplied the material for many reminiscences in his garrulous old age. He was so closely identified with art that he appears to have applied for the directorship of the Fine Arts Gallery at Manchester, being refused "on the ground that he was likely to buy too many Manets." His reputation as an art critic was consolidated in 1893 by the publication of *Modern Painting*, a selection of his articles in the *Speaker*, which was reviewed by Pater in the *Daily Chronicle* and MacColl in the *Spectator*, and generally accorded respectful consideration. The French Impressionists were only just coming into their own, *Modern Painting* was a useful handbook or guide for those who wanted to learn about them, and so it remains to-day. As Sir William Rothenstein says, "Moore had attuned his mind and eye to one kind of painting; to great dramatic or imaginative art he was insensitive." *Modern Painting* drew its inspiration directly from the enthusiasm nourished over a *demi-tasse* at the Nouvelles Athènes, and Moore had the gumption to realise the fact. When he was occupying his latter years in making masterpieces of the novels of his nonage, he resisted the temptation to tamper with *Modern Painting*. It stands as it stood in 1893, no longer blazing the trail of a new fashion, but out of date and somewhat uncouth—nevertheless a document in the history of art criticism.

Assured of a small income and a secure position as a critic, he could now afford to speculate in other literary stock with less terror of the bottom falling out of his market. He worked on a drama after Racine's manner, which apparently came to nothing, and he applied himself steadily to *Esther Waters*. He enjoyed writing the chapters on the Derby, "no racing, only the sweat and boom of the crowd—the great Cockney holiday," and his studies of English manners and character inspired him with at least one notable idea, which he intended should be the subject of "one more effort, the most serious I have yet made to do a book . . . a real piece of literature"—the conception of the Englishman in his "habit of instinctive hypocrisy"—"Pecksniff done seriously, and if the feat does not seem impossible, with love." He confided this to one of his brothers in July, 1893, thirteen years before Galsworthy published *The Man of Property*. But he never persevered with the notion, so it remains a matter for speculation as to what sort of a job Moore would have made of Soames Forsyte.

Romance really entered his life at this time. In the autumn of 1893, he picked up a girl of eighteen in France, and had an affair with her lasting five days. "That women may lose their virtue certainly makes life worth living," he observed with satisfaction. But the one recorded serious love of his life revealed him as the reverse of an accomplished amorist. Mrs. Pearl Craigie, well known under the professional pseudonym of "John Oliver Hobbes," wrote asking his advice upon the possible dramatising of one of her stories. In Moore there was no such kindness and courtesy as in Galsworthy, who conscientiously replied to everybody who wrote to him, and he did not reply to the letter till Arthur Symons told him that the signature was the pseudonym of a beautiful and gifted woman, who also had the attraction of being wealthy. He immediately visualised the possibility of such a romance as his vanity craved and his imagination created in innumerable fictions; if he was not actually in love with the lady before he saw her, he was in love with the notion of being in love with her. When he found a society beauty of twenty-seven living apart from her husband, he must have rubbed his eyes before believing such luck; he danced attendance on her everywhere, readily devising an excuse for intimacy by collaborating with her in writing plays. Afterwards he spoke contemptuously of her literary work, and his vanity prevented appreciation of anything not his own, but the collaborations produced one weakly offspring in a playlet called *The Fool's Hour: The First Act of a Comedy*, appearing in the first number of the *Yellow Book* in April, 1894, and another somewhat lustier in *Journeys End in Lovers' Meetings*, which was produced at Daly's Theatre on 5th June, 1894, with William Terriss, Sir Johnston Forbes-Robertson, and Ellen Terry in the cast. Moore subsequently professed to have supplied the idea of *Journeys End in Lovers' Meetings* and written the whole thing, Mrs. Craigie adding only "little liver pills" in the shape of epigrams and bits of dialogue. But Ellen Terry, who played in the piece, clearly regarded Mrs. Craigie as mainly its author, and the salient fact appears that this was Moore's solitary success in the theatre, while Mrs. Craigie had a notable triumph four years later with *The Ambassador*, and acquired a considerable reputation as a playwright.

For some two years Moore suffered under the sway of this charming woman, but much of his suffering was his own doing. Women fasten their passions on curious objects, and it is possible that Mrs. Craigie may have seriously considered the possibility of marrying this ungainly-looking, middle-aged man, though it is more likely that, in common with most women, she felt only liking, even affection, for an amusing companion with the gift of almost femininely sensitive understanding, without being more than momentarily moved to the suggestion of sex relations. But, before she could contemplate marriage with Moore or anybody else, she had to be freed from her first husband, and divorce in the 'nineties was a step only to be contemplated by women of courage. Mrs. Craigie had courage, and the machinery of the divorce court was set in motion on her behalf. But there were therefore the more cogent reasons that no breath of scandal should pollute the fragrance of her good fame, since the petitioner for divorce must pose like a lily for purity and seem never to have known other emotions than injured innocence. And Moore was not the type of male friend a woman could receive while maintaining appearances of discretion; he, who prattled incessantly of his imaginary amours, now shouted to the housetops of his familiarity with the beautiful Mrs. Craigie. Most likely she repeatedly cautioned and admonished him, before she was finally irritated into deciding that he was impossible; probably she insisted that they should meet only in public until her divorce was accomplished. Some such veto must have been imposed when, in March, 1894, the month of the publication of *Esther Waters*, he pronounced himself "too unhappy to write."

§ 2

Esther Waters provided the success for which he had longed, and taught him the difference between celebrity and the notoriety whose shadow he had mistaken for the substance in the days when he had revelled in shocking. Not only writers of the *Yellow Book* set, like Crackanthorpe and Lionel Johnson, but so important a pundit as Quiller-Couch hailed its coming with lavish praise. Calling *Esther Waters* "the most important novel published in England during these two years", "Q" felt it necessary to go back to the publication of Hardy's *Tess of the D'Urbervilles* in 1891 to find a book fit for comparison. He found that *Esther Waters* was more "philosophical" in the Aristotelian sense than *Tess*, because the tragedy of Tess "is not felt to be inevitable, but freakish", while that of Esther is felt to be "absolutely inevitable." Perhaps "Q" hardly realised that what he was trying to diagnose for praise was realism, or he might have been less bold in affirming that this was "the most artistic, the most complete, and the most inevitable work of fiction that has been written in England for at least two years." Andrew Lang was more cautious; perhaps because "Q" "called the book 'inevitable' I have avoided *Esther Waters*", he wrote in back-handed reproof of his friend, and though "seductions of servant girls by footmen may not be uncommon," he was not interested in the story of this seduction, because it "sounds unidyllic, and I have also no curiosity about the hospitals of maternity which are described." Though "Q" qualified his praise by asserting his disagreement with the popular estimate of *Tess* as Hardy's best book, Moore was greatly gratified by his praise, affording another instance of his insincerity as an artist, for in the *Confessions* he affected to despise Hardy, and the genuine artist can feel scant grounds for exultation in favourable comparison with work for which he feels no admiration.

Mudie's accepted the book, but Smith's found an excuse for banning it in the objection indicated by Andrew Lang to the chapter describing, Zola-like, the sordid surroundings of the maternity hospital. But Fortune, having elected to smile, gave generously, and after more than twenty thousand copies were sold, the book was baptised from the very fount of respectability in the shape of a postcard from Mr. Gladstone approving its morality, whereupon Smith's lifted the ban and received the book, thus cleansed as if by the waters of Jordan, upon their shelves. Moore estimated that Smith's lost £1,500 by their ban, and the proprietors adminstered a sharp rebuke to their unfortunate librarian for such financial sacrifice in the interests of morality, warning him against any such action in the future against books of which Mr. Gladstone was likely to approve.

Moore was thus on the top of the world. With his affected scorn for "facile success" and his avowed determination of "walking to the best of my strength, in the way of art," he might have been expected to sit down and proceed unperturbed with his "real piece of literature" about Pecksniff "done seriously" and "with love." But success went to the head of the cynic of forty-two as completely as if he had been a youth of twenty. Enriched by his royalties, he became modish in his dress, he moved from the Temple to more luxurious apartments in Victoria Street, he eagerly allowed himself to be lionised by fashionable hostesses in pursuit of the latest craze, and even got himself elected to Boodle's Club and made a point of using it frequently to emphasise his aristocratic associations. This conversion to club snobbery must have aroused smiles from those who remembered the sneer in the *Confessions* at the Club as an institution representative of Respectability, but Moore in his triumph was noticeably less irreverent towards Respectability, and though he had disdained to shelter behind the pretext of writing with a moral purpose in *A Mummer's Wife*, now he so far forgot his pose of paganism that he advertised himself as having written *Esther Waters* from "a love of humanity, a desire to serve humanity", and a quarter of a century later, he bragged about the book's "practical utility" in *Avowals*, displaying as much righteous self-satisfaction in the existence of an "Esther Waters Home for Girl Mothers" as a respectable maiden lady in her achievements as a welfare worker.

It must be allowed that his pursuit of Mrs. Craigie, almost as much as the intoxication of success, contributed to the alteration of his perspective. She was a lady of wealth and position, moving in fashionable circles, and Moore sought to adapt himself to her social atmosphere. If he had been content to remain true to his own individuality, he might have fared more fortunately in his suit, but his vanity inspired the desire to shine in her eyes as a figure of her own world, and blinded him to the obvious fact that a woman of her intelligence, accustomed to daily association with finished men of fashion, must instinctively discriminate at a glance between the genuine article and a ludicrously unhandsome imitation. Fate dealt him a cruel blow by providing him with a rival whose attributes, by comparison with his own physical limitations, must have afflicted Moore with bitter humiliation. This was no less a person that the Hon. George Nathaniel Curzon, afterwards the Marquess Curzon of Kedleston, one of the richest matrimonial prizes any woman of the time could hope for, not only brilliantly gifted and already regarded as a future Prime Minister, but one of the handsomest men of his day and among the last upholders of the aristocratic tradition. Not more than one woman in the world could have seen the two men and looked again at Moore; Mrs. Craigie was not that woman. "When a woman falls in love," Moore is reported to have said, "every previous thought or promise or obligation dissolves like a burnt thread," and he found himself "driven out by a handsome worldling."

Moore thus suggests, not only that Mrs. Craigie was in love with Curzon, but that she was never in love with himself. And apparently, as may be imagined of Moore, he did not take his dismissal gracefully. No doubt he continued to pester her with unwelcome attentions, pleading, protesting, cajoling, and frequently indulging his Irish temper; anyhow, he caused her to be so much the subject of gossip in his connection that, according to rumour, whatever intention of marrying Mrs. Craigie had been nourished by Curzon was extinguished. Probably the loss of the man she loved inspired the lady to such irritation that she banished Moore's hopes for ever, for Curzon married the mother of his beautiful daughters in April, 1895, a month before the death of Moore's mother, of which event he wrote in "Resurgam" of *Memoirs of My Dead Life:*

> "A man cannot lament two women at the same time, and only a month ago the most beautiful thing that had ever appeared in my life, an idea which I knew from the first I was destined to follow, had appeared to me, had stayed with me for a while, and had passed from me . . . Never one but she had the indispensable quality of making me feel I was more intensely alive when she was by me than I was when she was away."

If thus the facts fell out, Moore injured the women he loved with the worst possible hurt in causing the man of her heart to retreat from her, but characteristically it was himself whom he considered the injured party. In "Resurgam" he wrote of her as if she was the one woman who ever moved him to real passion, as indeed she was the only one whom he seriously thought of marrying, but his tenderness for her was less than pity for his injured vanity, and did not deter him from caricaturing what he conceived to be her worst failing in *Mildred Lawson,* the first of the three stories contained in *Celibates,* the book with which he followed *Esther Waters* in 1895:

> "Her appearance pleased her, and she wondered if she were worth a man's life. She was a dainty morsel, no doubt, so dainty that life was unendurable without her. But she was wronging herself, she did not wish him to kill himself . . . Men had done so before for women . . . if it came to the point, she would do everything in her power to prevent such a thing. She would do everything, yes, everything except marry him. She couldn't settle down to watch him painting pictures. She wanted to paint pictures herself. Would she succeed? He didn't think so, but that was because he wanted her to marry him. And, if she didn't succeed, she would have to marry him or someone else. She would have to live with a man, give up

her whole life to him, submit herself to him. She must succeed. Success meant so much. If she succeeded, she would be spoken of in the newspapers, and, best of all, she would hear people say when she came into a room, ' That is Mildred Lawson . . .'"

So Moore consoled his vanity; he was not rejected for another man or because he had occasioned her loss of the man she wanted, but because she was ambitious of success in her art, and jealous lest her success should seem secondary beside his, George Moore's!

Disappointment in love has changed the course of many lives, and it will be easy to argue that Mrs. Craigie marked an epoch in Moore's. If he had not known her, might he not have proceeded steadily with his idea of Pecksniff "done seriously" and "with love," and not merely have repeated, but exceeded, the success of *Esther Waters*? And if he had so proceeded, might he not have sustained the quality of *Esther Waters* and the Pecksniff book, and so come to be reckoned among England's major novelists? It is possible, but not likely. Moore was naturally an irregular artist capable of following brilliance with execrable balderdash, of the most sudden descents from considerable heights to incredible depths; he had not the remotest notion of gauging his own powers, or of maintaining a self-critical balance; he was inevitably fumbling feverishly in the reticule of his creative faculty, anxiously hoping that he would find the correct fare for where he wanted to go. He had followed such considerable novels as *A Mummer's Wife* and *A Drama in Muslin* with *A Mere Accident* and *Spring Days*; he thought he was writing a masterpiece when he was only writing *Mike Fletcher*; now he followed *Esther Waters* with *Celibates* and *Evelyn Innes*.

Celibates was probably a pot-boiler, hurriedly concocted to keep his name in the public eye. It consisted of the splenetic outpourings of his heart against Mrs. Craigie in *Mildred Lawson*, a re-hashing of *A Mere Accident* in *John Norton*, and an ugly story called *Agnes Lahens*, about an improbably neurotic girl, who takes refuge in a convent to escape being a bone of contention between a poor stick of a father and a libertine mother, which John Freeman thought "an anticipation of Tchehov", but seems rather a reversion to Moore's worst exaggerations in *A Mere*

Accident. Celibates was a failure; the condition of some copies turning up in the market suggests that unsold copies of the first edition were subsequently re-issued, as in the case of *Spring Days*. The book was a mistake, but of too slight a nature materially to injure the reputation of the author of *Esther Waters*.

Moore knew that it must not be repeated, however, and he took immense pains over *Evelyn Innes*, which was started in the summer of 1895 and occupied three years of work. Though he now affected contempt for Zola and posed as a disciple of Flaubert, he accumulated data for "local colour" with the assiduity of Charles Reade. Huysmans is reported to have smiled when he heard Moore was writing a novel about nuns, saying that, when he last met him, he "didn't know a Poor Clare from a Sister of Charity," but Moore told W. T. Stead, of the *Review of Reviews*, that he wanted "to meet someone who has been in a convent . . . a professed nun would be best of all," and Stead introduced him to a Mrs. Crawford, who was able to give him much useful information. Though he had started to learn the piano to please Mrs. Craigie and developed enthusiasm for Wagner, he knew little of music, but Sir William Rothenstein thinks he got the information he needed for the "musical parts" of *Evelyn Innes* from Arnold Dolmetsch, while he also discussed music freely with Arthur Symons, the closest friend he made from his connection with the *Yellow Book*. "To write a book about an opera singer," he told Symons, "without knowing one, and even sleeping with her, is to expose oneself to defeat," so he secured an introduction to Melba, who invited him to dinner "to tell him about her voice."

"It is a pleasure to write this book," he wrote to his brother, Maurice. "Hitherto I have had to drag myself to the writing table, now I can't drag myself away. I am making myself ill. The composition of this book is a pure joy. I cannot think what has come over me to write like this. It must be very bad or very good. I shall do a great book this time or cut the whole thing."

Written in 1895, the last two sentences had extraordinary significance three years later. He never knew whether his work was good or bad, and the bad was usually so intermingled with the good that he eventually realised the hopelessness of achieving a work of art with completeness and coherence of design, and took to his semi-autobiographical meanderings, shapeless, digressive, fiction and fact inextricably entangled, but here and there containing among endless junk a treasure of philosophy, imagery, or narrative. Now, in his earnest desire to sustain the success of *Esther Waters*, he wrote with the determination to tickle the public palate, unconsciously striving to supply such a book as was beloved by the circulating libraries he despised. *Evelyn Innes* was an excellent library proposition, for it was in the vein which Ouida had profitably marketed during the past quarter of a century; its exotic atmosphere is oddly reminiscent of *Moths*—it even displays solecisms worthy of Ouida, such as "almost thoroughbred horses" and the appearance of a man of fashion in town at noon wearing patent leather boots with tan tops. It sold fifteen thousand copies in the six shilling edition, a matter for self-congratulation in a commercial novelist.

But immediately after publication Moore sensed his failure to uphold the standard of *Esther Waters*. To Arthur Symons and W. B. Yeats, to whom it was dedicated as "two contemporary writers with whom I am in sympathy," he showed the book in proof, and they both found it "far better than they thought I could do." He himself conceived it as inferior to "Tourgournoff" and Balzac, but "better than Trashy Thackeray and rubbishy Dickens and pompous Eliot." But after reading the early reviews he confessed that he was "next door to believing that I had spent three years on the invention of an imbecility." His spirits rose a little as he saw it selling, but he knew he had committed an artistic *gaffe*, as he had formerly with *Mike Fletcher*. His resentment against the book's wounding of his vanity grew with bitter reflection; ten years later, he revised *Evelyn Innes* and its sequel, but though at first he characteristically trumpeted that he had "turned an eyesore into a beautiful thing," he soon decided, on finding that nobody was very much interested, that the revised version was after all inferior to the original. And when in 1922 he was preparing the "canon" by which he imagined he would be known to posterity, though he revised for reprinting such a feeble potboiler as *Celibates* and the ineffectual *Spring Days*, he selected *Evelyn Innes*, which is at least as good as *A Modern Lover*, and *Sister Teresa* to stand with the detested *Mike Fletcher* as the three works "not to be resuscitated."

§ 3

George Moore made old bones, dying at the age of eighty on 21st January, 1933. He had nearly thirty-five years of life after the publication of *Evelyn Innes*, and according to his little circle of fond admirers, there were still some years yet to pass before, at the age of sixty or so, he began to do his best work. But for the story of those thirty-five years, may it not be read in the many books of Moore about Moore, or more easily in Mr. Hone's fully documented and judicious biography? It can find no place here, for his subsequent life and works mattered nothing to the history of popular literature.

With *Evelyn Innes* Moore accepted his doom as a major novelist. He was forty-six; if he went on producing novels at intervals of three years, he might write another eight or nine books. If they were as successful as *Evelyn Innes*, they would bring him five or six hundred pounds each, but if they were no better than *Evelyn Innes*, it was doubtful if they would sell so well, for library subscribers require sensation, and if told by the smart young woman that it was "George Moore's usual—considered quite good," many would begin to say, "I won't bother then—I read his last, or last but one, and I want something new." Moreover, they might be worse than *Evelyn Innes*; how was he to know when he was going to produce another abortion like *Mike Fletcher*? Anyhow, he realised, with how much humiliation to his vanity, that he would never acquire the reputation of "trashy" Thackeray or "rubbishy" Dickens, or even Meredith or Hardy, whose work demanded to be read or skimmed because it was "the thing" to know about them. It would never be a reproach to the fashionably educated not to know one's George Moore; some might say, "You ought to read *Esther Waters* by a fellow named Moore—he's written lots of other stuff but this is really good," but they would be merely set down as exceptionally well-read people, who read out-of-the-way sort of books.

Moore's vanity must have writhed under the burden of such reflections. Better "cut the whole thing", as he had promised to do if *Evelyn Innes* was not "a great book". And as after the flop of *Mike Fletcher*, so after that of *Evelyn Innes*, he began to cast about him with a new line. The Boer War and the Irish Literary Theatre happened providentially. Kipling's star was high in the ascendant, and hating Kipling for his success as much as for his jingo journalism, he became a violent pro-Boer, which provided an excellent excuse for changing his course. He could say that society had dropped him on account of his unpopular political opinions, instead of admitting the truth—that society had decided that he was not a lion for lionising. So he decided, as he wrote in *Ave*, that:

> "It would be better to get away from London and waste no more time joining people in their walks, to try to persuade them that London was an ugly city, or to wring some ad-mission from them that the Boer War was shameful, and that England was on her knees, out-fought, vanquished by a few thousand Boers, about as many able-bodied men as one would find in the Province of Connaught."

Where should he get away to, but to Ireland? Yeats and Martyn had interested him in the founding of the Irish Literary Theatre, of which he was a director; the plays were to be produced in Dublin, and he was wanted to assist in the production.

He did not decide on the step in a hurry. He went over first to find out how the land lay, "wondering whether Ireland would accept me as a friend or as an enemy." But though he made haste to butter Irish feeling by declaring that he had threatened his nephews with disinheritance if they did not learn the Irish language, he found that Ireland did not care whether he existed or not; a dozen years had passed since the publication of *Parnell and His Island*, Parnell himself had long since been sacrificed on altars of respectability, and many malicious journalistic tongues had wagged since his. Probably his vanity was very disappointed that he was not an object of execration. But the enthusiast Yeats needed a literary ally and would help to blow his trumpet for him; besides, he wanted a little self-advertisement by writing to the papers about his pro-Boer opinions, and it would be safer to do it in Dublin than in London. So he worked himself into the same fanatical contempt for England before leaving it, as he had for Ireland before leaving it twelve years before: "England seemed to rise up before me in person, a shameful and vulgar materialism from which I turned with horror."

He dressed his departure with close attention to theatrical display. He posed as a disciple going forth into the wilderness because he had heard "the word". Such a farrago of self-concocted servility to egregious vanity appears nowhere in literature to compete with those last pages of *Ave*, where he describes himself haunted in Chelsea and his Victoria Street rooms by an unseen "presence", which repeatedly whispered, "Go back to Ireland! Go to Ireland!" how he "did not dare to look behind," and how at length "the presence seemed to fill the room, overpowering me," and forcing him, the devoted apostle of paganism, upon his knees to pray. "To whom I prayed I do not know, only that I was conscious of a presence about me and that I prayed." He had a farewell party given him by his painter friends, Tonks and Steer and Walter Sickert, who "pointed out to me that no man could break up his life as I proposed to break up mine with impunity." He replied that nothing they could say would change him, with all the airs of Sidney Carton doing "the far, far better thing" in *The Only Way*, or a crusader of the Middle Ages proposing a pilgrimage to Palestine in expiation of his crimes. He felt that "my manner must have impressed them; they must have felt that my departure was decreed by some unseen authority." They must indeed have been impressed; they probably reflected on the mercy of providence that Moore had not been bitten by the religious bug in his youth, or he might have got himself locked up for conceiving himself a reincarnation of Christ. They must have been impressed, too, by his histrionic ability; there can be no better tribute to the quality of Moore's prose at its best than to say that the reader of *Ave* is almost deluded into believing that the man really had an inspired mission to fulfil, instead of being merely bent on playing a losing hazard to gratify the yearnings of personal ambition.

"Modern Ireland! What of it as a subject for artistic treatment?" he wrote in the early chapters of *Ave*. And his going to Ireland marked the third stage of his literary life; he had failed as a sensation-shocking novelist, he had failed as a fashionable novelist, and he was now going to try his luck as a national novelist or dramatist. He was going to exploit Ireland—to see if he could make a name as a national bard, and go down to posterity as the pride of his native land, as Burns and Scott of Scotland.

He failed in this, as he had failed before. Remembering his former policy of not despising the bird in the hand, he completed the sequel to *Evelyn Innes*, but his heart was not in the work and he did not believe it could improve on its predecessor, so that it is small wonder that *Sister Teresa* proved a novel as dull as a wet month of February. In 1903 he published in England a book of short stories called *The Untilled Field*, which had been previously issued in Irish; the title inferred that Moore had discovered Ireland for the first time, and he described the book as "written in the beginning out of no desire of self-expression, but in the hope of furnishing the young Irish of the future with models." It is his best contribution to the art of short story, showing so marked an advance on *Celibates* that it seems the work of another writer; this and the short novel of *The Lake* published in 1905 were inspired by the same enmity to Roman Catholicism as *Evelyn Innes* and *Sister Teresa*, but instead of the artificiality of the one and the monotonous dullness of the other, the two later books are alive and breathing with the atmosphere of peat and bog and the tragedy of the Irish race. Among Moore's Irish peasants are the parents of characters now to be encountered in the works of Mr. Liam O'Flaherty, Mr. John Brophy, and other modern Irish writers, and *The Untilled Field* and *The Lake* are notable volumes in the library of Irish literature.

But while both books had merit, they had a narrow appeal, and as Moore's hopes of seeing himself a national idol, a sort of Goethe or D'Annunzio, began to ebb, he sickened of Ireland. A play written in collaboration with Yeats proved a damp squib, and the Irish Literary Theatre was wound up. He began to visit England again, and meeting Mrs. Craigie, collaborated with her in a play which became *The Coming of Gabrielle*, after being produced by the Stage Society in 1913 as *Elizabeth Cooper*; it was a flop in 1913, and ten years later was redeemed by the acting of such an artist as Miss Athene Seyler. This collaboration with Mrs. Craigie ended their acquaintance; according to Moore, a lovers' quarrel ended with the mature amorist of fifty-two kicking the lady "nearly in the centre of the backside" as she walked in front of him in the Green Park.

For some time he dallied alternately with the ideas of returning to London or settling in Paris, but it was not till 1911 that he finally shook the mud of Ireland from his boots and came to No. 121 Ebury Street. For he had at last found his medium in endless, formless posings with himself as their hero. His autobiographical fictions—or fictional autobiographies—from *Memoirs of My Dead Life* in 1906 and the trilogy *Hail and Farewell*, comprising *Ave*, *Salve*, and *Vale*, which occupied most of the years between 1906 and 1914, down to a *Communication to My Friends*, which he was writing at the time of his death, have a certain Gallic flavour about them which becomes explained when Anatole France is called to mind. Anatole wrote many better novels than anything of Moore's, but otherwise there was a curious similarity in their careers, for Anatole began with sensational novels and ended by writing volumes of embellished autobiography. He had, too, the same affection for fruity anecdote, and used much the same materials for getting himself acclaimed as a genius. Curious that Moore, with his familiar knowledge of French literature, never talked of Anatole France. He must have read him back in the 'eighties, just as he must have read Charles Reade then or earlier. Did he eschew discussion of his knowledge of Anatole France as he did of Reade, because his vanity revolted from the possible suspicion of being derivative?

Perhaps it was the recollection that Reade wrote a mediaeval romance called *The Cloister and the Hearth* which suggested his writing a thesis on the story of *Héloïse and Abelard*. For a thesis it is rather than a novel, digressing into endless garrulity in the same fashion as his autobiographical books, entirely lacking the saga-like power of Reade's narrative and failing to reproduce the mediaeval atmosphere so convincingly as many subsequent romances of the period, notably Mr. George Cronyn's *The Fool of*

Venus. More than half Moore's version of the Abelard story might have been entitled "Conversations in a Nunnery", for the latter part of the book is largely devoted to the gossip of Héloïse with her colleagues in the convent. His hatred of Roman Catholicism coloured much of his work after *Evelyn Innes*, and became so fanatical that he quarrelled with his brother Maurice on the subject. But his predilection for priests and nuns had another origin than religious bias. Avowedly he wrote to expose fanatical devotion to religion as "the most terrible of all forms of sensuality," but sexuality in monks and nuns obsessed him with an obscene fascination. He revelled as mischievously in telling tales of monkish lecherousness as Boccaccio or Balzac, and the notion of nuns indulging in unchastity appealed to his libidinous fancy as alluringly as to Casanova's.

Héloïse and Abelard appeared in 1921, but in the seven years since the publication of *Vale* in 1914, Moore had embarked on the fourth and final stage of his career. Expressing no surprise at a glaring solecism in *Evelyn Innes*, Oscar Wilde said, "The next time Moore will get it right. He conducts his education in public." When Moore happened to read the Bible on being presented with a copy by a friend, he was at once eager to announce his discovery of such an unsuspected masterpiece: he wrote a play called *The Apostle* on the idea of a meeting between Christ and St. Paul after the crucifixion. The idea was in his mind when, in 1913, he revised *Spring Days* and felt inspired with the desire to write another novel. In spite of all his new theories, he went to work in the old way learned from Reade and Zola; he did a sort of Cook's tour of Palestine in about six weeks to seek "local colour". The result was *The Brook Kerith*, which brought Moore once again into the news with a storm of controversy, and revealed that, though the pillars of Humbug's temple were mouldering to ruin, the old gods had not yet crashed to the dust. The time was not yet when the story of the gospels could be freely made the material of imaginative fiction as it was to be in the nineteen-thirties; the ecclesiastical pundits rose in their wrath, and still subservient as ever to the call of respectability, the libraries banned *The Brook Kerith.*

Naïvely John Freeman deplored the notoriety achieved by

The Brook Kerith, because its "notoriety obscured for a time" what he called its simplicity. The irony is that, if the ecclesiastical pundits had not made a martyr of Moore by their windy pomposity in the service of Humbug, he would never have been exalted by a small body of youthful enthusiasts into the comfortable saddle-bag of a Grand Old Man of Letters. The spectacle of a venerable man of letters pilloried by respectability in the cause of art—and Moore, of course, did not fail to strike this attitude when entering the lists of controversy—naturally appealed to the rising generation, which was revolting against the worship of the falling gods of Respectability and Humbug. Finding himself hailed as a hero by these young men, Moore remembered how he and Huysmans and Paul Margueritte and the rest hàd sat in the old days at the feet of Zola, and he studiously proceeded to act the part of "the Master".

His vanity now served him admirably. The young or middle-aged man who talks perpetually about himself and the quality of his work is regarded ironically as a bore, a buffoon, a bounder, or a pitiable eccentric by contemporaries—unless he is successful, and Moore had not been successful. But an old man thus talking about himself receives the respectful hearing due to his venerable years, and his youthful hearers are the more readily credulous, since they have neither matured independence of critical judgment nor motives of jealousy from rivalry with a survival from a senior generation. The contrast in the measuring of Moore by his contemporaries and by his youthful school of adorers finds illustration in the difference between John Freeman's verdict that "the English language has been brought to a new exercise in the prose of *The Brook Kerith*" and the contemporary Bernard Shaw's: "I read about thirty pages of *The Brook Kerith*. It then began to dawn on me that there was no mortal reason why Moore should not keep going on like that for fifty thousand pages, or fifty million for that matter."

So Moore found his bourn at last. His dreams of being recognised as a great writer by the public which read *Esther Waters* or by his countrymen of Ireland had long since vanished, and he was well satisfied to reign supreme in a little circle of adoring young men and women who hung on his words like

Boswell on Johnson's. The war affected him so little that in 1916 he proposed a trip with a feminine admirer through France and Italy, quite oblivious of its impossibility. He was as happy as a sandboy in his own little world, writing down imaginary conversations with his friends and putting all the plums in his own mouth, revising all his old books for the grateful reception of his adorers as perfected masterpieces, eternally talking volubly about himself in private and in print. And he formulated a new dodge for cheating his old enemies, the libraries, and at the same time prohibiting the possible discovery by his little band of admirers that they alone were interested in his work—the practice of publishing in expensive limited editions, which he taught his disciples to interpret as a manifestation of "his pride in the honour of English letters," which, said the devout Freeman, "extends to the outward form of a book, demanding the same conscience in the type-founding, type-setting and paper-making as he has himself come to observe in the diligent art of an author." Thus he not only avoided the humiliation of having his unsold copies "remaindered", or having them re-issued like *Spring Days*, but created the fictitious impression that a large public might read his works if only it could obtain them. For he could rely on selling the fifteen hundred copies of a limited edition; he had his two or three hundred regular readers, who stimulated sufficient interest to purchase, if not to read, in another two or three hundred, and the remainder went to that curious personality, the collector, who buys a reputation for refined literary tastes by accumulating books which he thinks will appreciate in value.

Not only was he happy in the reputation of a master within the bosom of his little circle, but this was financially the most profitable period of his career. His bibliography more than doubled, nearly trebled, in the last fifteen years of his life the number of books he had previously published in the forty years between 1878 and 1918. Almost all were revisings and reminiscences, except *A Story-Teller's Holiday*, an amusing imitation of Boccaccio after the manner of Balzac's *Contes Drolatiques*, *Héloïse and Abelard*, and *Aphrodite in Aulis*, a dull attempt to treat a classical theme as he had treated the mediaeval in *Héloïse* and the Biblical in *The Brook Kerith*. As he chuckled gleefully over

the proceeds from his limited editions in the cosy comfort of
Ebury Street, he may have been moved to reflect on the irony
of his career—on how he began as a pioneer in the campaign to
defeat the libraries' monopoly by selling direct to the public at
six shillings, and how he ended by again eluding the medium of
the libraries through reverting to the price of the old three
volume novel.

§ 4

In one of those flashes of candour, which appear fitfully from
a background of theatrical gasconading and deliberate laying of
false scents, Moore exclaimed with flamboyant sincerity: "Here
ye shall find me, the germs of all I have written are in the *Confessions*, *Esther Waters*, and *Modern Painting*." From corners in
Bloomsbury and Chelsea shrill voices are raised to protest the
claims of *The Brook Kerith*, of *Héloïse and Abelard*, of *Hail and
Farewell*, to acclamation as masterpieces of English literature
incomparable with any but Landor and Pater in the nineteenth
century and with none knows whom in preceding ages. But the
voices find no echo in the outer wilderness of less epicurean
tastes, which find Moore as he expected he would be found before
he enshrined himself in a splendid sarcophagus of expensive
limited editions.

The Confessions of a Young Man is an important book because
it is a contemporary document, reflecting the characteristics of
an epoch through a lens admittedly distorted, but coloured richly
by the revealing lights of an unusual personality. In the 'eighties
Moore was a "card", characterised by the same talent for opportunism as Arnold Bennett's Denry Machin, and the *Confessions*
is the frank autobiography of a card, impudently advertising
himself by scoring off conventional institutions with outspokenly
unconventional opinions. Knowing it for one of his successes,
Moore sought to repeat it in all his subsequent reminiscences:
he had neither judgment, nor the instinct of the genuine artist
which is a more than satisfactory substitute for judgment, and
failed to realise that such a success depends entirely on originality
and the dramatic soundness of the unexpected. When Denry

Machin in *The Regent* wanted to impress Mr. Seven Sachs, he wished he could have lighted his cigarette with a hundred-pound note as he had done to impress Sachs's agent, but he realised that "he had done the cigarette-lighting trick once for all," and that "a first-class card must not repeat himself." Moore showed himself only a third-class card by trying to repeat the effect of the *Confessions* in *Hail and Farewell*, and again when, finding *Hail and Farewell* attracted notice largely by his tattle about his friends, he went on tattling in *Avowals* and *Conversations in Ebury Street*. In 1888 the *Confessions* was the book of a card, and an original idea; before then nobody had thought of writing an autobiography before reaching the age of fifty. Moore set the fashion which has acquired the monotony of habit in the hands of Messrs. Robert Graves, Siegfried Sassoon, Douglas Goldring, Beverley Nichols, and many more, and nearly all the ink-dippers of the imitative sex, from the intellectually earnest Miss Vera Brittain to the commercially entertaining Miss Ethel Mannin.

Modern Painting, like *Impressions and Opinions*, also has value as a contemporary document. As his disciple, Mr. Humbert Wolfe, showing himself an apt pupil of his master in the card's device of sweeping generalisation, remarks: "All contemporary criticism is merely an exhibition of fugitive prejudice." *Modern Painting* and *Impressions and Opinions* retain interest as exhibitions of fugitive prejudice. Moore had a genuine enthusiasm and an individual understanding of the French Impressionists, and though to-day many of its arguments may seem crude and elementary, *Modern Painting* is a book of original criticism, reflecting more intellectual credit on its author than the whole gamut of theatrical gabble in *Avowals* and *Conversations in Ebury Street*, where he gambols up and down the garden of English literature, swinging his stick at the heads of flowers, like a larrikin let loose.

Esther Waters was his one big success and his one appreciable contribution to English literature. The epic tale of the servant girl touches the highest sort of beauty, the beauty of humanity; it is told with strict fidelity to reality, without exaggeration or the interpolation of anything foreign to the inevitable course of the narrative. Simple, straightforward treatment was necessary for such a subject; the whole thing might have been spoiled by a single digression such as the later Moore loved, like the insertion of the story of Gaucelm and Lady Malberge into *Héloïse and Abelard*. The girl's seduction, her practical resignation to her condition, her struggle against adversity to keep straight, her resistance and capitulation to her former seducer, and her life as a wife, taking the rough with the smooth as a matter of course, form a triumph of naturalistic narrative. And though the critics have habitually concentrated their praise on the character of Esther, the drawing of her husband as a type of the decent working-man, with a weakness for good-fellowship and sport, developing the vices of betting and drink, a victim of his crude animal senses, is even finer as a study in the lights and darks of character.

John Freeman is not alone among the admirers of *Esther Waters* in claiming that it marked an epoch in the history of the English novel, by giving it "form" and supplying a mode for subsequent fiction. These admirers seem to think that everybody had been following the formless, wandering fashion of Thackeray and Dickens, who had to keep the pot boiling through twenty-four monthly instalments of ten thousand words each, and Moore burst upon the world without warning with a novel conforming with the laws of unity of action and interest. But a reading of *Griffith Gaunt* and *Tess of the D'Urbervilles* will show that *Esther Waters* derived naturally from Reade through Hardy, and was merely a milestone in the journey of the novel from its early Victorian to its modern state. Moore ignored Reade, and disparaged Hardy as he disparaged Zola, but these three were the masters of whom he was the disciple in the writing of realistic fiction.

Nor was *Esther Waters* so revolutionary in outspoken frankness as it is commonly supposed to have been. Less courage was required to publish *Esther Waters* in 1894 than *Tess of the D'Urbervilles* in 1891 or *A Mummer's Wife* in 1885. Moreover, the story of *Esther Waters* showed virtue pleasantly rewarded, and soothed the tender susceptibilities of Respectability with the palliative of a moral purpose, which Moore was moved by commercial considerations to appropriate to himself, forgetting alike his pose of paganism and disinterested devotion to art;

whereas both *Tess* and *A Mummer's Wife* were tales of women brought to tragic ends through indulgence of the flesh, and however Respectability might approve their fate of retribution, it recoiled from the narrative of vice sympathetically recorded.

But *Esther Waters* did create a fashion for realistic treatment of lower-class life, which led to a loosening of prudery's shackles. Such good books as W. Somerset Maugham's *Liza of Lambeth*, Arthur Morrison's *Tales of Mean Streets*, and Richard Whiteing's *No. 5 John Street* gained a vogue with the public created by *Esther Waters*. And *Esther Waters* has well withstood the test of time; only in Mr. A. P. Herbert's *The Water Gypsies* has the psychology of the domestic servant been mirrored with equal naturalness and conviction.

The tragedy of George Moore was his incapacity to follow the fashion which he had himself created. In *Ave* he wrote:

> "*Esther Waters* was a bane—the book snatched me, not only out of that personal poverty which is necessary to the artist, but out of the way of all poverty. My poor laundress used to tell me every day of her troubles, and through her I became acquainted with many other poor people, and they awakened spontaneous sympathy in me, and by doing them kindnesses I was making honey for myself without knowing it."

With another of those rare flashes of candour, he declared that, in bidding his laundress of the Temple good-bye on moving to rooms in Victoria Street, "I bade good-bye to literature." He found no help from his smart parlour-maid, who thought he "ought to go into society." And he went into society, where he was inspired to write *Evelyn Innes*, a mere comestible for the maw of the libraries. Moore's only vital work arose from first hand knowledge; he drew the material for *A Mummer's Wife* from his personal experiences with Richard Mansell's opera company, of *Esther Waters* from his laundress and his memories of the betting and racing atmosphere of his boyhood at Moore Hall, of *The Untilled Field* from the peasantry on his Irish estate. From the types apt for inspiration of his imagination he divorced himself by his social phase at Victoria Street in the later 'nineties, and still further in the comfortable seclusion of Ebury Street during the last twenty-two years of his life. During those last twenty-two years, when he manufactured his great reputation with a little public, he was a purely bookish writer, deriving his material from reading and expressing himself as a bookman, divorced from reality, out of touch with life save the artificial society of the few bookish admirers who frequented the cosy hospitality of his drawing-room.

If he had not met Mrs. Pearl Craigie and been inspired by her with social ambitions, and if the success of *Esther Waters* had not provided the reputation and money for him to gratify his social ambitions, he might have pursued his artistic destiny by writing his novel about Pecksniff "done seriously" and "with love", so forestalling Galsworthy with his *Man of Property*. But he, who had battled against the libraries and the forces of Humbug for a dozen years, knuckled under to Respectability in his hour of triumph; fearing to offend and feverish to sustain his fashionable success, he wrote a nice novel for his library public, which committed him to the choice between a career of competent mediocrity and the new departure which he chose. If he had not been a "card", and so convinced a tiny majority with his limited editions that he was a genius, he would now be reckoned as a one-book author with *Esther Waters*, like Richard Whiteing with *No. 5 John Street*.

Of the tiny minority which saved him—at least temporarily —from this fate, some few may have suspected his true character as a "card". In his study of George Moore, published in 1931, Mr. Humbert Wolfe may be suspected of suspecting. Moore himself evidently suspected his disciple, as he looked at him "askance out of a frosty eye," of taking a rise out of him, as he himself had taken a rise out of Zola, as well as his Irish friends. Anyhow, for all outside the tiny minority, George Moore remains the author of *Esther Waters* and a "card", whose best achievement as a "card" was the *Confessions of a Young Man*.

CHAPTER FOUR

Stevenson Single

§ 1

FROM a comparison between the careers of George Moore and
Robert Louis Stevenson, it would appear that the most certain
way not to be recognised as a genius is to die, as most men do,
between the ages of fifty and seventy. For while Moore obtained
recognition as a genius by living to be eighty, and being worshipped as a Grand Old Man of Letters by an enthusiastic handful
of his juniors, Stevenson obtained such recognition by dying at
the premature age of forty-four, and being deified as a great
young man of letters by the vast majority of his surviving
contemporaries.

Stevenson was born in Scotland fifteen months before Moore
in Ireland—at Edinburgh on 13th November, 1850. In Edinburgh
of that date, De Quincey and "Christopher North" were still
living, and Francis Jeffrey but just dead. Edinburgh was very
conservative, and when Thackeray visited it in 1851, it had altered
little from the days when *Blackwood's Magazine* had disturbed its
serenity with a stormy entry, when "Christopher North" had
successfully contested his election to the university chair of
Moral Philosophy, and when North and Tickler and the Ettrick
Shepherd had foregathered for their *Noctes* at Ambrose's Hotel.
Thackeray found "a vast amount of toryism and donnishness
everywhere," and though Thackeray met only the cream of the
literate society which thronged his lectures on the *English
Humourists*, Edinburgh still proudly endeavoured to live up to
its reputation as the Athens of the North. Its upper class was
professional and academic—professors, doctors, lawyers, clergymen—the class which had formed the middle quality in the old
days between the aristocracy and the mob, but which came to be
promoted to the upper class by the new middle-classes created by
industrialism and trade. Gentility was their god before the wor-

ship of Respectability was introduced; they practised the gospel of Humbug with equal zeal, but with the additional quality of snobbery, impelling an attitude of unwilling condescension to all in trade or lacking genteel antecedents.

Into this society Stevenson was born, for his father, Thomas Stevenson, was an engineer by profession, like his father and grandfather before him, and his mother the daughter of the Rev. Lewis Balfour, of a family which had been gentry for generations. Christened Robert Lewis Balfour Stevenson, he dropped the Balfour himself, and Lewis became Louis because Lewis was the name of a prominent local Liberal politician, duly execrated by Thomas Stevenson in his character of "a stern and unbending Tory". The only child of his parents and delicate of constitution, Stevenson was the coddled darling of a fragile, frequently ailing mother and his bonny Scots nurse, Alison Cunningham, known as "Cummy"—a type of the faithful family retainer belonging to those days when servants came into service as girls of fourteen and stayed in the same place all their lives, becoming in time an essential part of the household, like Smither in *The Forsyte Saga* and Maggie and Amy in *The Old Wives' Tale*. Deriving from fine old Covenanting stock, Cummy was a rigid Calvinist, with lurid visions of the hell to which the wicked were damned springing from a picturesque imagination, which lent itself readily to superstition, and such tales of bogles, witches, and warlocks, as inspire an imaginative boy with a haunting terror of the dark. "A woman in a thousand, clean, capable, notable; once a moorland Helen, and still comely as a blood horse and healthy as the hill wind." So wrote Stevenson in *Weir of Hermiston* of Kirstie Elliott, an idealised portrait of Cummy.

"Her feeling partook of the loyalty of a clanswoman, the hero-worship of a maiden aunt, and the idolatry due to a god. No matter what he had asked her, ridiculous or tragic, she would have done it and joyed to do it . . . Like so many people of her class, she was a brave narrator; her place was on the hearth-rug and she made it a rostrum, mimeing her stories as she told them, fitting them with vital detail, spinning them out with endless ' quo ' he's ' and ' quo ' she's,' her voice sinking into a whisper over the supernatural or the horrific; until she would suddenly spring up in affected surprise, and pointing to the clock, ' Mercy, Mr. Archie!' she would say, ' whatten a time o' night is this of it! God forgive me for a daft wife! '"

In the childhood of Archie Weir, Stevenson recalled much of his own. He "stayed as little as was possible in his father's presence," and while there masked his natural brightness under a demurely serious demeanour; going reverently to church, he "took his place in the pew with lowered eyes," yet "could not follow the prayer, not even the heads of it," and his imagination wandered—"brightness of azure, clouds of fragrance, a tinkle of falling water and singing birds, rose like exhalations from some deeper, aboriginal memory, that was not his, but belonged to the flesh on his bones." Vainly in after years Stevenson sought a romantic strain in his paternal ancestry, but his father was true to the family type—the Stevensons were gloomy, taciturn, practical, unimaginative lowlanders. In his mother's blood lay the germ which made Stevenson a seemingly inexplicable aberration from his prosaic ancestry; the most satisfying of his many biographers, Mr. J. A. Steuart, discovered among his Balfour progenitors a turbulent laird of Blairgowrie and an adventuring French emigré, from whom came the romantic imagination and instinctive love of adventure which fed greedily on, and were fostered and developed by, the picturesque tattling of Cummy.

Cummy's personality enveloped his childhood. Her Calvinistic zeal inspired him to play at preaching in his nursery, improvising a pulpit with a stool and a chair, and at the age of six, he wrote a "History of Moses", with "illustrations by the author which showed the Israelites swaggering in top-hats and enjoying immense cigars." With Cummy he took his walks in the Edinburgh streets, carefully muffled up to guard his delicate throat and chest from the chill northern weather, pursued by the jeers of hardier urchins at his being taken out by his nurse. In Cummy's company he first pressed his nose to the window of the stationer's shop described in " A Penny Plain and Twopence Coloured" of *Memories and Portraits*, greedily gazing at the toy theatre set out within, "with a 'forest set', a 'combat', and a few 'robbers carousing', in slides." Greedily he eyed "the plays themselves, those budgets of romance", which "lay tumbled one upon another"; *Sixteen-String Jack* "troubled me awake and haunted my slumbers", and he hungered to possess *The Wreck Ashore* and *The Floating Beacon*. Occasionally his delicate mother relieved Cummy of her charge for an hour, and fondly recorded in a notebook the sayings and doings of her oddly precocious boy.

His delicate health much interrupted his schooling. At six he started at a small school near his home, to which he was doubtless daily escorted by Cummy; then he attended a preparatory school, from which, when he was not absent through illness, he made a practice of playing truant. At eleven, he went to the Academy for eighteen months of unprofitable misery; he was lazy at lessons, played no games, recoiled from fisticuffs and horse-play, and received the derisive label of a "softie". The only mark he left was his editing of a school magazine. In *Memories and Portraits* he wrote:

> "All through my boyhood and youth, I was known and pointed out for the pattern of an idler; and yet I was always busy on my own private end, which was to learn to write. I kept always two books in my pocket, one to read, one to write in. As I walked, my mind was busy fitting what I saw with appropriate words; when I sat by the roadside, I would either read, or a pencil and a penny version-book would be in my hand, to note down the features of the scene or commemorate some halting stanzas. Thus I lived with words. And what I thus wrote was for no ulterior use, it was written consciously for practice. It was not so much that I wished to be an author (though I wished that too) as that I had vowed that I would learn to write."

Whatever impressed him that he read, he felt he "must sit down at once and set myself to ape that quality," and from "bungling adaptions from Mayne Reid," he progressed to playing "the sedulous ape" to Hazlitt, Lamb, Wordsworth, Defoe, and many others, till he wrote an epic called *Cain* in imitation of Browning's *Sordello*, tragedies after Swinburne and Webster, and at the age of thirteen "tried to do justice to the inhabitants of the famous city of Peebles in the style of the *Book of Snobs*."

After the Academy, he spent one term at a boarding-school before pathetic appeals prevailed on his father to take him away and place him with an Edinburgh "crammer", at whose establishment he was reputed " a quick and bright, but somewhat desultory scholar," and figured eminently in a manuscript magazine, to which he contributed blood-and-thunder serial stories of the most bloody and sensational sort. His talents so impressed his parents that his father had printed *The Pentland Rising: A Page of History*, written when he was sixteen. Most of his early holidays were spent at Colinton Manse, the home of his mother's father, the Manse of *Memories and Portraits* and the prototype of Hermiston, the "great and roomy house," overlooking the churchyard, where "after nightfall 'spunkies' might be seen to dance at least by children," with a fine old garden where Stevenson and his cousins played Red Indians or hide-and-seek, and near at hand the cornfields where they romped before eating "strawberries and cream near by at a gardener's." But after his grandfather's death, his mother took him farther afield for the sunshine needed equally for his health as hers—to Torquay, the Isle of Wight, Italy, the Rhine.

In the autumn of 1867 his crammer succeeded in getting him into Edinburgh University. As an only son, naturally destined by his father to follow the family tradition by becoming a civil engineer, he attended the engineering class, presided over by Fleeming Jenkin, whose character lives in Stevenson's memoir of him. Playing truant was his principal occupation, and when he applied at the end of a term for a certificate of attendance at the Greek class, the presiding professor, J. S. Blackie, remarked, as he obligingly supplied the necessary document, that he did not know his face. The truant felt cynical triumph in prevailing upon Blackie thus to be an accessory to his deception of authority, but he confessed to shame on winning the same concession from Jenkin, who gave it unwillingly, making "no reproach in speech", but with a manner so eloquent that "it told me plainly what a dirty business we were in." He "never thought lightly" of Jenkin afterwards, feeling for him the respect due from one "sportsman to another".

Save for being a popular member of the " Spec.", the university literary and debating society, he pursued the same undistinguished career at the university as at school. But the school softie became at the university an eccentric bounder. He was physically "a slithering, loose flail of a fellow, all joints, elbows, and exposed spindleshanks, his trousers being generally a foot too short in the leg . . . so like a scarecrow that one almost expected him to creak in the wind." He so obviously exaggerated the oddity of his appearance that he clearly enjoyed being pointed out as an eccentric, and advertised himself as such. His habitual dress consisted of a shabby black velvet jacket, duck trousers, a black shirt, and a loose collar and tie; he affected "an offensive provocative attitude of sneering", regarded the university teaching as "an elaborate and stupid joke, fit only for asses", and irritated his critics with "the smile of disdain on his queer, foreign-looking face." Some put him down as a poseur, "so consumed with conceit he could not even walk properly, but must for ever go mincing and posing like a dancing-master"; others candidly considered him a little touched with insanity; all agreed that he was an oddity and a bounder. And he was regarded as the more outrageous on account of the impeccable respectability of his social standing; if he had come from distant parts, nobody knowing aught of his people, he might have been dismissed as a queer cuss, probably with something fishy about him, but he was the son of the highly respected and respectable Thomas Stevenson and grandson of the still more respected and respectable Rev. Lewis Balfour. There was no excuse for his oddity.

Contempt or derision usually has dangerous effects on a sensitive nature. Stevenson did not openly rebel; he recoiled from violence, and when tackled by one of his teachers, he subsided immediately without retort, contenting himself with an irritating, impudent sneer. Nor did he retire into timid seclusion, resigning himself to being a pariah, like De Quincey. He swaggered defiantly, concealing his feelings under a brave show of careless eccentricity; being thought mad, like Hamlet, he acted the part. His jokes had the savour of eccentricity, as when he and his cousin, Bob Stevenson, invented a fictitious Mr. Libbel, called at houses to inquire for him, left his card, and wrote letters over his signature to prominent people. Here again he was probably playing "the sedulous ape", having read of Theodore Hook's Berners Street hoax and its huge success.

For three years he drifted unsatisfactorily; then just as his father had reason to congratulate himself that his boy was showing some promise of success in his prospective profession, by winning a silver medal for a paper on "A New Form of Intermittent Light for Lighthouses", Stevenson informed him that he could not enter the engineering profession as a career. To the father, never doubting that his son would succeed him, as he had succeeded his father and his father his grandfather, the intimation came as an unbelievable blow. Though she had learned to realise something of her adored son's gifts during holidays spent at Swanston Cottage—a summer residence outside Edinburgh taken when Stevenson was seventeen, which figures in *St. Ives* as the home of Flora Gilchrist's aunt—his fond mother was horrified at his temerity in contravening the wish of his father, and vainly implored him to bow to the will which she had never dreamed of questioning. But Stevenson was firm; he wanted to write, but knowing that a man so practical and unimaginative as his father would regard the adoption of the profession of letters as an imbecile fancy, he proposed to study law. Wearing with dignity the outward signs of disappointment and disapproval, and the air of resigning his own hopes to allow his son's freedom of choice, the father consented, and while still attached to the university, Stevenson entered the office of a firm of Writers to the Signet in the spring of 1871.

His father's aloof attitude and sorrowful disapproval intensified Stevenson's sense of his eccentricity and proportionately his defiance. He saw himself an effronting eyesore to the conventional and respectable, and exaggerated his deformity in their eyes. Disdaining evening-dress as a uniform of respectability, he attended dinner-parties in his old velvet coat and tweed trousers; the casual passer-by in the street laughed at him, while friends of the family avoided acknowledging him, pitying his parents for being shamed by such a son. He began to haunt the slum districts of Edinburgh, becoming "the companion of seamen, chimney-sweeps, and thieves"; he professed to having been driven to consorting with low company by the poverty of his allowance, but the obvious reason lay in the attraction of courting the censure of respectability. There were streets in Edinburgh down which none respectable ever walked, down which none respectable could walk with safety after dark; there were districts in Edinburgh of which the respectable ignored the existence, the merest mention of which was a breach of good form, since the mere fact of their existence inferred a libel on enlightened democracy and a reproach to respectability and Mr. Gladstone. Thither went Stevenson, seeing life and thinking himself a devil of a fellow, getting drunk on cheap whisky in low taverns in the company of sailors and prostitutes. Down there in the dregs perhaps he occasionally encountered a member of the respectable class, furtively seeking relaxation from the bonds of respectability with a painted tart; perhaps in after years he himself, a distinguished writer and a respectable husband, felt a longing to taste again the bawdy excesses of the stinking taverns; certainly it was the recollection of these excursions into Edinburgh slums, their intriguing antithesis to the respectability of the society to which he belonged, and his knowledge of the impulse in a respectable man to escape occasionally from the atmosphere of respectability for a brief taste of its utmost contrast, that inspired the idea of the highly respectable professional man assuming a second self for the indulgence of his vices in *Dr. Jekyll and Mr. Hyde.*

Humbug dictated a habit of conscious dishonesty in Victorian biography, and the legend draped like a surplice about Stevenson's memory by his widow and his official biographer, Sir Graham Balfour, merely conformed with contemporary fashion. Mrs. Stevenson and Graham Balfour were less blameworthy than many others—than, for instance, the guardians of such reputations as Thackeray's, Dickens's, or Carlyle's. Mrs. Stevenson had been a restricting influence on Stevenson in life, and after his death she jealously cherished the reputation she had helped to make. She had the best of reasons, for Stevenson's sales depended commonly on his juvenile public, and respectability would have revolted from giving into the hands of its schoolboy sons the works of an author tainted with scandal. In encouraging the inference that she was the only woman in Stevenson's life, she was guilty of no greater Humbug than the average wife in respectable society, to whom a husband's life before marriage was a discreetly sealed book, and any subsequent infidelities were incidents of her wifely fate, to be silently suffered "for the sake of the children" or generally in the interests of respectability. Everybody who knew Stevenson well fully appreciated the necessity for the panoply of Humbug in the interests of respectability. To err being human, they also had been human, but they hoped and anticipated that their survivors would conceal the facts of their humanity with discretion as commendable as Mrs. Stevenson's. When, therefore, on the publication of Graham Balfour's eminently respectable memorial in 1901, William Ernest Henley alone raised his voice in protest against the inhumanising of his old friend as a "seraph in chocolate", respectability manifested such horror as if he had poked bawdy fun at a parson, or relieved himself audibly of flatulence in a drawing-room.

Healing time alone can smooth away the scars unsightly to Humbug's peering spectacles. If a man announces himself a remote descendant of Byron, Casanova, or Ninon de Lenclos, respectability exclaims "how interesting", but skirts are drawn aside, and doors closed to his face, and he is passed unacknowledged in the street, if he proclaims his affinity to a recently convicted bigamist or contemporary woman of notoriously elastic morals. Stevenson's widow died in 1914, and after the war period, Stevenson was a faded memory to a few elderly survivors, and as dead as Shakespeare to the modern generation. Hence, the truth, which reeked with the stench of obscenity from Henley's pen in 1901, could be introduced as a casual subject of academic discussion by Miss Rosaline Masson in 1923, Mr. J. A. Steuart in 1924, and Mr. G. S. Hellman in 1925. From that happy hunting ground to which the manuscripts of all important English writers inevitably gravitate, a New York saleroom, emerged a mass of Stevenson's unpublished verse and prose, giving important evidence of his early life.

In his excursions as a youthful Hyde, Stevenson must have fallen in with many women of the unclassed, but the researches of Mr. Steuart and Mr. Hellman disclosed a much more important affair than casual mercenary commerce, leaving a distasteful memory of a week or a month. He developed an attachment for a young prostitute named Kate Drummond, a Highland girl probably driven to her trade by the treachery of a seducer or some such indiscretion, which banished her to exile from a respectable home. She was described to Mr. Steuart as "slim and dark, very trim and neat, with jet-black hair and a complexion that needed no cosmetics to make it rosy and alluring." With his splendidly expressive eyes, his fragility, his natural charm, Stevenson was a type attractive and frequently fascinating to women, and he described himself as having been "distinctly petted" by the Edinburgh prostitutes. To this girl, not yet hardened to insensibility by continual degradation, and still instinctively shrinking alike from the lusty brutality of rough sailors and the limp pawings of dribbling old lechers, the velvet-coated youth, with the refined speech and manners of another world, represented the romance which her young heart craved, and which she saw forever slipping from her reach. Once in her arms, he learned that she had more to give him than other women of her sort; to him she gave freely from desire instead of suffering caresses for money. No doubt he became known as "her boy"; probably his presence with her often protected her from drunken manhandling. The knowledge that he represented love and all the brightness in her sordid life could not but flatter a young man, and with that knowledge her situation naturally invoked all his sense of chivalry. Besides, the idea of loving a prostitute, the most reprehensible of respectability's outcasts, suited his character of eccentricity. Had not Hazlitt loved a whore, and Propertius his golden Cynthia? And as Tibullus and Propertius eulogised in verse their courtesan mistresses, so Stevenson addressed verses to his Kate as "Claire", apostrophising her charms and all the sentiment, melting passion, and happiness he enjoyed with her.

Mr. Steuart was told that Kate was "many times scolded by 'the head of her establishment'" for wasting so much time in Stevenson's company, and "at last actually beaten". This probably excited Stevenson in his anger to the utmost recklessness of chivalry. Kate was eager to give up her way of living for his sake, and he proposed to marry her. The sensation of the suggestion in his family circle can be imagined. Thomas Stevenson, devout churchman and upright pillar of respectability, must have been more appalled than angry at the madness of the proposal. It is doubtful if he went so far as to threaten disowning his son if he persisted in marriage; so much was unnecessary, for Stevenson had nothing but his meagre pocket-money, and a threat to throw him upon his own resources was sufficient to squash the project. The young man surrendered, and in surrendering, suffered more than the agony of thwarted desire, for his resignation of Kate meant her inevitable dedication to a career of shame. For whatever sad fate she came to, he felt morally responsible; in a poem called *The Vanquished Knight* he wrote:

"I have left all upon the shameful field,
Honour and Hope, My God! and all but life."

The shame of his surrender afflicted his spirit as no derision or antagonism could have done. Buoyed upon the vanity that he possessed exceptional gifts and was destined to greatness, he could afford to sneer disdainfully at his mockers, but this blow humbled him, and in his humility he wrote that as "I do now recognise that I shall never be a great man, I may set myself peacefully on a smaller journey, not without hope of coming to the inn before nightfall." In his affliction, it was natural that he should feel resentment against his father as its cause, and he must have experienced the morbid sweets of vengeance in administering a still greater shock to the devout churchman by avowing his conversion to atheism.

Never since the priests of the Middle Ages terrorised the almost universally ignorant with the picturesque horrors of eternal damnation, has ecclesiasticism enjoyed such a vogue, as when it adapted to its uses the paraphernalia of Humbug in the Victorian era. But though the parsons were firmly entrenched behind the bulwark of respectability, there were engaged against them in damaging guerrilla warfare such doughty warriors as Huxley, Darwin, Tyndall, and Herbert Spencer. Huxley's *Lay Sermons* had appeared in 1870, and Spencer's *First Principles* had long enjoyed a vogue. Their doctrines provided food for speculation to unprejudiced youth, and Stevenson, frailly fortified against logical argument by Cummy's simple superstitious faith, readily fell to agnosticism, and thence through scepticism to atheism.

His mood favoured a renunciation of faith. His soul had received its first serious emotional bruise, which he felt with the soreness of sensitive youth. Compelled by considerations of respectability to cast his love to the certain fate of degradation and disease, he must have reflected bitterly on the farce of respectability's devout professions of adherence to the doctrines of the Christ who succoured Mary Magdalene. Moreover, the adoption of atheism suited his character of eccentricity, since nothing could be more shocking to the Presbyterianism of Edinburgh's respectability, and finally it would wound his father as his father had wounded him.

The effect of his bombshell evidently exceeded his expectations, for after his father had catechised him on the state of his beliefs and he had duly confessed his opinions, he told his college friend, Charles Baxter, that "if I had foreseen the red hell of everything, I think I should have lied as I have often lied before." The domestic scene can easily be imagined. Thomas Stevenson, a believer so devout that in another age he would have gone to the stake like a Latimer or a Ridley, might have forgiven his son for wrecking his life and scandalising society by a foolish marriage, but he would have soon as seen him a murderer as a heretic. If he did not actively threaten to disown his son and turn him out of his home forthwith, he told him that he could not leave his money to a holder of his opinions. Stevenson replied with youthful heat, and high words were flung between father and son over the head of the anguished mother, who tearfully beseeched the son on the one hand to retract his sacreligious views and the father on the other to mitigate his wrath against their only beloved son. The mother's pleadings must have prevailed with the father, for it was obvious that, if turned away from home, the son would probably go to the devil, while the blow would mean death to the fragile mother.

To relieve the domestic tension and in the hope of bringing him under favourable influence, Stevenson was sent to spend the summer vacation of 1873 with a cousin who had married the rector of a parish near Bury St. Edmunds. There he did encounter a beneficial influence, not in the clergyman, but in a fellow guest in the house, Mrs. Sitwell. She was not only a charming and gifted woman of about thirty, the age to attract a young man of twenty-two, but she had the additional charm of romantic appeal, being unhappily married, separated from her husband, and obviously the object of attention from a gifted young Cambridge don, Sidney Colvin. She was as charmed with him as he with her, and she engaged Colvin to share her interest in him. "To know him," said Colvin, "was to recognise at once that here was a young genius of whom great things might be expected."

"A slender, boyish presence, with a graceful, somewhat fantastic bearing, and a singular power and attraction in the eyes and smile, were the things that first impressed you; and the impression was quickly confirmed and deepened by the charm of his talk, which was irresistibly sympathetic and inspiring and not less full of matter than of mirth. I have known no man in whom the poet's heart and imagination were combined with such a brilliant strain of humour and such an unsleeping alertness and adroitness of the critical intelligence."

In later years, when Colvin became one of the literary pundits with Gosse, Lang and Saintsbury, he always "had a *protégé* of some kind." Unlike Gosse and Saintsbury, who rarely risked a judgment on anybody who had not been dead sufficiently long to have passed through the fire of ample posthumous criticism, Colvin looked eagerly for talent among his contemporaries and juniors, and generously encouraged it when he thought he recognised it. He made mistakes; he hailed poor Stephen Phillips as a genuis, and his *Paolo and Francesca* as the dawn of a new poetic era in 1899. But he also spotted many winners, who received encouragement and useful introductions in the salon presided over by his wife, the former Mrs. Sitwell, who figured in literary circles much like Mrs. Procter, the wife of "Barry Cornwall", in the 'thirties and 'forties. Stevenson was the first and most important of his discoveries, and Stevenson's first published article, on "Roads", appeared through Colvin's agency in the *Portfolio*, an art magazine edited by P. G. Hamerton.

The enthusiasm inspired by Colvin and Mrs. Sitwell's encouragement was speedily damped on his return home, and in
letters to Mrs. Sitwell he confided the misery of his antagonism
over religion with his father. Then he fell ill, a specialist diagnosed threatening tubercular symptoms, and he was "ordered
south". Alone in illness and depression at Mentone, he wrote to
Mrs. Sitwell that he felt like a man of seventy—"Oh! Medea kill
me or make me young again," he exclaimed—and to his mother,
"I lead the life of a vegetable; I eat, I sleep, I sit in the sun, I
read, alas! nothing but novels and newspapers." He gave up
"trying to walk and to work," resigning himself to "sitting in
the sun and George Sand." To relieve his nervous depression he
tried opium, and throughout his life he resorted to the drug in
bouts of illness and depression, though he never became an
habitual addict.

Rescue from his dark mood again came from feminine
company, when he made the acquaintance of two "brilliantly
accomplished and cultivated" Russian sisters, one of whom had
a little girl called Nelitchka. In his letters to Mrs. Sitwell, he
talks much of the child, but confessed that he found the attractions
of the elder lady, Madame Garschine, embarrassing. If he admitted as much to his feminine correspondent it is likely that
much more actually occurred. The natural charm which caused
him to be "petted" by prostitutes was equally effective on women
of another order; Fleeming Jenkin was doubtless duly astonished
when his wife announced her discovery of a "young Heine with a
Scottish accent" and introduced him to the truant of his engineering class, Mrs. Sitwell had at once felt her interest awakened, and
now he strongly attracted Madame Garschine. She was "much
of an invalid, consistently gentle and sympathetic," about forty,
and "an exquisite musician." Colvin said that she conceived for
Stevenson "a great quasi-maternal tenderness," and vividly
remembered "her sharp twitch of pain as I spoke one day, while
she was walking with her arm in mine, of the fears entertained
by his friends for his health and future." If she is coarse and he
a cad, the passion of a woman of forty for a boy young enough
to be her son presents a disgusting spectacle of lust, but Madame
Garschine's infatuation for Stevenson seems to have been like

Anna Stormer's for young Lennan in Galsworthy's *The Dark Flower* and the Jewess Miriam's for the hero of Mr. Compton Mackenzie's *East Wind of Love*—productive of an experience rich in romantic and poetic beauty for both, remaining a cherished memory for the ageing woman and marking an epoch in the boy's sexual education. In Stevenson's case the memory was not spoiled by bitter recriminations for the fading of ephemeral passion; he parted from her with a promise to visit her in Russia the following summer, but he neither went nor ever saw her again.

He was twice visited during the winter by Colvin, who then introduced him to Andrew Lang. Colvin confessed to feeling trepidation at bringing together two young men so unlike in temperament and training.

> "On the one hand the young Oxford don, a successful and typical scholar on the regular academic lines, picturesque by the gift of nature but fastidiously correct and reserved, purely English in speech, with a recurring falsetto note in the voice—that kind of falsetto that bespeaks languor rather than vehemence; full of literature and pleasantry but on his guard, even to affectation, against any show of emotion, and consistently dissembling the *perfervidum ingenium* of his race, if he had it, under a cloak of indifference and light banter. On the other hand the brilliant, irregularly educated lad from Edinburgh, to the conventional eye an eccentrically ill-clad long-haired nondescript, with the rich Lallan accent on his tongue, the obvious innate virility and spirit of adventure in him ever in mutiny against the invalid habits imposed by ill-health, the vivid, demonstrative ways, every impulse of his heart and mind flashing out in the play of eye, feature, and gesture no less than in the humorous riot and poetical abundance of his talk."

But after some signs of coolness at their first meetings, a mutual liking developed, and Lang remained a firm friend and devoted admirer to the end. Sometimes Stevenson's eccentricities strongly offended his sense of correctness, and there is an amusing story of how one day, wearing his shabby cloak and a smoking cap, Stevenson met him in Bond Street and hailed him with his usual gay abandon, whereat Lang refused to stop, saying, "My character will stand a great deal, but it won't stand being seen talking to a thing like you in Bond Street." Fortunately for Stevenson's reputation, the friendship survived all the storms he put upon it, for Lang's enormous influence and his exaggerated adulation of Stevenson's work contributed more than all else to stabilising his celebrity.

With Colvin he seriously discussed his chances of making a living by writing, passionately desiring to be independent of his father. As he indicates in the essay, "Ordered South", which he wrote in depression at Mentone and appeared through Colvin's influence in *Macmillan's Magazine* for the following May, he thought he was suffering from fatal symptoms, and death could not long be delayed, and his feeling against his father was such that he dreaded dying before he had been able to repay his father for the money given to him, which he regarded in the light of a loan.

On his way home from Mentone, he stayed in Paris with his cousin Bob Stevenson, who was studying art and introduced him to Bohemian life of the Latin quarter. He returned home in May to find his refreshed spirits speedily damped by his parents' attitude of disapproval and sorrowful concern. "I am always bad with them," he confided to Mrs. Sitwell, "because they always seem to expect me to be not very good; and I am never good, because they never seem to see when I am good." He confessed that "I never feel so lonely as when I am too much with my father and mother, and I am ashamed of the feelings, which makes matters worse." He escaped from the depressing home atmosphere to visit Colvin in London, where he received inspiring encouragement, for besides "Ordered South" in *Macmillan's Magazine*, he had a paper accepted for the *Fortnightly Review* by John Morley, and an article on "Victor Hugo's Romances" for the *Cornhill* by Leslie Stephen, while through Colvin's influence he obtained some book-reviewing from the *Fortnightly* and the *Academy*. Colvin introduced him to many literary notabilities, including Thackeray's daughter, Anne Thackeray Ritchie, who, he told his mother, "has a jolly big mouth and is good-humoured looking," and Leslie Stephen, who seconded Colvin in his early encouragement of Stevenson, tried to get him an interview with Carlyle, but found the old man in a black mood and "sick of visitors." With Colvin and Lang as his proposer and seconder, he was made a member of the Savile Club, where in later years he and his cousin Bob became familiar and popular figures, and his first letter on club notepaper must have been that to his mother of July 1874, in which he discussed the subject of returning home with the significant words, "This is hypothetical, mind you, like my father's plans."

In his heart he was determined on a literary career, but the impossibility of making even the barest living by writing prevented his announcing the decision. His father was equally determined that he should persevere with the profession he had himself chosen, regarded his writing contemptuously as a waste of time, and would immediately have cut off his allowance if he had finally given up the law for literature. So Stevenson vacillated and argued, while hoping for the best and playing as much as possible on his mother's secret pride in his literary gifts and aspirations.

§ 2

Through the winter of 1874-75 he continued his law studies while writing his essays on Whitman and Knox, the latter of which gave him malicious glee as he visualised the austere Calvinist licking his lips over "his godly females". In February, Leslie Stephen visited Edinburgh to lecture, and took Stevenson with him to call on W. E. Henley, who was lying ill in Edinburgh Infirmary with tubercular disease of the foot.

Just as Stevenson was the first and most famous of Colvin's discoveries, so he was the first and most famous of Henley's "young men". Though little more than a year Stevenson's senior, Henley had a vital, inspiring personality which moved stronger characters than Stevenson's to enthusiasm. As in the cases of many cripples, the energy which he was incapable of exerting physically found vent in extraordinary intellectual force. In the first paper on *Talk and Talkers* in *Memories and Portraits*, Stevenson paints a vivid portrait of him as "Burly".

"Burly is a man of great presence; he commands a larger atmosphere, gives the impression of a grosser mass of character

than most men. It has been said of him that his presence could
be felt in a room you entered blindfold; and the same, I think,
has been said of other powerful constitutions condemned to
much physical inaction. There is something boisterous and
piratic in Burly's manner of talk which suits well enough
with this impression. He will roar you down, he will bury his
face in his hands, he will undergo passions of revolt and agony;
and meanwhile his attitude of mind is really both conciliatory
and receptive; and after Pistol has been out-Pistol'd, and the
welkin rung for hours, you begin to perceive a certain sub-
sidence in these spring torrents, points of agreement issue, and
you end arm-in-arm, and in a glow of mutual admiration. The
outcry only serves to make your final union the more unexpected
and precious. Throughout there has been perfect sincerity,
perfect intelligence, a desire to hear although not always to
listen, and an unaffected eagerness to meet concessions."

Henley possessed unquenchable courage, which inspired
affection and enthusiasm in all who knew him well. Having
already lost one foot, he was told that the other must also be
amputated to save his life, but though desperately poor and ill,
he made the painful journey from his Gloucester home to
Edinburgh to ask the advice of Joseph Lister. Like many other
medical benefactors who have pursued experiment in contempt of
professional convention, Lister was then frowned upon by the
conservative body of his profession, though in years to come he
was to be loaded with honours, including a baronetcy and a
peerage, and he asked Henley why he had come to him. Henley's
reply was characteristic; he came, he said, because the rest of the
medical profession declared that Lister was, in effect, "totally
incompetent." Just as he bravely staked the chance of losing his
foot, and possibly his life, on his own judgment, in defiance of the
massed chorus of conventional opinion, so he backed his own
independent judgment throughout his literary career. The policy
did not pay in a worldly sense, for he reaped none of life's material
rewards; each of the journals he edited, stamped boldly with his
own vital personality and a fine scorn of accepted convention, were
brilliant failures, and his last years were saved from beggary only
by a civil list pension. Moreover, his fearless independence made
him many jealous enemies among the timid adherents to orthodox

convention, and his offence against propriety in raising a lone voice in favour of the struggling cause of biographical honesty, and in protest against Graham Balfour's portrayal of Stevenson as a "seraph in chocolate," coming two years before his death in 1903, provided an excuse for a conspiracy to kill the just survival of his reputation. Bearing "vivid news of the overflow of Henley's gall," the pundit Gosse led Henry James to suppose that Henley's article provided "rather a striking and lurid—and so far interesting case—of long discomfortable jealousy and ranklement turned at last to posthumous (as it were!) malignity, and making the man do, *coram publico*, his ugly act, risking the dishonour for the assuagement." That James was not completely gulled by Gosse's presentment of the matter, is testified by his implied rebuke in the same letter to the critics who were engaged in disservice to Stevenson's reputation by exalting, through "insistent publicity," his personality at the expense of his books. He also mentioned significantly that Graham Balfour found Henley's article "less bad than he expected," and "he apparently feared more." Balfour knew, as James suspected and Gosse either did not suspect or did not want to suspect, how much he had suppressed and distorted to present an ornamental view of only one side of the medal, and he probably expected more than Henley's protest, because his estimate of human nature was not so low as to suppose that only Henley would have the courage to value truth above Humbug.

Posterity has already recognised that Henley had justice on his side in this snarling over Stevenson's bones, and that he alone had not only the honesty and the courage to despise Humbug's suppression of facts, but also confidence in the quality of his dead friend's work to survive for its own sake, in spite of any reflections on his life and personality. And the time approaches when posterity will arrive at a just estimate of Henley's merits, an estimate which will reveal him as one of the most impressive and influential personalities in the contemporary world of letters, a champion of truth and honesty in an age of pharisaic Humbug, an editor and critic who by independent judgment and generous encouragement stimulated and fostered the careers of many talented writers, a master of fluent and vigorous prose, and a poet of no mean order. The success of the conspiracy to obscure his reputation is witnessed in the derision which greets the mention of his name as the author of " Out of the night that covers me," the verses included in the additions to Palgrave's *Golden Treasury*, which now represent all that is known of Henley by any save a handful of students. Knowing nothing of the man, and reading the verses with the supercilious superficiality which passes in Bloomsbury and academic circles as "critical detachment", facile critics seize upon the phrase "captain of my soul" to label Henley a truculent jingo, blowing a trombone in the imperialist orchestra, of which Kipling was first violin and Joseph Chamberlain conductor. It is true that Henley set Kipling's foot on the first rung of the ladder to success, as he set many another, by publishing *Barrack Room Ballads* when Kipling was unknown, that he championed individualism, that he preferred patriotism to the vacillating sentimentality of "enlightened democracy", and in later times would probably have been a Fascist. But how many of his critics realise that the "captain of my soul" verses were written in 1875, after nearly two years in hospital in Edinburgh, when he was only twenty-six, and when he owed the salvation of his one remaining foot to the skill of an individual to whom he had gone on the strength of his own judgment and in defiance of the counsel of accredited opinion?

For twenty months, from 1873 to 1875, Henley lay in the Old Infirmary at Edinburgh under Lister's care. When Stevenson was introduced to him, "the poor fellow sat up in his bed with his hair and beard all tangled, and talked as cheerfully as if he had been in a King's palace, or the great King's palace of the blue air." When he left Lister's charge with his foot saved, he remained for two years in Edinburgh lodgings till, in 1877, he went to London to succeed Robert Glasgow Brown as editor of the journal called *London*.

§ 3

Henceforward life in Edinburgh was less dull for Stevenson. He and Charles Baxter and Henley were three of an age with views in common, and talked together by the hour. When Henley was well enough, Stevenson took him for drives about the countryside; he also introduced him to his only congenial friends in respectable circles, the Fleeming Jenkins. A lover of literature and himself a stylist in prose, Henley did much to encourage him in the cultivation of that limpid clarity in writing, that unerring selection of the right word and combination of words, which became the primary quality of his power to enchant. From a literary point of view, Henley was even more important to Stevenson than Colvin, Stephen, or Lang. But from Thomas Stevenson's point of view, he must have seemed the devil's agent, for he confirmed Stevenson in his choice of writing as a career, and by his sympathetic friendship and encouragement aided and abetted him in his revolt against parental authority. During the next two or three years, Stevenson shared Henley's Edinburgh lodgings for at least two spells of several weeks, when his irate father had been provoked to fury and refused to have him in the house.

Though Kate Drummond had passed from his ken, he still persisted in his Hyde-like excursions to the Edinburgh slums, and during one of his sojourns with Henley, his friend had to nurse him through the virulent stages of a disease contracted in his adventures, which is said to have left a legacy to his constitution for life. He continually escaped from Edinburgh in travel; though his impressions of the lonely islet of Earraid, described in a paper of *Memories and Portraits* and introduced into *Kidnapped*, were gained in an expedition undertaken while he was studying engineering. Most of his intimate acquaintance with the Highlands, which he capitalised so profitably in *Kidnapped* and *Catriona*, was acquired on pleasure trips in these years, sometimes with Walter Simpson, son of the famous obstetrician who popularised the use of chloroform, sometimes with the Fleeming Jenkins, once or twice even with his father. In each of these years he also spent some time with his cousin Bob at the village of Grez, near Fontainebleau, a fashionable resort for the artists of Montparnasse, where Sir William Rothenstein found him well remembered in the 'nineties. His long, lean figure, cloaked and shabby, became well known in the Latin quarter of Paris, and one old restaurateur on the quais clearly remembered in 1922 how he would sit over a carafe of wine, busily turning the leaves of books in tattered paper covers. He bought books on the quais, for he was a prodigal book-buyer, having a horror of working in libraries, where he felt "like Esther before Ahasuerus."

The frequency and length of his visits to France increased after July, 1875, when he was called to the Scottish bar, for his being called seemed to show a definite step towards a settled career, and his father not only made him a present of a thousand pounds but liberally subsidised his travelling. He found an attraction to detain him there throughout the summer of 1876, for it was then, at Montigny, near Grez, that he met his future wife, Fanny van de Grift Osbourne. Like Mrs. Sitwell, she was unhappily married and living apart from her husband, and though he confessed to have fallen in love with her at first sight, the coincidence of her condition with that of the woman who had proved his most confidential friend must have presented an intriguing attraction. Stevenson was the sort of man requiring a predominant maternal element in a woman's love; he liked to be "petted", and felt a proud, sensual urge to be sole possessor of a woman rich in the experience of ripe maturity, which derived an added stimulus from her being the mother of another man's children. Like D. H. Lawrence, he had the irresistible preoccupation with sensuality, commonly found with constitutional tubercular tendencies, and his romance with Fanny Osbourne finds a curious parallel in that of Lawrence and his wife.

Fanny Osbourne was thirty-six, more than ten years Stevenson's senior, with a daughter of seventeen and a son of eight. An American by birth, with Dutch and Swedish blood in her ancestry. she was, in Colvin's description, "small, dark-complexioned, eager."

"In spite of her squarish build she was supple and elastic in all her movements; her hands and feet were small and beautifully modelled, though not meant for or used to idleness; the head, under its crop of close-waving thick black hair, was of a build and character that somehow suggested Napoleon, by the firm setting of the jaw and the beautifully precise and delicate modelling of the nose and lips: the eyes were full of sex and mystery as they changed from fire and fun to gloom or tenderness; and it was from between a fine pearly set of small teeth that there came the clear metallic accents of her intensely human and often quaintly individual speech."

Everybody who met her noticed that "firm setting of the jaw"; it clearly marked her as a woman to avoid crossing, it looms significant in the eventual breach between Stevenson and Henley, it intimidated men like Colvin into ready acceptance of the belief that she was an admirable custodian furnished by benign providence for an unstable character like Stevenson's, while it inspired that sphinx of subtlety, Henry James, long afterwards to apostrophise her as a "poor barbarous and merely instinctive lady." She was not a woman to be trifled with, the more so since she had already suffered unhappiness in marriage; she was prepared to be maternal in a firm, practical way, but Stevenson must soon have realised that she was not the sort of woman to allow sentiment or her senses to seduce her into an idyll. Hence her attraction for him was enhanced, not only by unsatisfied desire of possession, but by the power of a masterful, possessive personality over one weaker and more sensitive.

Except for the period occupied in the canoeing expedition with Walter Simpson described in *An Inland Voyage*, Stevenson figuratively sat at her feet throughout the summer of 1876, reading aloud while she reclined listening in a hammock, "looking prettier and prettier." In the autumn he tore himself away to return to Edinburgh, where for a few weeks or months he assiduously attended Parliament House in the hope of securing briefs. No doubt his motive was mainly, as suggested by Mr. Steuart, "to placate the paternal conscience," for his father still declined to countenance his adoption of a literary career, but in the sudden application to duty so alien to his inclination may be detected the first symptoms of Fanny Osbourne's influence. Independence was more than ever necessary if he was to secure possession of this woman, who had become the dominant desire of his life, for he dared not even mention to his orthodox parents a suggestion of his attraction to a married woman. From Henley, Colvin, and his other advisers, as well as his own little experience, he knew that there was no more hazardous career than writing, and in these days when his literary talent could be appreciated only by such blind faith as his mother's and Cummy's, or such individual judgment as Henley's and Mrs. Sitwell's, firm-chinned Fanny, nothing if not prudent and practical, probably counselled him to follow the eminently respectable profession of the law, in which the influence of his father's friends might assist his advancement.

But Stevenson soon found that, without stronger influence than merely casual friendships, without money, natural aptitude, and slices of luck, the law offered no more immediate prospects of an independent living than literature, and faced with the choice between two desperate hazards, he naturally chose the one for which he felt inclination and confidence in his abilities. He was not without encouragement to follow his literary destiny, for he was regularly appearing in print. Leslie Stephen was his principal source of encouragement, and following such travel papers as "Forest Notes" and "Walking Tours" in the May and June numbers, the first *Virginibus Puerisque* essay charmed readers of *Cornhill* in August 1876, and contributions over the initials "R.L.S.," which were widely rumoured as signifying the "Real Leslie Stephen", became an eagerly awaited feature of the magazine. Whether or not Stevenson took Thackeray's essays as a model, the *Virginibus Puerisque* essays closely resemble the manner of the *Roundabout Papers*, which had provided the magazine's liveliest charm in the early days of *Cornhill*, a charm entirely lacking in such subsequent features as Stephen's own academically formal *Hours in a Library*.

As an essayist in the Elian tradition, Stevenson thus already had a market and the making of a reputation. But he realised that the rewards of success in this channel amounted only to admiration within the narrow confines of cultured tastes and an inconsiderable income, and the spring of 1877 found him at work on a novel, *The Hair Trunk, or The Ideal Commonwealth*, "a most absurd story of a lot of young Cambridge fellows who are going to found a new society, with no ideas on the subject, and nothing but Bohemian tastes in the place of ideas." It was to include "burglary, marine fight, life on desert island on west coast of Scotland, sloops, etc.," and Henley laughed till he cried over the first chapter, but it was abandoned in a fragmentary state. But he made his bow as a writer of short stories in 1877, the story about Villon, *A Lodging for the Night*, rich in the eerie gruesomeness of Poe, being accepted by *Temple Bar*, to be followed in the same magazine by *The Sire de Maletroit's Door*. His study of *François Villon: Student, Poet, and Housebreaker*, a subject of obvious appeal to the Bohemian Stevenson, and one of the best critical studies he ever did, appeared in the same year in *Cornhill*, which printed among other essays of his, *An Apology for Idlers*, which he described to Mrs. Sitwell as "really a defence of R.L.S." In his letters he mentions several projects unfinished, abandoned, or rejected by editors, but he sent the story of *Will o' the Mill* "red hot to Stephen in a fit of haste . . . quite prepared for a refusal," and had it accepted as his first fiction in *Cornhill*, where Henry James read it and described it as standing "in the same relation to the usual 'magazine' story that a glass of Johannisberg occupies to a draught of table d'hote *vin ordinaire*." In May 1878 his first book, *An Inland Voyage*, was published by Kegan Paul, Trench, and Co., who paid twenty pounds for the copyright. He was surprised that the reviewers liked the book so much, and still more surprised in consequence, knowing yet little of the value of the average reviewer, that it sold so few copies that most of the small edition had to be remaindered.

"The world is such a dance," he said in the autumn of 1878, after two years spent mostly in France running after Fanny Osbourne, but continually crossing to Edinburgh. In later years, he worked best when sitting up in bed, but he always had the faculty of writing under any conditions—in train, boat, garden, on a railway station platform or at a roadside inn. Henley had left Edinburgh to edit *London*, in which *The New Arabian Nights* ran serially from June to October, 1878, and contributed largely to the journal's ruin. Henley, then engaged in enthusiastically publicising the merits of the authentic *Arabian Nights*, probably himself suggested the idea in outline to Stevenson, and Bob Stevenson is said to have originated the idea of the Suicide Club, but the whole fanciful, fantastic conception had no hope of appealing to the staid taste of the 'seventies, though sixteen years later such work by an unknown author might have been welcomed in the *Yellow Book*. As Andrew Lang generously admitted, probably Henley alone then "foresaw that Mr. Stevenson's *forte* was to be fiction, not essay-writing," and he alone had the courage to print *The New Arabian Nights*, which had to wait another four years for publication in book form. From June to December of the same year, *Picturesque Notes on Edinburgh* appeared serially in the *Portfolio*, the editor of which, P. G. Hamerton, then secured publication in a folio volume by Seeley, Jackson, and Halliday, and the valuable essay on Walt Whitman, having been on the stocks for four or five years, was published in the *New Quarterly Magazine* for October.

In the summer of 1878, while visiting Burford Bridge with his parents, Stevenson met George Meredith and gave him a copy of *An Inland Voyage*. Meredith wrote him an encouraging letter in praise of the book, and also asked him to convey to Henley his appreciation of Henley's praise of his work, remarking that "I, who have worked for so many years not supposing that any one paid much heed to me, find it extraordinary." Meredith felt sufficient appreciation of Stevenson's talents and personal liking to invite him to stay with him the following summer, and he also urged John Morley to offer him work in the *Fortnightly Review*.

But by that time Stevenson was too occupied with momentous affairs to pursue Morley. In the late summer of 1878, Fanny Osbourne left for California. There is no doubt that, though she had preserved impregnable her virtue in spite of all appeals to her heart and senses, there was a definite understanding between them, and she returned to America with the fixed purpose of obtaining a divorce in order to marry Stevenson. Though she won her way into respectable marriage with the man she desired after four years of waiting in patient fortitude, at an age when every year meant much to a woman, she paid a heavy price for her triumph. For one thing, the fair face of their romance was scarred by Stevenson's fugitive amours. Strong sensual instincts such as his could not suffer continual stimulation from being regularly in the society of the woman he passionately desired without assuagement, and since her strength of character fortified her virtue against nature, he sought the assuagement elsewhere. Mr. Steuart has traced at least two amours in this period of his life—with too good-looking though lower-class young women, the one a dark, slender daughter of an Aberdeen builder and carpenter, the other tall, fair, and handsomely proportioned, said to be the daughter of a Midlothian village blacksmith. Mr. Steuart also learned that the fair Roxana met the exotic Statira on at least one occasion, when "a scene of fury resulting in physical violence" took place between the rival queans near Swanston Cottage, when Stevenson was there with his parents.

These discoveries by Mr. Steuart strengthen the charge of hypocrisy against Stevenson for his unsatisfactory *Cornhill* essay on Burns, which he wrote at this time, and in which, in marked contrast with his sympathetic treatment of Whitman and Villon, he condescends to Burns as "a country Don Juan", with all the self-righteousness of a respectable pundit. But, as Mr. Steuart shrewdly suggests, he probably saw himself as just such another "country Don Juan" as Burns, and wrote the essay in a mood of self-flagellation inspired by shame and remorse. The emotions of his father, on witnessing a brawl between a brace of lusty wenches over the body of his son, can be imagined. Stevenson was probably only received back into the parental fold after many recriminations, and having given a strict undertaking to discontinue his connection with both women. He was of a sensitive temperament to shrink from scenes of violent emotion, and his inamoratas were obviously not wanting in passion. So he wrote with feeling of Burns's amour with Jean Armour: "It is the punishment of Don Juanism to create continually false positions —relations in life which are wrong in themselves, and which it is equally wrong to break or to perpetuate." Nor had he only shame and remorse for having injured his two mistresses; he had the additional shame and remorse for having been guilty of infidelity to his higher love in ephemeral philandering.

He spent a year apart from Fanny Osbourne, during which he wrote and published *Travels with a Donkey*, the story of an excursion in the Cevennes, undertaken immediately after Fanny's departure for California. In his writing, he vented the longing of a lover separated from his mistress in addressing many passages of pointed meaning to Fanny. The book was treated with scant

respect by most of the reviewers, though Meredith declared himself
and Morley "wonderfully pleased" with it, and like *An Inland
Voyage* it was fated to be remaindered. He was much with
Henley, both in London and Edinburgh, collaborating with him
in writing a play, *Deacon Brodie*, and while in London he applied
vainly for work on *The Times*.

Suddenly came news from California that Fanny Osbourne,
after starting divorce proceedings, had fallen seriously ill under
the stress of anxiety, and as suddenly Stevenson acted: he sailed
for New York on 7th August, 1879. His action suggests to Mr.
Steuart the "flint" which he and Lord Guthrie assume to have
lain among the foundations of Stevenson's character. He left
Edinburgh without a word to his parents, spent a few days in
London making preparations, and was seen off from St. Pancras
by Henley, *en route* for Glasgow, whence his boat sailed. In
London, Henley, Colvin, and Edmund Gosse vainly attempted to
dissuade him from his purpose, to which Mr. Steuart sees him
holding coolly and resolutely, with the determination of a man
in whom there was "flint", tempered by "a large admixture of
selfishness." But was not his conduct natural in an unstable
character, driven to a desperate decision by emotional stress and
longing? A strong, silent hero, of the type soon to be an essential
of popular fiction, would have gone to his parents and said,
"Father, mother, I go to the woman I love, who is a married
woman," and having waited with bowed head while his father
waxed near apoplexy, have kissed his weeping mother before
going forth, face upturned serenely to the wind, and conscience
clear. But Stevenson shrank from a scene, which could serve no
useful purpose; he was determined to go to Fanny Osbourne, he
knew his father would never countenance his going, and so it
was better to save his feelings and theirs from the harrowing
of a scene. Likewise, he refused to listen to his friends' arguments
with the obstinacy of a weak man committed to a desperate
undertaking; his state of mind when he boarded the ship, so far
from reflecting the serene confidence of a strong man adhering
stoically to a considered resolve, presented a pathetic confusion in
which despair was dominant—writing to Colvin, with an en-
closure for his father, he confessed to feeling incapable of "a

regret, a hope, a fear, or an inclination," and signed himself "the husk that once contained R.L.S."

The charge of selfishness was hard on him. He had very little money, for though his own expenses were not extravagant, he lacked any pretensions to native Scotch thrift, delighted to appear generous and open-handed, and never resisted an appeal for charity; hence the thousand pounds received on his call to the bar was gone. So long as he continued in his father's good books, he could rely on liberal subsidies; by offending his father and fleeing like a thief in the night, he threw himself entirely on his own resources. His health was bad; seeking to dissuade him from going, Colvin warned him that if the "spirit will go playing fast and loose with its body, the body will some day decline the association—and we shall be left without our friend." Finally Henley characteristically appealed not to sentiment or considerations of health, but to a common-sense view of practical policy; men like Morley and Stephen would give him work if he went hat in hand to woo them for it—he must "see that England and a quiet life are what he wants and must have if he means to make —I won't say reputation—but money by literature." It seems hard to call a man selfish, who thus, with his eyes open, gratuitously sacrificed parental favour, financial interests, welfare of health, and prospects of success in the career of his choice; he might surely have been more obviously convicted of selfishness, if he had decided prudently to preserve these advantages and wait comfortably at home, while the woman he wanted straightened out her own affairs and put herself in a condition to be respectably married.

What must have been Stevenson's feelings? He had allowed counsels of prudence to rob him of Kate Drummond, and so laid himself open to bitter agonies of self-reproach. He had recently felt ashamed of himself for behaving like a cad and a blackguard to the blacksmith's daughter and the Aberdonian girl. Should he now lay himself open to life-long regret and eternal reproach from Fanny by failing to offer her his comfort and counsel when she so needed them?

Stevenson travelled second-class, at two guineas more than the steerage fare of six guineas. During the crossing he wrote

The Story of a Lie, and made copious notes of his experiences and fellow-travellers with a view to the book called *The Amateur Emigrant*. For the sake of economy and material for his book, he crossed America on an emigrant train, "sitting on the top of the cars," always writing. He wore "nothing but a shirt and a pair of trousers," the shirt unbuttoned, he shared "a tin wash-bowl among four," he took laudanum to obtain sleep. "What it is to be ill in an emigrant train let those declare who know," he wrote to Henley; his illness was a "subject of great mirth to some of my fellow-travellers." Arrived at San Francisco, he found Fanny recovered of her illness and gone to Monterey, a hundred and fifty miles down the coast. He fell ill in the cross-country journey, and was found lying sick in his camp by two ranchers, who kept him at their goat-ranch for three weeks. In his letters he confessed to feeling lonely, despondent, even miserable, but to both Henley and Colvin he reiterated defiantly, "I am doing right."

At Monterey, a beautiful spot on the Pacific, with a population "mostly Mexican and Indian" and "about that of a dissenting chapel on a wet Sunday in a strong church neighbourhood," he lodged with a French doctor. In spite of illness, he worked incessantly. *The Pavilion on the Links* was sent off to Henley in October; "carpentry" he called it, "but not bad at that; and who else can carpenter in England now that Wilkie Collins is played out?" He needed money badly, for he was not only so poor that he reduced his daily expenditure on food to the equivalent of a shilling and tenpence-halfpenny, but was faced with the prospect of soon having a wife and stepson to support. "Dibbs and speed are my mottoes," he told Henley, but illness and anxiety were not the best conditions under which to work at high speed. When at Christmas, Colvin received the first part of *The Amateur Emigrant*, he found it " a spiritless record of squalid experiences, little likely to advance his still only half-established reputation." To poor Stevenson, recovering from a bout of pleurisy, dosing himself with aconite, and staying in bed all day because he "had no other means of keeping warm for my work," the verdict came as a crushing blow. No wonder he confessed to Henley that "at times I get terribly frightened about my work, which seems to advance too slowly." At times he felt that he could not survive the ordeal; "I am going for thirty now," he told Gosse, "and unless I can catch a little rest before long, I have, I may tell you in confidence, no hope of seeing thirty-one." His contraction of pleurisy in a climate so mild awakened him with a shock to the ravages worked on his constitution in these few weeks of hardship, and the ominous reflection that it was "six years, all but a few months, since I was obliged to spend twenty-four hours in bed," reminded him of the foreboding he had experienced in "Ordered South". At San Francisco in December he wrote:

"Death is no bad friend; a few aches and gasps, and we are done; like the truant child, I am beginning to grow weary and timid in this big jostling city, and could run to my nurse, even although she should have to whip me before putting me to bed."

Sometimes he wrote himself "into a kind of spirits," and even when he heard Colvin's verdict on *The Amateur Emigrant*, he determined to finish it, and remarking jokingly that "it bored me hellishly" to write it, decided it was only fair that it should "bore others to read it." "There shall be no more books of travel for me," he said; "I'll stick to stories." And "I'm not frightened," he protested bravely to Colvin; "if the *Emigrant* was a failure, the *Pavilion* by your leave, was not." Nevertheless, he plainly hinted that he hungered for encouragement.

"I don't spend much, only you and Henley both seem to think my work rather bosh nowadays, and I do want to make as much as I was making, that is £200; if I can do that, I can swim; last year, with my ill health I touched only £109, that would not do, I could not fight it through on that; but on £200 as I say, I am good for the world."

Often he felt home-sick; often pathos creeps heart-rendingly into his letters.

"Last night, when I felt so ill, the supposed ague chill, it

seemed strange not to be able to afford a drink. I would have
walked half a mile, tired as I felt, for a brandy and soda."

In February he was cheered by a "long and kind letter" from
Henley, which it must have cost Henley some compromise with
impatience to write. For Henley himself was having a struggle
to make his way in London, and Stevenson's self-imposed exile
seemed to him such a hopeless impediment to his chance of success,
that he asked Colvin to write to Stevenson for him, "being too
blasphemously given towards California and California things
to trust myself." But he was active in Stevenson's interest, and
suggested that he might find a publisher for a volume of his
essays. Stevenson replied with glee: "I am well, cheerful, busy,
hopeful; I cannot be knocked down; I do not mind about the
Emigrant." He had sent off his studies of Thoreau and Yoshida
Torajiro to Leslie Stephen for *Cornhill*; he had high hopes of two
stories, *A Vendetta in the West*, over which he toiled for weeks and
finally abandoned, and *The Greenwood State*, which was eventually
finished as *Prince Otto.*

But the phase of buoyancy was brief. In March his landlady's
little girl lay ill and dying, and sitting long hours by the child's
bedside, Stevenson himself fell dangerously ill. For six weeks
"it was a toss-up for life or death;" he was "on the verge of a
galloping consumption, cold sweats, prostrating attacks of cough,
sinking fits in which I lost the power of speech, fever, and all the
ugliest circumstances of the disease." Fanny Osbourne's devoted
nursing and the attending doctor's skill and assiduity pulled him
through, but as he lay convalescent, the doctor's orders were
uncompromising: "a sea voyage would simply kill him at once"
—he must "go to the mountains," which, as Colvin tersely told
Henley, "means lungs"—there was "no work to be done meantime." Fanny had no money of her own, and with Stevenson
temporarily incapable of earning anything, she addressed an
appeal to his parents. The answer came by telegraph in April:
"Count on 250 pounds annually."

Perhaps his parents thought that he had been sufficiently
punished for his romantic adventure, perhaps that marriage with
the writer of the common-sense letter received might prove the

safe anchor of a rudderless ship; in any case they were not prepared to allow their only son to die in a distant land for want of money. So Stevenson married Fanny Osbourne in May, 1880, and their honeymoon was his convalescing trip to the mountains. Firm-chinned Fanny, after four years of waiting, had won her way to respectable marriage with the man she wanted, but she paid her price. She wrote to Colvin at this time that she was "trying to take care of my dearest boy," and such was her daily task for the rest of his life. For the terrible struggle with illness and anxiety through the horror of that Californian winter left an indelible mark on his constitution; henceforth he walked with consumption as his shadow, and every one knew that life would not be long for him.

CHAPTER FIVE

Stevenson Married and Mature

§ 1

ON 7th August, 1880, a year to the day after his sailing from Glasgow, Stevenson left New York for Liverpool with his wife and stepson. They were met on the quay by his parents and Colvin, who thought "it made things pleasanter my being there." He found Stevenson "looking better than I expected, and improved by his new teeth; but weak and easily flustered," and so frail that "you could put your thumb and finger round his thigh." With Fanny he was not impressed; he told Henley that Stevenson's mother looked "the fresher of the two", and wondered "whether you and I will ever get reconciled to the little determined brown face and white teeth and grizzling (for that's what it's up to) hair, which we are to see beside him in future."

Behind the "little determined face" sheltered a determined little brain. She knew what she had to face from Stevenson's family and friends, who saw her as the sole reason for the escapade which had nearly killed him, permanently ruined his health, and seriously prejudiced his career. She knew she looked no Helen of Troy or Cleopatra, for whom the world might be "well lost"; she was grizzling and already a grandmother. But she had personality, brains, and the charm which had been sufficient to captivate the impressionable Stevenson. Colvin thought "the old folks put a most brave and most kind face on it indeed." Fanny knew that so much was bound to be so, since they had already forgiven and were welcoming their prodigal, but she knew that they were inwardly as curiously critical as Colvin. She felt that Colvin could wait; he was only staying for lunch, and she could tackle him later. Stevenson's mother was the typical Victorian lady, stoically subordinating the ruling passion of her life, her love for her only son, from a sense of duty to devotion and submissiveness to her husband. If she could win the father, the mother would want no winning, since all she desired was union between father and son, reconciling her devotional duty with her love.

So Fanny set herself to win the gander with the golden eggs. She profited by a probable predisposition in her favour on sight. With painful memories of poor Kate Drummond, the Aberdonian, and the blacksmith's amazon, Thomas Stevenson must have been forearmed with fortitude to welcome a painted harpy, and felt glad relief on seeing a demure, matronly little body, with all the apparent attributes of respectability. Perhaps she was hardly the daughter-in-law he had hoped for, but then Stevenson was far from all that he had desired in a son; that she was "grizzling" and a grandmother appeared advantageous, since there would be no nonsense about her, and her mature discretion would balance his son's eccentricity. With so many trumps in her hand, Fanny had only to play her cards well; her mother-in-law watched her play them, and found it "quite amusing how entirely she agreed with my husband on all subjects." Hence Colvin was able to record that "there sprang up between her and his father the closest possible affection and confidence."

Stevenson's marriage with Fanny thus provided happiness at least for his father. The old gentleman had less than seven years to live, and he had Fanny to thank that they were spent on terms of affection and intimacy with his son, such as neither had ever known before. No more was there strife, no more disgraceful entanglements, shocking outbursts against religion, and fitful comings and goings. The prodigal had returned with a vengeance; he was firmly fastened to the apron-strings of a rock of respectability.

The rest of the summer was spent with his parents in the Highlands. But Stevenson was so ill that he was warned against wintering in England and ordered by his doctor to Davos. On his way he and Fanny paused in London, and she girded up her loins for battle. Stevenson's friends flocked to see him, eager to decoy him to the Savile Club to hear the tale of his Californian adventures in such late sittings as he describes in "Talk and Talkers", and which Gosse long afterwards recalled as "worthy of the finest traditions of eager, cultivated communication." But

Fanny put her foot down; his state of health would not permit
late nights. No doubt she marked Henley and Bob Stevenson
as the two most boisterous spirits; the latter's influence she could
control, but she must have sensed in Henley a dominance menacing to her own. Already "blasphemously given towards California
and California things," Henley was not propitiated, and the
tale of his friendship with Stevenson from this time is its gradual
undermining by Fanny till its ultimate breakage.

Colvin, however, being at once more respectable and influential, and less formidable as a possible counter-influence than
Henley, she set herself to win. Within a few weeks, she was writing
to him from Davos, confiding all the sayings and doings of her
husband as to a special friend, flatteringly asking his advice, and
cunningly making herself the channel of communication between
him and Stevenson. It was not long before she addressed him
fulsomely as "dear friend" and "best friend", and sent her love
or was his affectionately. Like Thomas Stevenson, Colvin was
won: he saw "in Stevenson's wife a character as strong, interesting
and romantic almost as his own; an inseparable sharer of all
his thoughts, and staunch companion of all his adventures; the
most open-hearted of friends to all who loved him; the most
shrewd and stimulating critic of his work; and in sickness,
despite her own precarious health, the most devoted and most
efficient of nurses."

Mrs. Sitwell was not such an easy conquest. The editor of
Colvin's correspondence, Mr. E. V. Lucas, suggests that "it would
not have been unnatural had Mrs. Osbourne, as she was in 1876,
resented Stevenson's dependence upon her predecessor," but adds
that "I have no reason to suppose that she did." Whether Fanny
resented Mrs. Sitwell's previous influence or not, she was not
worried over the possiblity of such influence's continuance; she
knew to whose apron strings her husband was going to be securely
tied for the future. But she could not offend Mrs. Sitwell without
losing Colvin, whose usefulness she could not afford to sacrifice;
therefore she set out to propitiate her. Mr. Lucas prints "some
very affectionate letters" from Fanny to Mrs. Sitwell, naïvely
remarking that he has "no doubt, although none seem to exist,
that the replies were punctual and equally warm." That the

replies do not "seem to exist" may or may not have significance, but obviously "it would not have been unnatural" if Mrs. Sitwell had regarded with suspicion, and a ready tendency to adverse criticism, the woman who, already married and a mother like herself, and of the same mature age as herself, had yet surmounted respectability's obstacles to secure legal possession of the gifted young man, whom she had herself encouraged out of purely maternal affection. Fanny was much too shrewd not to be aware of this attitude, and the reader of her "very affectionate" letters senses the presence of claws, hidden but none the less ready to strike, in the caressing velvet of her paws. In her first letter to Colvin from Davos, she asks him to "give my dearest love to my pretty friend, who really (but that you must know as well as I) grows more lovely as time passes by. I wish I knew how she did it." No doubt Colvin ingenuously saw nothing in this beyond a sincere compliment to the lady of his heart, but when he conveyed the message, Mrs. Sitwell may be imagined to have smiled a little wryly.

There was no more confidential correspondence directly between Stevenson and Mrs. Sitwell. Mrs. Sitwell wrote, but Fanny answered, in strict accordance with the conventions. In his published correspondence appear only three letters from Stevenson to Mrs. Sitwell after his marriage, and two of them were obviously written under Fanny's eye. Shrewdly she seized the opportunities offered by his frequent illness to act as his amanuensis, so acquiring the freedom of his writing-desk as a natural habit; henceforth he wrote little which could escape her watchful eye.

Stevenson was very ill at Davos. Reading was all he was "fit for", and he wrote nothing throughout the winter except an essay for the *Fortnightly Review* on "The Morality of the Profession of Letters", his *Cornhill* essay on Pepys (remarkable autobiographically for its gibes at respectability, and the improbable but respectable supposition that Pepys's "period of gallantry" ended with his diary), and some newspaper articles on Davos. He meditated a *History of the Highlands*, for which his father industriously occupied himself in research, and though Stevenson progressed little beyond drafting a synopsis of the book, his notes, especially on the trial of James Stewart for the Appin murder, stood him in good stead when he came to write *Kidnapped* and *Catriona*. *The Amateur Emigrant* was printed, but withdrawn from publication at his father's expense, on the advice of Colvin and others that it might be harmful to Stevenson's reputation. Whenever illness affected his ability to work, his recovery was prejudiced by moods of depression, and he became so morbid that his friends were alarmed. John Addington Symonds, whose tubercular affliction had just driven him to settle permanently at Davos, advised him to try reviewing as an outlet for his urge to write; apparently both Symonds and Leslie Stephen feared that his mind might become unbalanced unless he obtained relief from the depression of inertia.

Returning to Scotland for the summer, he succeeded to getting down to work sufficiently to produce the splendid story of *Thrawn Janet*, *The Body-Snatcher*, and *The Merry Men*, which plainly reveal him as one of the most successful followers of Poe. But the prospect of his ever making a living by writing seemed so remote that he astonishingly offered himself as a candidate for the chair of Constitutional Law and History at Edinburgh University. He himself thought it "a mad thing", but was "advised on all hands to go on"; doubtless Fanny coveted the impeccable respectability of a university don's spouse. But university dons rarely confer their sinecures on men of imagination, and imagination was Stevenson's sole apparent recommendation for the post. He obtained testimonials from all his influential literary friends, Stephen, Colvin, Symonds, Gosse, Andrew Lang, and P. G. Hamerton; apparently Henley was not asked, being of insufficient eminence to impress academic authority. Among his professional sponsors was the educationist Meiklejohn; notable by his absence was Fleeming Jenkin, who presumably declined to associate himself with a hopeless project or to lend himself, even in friendship's name, to a barefaced attempt at place seeking. Stevenson's candidature failed abjectly; he received only three votes.

Late in the summer he was better in health and projecting a book of "Tales for Winter Nights", to include *Thrawn Janet* and others of the Poe variety—though he affected to be influenced, not by Poe, but by Wilkie Collins. In August he was "on another

lay", writing *The Sea Cook, or Treasure Island: A Story for Boys.*
He confessed that the idea was "purely owing to Lloyd", meaning
his stepson, Lloyd Osbourne. Always fond of children, as he had
shown in the case of Madame Garschine's little girl, he made a
friend and comrade of his stepson, an unconventional attitude in
those days of the heavy parental rôle. He was always natural
and at his ease with the boy, never condescending with obvious
effort to the intellectual level of his years, nor changing the
subject of conversation when he entered the room. He played
with him by the hour, at first with soldiers, later with a printing
press "managed by Samuel Lloyd Osbourne and Co.," and he
encouraged him in writing such blood-and-thunder stories as he
himself had written in boyhood. The idea of *Treasure Island*
occurred on a wet afternoon when he amused his stepson by
drawing a map of an imaginary island—the map which was to
figure as the frontispiece of the book.

Not to Colvin or Gosse could he confide that he, a published
Cornhill essayist, was wasting his time in scribbling a blood-and-
thunder tale for boys; it was to the more human Henley that he
wrote news of the story when he had finished two chapters, a little
ashamed of his enthusiasm for it and joking to hide his embarrassment. " If this don't fetch the kids," he said, "why, they have
gone rotten since my day." He found some difficulty in sacrificing
realistic effect to respectability's requirements; "Buccaneers
without oaths—bricks without straw. But youth and the fond
parent have to be considered." And another remark to Henley has
significance in view of the subsequent charge against Stevenson
of inability to draw characters of women: "No woman in the
story, Lloyd's orders; and who so blithe to obey?"

The character of Squire Trelawney he drew from his conception
of Walter Savage Landor, on whom Colvin was then writing a
study for the "English Men of Letters" series. Two years later
he told Henley that "it was the sight of your maimed strength
and masterfulness that begot John Silver . . . the idea of the
maimed man, ruling and dreaded by the sound was entirely
taken from you." Stevenson's impression of Henley's dominance
over his disability was shared years later by Mr. H. G. Wells,
who, on meeting President Franklin Roosevelt in 1934, was

reminded, by "the same big chest and the same infirmity," of when, forty years before, he had first interviewed Henley at his Putney riverside house, and seen his "magnificent torso upon shrunken withered legs."

For a month the story progressed apace to the nineteenth chapter, "no writing, just drive along as the words come and the pen will scratch." He talked of following it with a yarn called "Jerry Abershaw: A Tale of Putney Heath", thought the "Sea Cook" better than Marryat, and joked to Henley that he would be "the Harrison Ainsworth of the future." He received a visit from Dr. Alexander Japp, the biographer of De Quincey and friend of Mrs. Henry Wood, who had written a study of Thoreau and, disagreeing on some points with Stevenson's views, was invited down to discuss their differences of opinion. Japp had many connections with popular journalism, and expressing himself impressed by reading "The Sea Cook", he took away the finished chapters to offer them to a weekly paper for boys called *Young Folks*, the forerunner of countless "penny dreadful" papers issued in the 'nineties by Alfred Harmsworth, Arthur Pearson, George Newnes, and other enterprising caterers for the popular market.

The story was accepted, but Stevenson was a little dashed on hearing that, instead of the hundred pounds for which he had hoped, he would receive only "somewhere about £30," payment being at the rate of fifty shillings per page of 4,500 words. His lung troubles revived in the autumn, and he again went to winter at Davos, where he finished *Treasure Island*, which title was preferred to "The Sea Cook" by the editor of *Young Folks*. The story was only the secondary attraction of the paper, each instalment being squeezed into narrow columns of close print at the end of each number, pride of place being given to the adventures of *Don Zalva the Brave*, by Alfred R. Phillips, who was "the big man" for the paper's serials. It was not a success as a serial; as the editor, Robert Leighton, remarked, "it had not the serial trick," too long being taken in preamble before getting down to the business of the treasure hunt, so that the story was "carried on for at least six weeks by its alluring title." Leighton shrewdly judged that *Treasure Island* is "appreciated less by boys than by grown-up readers"; he never knew "a boy under sixteen read it a second time."

At Davos he and his wife were both frequently ill, but he did much more work than in the previous year. He wrote part of *A Child's Garden of Verses*, inspired by Kate Greenaway's *Birthday Book for Children*, *The Silverado Squatters*, written up from the diary he kept during his honeymoon, and several essays for the *Cornhill*, including "Talk and Talkers" and "A Gossip on Romance". He wanted to write a biography of Hazlitt, because he loved the subject and regarded him "as *the* English writer who has had the scantiest justice" (a just judgment in 1881), but though he entered into negotiations with Bentley the publisher, nothing came of the idea, perhaps for the same reason as Morley declined to let him write a volume for the "English Men of Letters" series—that he had not sufficient reputation. He had no belief in *Treasure Island*, viewing it, like Colvin and the others of his literary friends, with deprecation as a manifestation of his incorrigible eccentricity, and obviously hankered after a career as a bookman and essayist, like Gosse and Colvin. It is significant that he confided his plans of work at this time, not in Colvin, as he did in the case of his early *Cornhill* contributions, but in Henley, who acted as his unofficial literary agent. In 1882 Henley became editor of the *Magazine of Art*, and in spite of the ill effect of the *New Arabian Nights* on *London*, at once invited Stevenson's contributions, while in the same year he not only placed *The Silverado Squatters* with Chatto and Windus, but persuaded them to undertake a volume of Stevenson's *Cornhill* essays, which appeared as *Familiar Studies of Men and Books*, and to publish the *New Arabian Nights* in two volumes.

Stevenson returned to Scotland for the summer of 1882, after staying a few days with Meredith, but a serious hæmorrhage necessitated his being "ordered south" again, and dreading to return to Davos, which did not agree with Fanny, they sought a refuge in the South of France. During the winter, spent in Marseilles and Nice, he was too ill to work, nothing resulting except a few verses and a first draft of the story called *The Treasure of Franchard*. But in the spring of 1883 he found at Hyères a Swiss cottage called Chalet La Solitude, "two rooms below with a kitchen, and four rooms above, all told," but "healthy, cheerful, and close to the shops, and society, and civilisation." Here he had some luck, for Henley, succeeded in arranging with Cassell's, the proprietors of his magazine, to publish *Treasure Island* for "a hundred jingling, tingling, golden, minted quid," while Gosse obtained forty pounds from the American *Century Magazine* for the serial use of *The Silverado Squatters*. The news put heart into him and when he completed the story of *Prince Otto*, originally begun in San Francisco, he congratulated himself that "this year I should be able to live and keep my family on my own earnings." The sale of *Treasure Island* sent him back to writing boy's books, and he started work on *The Black Arrow*. A "tale of tushery" he called it to Henley, but he agreed with Henley that *Prince Otto* was "not a thing to extend my public on"—"it is queer and a little, little bit free; and some of the parties are immoral"—and he set about *The Black Arrow* purely as a piece of commercial carpentry, writing it specially as a serial for *Young Folks* in deliberate imitation, as he freely admitted in the preface to the book in 1888, of the style of Alfred R. Phillips. The story ran in *Young Folks* between June and October, appearing under the pseudonym of Captain George North; its publication in book form under his own name was delayed till 1888, probably on the advice of Colvin, who told Henley that he found it "rather *less* good than I thought and I'm afraid might do him harm on the whole."

The publication of *Treasure Island* in the autumn of 1883 proved his first financial success. It created no sensation such as might be expected from its subsequent popularity; there were no phenomenal sales like those of Dr. Cronin's *Hatter's Castle* and *The Citadel*, Miss Mitchell's *Gone With the Wind*, or Mr. Hutchinson's *If Winter Comes*—it had nothing like the instantaneous success of its successor and confessed imitator, Rider Haggard's *King Solomon's Mines*. But a second edition was called for in 1884, the first illustrated edition appeared in 1885, and sales continued steadily year after year till, in 1897, seventy-five thousand copies had been sold.

Treasure Island won for Stevenson the valuable allegiance of Andrew Lang. Lang made a habit of destroying letters, and he is meagrely represented in Colvin's collection of Stevenson's correspondence; hence it is difficult to gauge the degree and duration of his intimacy with Stevenson. But though they had met at Mentone in 1874 and probably met often in Stevenson's Savile Club days, it is likely that Lang's interest was first arrested at this time, when he wrote enthusiastically to the author of *Treasure Island* that, "except *Tom Sawyer* and the *Odyssey*, I never liked any romance so much."

Henceforth Lang never allowed a new book of Stevenson's to pass without notice from him, and the weight of his enormous influence bore down the scales of popular opinion heavily in Stevenson's favour. His good offices were also of direct service to Stevenson in marketing his writings. Leslie Stephen had resigned from the editorship of *Cornhill* in 1882, and was succeeded by James Payn. If never a close friend, Payn knew Stevenson and did not dislike him. But a change of policy was dictated under the new editor. When *Cornhill* started under. Thackeray, the first issue sold the phenomenal number of 120,000 copies, but under Stephen, the circulation steadily declined till it fell as low as twelve thousand. The fault was not Stephen's, unless he is accused of not having kept up with the changing taste of the time; he maintained the magazine in the same style as when it began, but the public changed. People now wanted the lightest form of fiction, with gossiping articles about personalities or trivial topics, lacking any pretensions to literary quality, such as they found in the popular "family" magazines, illustrated with process blocks. Payn assigned the decline of *Cornhill* mainly to "the failure of the literary, and especially the classical, essay to attract the public"; hence the services of the author of *Virginibus Puerisque* were among the first to be dispensed with.

It happened fortunately that Stevenson suffered nothing from the loss of this market. For one thing, Henley became editor of Cassell's *Magazine of Art*, to which Stevenson contributed such different papers as "By-ways of Book Illustration", a sketch of San Francisco as "A Modern Cosmopolis", and, most important, his "Note on Realism". But it happened also that *Longman's Magazine* came into being in November, 1882, and Lang was employed as reader and literary adviser to the firm of Longman.

The first number included "A Gossip on Romance", written for, and presumably rejected by, *Cornhill*, and Stevenson became a cherished contributor to the magazine, which made a last valiant struggle to uphold the literary tradition of the old Victorian monthly periodical. During 1883 *The Treasure of Franchard* and *Across the Plains*, which was concocted out of *The Amateur Emigrant*, appeared in *Longman's*; in 1884 "Old Mortality", reprinted in *Memories and Portraits*, and "A Humble Remonstrance on Henry James's ' Art of Fiction '"; in 1885 *Prince Otto* ran as a serial. He also received valuable publicity from Lang's monthly commentary in the magazine, called *At the Sign of the Ship*, as Lang, in his chatty digressions about books in general, regularly referred to Stevenson and his different writings as illustrations to point his arguments, thereby implying that he was an established writer, with whose work he supposed as a matter of course that his readers must be acquainted. More than all that favourable reviews could do was achieved for Stevenson's reputation by this habit of Lang's in persistently, casually, and unobtrusively keeping his name before the public; it was an instance of auto-suggestion—Lang talked of Stevenson as if everybody must know his work; therefore everybody felt ashamed of their ignorance and hastened to correct the defect in their literary education.

Treasure Island also derived benefit from Gladstone's appreciation. In recent years a Prime Minister with literary aspirations created a vogue for the stories of the late Mary Webb; in the 'eighties Respectability deemed it a duty, and a verification of individual respectability, to read anything of which its High Priest recorded his approval. Gladstone announced that he sat up "till two in the morning to finish" *Treasure Island*. When Stevenson heard of Gladstone's praise, he said scornfully that "he would do better to attend to the imperial affairs of England." He loathed Gladstone, not only because he himself inclined to an old-fashioned Toryism like Walter Scott's, but because he saw in Gladstone the emblem of the respectability he despised. When, in 1885, he was commissioned by Lang to write a biography of Wellington for the "English Worthies" series, he hesitated for some time to write to Gladstone, asking for his personal reminiscences of Wellington, and finally decided not to do so when the news came of General Gordon's abandonment at Khartoum. He felt that he could only sign his letter "your fellow-criminal in the eyes of God," and in a letter to Symonds he bitterly derided Gladstone as a *bourgeois*, and then assailed himself for being likewise a *bourgeois*, since he did nothing to protest against the *régime* of the *bourgeois*.

This reflection upon himself provides one of the rare instances when he revealed a glimpse of his secret feelings of dissatisfaction concerning his intellectual integrity. In 1881, in a white heat of anger at the Boers having been attacked at Majuba, he had written a "Protest on Behalf of Boer Independence". The manuscript turned up years after his death, and the "Protest" has since been included in his collected works. But at the time it was suppressed, almost certainly, as Mr. Hellman and Mr. Steuart believe, at Fanny Stevenson's instigation. Her practical mind argued that such an explosion against popular opinion would injure Stevenson as an affront to Respectability; he could not afford to offend the public which he wanted to provide his living by reading his books. From a practical point of view, she was right, but just as majorities are invariably wrong, the instinct of the true artist rarely leads directly to the commercial or practical. Stevenson believed in what he had written, and knew he was a traitor to his own integrity by not publishing it; hence he could not conscientiously decry Gladstone as a *bourgeois*, since he had allowed Fanny's prudence to stamp him with the same die.

Prudent Fanny was ever on the side of respectability. At Hyères during 1883, while scribbling *The Black Arrow* for commercial reward, Stevenson sought to satisfy his artistic conscience by working on *Prince Otto*, for which he had small hope of commercial success, but which satisfied his self-criticism as an artist. But *Prince Otto* went forward slowly, and he started another novel, *The Travelling Companion*. A publisher who saw this novel described it as "a work of genius, but indecent"; two years later Stevenson professed to find it "a gross, bitter, ugly daub", and consigned it to the dustbin. Another novel, with a common prostitute for heroine, was immediately destroyed, either by Fanny herself or by Stevenson in disgust at Fanny's objections to it. Obviously he began this with Kate Drummond in mind, and intended to attempt some such study in romantic realism as Daudet's *Sapho*, which appeared in the following year. He was closely in touch with the latest theories of the novel, as his "Note on Realism" shows, and though he then disparages realism as liable to degenerate in such hands as Zola's "into mere *feu*x-*de-joie* of literary tricking," he probably had the idea of taking a Zola subject and illustrating his theory that the treatment should be "both realistic and ideal."

But Fanny again intruded practical advice. This was two years before George Moore published *A Mummer's Wife*, eight years before Hardy's *Tess*. A novel faithfully based on such a romance as his with Kate Drummond would have invoked the ban of Mudie, and did he not urgently need commercial success? A banned book would mean a dead loss; he might even be compelled to share the expense of the loss with the publisher. Such a book would awaken horror in his father; did he wish to alienate his father, cut off the rich source of subsidy, and undo all the good work in reuniting him with his parents achieved by Fanny's tact? Such were clearly Fanny's arguments, while secretly she trembled at the thought of the scandalous gossip, which would arise about the personal knowledge of prostitutes implied by such a book, and the consequent mud disfiguring the respectability of her marriage. Stevenson gave way, but he suffered in consequence. All his subsequent critical writings have to be regarded with suspicion, for he must always be suspected of making out a case for himself, embroidering theories which excused his own treatment of fiction and sprang from no honest conviction. And towards Fanny he assumed the attitude of the dog in the manger; "my wife . . . hates and lothes and slates my women", he wrote from Hyéres to Henley, so he left the feminine element out of his novels altogether.

§ 2

In the new year of 1884, he was visited at Hyères by Henley and Charles Baxter, and joined them in an excursion to Nice. It was like a return to old times to be thus on a jaunt with his old friends, and he revived the old pleasures, sitting up late over talk and bottle and revelling in boisterous exchanges with Henley. But his constitution was no longer equal to such strain; on his return to Hyères, he was for three months as dangerously ill as he had been in San Francisco. Fanny not unnaturally blamed Henley for lack of consideration; she always had reason on her side.

His recovery was slow. Owing to the congestion of the lungs, his right arm was strapped to his side for safety's sake, and he was forbidden to speak. In convalescence, when he could speak in whispers, he dictated to Fanny some part of the story which eventually became *The Dynamiter*. By July he was sufficiently recovered to travel, and since his father was now too infirm to visit him on the Continent and it was unwise for Stevenson to venture to Scotland, a compromise was arranged by meeting at Bournemouth. Though they remained throughout the winter at Bournemouth, the air seemed to suit Stevenson better than that of Switzerland or France, and in the spring of 1885 his father bought a house there, which they rechristened Skerryvore, after one of the lighthouses built by the Stevenson family, and which he presented to his daughter-in-law, along with a gift of five hundred pounds for furnishing expenses.

During his first months at Bournemouth, he spent most of his time collaborating with Henley in writing plays. Henley believed in a theatrical revival, he had a brother on the stage, and hearing the actor's perennial plaint that the theatre was dying for want of good plays, he assured Stevenson that fortune was waiting to fold them as dramatists to its opulent bosom. *Deacon Brodie*, the fruit of their collaboration before Stevenson's marriage, was produced in July, 1884, at the old Prince's Theatre, with Edward Henley in the lead, but had little success. Lloyd Osbourne said that Stevenson "entered enthusiastically" into the collaboration, though never wholly sharing Henley's belief in their success as playwrights. But Henley was his literary adviser, and also the collaboration brought his congenial company regularly to the invalid at Bournemouth.

"Henley came—a great, glowing, massive shouldered fellow with a big red beard and a crutch; jovial, outstandingly clever, and with a laugh that rolled out like music. Never was there such another as William Ernest Henley; he had an unimaginable fire and vitality; he swept one off one's feet. There are no words that can describe the quality he had of exalting those about him; of communicating his own rousing self-confidence and belief in himself; in the presence of this demi-god, who thrilled you by his appreciation, you became a demi-god yourself, and felt the elation of an Olympian who never until then had known the tithe of what was in him."

So wrote Lloyd Osbourne, who, as a boy, "idolized" Henley, "the first man I had ever called by his surname." He remembered how *Beau Austin* was written in four days, and how Henley read it aloud "so movingly, so tenderly, that my eyes were wet with tears."

Fanny Stevenson stood by in disapproval, probably impatient of the admiration and affection inspired by this man in her husband and her son. She neither liked nor believed in Henley, and in the latter feeling at least she again had reason on her side. Neither Henley nor Stevenson had much practical knowledge of the stage, and nobody could nourish the remotest hope of success with the literary "drama" in such an age of theatrical clap-trap, when, as William Archer said, it was wonderful "to conceive how any one with the smallest pretension to intelligence could in those years seriously occupy himself with the English theatre." But Henley had the beneficial effect of cheering Stevenson and inspiring him to energy—so much so that the cautious Colvin, primed by Fanny, warned Henley against "letting him work too hard." When he caught cold in the winter (from his mother, according to Fanny), even Fanny welcomed his breezy company to relieve the depressing atmosphere, telling Colvin that Henley "might as well bring his influenza here, and join us, as he can do no harm."

Henley tirelessly hawked the plays round the London theatres, and succeeded in interesting Beerbohm Tree sufficiently for the actor to visit Bournemouth. Tree did eventually produce *Beau Austin*, but not till 1890, when the taste of theatrical fashion had somewhat improved. Henley's confidence was thus far justified; he might have argued that they were before their time. But at the time the plays were unwanted, and Stevenson, doubtless under Fanny's promptings, protested against Henley's persistent hawking to theatrical managers, fearing that his reputation might suffer, and expressed disparaging opinions on the merit of the plays. Henley was hurt, and the narrow end of the wedge was thus driven into their friendship.

Of his other old friends, apart from Baxter in distant Edinburgh, only Colvin remained. Gosse had drifted away of his own accord; during the miserable experiences in San Francisco, he had been a faithful and heartening correspondent, but during 1881, he ceased to be Stevenson's "dear Weg" and became simply "my dear Gosse", after which correspondence became gradually less frequent. It seems as if Gosse began to doubt that the real stuff was in Stevenson, to wonder if he was not doomed merely to be a tiresome invalid, and to wonder if the friendship might not be an unnecessary pendant to his own rising star. So Stevenson evidently thought, for there comes a savour of sarcasm into his letters, gibing a little at Gosse's success, especially after he heard the news in 1883 that Gosse had been invited by W. D. Howells to lecture in America. Moreover, it is known that there existed a strong antipathy between Gosse and Henley; Gosse had a liking for fashionable society and great names, a trait calculated to rouse pungent expressions of scorn from Henley. When in the 'nineties, with its vogue for "At Homes" at which singers and musicians were paid high fees as professional entertainers, Gosse became a lecturer in fashionable drawing-rooms, the comments of Henley may be imagined to have echoed those of Carlyle on hearing that Thackeray had secured a free passage for his trip from "Cornhill to Cairo"—that he was degrading the profession of letters by acting like "a blind fiddler going to and fro on a penny ferry-boat in Scotland, and playing tunes to the passengers for half-pence." Possibly discord fell between Gosse and Stevenson over Henley; Gosse had a feline *flair* for satire, as is witnessed by his letter to Stevenson in 1884, guying the "triumph at the new Museum" of another mutual friend.

A new and valuable friendship was begun in December, 1884.

Henry James's essay on *The Art of Fiction* appeared in *Longman's Magazine* for September, 1884, and Stevenson replied in December with *A Humble Remonstrance*, which deprecated James's definition of a novel as "a personal impression of life," arguing that art cannot "compete with life," because "life is monstrous, infinite, illogical, abrupt, and poignant," while art is "neat, finite, self-contained, rational, flowing, and emasculate"—that, in fact, the novelist's business is not to be concerned, like James, with "the statics of character," but simply to tell a story. The "remonstrance" was possibly suggested by Lang; certainly it reflected his taste, which demanded "more claymores, less psychology," as he afterwards complained of *Catriona*. But Stevenson wrote it in his public character as the author of *Treasure Island*, not as the artist who laboured long with *Prince Otto*, and the *Remonstrance*, viewed biographically, is a pathetic effort at self-justification.

Henry James, however, wrote a courteous letter, suggesting that they might continue privately the discussion begun in print, and was accordingly invited to Bournemouth. Fanny told Colvin that she thought "there is no question but that he likes Louis," and there was certainly no question that Fanny liked James. "He seems very gentle and comfortable," she said, "and I worship in silence." Few men resist the flattery of woman's admiration, especially when she has the tact to leave the talking to them, but James, while he seems to have liked her well enough, had no illusions about her. It was a hard reward for her adulation to leave the impression of a "poor barbarous and merely *instinctive* lady," and when, many years later, he gave a friend an introduction to Stevenson's widow, he added the warning that "*she* (with all deference to her) was never the person to have seen, it was R.L.S. himself." But Fanny saw in him a friend worth cultivating; he was a man of means and already established reputation, eminently respectable—quite different from Henley. Soon, therefore, she announced that she and Stevenson were "devoted to him," and professed rapture for James's latest novel, *The Princess Casamassima*, "not but that I have always liked his other work." As his sister was living at Bournemouth, James became a regular caller—"sitting like a beneficent deity, a sort of bearded Buddha," as Gosse described him at this time, listening to Stevenson's eager, lively talk—and he became the most valued of Stevenson's literary friends in his later years.

Commissioned to write a story for the Christmas issue of the *Pall Mall Gazette*, Stevenson submitted *Markheim*, but this was declared too short, and being unable to write another in time, he sent *The Body-Snatcher*, which had laid by for three years. The newspaper accepted the story, and advertised it with posters so lurid that they were suppressed by the police, but in spite of Henley's protests, Stevenson declined to accept the forty pounds paid for the commissioned story. "I took that as a fair price for my best work," he said; "I was not able to produce my best; and I will be damned if I steal with my eyes open." Henley naturally argued that, if the newspaper was satisfied and prepared to pay, it was pointless quixotry to refuse it, especially as he needed money. But Stevenson had his father's bank balance behind him, and probably seized this opportunity of appearing fastidious about his work to convince his friends of his belief in his avowed theories of fiction, so diverting possibility of their suspecting the secret qualms of his artistic conscience.

His *Child's Garden of Verses*, dedicated to Cummy, appeared in the spring of 1885; he finished *Prince Otto*, and was working on his biography of Wellington, a story called *The Great North Road*, and *More New Arabian Nights*. Of these projects, only the last matured, and owing to his illness, these stories, except "The Explosive Bomb", were largely Fanny's work. During the summer he began *Kidnapped*, but fell ill and put it aside. He had neither the health nor the heart for writing a long story. Secretly he had built great hopes on *Prince Otto*, over which he spent more time and pains than any other work he ever wrote, and *Prince Otto* had proved a flop; Henley reviewed it with such praise that Stevenson wondered "whether (considering our intimate relations) you would not do better to refrain from reviewing me," but other reviewers either damned with faint praise or loaded it with contempt, and whatever encouragement he felt on receiving a letter of praise from Meredith, was discounted by Gosse's condescending flippancy that "it is a wilful and monstrous sacrifice on the altar of George Meredith, whose errors you should be the last to imitate and exaggerate." This failure was the

bitterest pill for Stevenson in his whole literary career; the work
in which he believed, and on which he hoped to build his reputation, was ignored by the public and despised by the critics.

"You aim high, and you take longer over your work, and
it will not be so successful as if you had aimed low and rushed
it. What the public likes is work (of any kind) a little loosely
executed; so long as it as a little wordy, a little slack, a little dim
and knotless, the dear public likes it; it should (if possible)
be a little dull into the bargain. I know that good work sometimes hits ; but with my hand on my heart, I think it is
by accident. And I know also that good work must succeed
at last ; but that is not the doing of the public ; they are only
shamed into silence or affectation."

He would rather that *Treasure Island* had never sold a copy, if
he could have had its success for *Prince Otto*. This was his thesis
to qualify for the degree of a Thackeray or a Meredith; was he
to be no more than a Marryat or an Ainsworth, a mere writer of
boys' books?

During 1885 he wrote only two stories, *Olalla* for the Christmas
number of the *Court and Society Review*, and *The Strange Case of
Dr. Jekyll and Mr. Hyde*, which was published by Longman's as
a "shilling shocker" in the new year of 1886. It was ironical that
the fame he hoped to earn with the carefully written *Prince Otto*
should come with a shilling shocker, written because he felt he
must keep earning money and yet felt unable to concentrate on a
longer story. *Jekyll and Hyde* was written, re-written and printed
in the space of ten weeks. When he read the first draft to Fanny,
she so irritated him by her criticism that he had used an allegory
for a commonplace thriller, that he threw the manuscript into
the fire. He told her afterwards that her criticism was right, and
he re-wrote the story in the light of her remarks, but probably
Fanny neither realised the reason for his anger nor understood
the conception of the story. *Jekyll and Hyde*, masquerading in
the guise of a mere thriller, is one of the most shrewd and daring
satires on Respectability between Thackeray and Galsworthy.
Jekyll, the figure of monumental respectability, seeking relief
for his suppressed instincts in the guise of Hyde, represented any
highly-respected citizen of the purest suburb—as Stevenson

meaningly told his friend W. H. Low, he might "answer to the name of Low or Stevenson." The thousands who kept mistresses at Richmond or Clapham unknown to their families at Highgate or Streatham, the hundreds of thousands who led lives of impeccable respectability, and grew soured through suppression of their natural selves, because they feared to flout the laws of convention, the millions who yearned hopelessly for relief from the thraldom of the inevitable daily routine—all could appreciate the motives for Jekyll's sinister device. Andrew Lang told the readers of *Longman's Magazine* that the idea of Hyde came to Stevenson in a dream, which he related to a friend ten years before. Almost certainly the idea first occurred to Stevenson some ten years before, not so much in a dream as in satirical reflection on his own escapes from the respectable surroundings of his home to the brothels of Edinburgh slums, and on seeing sundry pillars of respectability furtively seeking recreation in those resorts of vice.

Characteristically the Victorians declined to recognise the satire as such, but respectably labelled it as "drawing a moral." Hailing the story as "a work of incontestable genius," James Payn declared that "nothing by Edgar Allan Poe is to be compared to it," adding the irresistible inducement that "what is worth mentioning, otherwise a good many people would miss it, is that a noble moral underlies the marvellous tale." Lang said much the same; it seemed to him "a masterpiece of the terrible and grotesque, and to possess withal an unobtrusive and salutary moral." Where Lang and Payn led, the smaller fry of critics followed; some varied the comparison with Poe by comparison with Bulwer, but all emphasised the "moral". An ecclesiastical pundit took it up, and preached a sermon on the moral; soon all sorts and conditions of the clergy were spouting the parable from their pulpits. *Jekyll and Hyde* was the talk of the town and the success of the publishing season; fifty thousand copies were soon sold, and by the end of the midsummer quarter, Stevenson told Symonds that he had made £350 from the shilling copies.

Stevenson's name and fame were made, and he neither paused to bask in the sunshine of success nor failed, like so many novelists, to sustain his vogue. He made hay while the sun shone. With his

spirits stimulated by success he grappled enthusiastically with
Kidnapped, which appeared serially under his own name in
Young Folks between May and July of 1886. Unlike the despised
Treasure Island, *Kidnapped* was the leading feature of the periodical,
and Stevenson, trading on his increased reputation, demanded
and received thirty shillings a column for it. Like *Treasure
Island* before it and *The Black Arrow* two years later, *Kidnapped*
was published in book form by Cassell's, but in a six-shilling
edition, thus providing an early instance of other publishers
following the example of Vizetelly's Six Shilling Novels, amongst
which George Moore's first novels were then appearing.

Kidnapped is not only one of the best adventure stories for
boys ever written; like *Treasure Island*, it appeals equally to all
ages, and the man of forty finds in its re-reading the same enjoyment as when he read it as a boy. Stevenson wrote it in a burst
of care-free energy, and knowing his materials intimately, he
enjoyed the writing. Hence it has a vitality and verve superior
to *Treasure Island*, which not only dallies at its start, but marks
time during the siege of the stockade, as if the author was not
quite sure whom to kill off in the fighting. *Kidnapped* does not
at once get under way, like *The Black Arrow*, but from the appearance of Alan Breck in the ninth chapter, a breathless interest
prevails to the end, and much midnight oil has been burned to
finish it at a sitting. Henley wrote of it in *Longman's:*

> "Mr. Stevenson's new book—which these eyes have been
> privileged to see in proof—is in some ways his best. The
> material is inferior to that of *Treasure Island*—is not that
> common yet eternal stuff of romance which counts for so much
> in the interest and charm of the older story; nor have the
> adventures of David Balfour that element of plot which attaches
> us so closely to the study of those of Jim Hawkins and Long
> John. But the whole thing is full of delightful invention,
> and is touched, besides, with a humanity which I do not think
> Mr. Stevenson has ever realised before. The manner of the
> book is, of course, the manner of Defoe; by which I mean that
> there is, as in *Robinson Crusoe*, perhaps a little too much psy-
> chology, especially the psychology of suffering. The two
> heroes, Alan Breck and David, have a dreadfully hard time of

it, and their aches and pains and tribulations are, it may be, a trifle too well realised. One thinks with a sigh of the cheerful and gallant fancy of Dumas; of the smiling indifference of the details of hunger and fatigue which distinguishes the experiences of Chicot and D'Artagnan . . . In two passages at least—the Fight in the Round House and the Quarrel in the Heather—Mr. Stevenson has surpassed himself in the matter of brilliant narrative—has gone higher indeed than is within the flight of any of his contemporaries—and produced a couple of chapters that are *tout bonnement* a couple of masterpieces. As for the style—a most quaint, elegant, and delightful compromise between Scotch and English—it recalls, with certain differences, the manner of Jedediah Cleisbotham (of Gandercleugh), and is good enough, as it seems to us to take high rank and live long as a literary creation."

Coming hard on the heels of *Jekyll and Hyde*, such a book was assured of acclamation, and just as its predecessor had been compared with Poe and Bulwer, *Kidnapped* was reckoned worthy of Defoe and Scott. With the royalties of two best-sellers, though one was only a shilling book, Stevenson should have been well off, but cautiously he told his father only that he hoped to "see the year through without help." He had scant faith in popular favour and less in his health; if he had a bad winter he might be able to write nothing to keep his name before the public, and so again fall short of money. For the moment he enjoyed himself as he had had neither health nor leisure for doing since his marriage; he stayed with Colvin in London, meeting Browning and James Russell Lowell, and being lionised in Bloomsbury society; he made a trip to Paris with Henley, mainly to meet the sculptor Rodin. Whether or not the pleasures of this trip again overtaxed his strength, he was ill on his return and had the bad winter of his worst anticipations. He completed the memoir of his friend Fleeming Jenkin, which occupied him after *Kidnapped;* his only fiction for the rest of 1886 was *The Misadventures of John Nicholson*, of which he said that "some of it is passable in its mouldy way."

His frequent hæmorrhages and the attendant exhaustion convinced him that Bournemouth, after all, was no more salutary than Hyères or Davos, and he had already decided on a change of air when his father died in May, 1887. This severed the one unbreakable tie which bound him to Great Britain; his father would never have countenanced the notion of living far from Scotland, and Fanny would never have risked offending him with the suggestion. But she had spent years in exile from her family connections, and seized her chance of repatriation. The doctors advised a change from Bournemouth; why should they not try the healthy mountains of Colorado? Stevenson's mother would go anywhere with her son; she would also pay the expenses of the trip, as she was to "get some money from the business."

So they sailed in August—Stevenson, his mother, Fanny, Lloyd Osbourne, and a servant. Seeing them off from Tilbury, the faithful Colvin thought it was only a parting for the winter, but it was his last sight of Stevenson, and Stevenson's last of England, as the tall, painfully thin figure leaned waving over the boat's rail.

§ 3

Like Thackeray, Reade, and many other novelists, Stevenson's work had received quicker and more generous appreciation in America than England, though the absence of an international copyright agreement, in spite of Reade's fierce crusade for a quarter of a century, brought no income with American popularity. *Kidnapped* had just appeared over there, pirated editions of *Jekyll and Hyde* sold in thousands, and Stevenson was greeted as a lion on arrival. He was amused by "the poor interviewer lads", who were "no more vulgar in their reports than they could help." But, "Lord, what a silly thing is popularity!" he exclaimed, and regretted "the cool obscurity of Skerryvore." He was "not busted, but medallioned" by the sculptor St. Gaudens, and he found American editors much more generous than their London compeers. He refused an offer of two thousand pounds a year from the *New York World* for a weekly article, as his health was unlikely to permit work of such regularity, and though he accepted the offer of seven hundred pounds for twelve monthly articles for *Scribner's Magazine*, he confided to Henley his fear that "the slavery may overweigh me." He also signed a contract with S. S. McClure, by which he was to receive one thousand six hundred pounds for the serial rights of his next story.

Meantime, though he had written little for a year, his name was before the public in England by the publication of his second volume of verse, *Underwoods*, his *Memories and Portraits*, the book of stories called *The Merry Men*, and a new edition of *Virginibus Puerisque*. Of the stories in *The Merry Men*, Andrew Lang declared *Thrawn Janet* to be "written in the best Scotch since the pen fell from the hand of the author of *Wandering Willie's Tale*," *Markheim* "as good as Hawthorne", and *The Merry Men* worthy of Hawthorne "if he had been a kindly Scot." *Underwoods* provided an opportunity for Gosse to write of "Mr. R. L. Stevenson as a Poet"; now that *A Child's Garden* was followed by such "an easy book to appreciate and enjoy" as *Underwoods*, he declared that Stevenson claimed consideration as a poet and "a candidate for the bays." He hesitated "to decide whether or no Mr. R. L. Stevenson's poems will be read in the future," but he found them "so full of character, so redolent of his own fascinating temperament, that it is not too wild to suppose that so long as his prose is appreciated those who love that will turn to this." Feline irony lurks in nearly every paragraph of the article, as Stevenson was quick to perceive, for he wrote a bantering letter to Gosse, doubting if he "ever wrote anything so funny."

Finding the cold of Colorado "too rigorous", he settled for the winter on Saranac Lake, in the Adirondacks. He felt that his essays for *Scribner's* bore "many traces of effort"—"the ungenuine inspiration of an income at so much per essay, and the honest desire of the incomer to give good measure for his money" —though he thought his "Darwinian sermon", *Pulvis et Umbra*, "pulled off after a fashion." At Christmas he announced himself to have "fallen head over heels into a new tale, *The Master of Ballantrae* . . . to me a most seizing tale . . . a dead genuine human problem . . . It will be about as long, I imagine, as *Kidnapped*." As with *Treasure Island* and *Kidnapped*, he started off on this story at a great pace, but having written enough for four monthly instalments, he paused, probably on account of a bout of illness, found himself unable to get down to it again, and told

Burlingame, the editor of *Scribner's*, that he had to put it aside, "as I was quite worked out." He was better in health; up to Christmas he had not brought up "one drop of blood from his lungs since leaving England." But the monthly articles for *Scribner's* weighed on him, and lacking the energy for creative work on his own account, he occupied the rest of his time in correcting and adding to a story written by Lloyd Osbourne, which eventually appeared as *The Wrong Box*, the first published work of his collaboration with his stepson.

In the spring came a saddening blow which left an ache in his heart to the end of his life—the final rupture of his friendship with Henley. Details of the affair were long suppressed—to Henley's disadvantage—but Mr. Steuart's biography provides an account sympathetic with both sides. Some years before, Stevenson's cousin, Katherine de Mattos (to whom he dedicated *Jekyll and Hyde*), had written a story, which Henley hawked round editors and publishers along with Stevenson's work, till the authoress, in disgust, declared herself "done with it." At this time, Fanny Stevenson remembered the story, wrote it up on her account, and had it accepted. In Henley's next letter to Stevenson, after talking of other matters in his usual manner, he expressed "considerable amazement" at seeing Fanny's story without at least the acknowledgment of "a double signature." He added that he did not wish his letter to be shown "to anybody," meaning Fanny, but it seems that Stevenson ignored the request. Fanny's anger can be imagined; she disliked Henley, and her nerves were also on edge from having been ill most of the winter. She exasperated Stevenson into writing a most uncharacteristic letter, demanding "a proper explanation and retraction" of "an abominable accusation", which was aggravated by a request for secrecy. Henley replied in affectionate dismay; he did not know whether to laugh or cry at Stevenson's "heart-breaking" letter; he had mentioned the story casually, and though he felt he had grounds for his remark, his friendship and affection remained unaltered, and he asked forgiveness.

Such generous frankness from a much less valued friend than Henley would normally have won from Stevenson a warm and equally generous response, and Fanny's firm chin looms plainly in his attitude. Henley asked forgiveness; he made no retraction. The aspersion on Fanny's literary good faith remained, and she was not the woman to overlook an insinuation from anybody, much less from a man she disliked. As if to make sure that the wedge was driven firmly home to split the old friendship, Fanny herself wrote in terms of bitter resentment to Henley, who then realised the utter hopelessness of the situation. If he won Stevenson by appeals to his generosity at the cost of sinking his own pride, Fanny's enmity would only be enhanced by her husband's forgiveness of his friend in spite of her; he would be a bone of contention between husband and wife. Better for Stevenson if he held his peace, rather than enter the lists against a woman and ask the husband to choose between his wife and his closest friend.

Stevenson immediately recognised the false position in which he had placed himself, and wrote a succession of hysterical letters to his friend and Henley's, Charles Baxter. He made himself ill with worry, and then blamed Henley as the origin of his illness. He was reminded, perhaps by Fanny, of the danger of quarrelling with this friend who knew so much of his private past; Henley possessed those early love-verses of his, addressed to "Claire", and had ignored Stevenson's request that they should be destroyed. When his better nature asserted itself, and he exclaimed to Baxter, "Lord, man! I can't help loving the man; I know his merit—damn him!" he must have recalled with sad irony the similar nature of the quarrel described by himself in *Kidnapped* between David Balfour and Alan Breck.

In the years following, he regularly asked Colvin to convey his affectionate remembrances to Henley; twice he wrote directly to him—on the death of his daughter and on the publication of his *Song of the Sword* in 1892—evidently earnestly hoping that the breach might be healed. But Henley was deeply wounded and doubtless felt, as he felt when Stevenson had made his wild venture in 1879, "too blasphemously given towards California and California things" to have any hope of perpetuating the friendship. Stevenson was now successful, with no further need for Henley's indefatiguable services in placing his manuscripts and procuring notices of his books; Henley knew Stevenson too well to suspect his dropping him on this account, but he probably imputed it to Fanny as a potent motive for her prompting Stevenson to pick a quarrel with him. When, in 1901, he wrote his famous protest against Stevenson's deification as a "seraph in chocolate," the majority sided with Gosse in imputing to him the petty motive of envy that Stevenson had left him so far behind in the race for fame, and had virtually deserted him, like a footsore cripple, at the wayside. He had contributed much to the making of Stevenson, and Stevenson was not the only writer he started on the road to success. Barrie, Kipling, Charles Whibley, W. B. Yeats, and Bernard Shaw were all put through their early paces by Henley, who could say of them proudly; "My young men outdo me and they write better than I." Mr. Steuart knew Henley well, and thinks that he intended to return to the subject. Nobody was so well fitted to have written Stevenson's biography, and it is interesting to conjecture what might have happened if their quarrel had not happened and their friendship had endured to the end. Henley, not Henry James, would then have been left Stevenson's literary executor, and whatever suppressions Fanny might have demanded and secured, there would have been no seraphic legend. But reason, as always, was on Fanny's side; however compromised were the ethics of literary biography by her and Graham Balfour, they did well by Stevenson's popular fame.

Anguish over the quarrel upset Stevenson's health; he fell ill, and resorted to drugs to relieve depression. Fanny had been ill all the winter; both needed a change. So Stevenson resolved on a big-scale effort to restore his health. His father had left him three thousand pounds; he wrote to Baxter for two thousand, and acquired a millionaire's pleasure yacht. Early in June, he once more made the journey from New York to San Francisco, travelling *de luxe* this time instead of in an emigrant train, and at the end of the month (June, 1888) he sailed for the Marquesas. The voyage was avowedly a trip in search of health; he expected to be away for seven months, and if it "fails to set me up, well, £2,000 is gone, and I know I can't get better."

He enjoyed the life on the yacht, and on arriving at the Marquesas, delighted not only in the climate and surroundings, but in the characters of the natives. He found it thrilling to sit at the same table with a tattooed queen, a beauty in her day, who had passed from captor to captor, or husband to husband, like Helen of Troy, who had been a cannibal in the days before her conversion, and had kept "cold missionary" on her sideboard. He did no work before Christmas, when the need for finishing *The Master of Ballantrae* became pressing, since it had begun as a serial in *Scribner's* for November. In April at Honolulu, "this cursed end of *The Master*" hung over him "like the arm of the gallows", and the trouble he found in finishing it is unfortunately reflected in the story. Two-thirds of the book sustains the breathless interest of *Kidnapped*, allied with a deeper emotion—a sense of fatality and foreboding, a consciousness of impending tragedy, which gather impressiveness from the finely limned background of enveloping gloom; but from the moment of the appearance in the story of the Indian, Secundra Dass, the illusion becomes unconvincing as if by the intrusion of the incompatible, a straining for effect supervenes, and the story is forced to an ending of disappointing pathos. In his reviews, Lang tempered enthusiastic plaudits only with the characteristically irrelevant regret that Alan Breck could not have figured in a brandishing of claymores in mortal combat with the Master. But in his considered estimate of "Mr. Stevenson's books", included in his volume of *Essays in Little*, he laid his finger on "obvious weak point" in Secundra Dass, which prevented the book from being a "victory all along the line" and so qualifying as "Mr. Stevenson's *Bride of Lammermoor*." If the fragment of *Weir of Hermiston* be excluded, *The Master of Ballantrae* represents Stevenson's most ambitious effort in the novelist's art; as Lang said, he made "a gallant effort to enter what I have ventured to call the capital of his kingdom," for "he does introduce a woman" and makes "a remarkably daring attempt to write the tragedy, as in *Waverley*, Scott wrote the romance of Scotland about the time of the Forty-five." Though Scott may remain forever unassailable in Scottish enthusiasm as the supreme national interpreter, to one Nottinghamshire born of Kentish stock, *Kidnapped* and *The Master of Ballantrae*, separately, or collectively, convey a more vivid atmospheric impression of eighteenth-century Scotland than *Waverley* and *Rob Roy*.

The Master was finally finished in May, 1889, and conscious of its unsatisfactory ending, Stevenson qualified his satisfaction by pronouncing it to contain "more human work than anything of mine but *Kidnapped*." Before starting the cruise, he had received an offer from McClure for a series of articles on his experiences, and he now wrote much of the book which became *In the South Seas*. He also wrote many of the poems afterwards appearing in the volume of *Ballads*. In February he spoke of being home in May or June, and looked forward to a trip to Paris. He found even Honolulu "too cold for me," but he was so well in the southern islands that, "as Tahiti is too complete a banishment," he planned to settle on his return at Madeira, which would be "only a week from England." But he was having "more fun and pleasure of my life these past months than ever before, and more health than any time in ten long years," and by April he announced that he was "not coming home for another year," which he intended to spend cruising among the islands between Honolulu and Sydney, and then working back to Tahiti by way of the Fijis. In June he sailed for the Gilbert Islands in a trading schooner; at Samoa by the end of the year, he fell so much in love with the island and its natives that he "bought 314½ acres of beautiful land in the bush behind Apia," where he intended to build a house and establish a farm, to which he could return in the future on similar trips for health. But when in February he visited Sydney, he at once fell ill, having a bad bout of fever and hæmorrhage such as he had in England, and he felt "sure I shall never come back home except to die." In April he started on another voyage to recover from his illness, visiting New Caledonia, but on returning to Sydney in August, 1890, he made up his mind finally to renounce any hope of returning to England and to make his home at Samoa, writing to Henry James:

"I must tell you plainly—I can't tell Colvin—I do not think I shall come to England more than once, and then it'll be to die. Health I enjoy in the tropics; even here, which they call sub-or semi-tropical, I come only to catch cold. I have not been out since my arrival; live here in a nice bedroom by the fireside, and read books . . . But I can't go out! The thermometer was nearly down to 50° the other day—no temperature for me, Mr. James: how should I do in England? I fear not at all. Am I very sorry? I am sorry about seven or eight people in England, and one or two in the States. And outside of that, I simply prefer Samoa . . . I was never fond of towns, houses, society, or (it seems) civilisation . . . The sea, island, the islanders, the island life and climate, make and keep me truly happier . . . It is plain, then, that for me my exile to the place of schooners and islands can be in no sense regarded as a calamity."

So on October, 1890, he returned to Samoa to settle on his estate of Vailima, and entered upon the last stage of his curious life.

Always impressionably sensitive to his surroundings Stevenson acquired an increase of egotism from the narrowness of his interests on Samoa. To Colvin, Baxter, Henry James, and others (probably including Andrew Lang, but Lang destroyed letters), he wrote minute accounts of his daily doings, and even the patient Colvin at length ventured a protest against his preoccupation with the parochial interests of the islanders. Stevenson replied that Colvin must "remember that my life passes among my ' blacks or chocolates,' " and must "put yourself, perhaps with an effort, into some sort of sympathy with these people, or how am I to write to you?" His situation appealed to his romantic imagination; he saw himself as a Robinson Crusoe, or rather as a Fletcher Christian of Pitcairn, and saw the enormous value of literary talent in such a character. He knew the documentary value of such books as Captain Cook's *Voyages*, and Bligh's memoirs of the mutiny in the "Bounty" and *Voyage to the South Seas*; such a work by a writer of talent must surely be a book unique in literature. He therefore decided early "to send a long letter every month to Colvin," which letters would form a journal and eventually a book for publication. Colvin did make a book of them after his death as *Vailima Letters*, and they possess precisely the same curious interest as any other exile or explorer's journals, a documentary value, but none of the attraction of a work of art, such as he might have created by writing up his notes into a narrative form and design.

His environment awakened in him the instinct to legislate and govern, which has made the British the greatest race of empire-builders since the ancient Romans. As the principal white resident on Samoa, he became virtually the ruler of the island, and by sympathy and understanding acquired such dominance over the natives that his position appeared very like that of the patriarchal chieftain of a Highland clan. Known to the islanders as Tusitala, the teller of tales, he was credited with almost supernatural powers, and he became loved and revered as their protector and prophet for championing their grievances against the corrupt practices of the governing whites. His literary friends at home deplored his obsession with local politics as a prodigal waste of his talents, and truly such a work as his *Footnote to History*, an account of the abuses and grievances to which the Samoans were subject, in the the form of a plea to the great powers for better conditions of government, might well have been entrusted to a special commissioner of the civil service. When, too, in 1890, his narrative of his cruises, *In the South Seas*, appeared serially in *Black and White*, it proved to be the work of a specialist, more suitable for publication in the quarterly journal of a learned society, by a university press, or as a government report from H. M. Stationery Office, than as the picturesque impressions of a popular novelist in a sixpenny magazine. Bowing his way into drawing-rooms within "a three-mile radius of Charing Cross," Gosse decided that "the fact seems to be that it is very nice to *live* in Samoa, but not healthy to *write* there."

Nor were the *Ballads* a success. "Between you and me and Lake Michigan," confided Gosse to a receptacle of his great thoughts, "the versification is atrocious." He disparaged "the effort to become a Polynesian Walter Scott," and when Stevenson wrote for his opinion on the *Ballads*, he did not reply. He professed not to have received Stevenson's letter, though it turned up all right when Colvin came to edit the correspondence. Gosse evidently thought Stevenson a waning flame; anyhow, he was interestedly watching the rising star of another of Henley's young men, Kipling, and not inclined to bother his head over a man he was not likely to see again.

In his distant exile Stevenson kept himself informed of

literary affairs. He thought Kipling "by far the most promising young man who has appeared since—ahem—I appeared;" he read Hall Caine's *Bondman*, Marion Crawford, William Morris, and Henley; he was an ardent admirer of Barrie, to whom he wrote in friendly commendation; Henry James sent him his novels as they came out, and Stevenson called him, Barrie, and Kipling, "my Muses Three."

He had begun in 1889 two novels in collaboration with his stepson—*The Wrecker* and *The Ebb-Tide*, the latter at first called *The Pearl Fisher*. Having long dallied over its writing, he forced *The Wrecker* to a conclusion with much trouble during 1891, in August of which year it began as a serial in *Scribner's*. Since he left England, *The Master of Ballantrae* and *The Wrong Box* were his only works of fiction; knowing that he must continue to produce to sustain his popularity, he drove himself to finish *The Wrecker*, taking little pleasure in its writing, and he described it as "a machine, and a police machine," though he chuckled over the ending as "one of the most genuine butcheries in literature." It appeared over the signatures of "Robert Louis Stevenson and Lloyd Osbourne," but while his stepson supplied the original plot, *The Wrecker* bears more distinctly the impress of Stevenson than the subsequent *Ebb-Tide* and much more than *The Wrong Box*. Richard Le Gallienne, praising it as a successful effort in a new field, the "blend of the novel of manners and the pure 'adventure' romance," shrewdly suspected that, while his collaborator had worked on the plot and "thrown in out-of-the-way experience of ships and shipmen," Stevenson had "done all the writing." As a serial and as a book it was a signal success, for, as Lang said, "it is a magnificent yarn," and "a splendid novel for a magazine, because one was always panting after the secret, as in the old days of Wilkie Collins."

Earlier in the year, the short story of *The Bottle Imp* had been a magazine success; in October, 1891, while still labouring to finish *The Wrecker*, he announced that "*David Balfour*, the second part of *Kidnapped*, is on the stocks at last." Throughout 1892 he worked hard; he finished *A Footnote to History*, which was published the same year with *The Wrecker* and a volume containing his *Scribner's* essays called *Across the Plains* (which moved Le

Gallienne to believe that Stevenson's "final fame will be that of an essayist, nearest and dearest fame of the prose writer"); he began and finished *David Balfour*; he wrote much of his grandfather's life, which appeared posthumously in *A Family of Engineers*; he wrote and published *The Beach of Falesà*, which he valued more than any work of his since *The Master of Ballantrae*; he started two other novels, *The Young Chevalier*, which was found after his death to be a fragment of brilliant promise, and *The Justice-Clerk*, the title of which was changed at Colvin's suggestion to *Weir of Hermiston*.

Unlike *The Wrecker*, *David Balfour* was not a success as a serial, and though the title was retained in America, the book was published in England by Cassell as *Catriona*. It was one of the publishing successes of the year, for the same reason as Le Gallienne praised *The Wrecker*; by blending "the novel of manners and the adventure romance," Stevenson captured the whole reading public, for he was "light" enough to appeal to the masses who demanded merely entertainment, while his fine prose and artistry satisfied the fastidious, who could echo Henry James's reflection that, while literary taste in general grew "systematically vulgarer and baser," it was a "a blur of light" that Stevenson was popular, and "if it hadn't been for *Catriona* we couldn't this year, have held up our head."

By contrast with 1892, Stevenson worked badly in 1893. There was unrest among the Samoan natives, and as appears in *Vailima Letters*, he was much occupied in their affairs. But his inability to concentrate was due to dissatisfaction as an artist with his work. He fell into moods of depression such as those which had stifled his powers of work at Davos in the days of *Prince Otto*. He started many projects—*The Shovels of Newton French* was to be a magnificent "opus" on the scale of Sir Hugh Walpole's *Herries Saga*, beginning with one hero in 1664 and ending about 1832 with his great-great-grandson's "second marriage to the daughter of his runaway aunt"; *The Young Chevalier* was "to be part in France and part in Scotland, and to deal with Prince Charlie about the year 1749"; *Heathercat* was "an attempt at a real historical novel, to present a whole field of time," showing his own race, "the west land and Clydesdale blue bonnets, under the influence of their last trial"; *Weir of Hermiston* was "a private story of two or three characters in a very grim vein." With none of these major tasks could he make progress in his depressed state, and as he had turned to *The Wrong Box* when unable to proceed with *The Master of Ballantrae*, he now worked on Lloyd Osbourne's story of *The Ebb-Tide*.

He was making four or five thousand pounds a year from his work, but in his despondence he developed worries akin to those of the nightmare days in San Francisco. Suppose he had worked himself out? Suppose he lost his public through indifferent work? Suppose his faculties were declining? News of his popularity in England and America was heartening; Gosse regretted his haste in supposing him a declining force, and resumed correspondence by dedicating a book to him; when he paid a visit to Sydney, he found his fame "much grown", and felt it "very queer" how "people all looked at me in the streets." But he derived no enthusiasm from any signs of encouragement; on finishing *The Ebb-Tide*, he called it "a dreadful, grimy business" and the characters "such a troop of swine." "The truth is," he declared, "I have a little lost my way, and stand bemused at the cross-roads." His lungs were "pretty right", but "his stomach nowhere"; he despised himself as "a white-livered puppy" for giving up drinking and smoking, and did "not like to think of a life without the red wine on the table and the tobacco with its lovely little coal of fire." When, towards the close of 1893, he got to work on *St. Ives*, which was completed after his death by Quiller-Couch, he despised it as "in no style in particular, a tissue of adventures, the central character not very well done, no philosophic pith under the yarn." He decided that he would "never do a better book than *Catriona*"; that was his "high-water mark," and "for the top flower of a man's life it seems to me inadequate. Small is the word; it is a small age, and I am of it." He felt that he "ought to have been able to build lighthouses and write *David Balfours* too"—that he had little to look back upon, and less to look forward to. His bolt was shot, and he saw himself declining gradually in popular favour.

"I begin to grow old; I have given my top note, I fancy

. . . The little, artificial popularity of style in England tends,
I think, to die out; the British pig returns to his true love, the
love of the styleless, of the shapeless, of the slapdash and the
disorderly."

When his several London publishers paid him the compliment
of uniting to issue the Edinburgh Edition of his collected works,
his friends were disappointed at his lack of enthusiasm. He
wrote prefaces for *Treasure Island* and *The Master of Ballantrae*,
and promised to do so for others of the volumes, but "*Prince Otto*
I don't think I could say anything about, and *Black Arrow* don't
want to."

Colvin emphasised that he vented his depression only in
writing; significantly he imparted none of the worries over his
work to Fanny, and "to those about him, whether visitors or
inmates, he remained the impersonation of life and spirit, maintaining to the last the same gaiety as ever, the same happy
eagerness in all pursuits and interests." The suddenness of his
end was thus the more shocking to his household. In October,
1894, he laid aside the unsatisfactory *St. Ives* and took up *Weir
of Hermiston* in a burst of creative energy. Throughout November
he worked exultantly, enjoying "a consciousness of perfect
command over his subject and his means." On Monday, 3rd
December, he wrote hard at *Weir of Hermiston* all morning; in
the afternoon he wrote letters. At sunset he came down, full of
spirits, to help his wife in preparing supper:

"He was helping his wife on the verandah, and gaily talking,
when suddenly he put both hands to his head and cried out,
'What's that?' Then he asked quickly, 'Do I look strange?'
Even as he did so he fell on his knees beside her."

He never spoke again, and died the same evening; the medical
verdict was apoplexy, followed by paralysis of the lungs.

§ 4

The news of Stevenson's death made a deep impression on the
English reading public. The romance of his latter days appealed
to *bourgeois* sentimentality. Here was a man who had made name

and fame in defiance of malignant disease, against which he had struggled heroically, to defeat which he had gone, with the adventurous courage of a hero in one of his own romances, from the snug suburban villas of England to seek health and strength in the savage wilds of the South Seas. To Clapham and Highgate, he might as well have gone to Mars; it was equally romantic. Here was a writer of romance who was himself a hero of romance. Lang spoke of his "dauntless courage which overcame so many evils," and the public took him to their hearts as a gay adventurer who had gallantly fought his way to their appreciation with a brave smile hiding the pain of his poor, diseased body.

They were not allowed to forget him, either. *The Ebb-Tide* was still fresh, having been published in the autumn before his death, and Colvin quickly edited and issued *Vailima Letters*. The greater public did not read *Vailima Letters*, but they read the reviews, which enhanced their romantic view of the man, showing how, while he was catering for Mr. Mudie, he was busily concerned with the welfare of the poor natives, and was almost a King of the Cannibal Isles. Regularly, at intervals, volumes of the Edinburgh Edition of his collected works appeared to parade the old favourites before the public view; his *Songs of Travel* were published, his *In the South Seas*, and *Weir of Hermiston* appeared with an impressive editorial note by Colvin, relating how the last words, "a wilful convulsion of brute nature," were dictated "on the very morning of the writer's sudden seizure and death," comparing it in Stevenson's canon with *Edwin Drood* in Dickens's and *Denis Duval* in Thackeray's, and rightly pointing out the merits of what might have been a masterpiece. In the same spirit of reverence for the work of a master, Sir Arthur Quiller-Couch performed "the delicate task" of finishing *St. Ives*, with which he was "entrusted" after momentous consultation among the custodians of Stevenson's reputation. Finally, after some six years, appeared the massive tomes of Sir Graham Balfour's official biography, setting the seal of authority upon the legend already fostered in the public mind. No wonder Henley's lone protest against the lauding of a "seraph in chocolate" sounded like a rude noise in a drawing-room.

Even after Stevenson's death, Fanny had reason on her side;

the policy followed by her and Colvin and their counsellors insured Stevenson's permanent place among the great writers of English literature. Forty odd years after his death, it is still a subject for debate whether or not his achievement has been exaggerated and his acclamation undeserved. There are still many admirers who rate him among the greatest romantics of English fiction. What is his title to such consideration?

His reputation as a novelist rests upon four novels—*Treasure Island*, *Kidnapped*, *Catriona*, and *The Master of Ballantrae*, a long short story, *Dr. Jekyll and Mr. Hyde*, and a fragment, *Weir of Hermiston*. *Treasure Island* and *Kidnapped* are boys' stories, classics of their kind, but if he had written nothing else but these and such as *The Black Arrow*, Stevenson could be reckoned no more than a boys' author, a greater but less prolific Captain Marryat. But he wrote much besides; he wrote verse at least equal to any but the great poets of his day; he wrote essays comparable with *Elia* and Thackeray's *Roundabout Papers* and superior to any of their kind in his own day; he wrote in *Dr. Jekyll and Mr. Hyde* a gem of satirical allegory, which challenges the best of Poe as a masterpiece of macabre and stands unique as a *tour de force* in its generation.

Thackeray would still be rated a great writer if he had written only *Vanity Fair*, Fielding if only *Tom Jones*, Scott, perhaps, if only *Waverley*, Arnold Bennett if only *The Old Wives' Tale*. But Stevenson's fame derives from his collective achievement; if his works are individually analysed, he achieved no masterpiece comparable with those of Thackeray, Fielding, Scott, or Bennett. If he had lived longer, it is frequently argued, he might have written such a masterpiece, and *Weir of Hermiston* has the makings of a masterpiece. But would the end of *Weir* have sustained the power of its beginning? Stevenson's best work was written rapidly while the mood was on him, as he wrote all that exists of *Weir of Hermiston*; if circumstances, usually illness, intervened to interrupt his concentration, he needed endless effort to gather together the threads of the narrative. Consider the impressiveness of *The Master of Ballantrae* if it had been left unfinished; for half the book, it is a masterpiece, and fails only in its forced, unconvincing conclusion. *Treasure Island* likewise tails off; *Kid-*

napped lacks an ending of any sort, leaving off abruptly with the promise of a sequel; as for *Catriona*, its endings flag less obviously only because its beginning and middle lack the verve and inspiration of any of the other three stories.

With its unsatisfactory ending, *The Master of Ballantrae* is the best finished novel of Stevenson. He himself thought *Catriona* his best, but his judgment was prejudiced by his point of view. At the time of writing *Catriona*, he was conscious that the absence of women from his fiction was a serious flaw in his art, and both the heroine of *Catriona* and Lady Barbara Grant, the one with obvious limitations, the other within narrow limits, were at least women of flesh and blood. Previously he had never satisfied himself in drawing women except with the small characters of the Countess of Rosen in *Prince Otto* and Anastasie in *The Treasure of Franchard*.

In his *Humble Remonstrance* to Henry James on " The Art of Fiction," he stated categorically his belief that " the dramatic novel" must be founded on "one of the passionate *cruces* of life, where duty and inclination come nobly to the grapple," and cited as examples Meredith's *Rhoda Fleming*, Hardy's *Pair of Blue Eyes*, and Charles Reade's *Griffith Gaunt* and *The Double Marriage*. Probably he had intended such a theme in the novel about a prostitute which Fanny compelled him to destroy; after he came to know Henry James, he became more and more conscious of the flaw in his art produced by his avoidance of women, and the original plot of *The Master of Ballantrae*, the first of his novels to introduce a woman after Fanny's veto on the prostitute's novel, was the motive of struggle between duty and inclination in the characters of Lord Durrisdeer and his wife. So far as he followed this theme, *The Master of Ballantrae* is magnificent human tragedy; whether Fanny intervened or whether Stevenson himself feared to offend prudery by frankness too naked, he shunned and shelved the logical outcome of the story, invoked the *deus ex machina* of Secundra Dass, and descended to the platitudes of common melodrama. Lang sensed the failure when he described Alison Durie as " the best woman among Mr. Stevenson's few women; but even she is almost always reserved, veiled as it were."

O.G.F.   M

Stevenson knew his failure; his difficulty in finishing *The Master* was palpably due to disgust with himself at his compromise with conscience; his lack of enthusiasm for the book when it was finished arose from his knowledge of failure to carry out the original theme of the story. Following *The Master*, his long periods of inaction and inability to concentrate were undoubtedly due to his obsession with the problem of how to be faithful to his conception of art without offence to Fanny and the forces of respectability. Expressing admiration of Adela Chart in Henry James's story of "The Marriage" in *The Lesson of the Master*, he exclaimed bitterly, "What a different line of country to be trying to draw Adela, and trying to write the last four chapters of *The Wrecker!*" Of all his work at this time he thought most highly of *The Beach of Falesà*, because there, against a vital background of South Sea island life, he depicted honestly and naturally the sensual love of the white trader Wiltshire for his Kanaka girl.

In one of his rare flashes of genuine discernment as a critic, George Moore said of Henry James that, "although he had conceded much to the foolish, false, and hypocritical taste of the time, the concessions he made had in little or nothing impaired his talent." Moore added:

"The very opposite seems to me the case with Mr. Stevenson. For if any man living in this end of the century needed freedom of expression for the distinct development of his genius, that man is R. L. Stevenson."

Moore was writing in 1887, before *The Master of Ballantrae*, and his reference to Stevenson's "direct indebtedness to Edgar Poe" shows that he had *Dr. Jekyll and Mr. Hyde* uppermost in his mind. Henry Sidgwick, a Cambridge don of impeccable respectability, saw the same flaw on reading *Dr. Jekyll and Mr. Hyde*, thinking "it might have been better if English taste had allowed a little more 'realism.'"

Stevenson was well aware of the truth in Moore's criticism. In the *Humble Remonstrance* he took Henry James to task for the very concessions which Moore remarked—the method by which

James contrived that "the great struggle, the true tragedy, the *scène-à-faire*, passes unseen behind the panels of a locked door." This method, which Moore regarded as a compromise with the requirements of respectability, was impossible to Stevenson, being antagonistic to his theory of his art; as he told James himself, replying to James's criticism of *Catriona* in December 1893, "I *hear* people talking, and I *feel* them acting, and that seems to me to be fiction." If Stevenson was to write a dramatic novel, he had to deal with "one of the passionate *cruces* of life," and if he was to introduce passion, he had to let it develop naked and unashamed before the eyes of the audience. How then was he to fulfil himself as an artist without mortal offence to "the foolish, false, and hypocritical taste of the time?"

Such was his problem, which became an obsession in those last years of inward intellectual struggle at Samoa. Stevenson had much of the native reticence of the Scot; moreover, he was as loyal as his own Alan Breck. To none of his friends would he betray the truth about his domestic relations, the eternal antagonism against Fanny on the theory of his art; only Henley suspected, from his intimate knowledge of Stevenson before his marriage. The barest traces of that antagonism may be scented in his letters over a period of years—little more than the statement to Henley from Hyères, after destroying the prostitute's story, that his wife "hates and loathes and slates my women." Fanny's own letters betray more; she told Colvin how she "begged to have a few things marked out" in *Prince Otto*; from Samoa she recorded how "he says I do not take the broad view of an artist, but hold the cheap opinions of the general public that a book must be interesting." The subject under discussion was *In The South Seas*, which Fanny wanted to be light articles of personal trivialities infused with what newspapers call "human interest", usefully advertising himself and his fiction, whereas Stevenson wanted to interpret his enthusiasm for the natives, their lives, manners, customs, and conditions. So, when he was writing fiction, Fanny may be seen arguing in favour of food for Mudie, while Stevenson wanted to express himself without let or hindrance.

Fanny's determination and habit of getting her own way

were visible in her firm chin. "If you don't get on with her it's a pity about your visit," wrote Stevenson to a prospective visitor to Samoa; "she runs the show." But there were signs towards the end of Stevenson's increasing restlessness under the yoke. "Louis is coming round now to my view of his book of travels," Fanny told Colvin with serene confidence, and thought that soon, doubtless after more haranguing from her, he would "look as coldly upon the scientific aspect as ever I have done." But Stevenson disappointed her by sticking to his own view and declining to make *In The South Seas* a condiment for the circulating libraries. And in *The Beach of Falesà* he sailed very near the wind of impropriety in describing the trader's animal passion for his Kanaka wife, as he did again in the elder Kirstie's appreciation of her luscious charms, as she rose from bed to go to Archie's room.

Hardy's *Tess* in 1891 was a bold stroke for freedom of expression which Stevenson in Samoa hardly recognised; if he had lived long enough to see the effect of such as *Jude the Obscure* in 1896, Maugham's *Liza of Lambeth* in 1897, *The Man of Property* in 1906, and Wells's *Ann Veronica* in 1909, he would almost certainly have left greater work than anything he actually achieved. Though he compromised with propriety by delaying the physical consumation of Catriona's love till after she was respectably married, he persevered with the theme of *Catriona* where he had shied away in *The Master of Ballantrae*; in *The Beach of Falesà* and *The Ebb-Tide* he showed an increasing tendency to sacrifice mere incident to psychology, and foreshadowed the coming of Joseph Conrad; in *Weir of Hermiston* the stage was set for such a subject as Hall Caine treated as melodrama, but which Stevenson as an artist would have made into moving tragedy.

Speculation is idle, but Stevenson's marriage was obviously the controlling influence of his literary career as well as his life. If he had not packed off on his romantic adventure to California, his health would not have been ruined; if he had not married Fanny Osbourne, he would have been free to follow his own natural medium of expression. And who can doubt that the eccentric youth who faced social ostracism in Edinburgh would have defied the ban of Mudie as George Moore defied it? And remembering the achievements of George Moore, while comparing his second-rate talent with Stevenson's genius, who can measure the loss to literature by Stevenson's marriage, which introduced to his domestic hearth a watchful ambassadress of respectability, a spiritual god-daughter of Mr. Mudie and Mr. Gladstone?

CHAPTER SIX

Andrew Lang and other Critics

§ 1

THE legend of Stevenson as a "seraph in chocolate" attained to such a degree of sanctity that Colvin wrote in private protest when Maurice Hewlett, as late as 1922, ventured to suggest the now prevailing opinion that Stevenson's reputation was distorted out of reasonable proportion by the idolatry of his friends. Hewlett was of the generation which followed Stevenson; apart from having seen Stevenson once at the Savile Club, he confessed to Colvin that he had no idea of him, and the legend of "the romantic and endearing figure" was a "revelation" to him as to the general public. "The idea which I then obtained," wrote Hewlett to Colvin, "was surely largely owing to the generous warmth with which you, Lang, and in a lesser degree Gosse and Mr. Graham Balfour praised . . . your friend."

Colvin's services were those of the devout editor of Stevenson's works and correspondence, Balfour's of the even more devout family biographer; many other editors and biographers have been equally devout without being able to achieve the general acceptance of their special pleading, and Colvin and Balfour could not have achieved the Stevenson legend without the alliance of Andrew Lang. Lang did not confine his advertisement of Stevenson to laudatory reviews of his books; he talked endlessly about him, mentioning his books as standards of comparison when praising another writer's work, recalling remarks made by Stevenson as being incidentally suggested by a subject of discussion, continually referring to characters and incidents in his stories. Thus the bare statement of a publisher's announcement that Quiller-Couch was to finish *St. Ives* enabled Lang to discuss the impossibility of anybody's completing *Weir of Hermiston*, to suggest mockingly that a national memorial to Stevenson should take the form of a group of statuary representing George Moore in the act of instructing Stevenson in the art of writing, to remark that Stevenson never sought cheap publicity by lending himself to tradesmen's advertisements, and to relate the circumstances of the publication and reception of *Jekyll and Hyde*. Lang lost no opportunity of talking about Stevenson; therefore Lang's readers became educated to Lang's estimation of Stevenson, and Lang's readers were the great majority of the reading public.

For Lang occupied an unique position in the literary world of his day, wielding a dominant influence beyond that of any individual critic before or since. Relating how an obscure shilling book on dining-out in London was made popular into a big success by a notice of Lang's in the *Daily News*, Mr. Grant Richards remarked in his *Memories of a Misspent Youth* that, excepting Arnold Bennett's *Evening Standard* articles in the last years of his life, "no man alive, no newspaper, has all that power." Lang contributed largely to the making of Stevenson's reputation; he contributed equally to the making of Rider Haggard's; he started the sensational success of Anthony Hope's *Prisoner of Zenda*, the vogue of Stanley Weyman, and the selling of S. R. Crockett's novels. The secret of his power is far to seek in the constitution of a curious individuality. He commanded the respect of all classes by the profundity of his scholarship, the extent and variety of his reading; the barbs of his wit and sarcasm opponents were chary of challenging; he possessed an easy grace of style which won the envy of highbrows, and charmed the masses by its unpretentiousness, its familiarity, its lack of conscious superiority and condescension; he was not himself a popular writer, but he was a voluminous author in so many fields, with so much distinction, that he created the impression that he might do anything if he chose, and was therefore admirably qualified to assess the achievements of others. The humanity and variety of his interests captivated the general public; he was a bookman without the mustiness of the bookworm, for while he could argue with sedentary pundits the most abstruse difficulties of the classics, he expressed a preference for the swashbuckling in fiction, and while he was known to indulge in the pastime of poetry, the province of the long-haired, unwashed decadent, he loved nothing better than watching the cricket at Lords' or a day with the fly on the streams of his native Scotland. He was the Admirable Crichton of letters, the gallant cavalier of literary critics.

Ironically, for one who wrote several biographies, including the standard *Life and Letters of John Gibson Lockhart* and the politically useful *Life, Letters and Diaries of Sir Stafford Northcote*, Lang desired that no biography should be written of him. Like Thackeray, he revolted from the idea of having erected over his remains one of the heavy monuments of dull pomposity in two unreadable volumes, such as a distinguished Victorian's surviving relatives deemed a pious duty, as essential as the accordance of decent burial, and usually served to obliterate his memory in the foggy shroud of its dullness. To Edward Clodd he once confided that he wanted "some short way with the ' Life and Letters ' plague." He stated his view of biography plainly: "A biographer must be truthful or hold his hand altogether." But he argued the obvious objection that a "limit on ' the whole truth ' is placed by the feelings of other people." The hero's letters contain remarks about other people, which are fairly relevant, since they illustrate the hero's character or point of view, but their publication may cause pain or embarrassment to survivors closely connected with the objects of criticism. Lang had a sardonic wit; he knew that he had frequently passed uncomplimentary comments on acquaintances, and disliked the idea of remarks confided privately to friends, which he would never have dreamed of broadcasting, being made into public property after his death.

Though an official biography is wanting, ample material for a reconstruction of Lang's life and personality appear in the memoirs of contemporaries. He was born at Selkirk on 31st March, 1844, a longer time ago than any of the other writers under discussion in this book; his father was sheriff-clerk of Selkirkshire, his grandfather had been likewise sheriff-clerk and acquainted with Walter Scott, and his mother was a sister of William Young Sellar, professor of Latin at Edinburgh, of whom Lang wrote a memoir. He went to Selkirk Grammar School and Edinburgh Academy before matriculating in 1861 at St. Andrews, where he remained three years before moving to Glasgow University in order to enter for an exhibition to Oxford. He went up to Balliol as an exhibiter in 1865, and in 1868, having taken a double first in Honour Moderations and Greats, was elected a fellow of Merton. In the chapter of intellectual autobiography which gave its title to the volume of essays, *Adventures Among Books*, he reveals the insatiable love of reading, springing spontaneously from personal taste and fancy, which not only disqualified him for the unimaginative don's confinement within a prescribed syllabus, but led to his unique influence as a critic and the frustration of his individuality as a man and writer. He taught himself to read at the age of four, by learning the elegy of Cock Robin till he knew it by rote, and then picking out the letters and words in the printed text. His first reading was fairy tales and penny chap books, but such frivolity was forbidden on Sundays, when the Bible was the only book allowed, and in an illustrated family edition he read "the fightingest parts," the Apocrypha, and "stories like that of the Witch of Endor." His love of fairies and an illustrated Shakespeare led him to *A Midsummer Night's Dream*; family reverence for Scott enabled him to come early upon the *Lay of the Last Minstrel* and *The Lady of the Lake*. "After learning one's first lesson in history from the *Tales of a Grandfather*," he wrote, "nobody, one hopes, can criticise him in cold blood, or after the manner of Mr. Leslie Stephen, who is not sentimental."

He read everything that came to hand; he read even Pinnock's *History of Rome* for pleasure, and won golden opinions from his teachers till he arrived at an age when he could lay hands on books of his choice. From the hour that *Pickwick* was brought into the house, "it was all over, for five or six years, with anything like industry and lesson-books." He read "every kind of light literature that I could lay my hands upon." Authority forbade his reading of novels, but the ban was withdrawn when it was found that he was merely reading Byron's *Don Juan* instead. He had to read *Vanity Fair* surreptitiously, though he could not understand why it was esteemed a wicked book, harmful to the young. Thackeray "became the chief enchanter;" he read *The Rose and the Ring* when it first came out—"it was worth while to be twelve years old, when the Christmas books were written by Dickens and Thackeray."

Only "a constitutional dislike to being beaten on the hands with a leather strap" urged him to struggle with his Latin grammar.

> "While we were deep in the history of Pendennis we were also being dragged through the Commentaries of Caius Julius Cæsar, through the Latin and Greek Grammars, through Xenophon, and the Eclogues of Virgil, and a depressing play of Euripides, the *Phoenissae*. I can never say how much I detested these authors, who, taken in small doses, are far, indeed, from being attractive. Horace, to a lazy boy, appears in his Odes to have nothing to say, and to say it in the most frivolous and vexatious manner. Then Cowper's *Task* or *Paradise Lost*, as school-books with notes, seems arid enough to a schoolboy. I remember reading ahead, in Cowper, instead of attending to the lesson and the class-work. His observations on public schools were not uninteresting, but the whole English school-work of those days was repugnant. One's English education was all got out of school."

So little have the educationists learned, that Lang's observations are as applicable after eighty years. It was this instinctive revolt against curriculum which assured his incompatibility with a don's life, just as it was the continuance of his boyish inclination to read for enjoyment, regardless of convention and the dictates of desirability, which won him popular favour as a critic. For years Greek seemed to him "a mere vacuous terror," but after he learned the romantic delights of Homer from a crib in Bohn's series, "Greek was no longer tedious." In an age of pomposity, when Leslie Stephen, Saintsbury, Gosse, and Lang himself were objects of reverence as scholastic pundits, there was an irresistible charm in the gay independence of Lang's careless confession "to having learned the classical languages, as it were by mere accident, for the sake of what is in them, and with a provokingly imperfect accuracy"—still more in the shameless addition: "Cricket and trout occupied far too much of my mind and my time: Christopher North, and Walton, and Thomas Tod

Stoddart, and 'The Moor and the Loch' were my holiday reading, and I do not regret it." This was the charm which won for him the allegiance of the great unlettered; he wore his learning with the careless ease of the born aristocrat, he never survived his zest for reading what he liked, and he was unafraid to confess even his most puerile pleasures.

His first book, *Ballads and Lyrics of Old France*, appeared in 1872, his "last undergraduate literary discoveries" having been of France and the Renaissance, the latest fashion of aesthetic Oxford in the late 'sixties, with the elfin Swinburne for its prophet, shocking the suburbs as with the gambols of a naked Cupid. Lang picked up *Atalanta in Calydon* in the Union reading-room; for him it represented ever "the best, the most beautiful, the most musical" of Swinburne. Lang and others of his time were sent by Swinburne to the ballade, the rondeau, the triolet, to reading Du Bellay and Ronsard, and thence to Alfred de Musset, Gautier, and Theodore de Banville; they founded "out of old French, and old oak, and old china," an aesthetic movement which supplied "an early purchaser of Mr. William Morris's wallpapers." They bridged the gulf between Pre-Raphælitism and the *Yellow Book*, between Rossetti and Beardsley; if George Moore had not been too busy in Montmartre to know of them, he might have conceded that they created the public for *Confessions of a Young Man*. But Lang was no longer of the movement in 1888, when nobody found Moore's *gaucherie* more offensive than the fastidious scholar who, characteristically independent, declined even to read *Esther Waters*, and only condescended to notice Moore's existence by snubbing him for writing about Gælic and Erse old literature without knowing his subject, and for the idiotic strictures on Fielding which Moore reprinted twenty-two years later in *Avowals*.

For Lang this aesthetic movement was a phase, to which he contributed notably and gracefully in his first book and in his later *Ballades in Blue China*. His mediaeval reading led him into the deeper waters of folk-lore and anthropology, the first fruit of which life-long study appeared in an article on "Mythology and Fairy-Tales" for the *Fortnightly Review* of May, 1873. Already he was writing regularly for magazines and weekly journals, and when he married in 1875, he resigned his Merton fellowship and settled in London to earn a living by journalism.

Lang had the glib pen of a born journalist. In a pavilion of chattering cricketers, he would stand beside the scorer and write an article while awaiting his turn to bat. Rider Haggard related how he once saw him write in half-an-hour a leading article for the *Daily News*, which "involved many allusions and much quotation," and on another occasion he wrote a *Saturday Review* article in a railway carriage, while sustaining an argumentative conversation with his fellow-travellers. His facility was equalled only by his versatility; to him alone of his generation descended from the famous Scotch reviewers—from Jeffrey, Lockhart, Maginn, and Christopher North—the faculty of writing knowledgeably on anything. On only two subjects he never touched in journalism—politics and religion. In his boyhood reading of Macaulay's *Lays of Ancient Rome*, his sympathies were with the exiled kings, and finding beside the slaying of Valerius by the youngest Tarquin the boyish marginal note, "Well done, the Jacobites," he remarked long afterwards, "Perhaps my politics have never gone much beyond this sentiment." In Professor George Gordon's apt phrase, Lang's "chance of politics was gone with Culloden." He once wrote to Rider Haggard:

"Abstain from politics; let civilisation die decently as die it must, and as we have no fight in us. I don't belong to the Voting classes. *Ni Elettori ni Eletti.*"

Of all the classics read as an undergraduate, Aristotle's *Politics* left the most lasting impression, and he wrote in *Adventures Among Books:*

"Probably politicians are the last people who read Aristotle's *Politics*. The work is, indeed, apt to disenchant one with political life. It is melancholy to see the little Greek states running the regular round—monarchy, oligarchy, tyranny, democracy in all its degrees, the 'ultimate democracy' of plunder, lawlessness, license of women, children, and slaves, and then tyranny again, or subjection to some foreign power. In politics, too, there is no secret of success, of happy life for all. There is no such road to the City, either democratic or royal. This is the lesson which Aristotle's *Politics* impresses on us, this and the impossibility of imposing ideal constitutions on mankind."

This contempt for illusion characterised Lang's attitude, not only to politics, but to religion and the whole business of life. His studies in folk-lore and comparative mythology—which found expression in his books on *Custom and Myth* (1884), *Myth, Ritual, and Religion* (1887), and *The Making of Religion* (1898), and which Edward Clodd considered his work of most abiding value—taught him that all the religions of the world have a common origin in the practical needs of human ignorance, each religion having been formulated by an imaginative leader, whether Mohammed, Christ, or Buddha, as a code for the regulation of a community's conduct—to supply, in fact, general principles of guidance for the vast majority in every community lacking the intelligence and imagination to evolve an independent philosophy. To Lang, as to any other intelligent student of history, the petty bigotry and squabbles of religious faction presented the futility, without the dignity, of political idealism. When Papal authority caused his *Myth, Ritual, and Religion* to be listed on the *Index Expurgatorius*, he requested an episcopal explanation, which was naturally not forthcoming, since bishops are educated only for the pulpit of declamation and not for the arena of logical debate; when the biologist St. George Mivart was excommunicated by Cardinal Vaughan, Lang was moved to irreverent levity; he supported Rider Haggard's opinion that the Christian missionaries ruined the Zulu race, by converting to monogamy a people whose high standards of morality depended upon the more natural condition of polygamy. He was a sceptic, conscious of the agnosticism which is the logical realisation of the intelligent scholar.

Meredith said of Lang that he "had no heart, otherwise he might have been a good poet." This Clodd, who knew him better than Meredith, denied, citing the verses in memory of his sister-in-law in *Rhymes à la Mode* as evidence of Lang's depth of feeling. But Meredith was right in thinking that Lang lacked the passion to write inspired poetry. Passion flourishes only in the soil of unreason; it cannot flower without illusion. Lang had the cynical serenity of wide and varied knowledge; he was too acutely conscious of his own littleness, and the littleness of the contemporary world [by comparison with the colossal scheme of eternity, to excite himself with idealist emotions. The "superciliousness" of manner, detected by the writer of his obituary notice in the *Times*, was the impression upon the undiscerning of this serenity, giving a sense of aloofness, and the sardonic humour with which he habitually looked on life. He despised the age in which he lived, with its humbug and hypocrisy, its graft, and its unnatural respectability, but he did not seek to alter it, like the reformers, nor score off its deficiencies, like George Moore—he merely accepted it for what it was, the age in which he was born to live his life.

And he got the best out of his life within the limits of his fate. He appreciated [beauty—the *Chanson de Roland*, a woman's delicate hand, the sun setting over a peaceful trout-stream—but he was content to enjoy the beauty beside him without wasting time in longing for greater beauty beyond his reach. He enjoyed the sunsets on Hampstead Heath without wishing that he was overlooking the Bay of Naples or the wooded cliffs of Lynton; one suspects that when he went to cricket and it rained, he did not linger in impatient pavilion raillery against the weather, but took a mackintoshed walk in a fresh-smelling lane, or retired to a corner to lose himself in the heather with Alan Breck. Perhaps he would have preferred to live in the days of Bolingbroke and Congreve; at least he preferred to read about the best and brightest of the eighteenth century in Dumas and Stanley Weyman, rather than the worst and saddest of his own day in Hardy and Gissing. The clear critical discernment of his culture fairly measured the artistic achievement of Hardy and Gissing, but he felt discomfort at the reproach of their preoccupation with life's sordidness. Why should art be wasted on ugliness, with so much beauty in the world? And what was artistic achievement anyhow if more pleasure was procurable from a plain-spun yarn of improbable adventure in lands remote from Fleet Street? "More claymores, less psychology, suit a simple taste," he wrote of *Catriona*, which may be taken as his slogan as a critic, and earned him the execration of serious novelists. "Lang," wrote

Henry James to Stevenson, "in the D.N. (*Daily News*) every morning, and I believe in a hundred other places, uses his beautiful thin facility to write everything down to the lowest level of Philistine twaddle—the view of the old lady round the corner or the clever person at the dinner party."

James's accusation was hardly exaggerated, even to the "hundred other places." Self-righteous researchers, sentimentalising over the injuries sustained by the fragile Keats, and even the formidable Hazlitt, at the hands of *Blackwood's* anonymous reviewers, piously congratulated the apostles of progress that such iniquities as those of Wilson, Lockhart, and Maginn are unknown to subsequent generations. But if Lang never punished with his left hand what he had praised with his right, as Maginn might have done, he shamelessly used the cloak of anonymity to reiterate the same view of the same book in half-a-dozen different papers. The abuse prevails to-day, since few reviewers can afford to quarrel with their bread and butter; while editors lack the judgment and enterprise to secure the exclusive services of new critics, and prefer to rest content with the second-hand work of tried old-timers, the abuse must and will continue. Another still prevalent abuse, that of the reader-critic, was shamelessly practised by Lang; he was literary adviser to Longmans, and rarely failed to boost a Longmans book as a reviewer. When Haggard proposed to dedicate *She* to him, Lang warned him that he would only be able to review it "with my name signed thereto and my honest confession," naïvely inferring that, without the dedication on his conscience, he would have followed his usual practice of reviewing the book in sundry places.

His tendency to write what he disliked "down to the lowest level of Philistine twaddle" sprang from a cultivated practice in his critical art; he was a master of ridicule. His guying of Tolstoy's *Kreutzer Sonata* is a masterpiece of destructive satire. He found the book in Sutherland Edwards's translation "very much like other shilling novels, not only in price, but in absence of humour," but mockingly reproached admiring critics who supposed that Tolstoy himself "held the ideas of his murderous hero, Pozdnisheff, about love, marriage, and those fair beings whom Guy Heavistone dismissed as ' poor little beasts.'"

"It is not to be imagined that the Count wishes to see the human race die out, for purely moral reasons, as Podsnapoff or whatever his name is, desires; and we are not to credit him with all Pod's wild criticisms of men and women. Why should he not be satirising rather than sympathising with this nonsense? To think he is a sympathiser is not to honour the famous Russian romancer, who is so dear to persons of secondhand 'culture,' and who really has great qualities, in spite of his admirers."

One good quality he found in Tolstoy, "not usual in his work," by reading him in a shilling edition—"he is short!" And having spent three hundred words in poking fun at "Pod's" comicalities, he proceeds to discuss "how different, how much more genial, if equally absurd, is Miss Florence Warden's shilling tale, *Nurse Revel's Mistake*!" Not till Frank Harris engaged Bernard Shaw on the *Saturday Review*, was there another critic who ventured on such impudent *badinerie*, much less one of the skill and prestige to get away with it.

Lang disliked Tolstoy and all the Russians. In *Anna Karenina* "there is a disconnected profusion, a crowding, a lack of proportion which no impartial critic, however favourable, can overlook." When Besant asked why he was "always tilting at Russian novelists," he admitted that Tolstoy, Turgeniev, and Dostoievsky had genius, but declared "they deserve the punishment which Dante assigns to those who deliberately seek sadness." Previously he had written that "the famed foreigner, Dostoievsky, and M. Zola, and M. Maupassant often seem to be in the mood when man delights them not, nor woman either. A piercing consciousness of the misery in the world fills their pages, and to read them is about as gay as to read the daily papers." Lang had masculine taste; if he had been born forty years later, he would have shared the golfing man's fondness for "Sapper" and Edgar Wallace. He rarely chose to remember that women formed the bulk of the library subscribers, that women made the huge sales of all the pilers-on of agony from Mrs. Henry Wood and Hall Caine down to the hero of Mr. A. S. M. Hutchinson, whose favourite recreation Barry Pain described as "suffering."

Lang liked to be entertained, and probably the only dolorous contemporary novels he ever praised were George Douglas's *House With Green Shutters* and W. E. Tirebuck's *Dorrie*. He describes Gissing as a realist—that is, "one of the 'idealists' who select and present the more disagreeable facts of life"—and frequently disparaged "that woebegone work *The Story of an African Farm*, a farm on which people were always tackling religious problems, or falling in love on new and heterodox lines, instead of shooting deer, and finding diamonds, or hunting up the archæological remains of the Transvaal." He deplored the tendency of the modern novelist to "gummidge", and when highbrow critics mocked "modern novels of hard blows as a recrudescence of barbarism," he retorted that polyandry was likewise "a recrudescence of savagery in its worst and least human form," and though "nothing could be much more disagreeable, in practice, than either antique diversion," he preferred "to read about fighting rather than about free love."

He never flinched before attack, and deprecating violence in criticism, held an enormous advantage over his adversaries, apart from his armoury of wit and the superior scope of his reading, in never allowing his urbanity to be ruffled. When Hardy inserted a preface to the fifth edition of *Tess of the D'Urbervilles*, taunting Lang with "gentility" for objecting to the novel's offences against respectability, he replied with a marshalled array of his objections to *Tess*, supporting them with the strictures on *Two on a Tower*, which he found equally "forbidding in conception," and concluded by coolly intimating that he did not intend "to speak again about any work of Mr. Hardy's." He likewise avoided reviewing the novels of Henry James and W. D. Howells, but he kept up continual warfare with Howells in his critical capacity as literary commentator of *Harper's Magazine*. He derided Howells's view that "the art of fiction, as Jane Austen knew it, declined from her through Scott, and Bulwer, and Dickens and Charlotte Brontë, and Thackeray, and even George Eliot, because the mania of romanticism had seized upon all Europe."

"Miss Austen is supreme in her own dominion. But there are other dominions; in this house of art there are many mansions. We can hardly regard Scott, or Thackeray, or the rest as persons who decline from the ideal of Miss Austen, because they attempted hundreds of things on which she never ventured, and did them admirably well."

Wh n Howells asked how England, having known "the refined perfection of Miss Austen," could "enjoy anything less refined and less perfect," Lang retorted, "How did America, once familiar with the refinement and perfection of Hawthorne, ' come to enjoy anything less refined and less perfect?'" And again, after defending historical novels from abuse by Howells, he reminded him suavely that "even the novels of Mr. Howells must one day become historical."

There was none of the august pundit's traditional snobbery about Lang. When the youthful pessimists of 1888 lamented that the popular novelists of the day were played out, he remarked that "Mr. Christie Murray, thank goodness, is still writing excellent novels, as good as *Rainbow Gold*, which is very good indeed." Though he lamented in his obituary notice of Grant Allen that he was "born to differ from Allen on almost every conceivable point," and once turned on him the full force of the batteries usually reserved for Howells, when Allen asserted that "the universal novel must ever hereafter travel in the very self-same path as Mr. Henry James and Mr. Howells," he vigorously defended Allen's *What's Bred in the Bone*, when high-brows affected to despise it for having won a prize competition in *Tit-Bits*. "To judge by the language of some haughty critics," he wrote, "one might think that to write a novel of this kind is an easy thing, which anyone can do," but "the special narrative genius" is "as rare a gift as the composition of the most ' cultured ' fiction." In his flippantly provocative vein, he praised Miss Braddon, though she "is not reckoned with the great masters of the human intellect, such as a Hall Caine, a Miss Corelli, an Ian Maclaren," because she could tell a story and drew men, not as they are, but as they should be. When Edward Garnett, in the *Monthly Review* for December, 1901, attacked him for liking only "what is old and seasoned," and striving "to close with his strait creed the mouth of this unworthy generation," Lang

did not adopt the usual pundit's course of ignoring the impertinence of a youthful beginner with the Olympian disdain of a
distinguished veteran. Nor did he reply with the condescension
of a wise elder to irresponsible youth, who recklessly proposes
to instruct his grandmother in sucking the proverbial egg. He
gracefully recognised Garnett as "a writer of weight and earnestness," reminded him that Stevenson, Kipling, Robert Bridges,
and others "were new and unseasoned in my time," and coolly
entered into reasoned argument, as with an equal, to prove his
view that "better novels were produced between 1814 and 1860
than in 1860 to 1901."

It was unjust to accuse Lang, as Gosse and Saintsbury could be
fairly accused, of praising only that which had stood the test of
time, for no reviewer of his day read more contemporary fiction.
Apart from being among the first to recognise Stevenson,
Kipling, Bridges, and Barrie, he virtually made the reputations
of Rider Haggard, Stanley Weyman, and S. R. Crockett, and
The House With the Green Shutters and Anthony Hope's *Mr. Witt's
Widow* were not the only novels by little-known writers to which
he drew timely attention—he praised *Love and Mr. Lewisham*,
though he had not liked "Mr. Wells's apocalyptic and extra-
natural romances about Mars and the future," and declared Rolf
Boldrewood's *Robbery Under Arms*, then unknown, to have "all
the merit of *Jack Sheppard*, or *Rookwood*, with an exemplary
moral thrown in," which was cunning eulogy, since Victorians
loved a moral to excuse entertainment with a pretence of deriving
enlightenment and had never been comfortable about enjoying
Jack Sheppard since John Forster attacked its moral tendencies.
He protested acidly when an American pundit stigmatised
Tirebuck's *Dorrie* as "not a book to lie on the family reading-
table;" "I am no judge of the family reading-table," he said,
but Tirebuck's heroine was "the most absolutely original and, in
her way, the most taking figure in recent fiction," though he
deplored the "realism, or naturalism probably," which required
"the wreck of beautiful, wilful, wanton Dorrie."

None can deny that Lang was instinctively conservative in
taste, or that he obstinately insisted on limiting the scope of the
novelist's function. When the *Athenæum* for 30th July, 1892,

complained that English literature was "gagged", and novelists "must work under painfully soul-killing restrictions," Lang argued that "a novel is not a treatise," and if "an author is a Malthusian, or a Free Lover, or has a just and natural desire to reform the world," he should state his theories "simply, directly, with all authorities and evidence," and "they ought not to be mixed up with flirtations, love affairs, and fanciful episodes."

"*Nana*, for example, may contain what we should know, and circumstances which we should endeavour to rectify. But a reform of morals would not be aided by letting *Nana* circulate among the readers of Miss Yonge."

Why the principles of Malthus, the practice of promiscuity, or the career of a prostitute should not enter the province of the novelist as freely as the animal fashion of Victorian procreation, the vicissitudes of matrimony, or the misdeeds of thieves and murderers, Lang never deigned to explain. Nor did he apparently recognise that the reformer reached a wider public with a novel than a treatise, and that Dickens with *Oliver Twist* and Reade with *Hard Cash* achieved more towards the correction of abuses respectively in workhouses and lunatic asylums than many treatises and commissioners' reports. And his trite remarks about *Nana* echo the hackneyed argument of the intellectual ostrich, indicted by Reade as the "prurient prude", who has flourished in every age from Jeremy Collier to the censors of *Ulysses*, *Lady Chatterley's Lover*, and *The Well of Loneliness*, though he was doubtless right in thinking that the reactions of Miss Yonge's readers to *Nana* would be unproductive of moral amelioration, even if the conclusion reflects unfortunately upon the achievements of education in an enlightened democracy.

Lang allowed his personal preference for romance and tales of adventure to force him into a position of prejudice so unjustifiable that he merited the disgust expressed by Henry James, and shared by most serious students of the novel's artistic development. He declined to review Olive Schreiner's *Trooper Peter Halket* "because you cannot argue fairly on a political topic in a romance," and though he was interested in Israel

Zangwill's *Children of the Ghetto* as a study of the "polyglot cosmopolitan modern Israelite," finding the book "more full of words needing a glossary than the early Anglo-Indian tales of Mr. Kipling," he asked "why did he not write a treatise when he might have done it so well?" It did not occur to him that many of his admired historical romances argued politics of past ages, and that some of the volumes in the "Standard Edition" of the Waverley Novels are furnished with copious glossaries. Nor was he always ingenious in his defences of romance. When Grant Allen saw in the revival of the historical novel a result of the "recrudescence of barbarism and Jingo reaction," Lang forgot his usual candid argument for pure entertainment, and attempted to attribute its revival to "the revival of historical studies." He admitted that Besant and "the authors of *The Splendid Spur* and *Micah Clarke* . . . would probably have written whether history was being more closely and widely studied or not," but mentioning Stevenson's *Kidnapped* and Haggard's *Cleopatra* as instances where "the history is not ' got up ' for the novel, the novel comes out of the knowledge of history," he cited *John Inglesant* as the cardinal example of a romance with "a real and ardent historical motive." Yet this was the only good word he ever had to say for Shorthouse's celebrated book. When *John Inglesant* came out, he did not read it because he "detected a tendency to pulpit oratory;" when *Blackwood's Magazine* praised it as "the most beautiful sermon in all fiction," he gibed that "one does not go for sermons to novels;" when it was said that *John Inglesant* was "loved for the sake of its exposition of the ideal perfection of the Church of England," and its first part "is concerned almost entirely with spiritual crises," he understood why "one was not attracted"— "efficiency, not spiritual crises, is what most people desire in a young hero of Royalist romance," and Queen Henrietta Maria should have chosen for her mission somebody like D'Artagnan or the Chevalier Wogan of Mr. Mason's *Clementina*, instead of that "dawdling creature" Inglesant.

Though he wished to make novelists only purveyors of entertainment for athletic undergraduates, and refused to allow that contemporary Humbug "gagged" expression, Lang shared no fellow-feeling with the gaitered moralist, who advertised having

put *Jude the Obscure* on the fire with the tongs. Though he never
missed a chance to gibe at Zola, he felt uncomfortable when
Zola was banned. His sense of sportsmanship revolted from the
mediaeval bigotry of forcibly silencing a man because he did not
agree with the majority, and his intellectual independence resented
authority's dictation about what was good for him. So, while
repeating his remarks on the inadvisability of turning Zola
loose on Miss Yonge's readers, he approved the morality of Zola's
intentions, and asserted that "grown-up readers are much more
likely to be disgusted than to be depraved" by Zola. And, with a
burst of spleen against Humbug, he added sarcastically, "when one
considered what is published daily by the press, there seems a
want of complete consistency in forbidding the publication of any
literary work."

Probably it tickled his taste in irony that he should earn his
living from a source for which he never concealed his contempt.
His mockery of Zola, of the Russian novelists, of Howells and the
intellectual critics, always rang whimsically flippant and ironic,
but his tone assumed the intensity of loathing when he tilted at
another favourite butt, the sensationalism of newspapers. He
went out of his way to praise Richard Whiteing's *The Island*, a
novel outside his usual taste, for the pleasure of quoting its attack
on the "cool devilry of mocking headlines, as though all the
woe and all the folly of the world were but one stupendous joke."
To Lang newspapers reflected the worst vice of contemporary
society: "we all sit in the Ear of Dionysius," he wrote, "in the
whispering gallery of the world, and hear the reverberations of
every mad word and deed, of every sorrow and disgrace."

Though his instincts were unlighted by even the faintest
flicker of the reformer's fire, and in literature, as in life, he
accepted existing conditions with lazy cynicism, he was unafraid
to utter startlingly unconventional comments, which came the
more forcibly from one who was not given to explosiveness.
When Churton Collins lamented the state of literary decadence
in 1901, Lang, though always finding some new book to praise,
not only admitted the fact of the decadence, but coolly added the
discomforting truth that "our literary decadence is partly the
result of education." He rarely attacked a book or scored off an

author, because he avoided reviewing books he did not like. He
believed an editor should "request his reviewer to leave the bad
books alone, except when some Robert Montgomery needs
exposure." Usually he only attacked books and authors when he
thought they were being generally praised beyond their merits,
as when he guyed Tolstoy, or when, everybody in the late 'nineties
being ready to acclaim everything by Kipling as the work of
inspired genius, he remarked that the heroes of *Stalky and Co.*
"are not normal schoolboys," and preferred the characters in
Eden Phillpotts's *The Human Boy.* In his experience, "most
reviewers are like cat-doctors—they do not know much." He
believed that "a critic ought to be able to correct an author
where his author is wrong, and to add, if only a little, to the
information." But he found that few editors liked a review "full
of condensed knowledge" which might be "even harder reading
than the book itself"; many preferred that their reviewer should
"only give a summary of the book's contents and say whether it
interests him, by style and manner, or not," which though "it
is not criticism," forms "the not useless function of the ' newsman
of the Republic of Letters.'" But too often Lang found that
editors lacked the knowledge and conscience to secure even so
much as this, and were content to print "the vapid jottings of a
weary, uninterested, ignorant hack, who dare not venture on an
original remark for fear of ' putting his foot in it.'"

Though he concentrated on books in which he could find
fruit for praise, he was impatient of the conventional findings of
reviewers. "Novels," he said, "are seldom so good, and perhaps
not often so bad as the reviewers declare."

> "There exists a set of advertisements, consisting of extracts
> from reviews of a pretty ordinary batch of novels, about
> eight extracts to each book. Say there are ten books, then there
> are about eighty extracts, in which each of them is called
> ' masterly ' or ' a masterpiece.' Masterpieces are not, really,
> quite so common."

Seemingly the practice of reviewing has made little progress
since Lang's day; his remarks on reviewing, in *Longmans's
Magazine* for March 1897, remain so apt that a publisher might

find them all well worth reprinting in a selection of Lang's essays.

Mr. Humbert Wolfe has been recklessly guilty of the generalisation that "all contemporary criticism is merely an exhibition of fugitive prejudice." Since there are exceptions to every rule, any generalisation can be made to seem an utterance of congenital idiocy, and it is idle to argue how much of the work of Coleridge, Hazlitt, De Quincey, Carlyle, and Macaulay, is not merely "fugitive prejudice." But even fugitive prejudice figures importantly in the province of the critical historian, and though Andrew Lang may be generally remembered only by a few bits of verse, his treatises on mythology, and his translation of the *Odyssey*, his importance in a study of the literature of his time rests on his reviewing. He was not a great critic; except Stevenson, he did little to assist recognition of any man of outstanding genius—Conrad, Bennett, Galsworthy, Shaw, all failed to impress him, and he disliked Meredith only less than Henry James and Hardy. But he assumed a dominance over public taste by reason of the alliance between obvious limitations and gifts curiously inappropriate in a popular journalist. His power lay in his avowed preference for light literature coming from one of the most accomplished scholars of the day, who was admitted even by his bitterest opponents to be incapable of writing otherwise than with grace and charm. The new middle-classes, eager to acquire a veneer of culture, were delighted to find a pundit whose reputation for scholarship commanded universal reverence, who astonishingly encouraged their improvement with books of entertainment —he appealed alike to their snobbery and inclination.

Of the brilliance of his intellect no writer left a greater variety of evidence. The most celebrated result of his classical studies is his translation of the *Odyssey* in collaboration with S. H. Butcher, published in 1879 and familiar to all readers of Homer as "Butcher and Lang;" his other translations were his Theocritus, *Homeric Hymns,* and in collaboration with Walter Leaf and Ernest Myers, the *Iliad,* while he wrote critical studies of *Homer and the Epic, Homer and his Age,* and *The World of Homer.* His most ambitious poem was *Helen of Troy* (1882), an epic in six books, but his best verse is to be found here and there in his two books of ballads and the subsequent collections called *Rhymes à la Mode* and *Grass of Parnassus*. With characteristic lack of illusion he told Haggard: "I have a hideous conscience which knows that a ballad or a leading article are the best things I have done, though I'd prefer to prefer *Helen of Troy*. But she's a bandbox." His valuable contribution to the study of mythology appears in three books, *Custom and Myth* (1884), *Myth, Ritual, and Religion* (1887), and *The Making of Religion* (1898); he called himself a "psycho-folklorist" and tried to establish an alliance between the Folklore Society and the Society for Psychical Research, of which he was a founder and president in 1911, though Clodd affirmed that "his attitude towards the whole business of the occult was that of the doubter." Besides his biographies of Lockhart and Northcote, he wrote several historical biographies, which were byproducts of his *magnum opus* as a historian, the four-volume *History of Scotland from the Roman Occupation to the Suppression of the Last Jacobite Rising*, published between 1900 and 1907. These offshoots of his *History*, which include a study of *Prince Charles Edward* ranking among the best of innumerable books on the subject, were characteristic of his habit of work. When Stevenson wrote from Samoa asking for "something about the Jacobites," Lang in his search was intrigued by the mystery attaching to the identity of the Jacobite spy mentioned by Scott in the introduction to *Redgauntlet*, and his investigations resulted in *Pickle the Spy*, identifying the spy as the Macdonell known as Young Glengarry. Throughout his life he retained his boyish zest for reading what he liked, so accumulating a vast store of miscellaneous knowledge, which provided the best possible equipment for a writer of gossip about books. No contemporary possessed this quality to anywhere near the same degree, and in a later generation probably Sir John Squire alone competes in the same field.

Lang was at work up to the day of his death, 20th July, 1912, in which year was published his *History of English Literature*, a readable and useful manual in its singularly unsatisfactory class, and a venture into the perennial Shakespeare-Bacon controversy, *Shakespeare, Bacon, and the Great Unknown*, defending Shakespeare against the Baconians. Except a play and a sermon, he attempted pretty well every form of literary expression. Though he believed himself lacking in the faculty of invention necessary to success as a novelist, he collaborated with Rider Haggard in *The World's Desire* and with A. E. W. Mason in *Parson Kelly*, while his solo efforts were *The Mark of Cain* in 1886, and *The Disentanglers*, a Victorian foretaste of P. G. Wodehouse, which ran anonymously in *Longmans's Magazine* during 1902. His poems have been collected in two volumes since his death, and there are still children lucky enough to possess copies of his many volumes of fairy stories, but there remains to be published a representative volume of his "fugitive prejudice," to be selected from the monthly *causerie*, *At the Sign of the Ship*, which he contributed to *Longmans's Magazine* for twenty years, beginning in 1886 and ending only with the discontinuance of the magazine in October 1905.

§ 2

Both Edmund Gosse (1849-1928) and George Saintsbury (1845-1933) were highly reverenced as scholarly pundits, but neither ventured much upon "fugitive prejudice", preferring discretion to enterprise as far as English literature was concerned, by keeping to well-trodden paths of criticism, where the pitfalls had been explored and mapped by sundry predecessors. Even so, Gosse did not escape accident. The son of a distinguished zoologist and bred in an oppressive atmosphere of piety, he escaped at eighteen to a post at the British Museum, and gained an introduction to the Pre-Raphælite circle. His verse in *Madrigals, Songs, and Sonnets* (1870) and *On Viol and Flute* (1873) won for him notice as a poet of promise, but he laid a firmer foundation stone to his subsequent reputation as the first English publicist of Ibsen. A Scandinavian holiday in 1871 introduced him to the study of Ibsen, and his magazine articles during the 'seventies forestalled the later advocacy of Ibsen by William Archer and Bernard Shaw. The publication in 1879 of *Studies of the Literature of Northern Europe* marked him as an authority on Scandinavian literature, and his monograph on Gray in the "English Men of Letters" series and his *Seventeenth Century Studies*, which caught the first flush of the revival of interest in seventeenth-century drama, so increased his scope and reputation as a critic that he was invited in 1884 to lecture in America. On his return, he succeeded Leslie Stephen as Clark lecturer at Cambridge and delivered the lectures published in the volume, *From Shakespeare to Pope*, which was ferociously attacked for inaccuracy by Churton Collins in the *Quarterly Review*.

From this charge, Gosse's reputation never really recovered in the eyes of his contemporaries, and his subsequent work endorsed rather than refuted the accusations of inaccuracy against his scholarship. His *Life of Congreve*, published in 1888, makes a pretentious parade of research, which is found to be painfully superficial by anybody intimately acquainted with the subject. He was handicapped at the outset by having no genuine inspiration to write about Congreve, whom he conceived as "no very fascinating or absorbing human being;" apparently he merely chose the subject because Congreve was one of the most eminent writers of a period in the study of which he wished to be esteemed a specialist. It would be tedious here to enumerate the errors and shortcomings of the book, even as a work of research, apart from its utter failure to present an adequate portrait of Congreve's character; it is sufficient to remark that, like Mr. Bonamy Dobrée and Mr. Crane Taylor after him, he failed to recognise that Congreve's letters in Monck Berkeley's collection were dated according to the "old style" calandar, and that he neglected to consult the files of contemporary newspapers in the Bodleian Library.[1] Ten years later, the publication of his short *History of Modern English Literature* again invoked the wrath of Churton Collins, who compiled an appalling "list of blunders and absurdities" to show that "to call this compilation a *History of Modern English Literature* is ludicrous." Collins's summary of Gosse's deficiencies and qualities, as reflected in this book, fairly applies to the body of his work as a critic. He possessed

"a vague and inaccurate but extensive knowledge of our seventeenth, eighteenth and nineteenth century Belles-lettres;

[1] Mr. D. Crane Taylor found Gosse's book "lacking in accuracy and completeness," and Mr. Crane Taylor's own book on Congreve, as the present writer demonstrated in the *London Mercury* of November, 1931, is far from exhaustive in research. Mr. John C. Hodges, of Tennessee University, is about to publish a biography of Congreve, on which he has worked for some years, and which will include much material overlooked by both Gosse and Mr. Crane Taylor.

and here, as a rule, he can acquit himself creditably. Though far from a sound, he is a sympathetic critic; he has an agreeable but somewhat affected style, and can gossip pleasantly and plausibly about subjects which are within the range indicated. But at this point, as is painfully apparent, his qualifications for being an historian and critic of English Literature end. The moment he steps out of this area he is at the mercy of his handbooks; so completely at their mercy that he does not even know how to use them. And it is here that Mr. Gosse becomes so irritating, partly because of the sheer audacity with which mere inferences are substituted for facts and simple assumptions for deduced generalisations, and partly because of the habitual employment of phraseology so vague and indeterminate that it is difficult to submit what it conveys to positive test."

Gosse was, in fact, a superficial scholar, who, unlike Lang, read not what he wanted to read, but what he thought he ought to read, and so frequently either scamped the reading, or satisfied himself with second-hand knowledge from another critic's account of a work. He was victimised by the qualities which brought him success. He was always in the fashion, admiring what he ought to admire, and assiduously cultivated the acquaintance of "the right people." A brilliant talker, he was able to impress people with the idea that he knew much more than he really knew, and with his "agreeable but somewhat affected" style, he thought to achieve the same facile impression as a writer.

The battery of Churton Collins ruined his chance of ranking as a popular pundit in the time of his own generation, a position for which he seemed to be qualifying in the early 'eighties. His gifts as a conversationalist and an after-dinner speaker procured him popularity in society, and he was in great demand during the 'nineties as a literary lecturer in West End drawing-rooms. Not till his old age, when in 1918 the *Sunday Times* engaged him as its leading writer on books, a position held since his death by Mr. Desmond MacCarthy, did he become a fully fledged pundit. By then a generation had risen which remembered nothing of Churton Collins and his damaging exposures, which revered him as the author of that sombre picture of his own boyhood, *Father and Son* (1907), a little masterpiece of crewel embroidery, and which eagerly sat at his feet in admiration, to listen to entertaining gossip about all the great literary figures of the past fifty years from the one man living who had known them all in the flesh. Like George Moore, longevity procured him a reputation which must have aroused uproarious laughter among contemporaries across the Styx.

His biographer, the Hon. Evan Charteris, justly claims that "Gosse excelled in literary portraiture." He had been intimately acquainted with almost every writer from Swinburne and "Orion" Horne to Squire and Siegfried Sassoon, he was a shrewd observer, and he possessed a woman's knack of reading a man's secret weaknesses. The best of his articles in the *Sunday Times* available in such volumes as *Silhouettes* and *Leaves and Fruit*, are those dealing with writers whom he knew, like Stevenson, Saintsbury, O'Shaughnessy, Leslie Stephen, Lang, Howells, Austin Dobson, and many more. His verdict on Lang offers an illuminating sample:

> "Like Gray, it may be said of him that ' he never spoke out.' He shrank from a close examination of life, and from passion as from a devouring flame. He seemed to take refuge in literature from any such disillusion as too close a scrutiny of experience would have brought with it. Hence, he was tempted by his amazing facility of expression to gloze over emotions and to suppress facts that were inconvenient. The texture of his poetry was thus made smooth and flexible, but at the cost of richness . . . Lang should be regarded as a lyrist of artifice, to whom the visible and toiling world was a mystery over the surface of which he hung in a trance of curiosity, without attempting to penetrate it, and for whom everything human was a subject of lightly flying, flashing verse, half humorous, half melancholy. If we consider him too gravely, we lose him altogether."

In accepting Gosse's judgments must always be remembered his feline tendency. Mr. Charteris admits "an element of sparkling malice apparent at times in his conversation and a proneness to take offence," which can be read, for instance, in his relations with Stevenson; one who knew him well, and ever speaks enthusiastically of the fascinating charm of his conversation, has remarked that, "though concealed within the silken velvet pads, the claws were there, ever ready to strike." With this characteristic in mind, it is unjust to find fault with his *Life and Letters*, compiled by the Hon. Evan Charteris and published in 1931, an unwieldy volume of clumsy and unconsecutive arrangement, for Mr. Charteris obviously had a delicate task. Probably if he had used all available, he might have filled three volumes with letters, but there are still too many people living who would suffer from Gosse's claws. Some day, when his poetry and criticism are forgotten, three or more volumes will appear, and Gosse will live by virtue of his letters as the Horace Walpole of his time.

§ 3

The critic who caught Gosse tripping, John Churton Collins (1848-1908), was a hard-working educationist who went straight into journalism on leaving Balliol. He swayed a wide public as a University Extension lecturer and as a copious contributor to high-class reviews like the *Quarterly* and the *Nineteenth Century*, literary magazines like *Cornhill* and *Temple Bar*, weeklies like the *Saturday Review*, and to the *Pall Mall Gazette*. A conscientious scholar, with a genuine appreciation of English poetry, he was a militant champion of his theories and trod on other toes than Gosse's; his relentless agitation for recognition in the universities, of literature as a study independent of philology, earned him the execration of academicians hide-bound by tradition. He campaigned fearlessly against the growth of evils in the world of letters, the superficiality encouraged by the gullible ignorance of the new public created by cheap education, the log-rolling of cliques, the publication of bad books, often with a university's *imprimatur*, and the conscienceless carelessness of discrimination by critics. Consequently a tacit conspiracy succeeded in obscuring after his death the merit of his work, not only as an editor of classics sadly in need of revival, like Dryden, Tourneur, Greene, and Herbert of Cherbury, but as a publicist of good books. He made mistakes, like his extravagant eulogy of Stephen Phillips, but these were exaggerated by his enemies out of all proportion to the mass of his honest and useful work as a critic.

George Saintsbury received a drubbing from Collins for his *Short History of English Literature*, a tedious text-book which not only merited the worst Collins could say of it, but lends colour to his charges of lack of conscience in university authorities, since it long continued to be recommended to students. Saintsbury was far superior to Gosse in scholarship, but he was handicapped by a slipshod, meandering, parenthetical style, which Collins not unjustly called "a very well of English defiled." He was a prodigious worker and wrote knowledgeably of all periods of English literature, but nobody who has once grappled with his tortuous periods will ever again read Saintsbury if anybody else is available on a subject. But he is likely to be long indispensable to the student of French romance, for he is unrivalled among his countrymen in his wide reading and appreciation of French novels. He had also a connoisseur's taste in wine, and his *Notes on a Cellar Book* (1920) is the most readable of his voluminous works.

Apart from Lang and the young men of the *Yellow Book*, Henley was the greatest influence during the 'nineties. He came from Edinburgh to London in 1877 to edit *London*, a journal which failed in the following year, largely owing to a preponderance of high quality aesthetic criticism and the unpopularity of Stevenson's *New Arabian Nights*. He was so poor that at one time he and one of his brothers faced starvation in miserable lodgings, but though he had no means after the failure of *London* save the pen of a free-lance, and as the eldest brother, had "his family on his back," he ventured with characteristic pluck into marriage and never regretted the step. For four years he earned a precarious living by writing for the *Saturday Review*, the *Athenæum*, the *Pall Mall Gazette*, *Vanity Fair*, and other papers, pursuing such a Grub Street career as the Irish journalists in *Pendennis*. In 1882 he became editor of the *Magazine of Art*, and threw open its pages to that individual art critic, R. A. M. Stevenson, on whose death he wrote a beautiful and moving tribute in the *Pall Mall Magazine* for July 1900. On his own account, he introduced to this country a knowledge of Rodin's work, and did so much to establish Whistler's reputation that, years later, Heinemann proposed him as the artist's biographer, though Whistler vetoed him as likely to be "too critical."

Apart from his plays in collaboration with Stevenson, his first book was *A Book of Verses* in 1888, mostly work written on his sick bed at Edinburgh, for he declared that "I found myself (about 1877) so utterly unmarketable that I had to own myself beaten in art, and to addict myself to journalism for the next ten years." He owed the publication of his poems, which had been "rejected by every editor of standing in London," to the enthusiasm of David Nutt, a small publisher of scholarly tastes, who finds no place among the state burials in the *Dictionary of National Biography*, but receives a graceful appreciation in Mr. Grant Richards's *Author Hunting*. In a short, modest, but distinguished career, Nutt published, besides all Henley's poetical works and two volumes of his collected essays, *Views and Reviews*, Moore's *Impressions and Opinions*, Alfred Nutt's annotated edition of Lady Charlotte Guest's *Mabinogion*, Andrew Lang's *Aucassin and Nicolette*, Oscar Wilde's book of stories, *The Happy Prince*, and the best of Arnold Bennett's early novels, *Whom God Hath Joined*.

In 1889, Henley returned to Edinburgh to edit a sixpenny weekly called the *Scots Observer* at the invitation of its principal proprietor, W. B. Blackie, then head of the Constable firm. In the hope of increasing its circulation, the journal's headquarters were moved to London in 1891 and its name changed to the *National Observer*, but it was sold as a declining property when Henley resigned in 1894. The *National Observer*, lasting five years, was a brilliant failure as the *Yellow Book*, lasting three years, was a brilliant failure; the decadence induced by cheap education left a cultured public too small to sustain periodicals of intellectual appeal, and the ironical situation appears that, with millions able to read and write where there had been thousands in 1817, the fifteen thousand subscribers to *Blackwood's Magazine*, in the early days of Wilson and Lockhart, had dwindled to a handful of hundreds in the time of the *National Observer*.

Yet Henley was an editor of even higher mettle than Jeffrey, Lockhart, or Maginn. He gathered round him a rare collection of writers, beside which the fraternity of the much-advertised

Yellow Book appears a pale coterie of long-haired dilettantes. Among established writers were Swinburne, Hardy, Lang, and T. E. Brown, while those who owed their first encouragement to Henley, and become known as "Henley's young men," included Barrie, H. G. Wells, W. B. Yeats, Kipling, G. W. Steevens, Arthur Morrison, H. D. Lowry, and Charles Whibley. His "young men" gave him a whole-hearted loyalty won by admiration for his courage, vigour, and magnetic personality. Yeats long afterwards told Wilfrid Blunt that "the three persons he had known who most impressed him with their power were William Morris, Henley, and Madame Blavatsky," and Wells gives a characteristic glimpse of him talking "richly and agreeably," while "he emphasised his remarks by clutching an agate paper weight in his big freckled paw and banging it on his writing table."

The *National Observer* was a fresh breeze in the fetid drawing-room atmosphere of the 'nineties, representing the best traditions of letters, shrewd criticism, honesty of outlook, and hatred of Humbug. Mr. Wilfred Whitten wrote wistfully afterwards:

> "The *National Observer* may not fill in the memory quite the same place that it filled in the eyes of its handful of pur-chasers; but what a bliss it struck upon the week. We were relatively poor then, my friend and I, and we clubbed our money week after week to buy the paper. How we shouted and wrote each other notes about Mrs. Meynell's ' Rejection ' and Mr. Kenneth Grahame's ' Orion ' and Kipling's ' Tomlin-son ', and the trail of Henley over all."

It was too good for a public insufficiently educated to dis-criminate between the real article and engaging counterfeits. When it died, that enterprising publisher, William Heinemann, invited Henley to edit the *New Review*, a monthly periodical which made its bow under Henley's guidance about the same time as Heinemann's rival, John Lane, launched the *Yellow Book*. Lane's venture endured exactly three years; Henley's lasted eight months longer, finishing in December 1897, its final number including the final instalment of Joseph Conrad's *Nigger of the Narcissus*. For Conrad was the last of "Henley's young men;" though he professed himself unable to get beyond the first sixty

pages of *Almayer's Folly*, Henley was the obvious buoy for a
struggling swimmer and Conrad, advised by Edward Garnett,
sent him all his stories till he accepted the *Nigger* as a serial.

When the *New Review* ended, George Wyndham, reckoned
the most brilliant of promising young statesmen and carrying
the hope of the young intellectuals with much the same prestige
as Charles Masterman some fifteen years later, started a weekly
paper called the *Outlook* " as a ' raft ' on which to save the fortunes
of Henley and other writers wrecked in the *New Review*." But
Henley's career as a maker of reputations was ended; he was
released from his twenty-years' bondage to journalism by a civil
list pension, doubtless procured by Wyndham from Balfour, and
passed the last five years of his too short life in poetry and—except
the horror excited by his Stevenson article—peace.

Francis Thompson happily termed Henley "the Viking Chief
of Letters." The magnificence of his powerful torso, the splendour of his massive head and bearded, blue-eyed countenance,
fittingly matched the majesty of a personality which brought to
a mean and artificial generation of letters the nobility, sincerity,
integrity, and fine disdain of falseness, without which even genius
must wither. His enemies disliked and feared his truculence,
for an age abandoned to soulless worship of artificial convention
recoiled from his savagely outspoken contempt for Humbug;
Wilfrid Blunt, who found him "a bitter talker, but a sayer of
good things," disliked him, though Henley did him a service by
editing his poems, as "both physically and intellectually
repugnant."

He was the most vital and commanding figure in literature
during the last two decades of the nineteenth century—a supreme
subject for biography. Yet the only book about him is L. Cope
Cornford's monograph in Constable's little series of "Modern
Biographies". It may be that he will be remembered as a poet
only for a few short lyrics, but his criticisms of contemporary
literature were anything but "fugitive prejudice", and rank with
the best in Hazlitt and Coleridge. Meredith said of him:

"As critic, he had the rare combination of enthusiasm and
wakeful judgment. Pretentiousness felt his whip smartly,

the accepted imbecile had to bear the weight of his epigram. But merit under a cloud or just emerging he sparkled on or lifted to the public view. He was one of the main supports of good literature in our time."

As a stylist in prose, he was a survivor of the golden age, a lone champion of the tradition of De Quincey and melody with meaning. Few in his time could construct a long sentence so crystal of clarity, so harmonious, so simple and yet so pregnant with impression, as this on Rodin:

"The hand that modelled these austere yet passionate statements of virile force and suffering and endowment, and expressed their sculpturesque quality in such terms of art as recall the achievement of Donatello himself, can on occasion create such shapes of beauty, and such suggestions of elegance and charm, as put the Clodions and the Pradiers to the blush, and enable you to realise, in the very instant of comparison and contrast, the difference between the art that is great whatever its motive and its inspiration and the art that only passes for great because it happens to be gracious and popular."

As a sample of the shrewd judgment and enduring quality of his criticism, a few sentences from his masterly essay on Meredith suffice:

"Mr. Meredith is one of the worst and least attractive of great writers as well as one of the best and most fascinating. He is a sun that has broken out into innumerable spots. The better half of his genius is always suffering eclipse from the worse half. He writes with the pen of a great artist in his left hand and the razor of a spiritual suicide in his right. He is the master and the victim of a monstrous cleverness which is neither to hold nor to bind, and will not permit him to do things as an honest, simple person of genius would. As Shakespeare, in Johnson's phrase, lost the world for a quibble and was content to lose it, so does Mr. Meredith discrown himself of the sovereignty of contemporary romance to put on the cap and bells of the professional wit. He is not content to be plain Jupiter; his lightnings are less to him than his fireworks; and his pages so teem with fine sayings and magniloquent epigrams and gorgeous images and fantastic locutions that the mind would welcome dullness as a bright relief. He is tediously amusing; he is brilliant to the point of being obscure; his helpfulness is so extravagant as to worry and confound. That is the secret of his unpopularity."

Is this "fugitive prejudice"? Or is it not rather a classic estimate of a classic writer? But it matters little to Henley's memory if the pimps of transparent modern culture cannot recognise the virtue in art's appreciation of art, for it requires neither a Boswell nor a Lytton Strachey to help Henley to live forever, like Dr. Johnson, as a personality apart from his works.

§ 4

Henley's assistant editor on the *National Observer* was Charles Whibley (1859-1930), a critic who absorbed from his chief the prevailing characteristic of independence. On leaving Cambridge he was a reader on Cassells's staff, and probably the representative to whom Henley referred Rider Haggard with the manuscript of *She*. He collaborated with Henley in the work of editing the *Tudor Translations*, and some time after the end of the *New Review*, established a connection with *Blackwood's Magazine*, to which he contributed monthly articles, *Musings without Method*, for about twenty-five years. He was a late survival of the old school of periodical essayists, a writer of polished style, strict intellectual integrity, and, though susceptible to occasional violent prejudice, of ripe and varied scholarship. Much of his best work appears in introductions to the countless books he edited, and even in such slight undertakings as his monograph on Thackeray in Blackwood's "Modern English Writers" series, he is uniformly competent, readable, and reliable. His most ambitious book was his two-volume *Lord John Manners and His Friends*, a document of political history and a skilful study in period portraiture, and there is much of value in such collections of his critical essays as his early *Studies in Frankness* and his post-war *Literary Studies*.

After Henley no other editor entered into his category as a literary force till Sir John Squire founded the *London Mercury* in 1919, but W. L. Courtney (1850-1928) upheld with dignity and taste the best traditions of editorship during his thirty-four years' conduct of the *Fortnightly Review*. At Oxford, Courtney was a "Univ." man, who took a double first and became a colleague of Lang's as a fellow of Merton. After a period of schoolmastering, he returned to Oxford as a philosophy don at New College, and in 1884 was associated with Arther Bourchier in founding the Oxford University Dramatic Society. *The Dictionary of National Biography* finds only five words for his work as a dramatist, but about a dozen of his plays secured London production, among them *Oedipus Rex* (1912), subsequently repeatedly performed by Sir John Martin Harvey, and an adaption of Stevenson's *Markheim*, taken on tour by H. B. Irving. Journalism and the stage weaned him away from Oxford in 1890, when he joined the staff of the *Daily Telegraph*, on which he acted as dramatic critic and literary editor for thirty years. His weekly book reviews over that period maintained a wonderful equality of competence, urbanity, and temperate judgment; he never had a powerful influence like Lang's, but a notice from Courtney assured a book's receiving due attention. As an editor, he chose contributors and subjects with careful discrimination, and earned their gratitude and loyalty, as he won the liking of his acquaintance, by his sincerity and charm of manner; he must have been the last of his profession to reply personally to unsolicited contributions, writing letters with his own hand and beginning with the Dickensian "My Dear Sir."

With the new century came a new generation of editors and critics. G. K. Chesterton was reviewing regularly in the *Speaker*, the *Bookman*, and the *Daily News*. Hilaire Belloc published his *Danton*, the first of how many brilliant historical biographies, in 1899, and *Caliban's Guide to Letters* in 1903; E. V. Lucas passed from the *Academy* to *Punch* about 1901, and soon afterwards made a corner in Charles Lamb; Ford Madox Hueffer was writing novels, started the important *English Review* in 1908, and published his interesting book on *The Critical Attitude* in 1911; Arnold Bennett found a weekly pulpit in the *New Age* in 1908; Robert Lynd published *Portraits and Impressions* in 1908; J. C. Squire became literary editor of the *New Statesman* in 1913. All these were bottled but still maturing in 1914; even that great modern editor, J. L. Garvin, who edited the *Outlook* as far back as 1905 before beginning his long dominion over the *Observer* in 1908, had still to find the fullest scope of his influence after 1914.

There remain two critics inevitably associated with the *Yellow Book* circle, Arthur Symons and Richard Le Gallienne. Unlike George Moore, who stumbled on symbolism and seized upon it as a new notion when he was tiring of Zola's naturalism, Symons gravitated naturally to symbolism by the transition from Browning, the Rossettis, and Coventry Patmore to Villiers de l'Isle Adam and Verlaine. His book on *The Symbolist Movement in Literature* in 1899 expressed the creed of the young writers of the *Yellow Book*, though all his colleagues who wrote fiction—Hubert Crackanthorpe, "George Egerton", Henry Harland—strayed from the true ideal in a way Symons cannot have approved. Ironically, perhaps the *Yellow Book* associate who approximated most nearly to Symons's definition of symbolism, as "a representation which does not aim at being a reproduction," was William J. Locke in the more flimsy of his romances after *The Morals of Marcus Ordeyne*. A writer of beautiful prose, Symons as an advocate of symbolism had to wait many years to see his theories practised by writers like Mr. David Garnett, Mrs. Virginia Woolf, and the apostles of the "new" short story in the nineteen-thirties.

Richard Le Gallienne is a romantic figure of mystery to his juniors. In many ways the most characteristic young man of letters in the Beardsley period, one of the most brilliantly gifted, most versatile, most prolific, certainly the most picturesque —he survived nearly all his ill-fated associates and yet appears a more elusive legend than any. Born in 1866 at Liverpool, he served for seven years under articles to a chartered accountant before coming to London to earn a living by journalism. His book of verses, *Volumes in Folio*, was the first book issued by John Lane; it was followed in 1890 by *George Meredith: Some Characteristics*. It seems incredible that a novelist of genius, who had been producing regularly for over thirty years, should owe his recognition to the appreciation of an unknown young man of twenty-four, but the fact emerges unmistakably that, while Meredith, as a result of Henley's praise, had accumulated increasing reputation within the narrow confines of an intellectual public during the 'eighties, it is only after the publication of Le

Gallienne's book that he entered upon his kingdom as a master among novelists. The book rang a novel note of criticism; it betrayed a poet's appreciation with poetic imagery; it spoke of Meredith as a modern in advance of the moderns, so that the devotees of fashionable culture were bewildered by the discovery that he had been writing since the days of *Bleak House* and *The Newcomes;* it whispered sensuousnesses subtly suggestive, as in saying that Meredith "sings of nature, not because he worships her in some vague way afar off, as one might the abstract woman, but because he has loved and worshipped her as a man his wife, lying in her arms, eye to eye, breath to breath." Surely this savoured of the "naughtiness" for which the 'nineties were ripe!

The book drew attention to the author as well as the subject, and in the following year Le Gallienne succeeded C. K. Shorter as literary critic of the *Star*. He was also John Lane's trusted literary adviser; Le Gallienne, not Oscar Wilde, was the inspiration behind the *Yellow Book*. "Lane," says Mr. Lewis May in *John Lane and the Nineties*, "had an almost romantic affection for Le Gallienne," and the same feeling was inspired in all the young men assembled by Lane, especially in rugged, tragic John Davidson, whose end, like Crackanthorpe's, recalls the pathos of Chatterton's. He was a picturesque figure, a mark for caricature, with his classically beautiful profile, his air of delicacy and distinction, his shock of dark curls, soft collar, and floppy tie of black silk—"he looked like Botticelli's head of Lorenzo," says Sir William Rothenstein, who adds that "Le Gallienne's name then stood for the 'new' poetry as Hubert Crackanthorpe's stood for the 'new' short story." He dressed and looked the part as author of his poetry and criticism; he was the embodiment and spiritual leader of the "decadence", and as such earned the special execration of Henley and the men of the *National Observer*. The "decadents" revered him as their prophet, for he was their principal publicist, the only one of their group who addressed the greater public; he wrote much exquisite verse, and in 1896 he achieved in *The Quest of the Golden Girl* the one successful effort in true symbolist fiction, an artificial essay in picturesque romance, delicately blending the naïvety and suggestiveness of Sterne with the grace and sweetness of poetic idealism, which distils the quintessence of the decadence and remains the most representative achievement of the movement of its inspiration.

It seemed that this young man, so rich in achievement before he was thirty, from being the prophet of a clique, might become the inspired leader of a new Romantic Movement in the approaching twentieth century. But he and nearly all his colleagues vanished away like so many Cinderellas, as if their mission was veritably *fin-de-siécle*, and the end of the century their midnight hour. Crackanthorpe's body was found in the Seine near Christmas of 1896, Ernest Dowson died in 1900, Harland in 1905, Davidson in 1909—Le Gallienne lived on, but went to America, whence he rarely reminded his countrymen of his continued existence.

As "Log-Roller" of the *Star*, he wielded a potent and healthful influence; he necessarily reviewed all qualities of books, but his selection and judgment were so equally guided by shrewdness and taste that the two-volume selection of his articles, *Retrospective Reviews: A Literary Log*, published by Lane in 1896, not only achieved its avowed purpose of providing "a sort of literary diary" from 1891 to 1895, but ranks with Henley's *Views and Reviews* as the most vital and illuminating collection of contemporary criticism. The permanence of its interest, as well as the standard of Le Gallienne's judgment, are reflected in the names of the authors criticised—Meredith, Hardy, Churton Collins, Tennyson, Gosse, Henley, Stevenson, Yeats, Pater, Anatole France, Alice Meynell, Austin Dobson, Symons, Crackanthorpe, Kipling, J. A. Symonds, Coventry Patmore, Henry James, Francis Thompson, Tirebuck, Birrell, Grant Allen, Swinburne, Lionel Johnson, Lowry—not a name which does not merit a certain meed of attention forty years afterwards. Unlike the young critic of to-day, he did not show off by "debunking" his subjects; in his view, the school of criticism "that praises is the more important," and many of the writers criticised stood then in sore need of such apt and able appreciation as Le Gallienne's, whose verdicts well withstand the test of time. He felt "the breath of Ireland's immemorial sadness" in Yeats's *Countess Cathleen*, he remarked in Crackanthorpe "the objectivity of his method," which made him a pioneer of the modern short story, he recognised "a real enthusiasm for humanity" in Grant Allen's *The Woman Who Did*, he found Francis Thompson's "the most fascinating poems that have appeared since Rossetti." A fine critic was lost to English letters by Le Gallienne's untimely retirement from journalism; few young men of genius have so generously appreciated genius and talent in others, fewer still have expressed appreciation so gracefully, serviceably, and well.

CHAPTER SEVEN

Our Boyhood's Favourite: Rider Haggard

§ 1

HENLEY, the discoverer of Kipling, detested Le Gallienne as the apotheosis of decadence, but neither Henley's dislike nor his own "decadence" prevented Le Gallienne from appreciating "the tremendous verve, the grasp, the fertility of Mr. Kipling's gift." *Plain Tales from the Hills* appeared in 1887, but Kipling's vogue really began in 1891 with Henley's boosting and publication of *Barrack Room Ballads* in the *National Observer.* He was the topic of the hour, everybody was reading him, the circulating libraries needing the storing resources of a pelican, while Henry James sent him to Stevenson in Samoa. Kipling is lately dead, and the tendency to-day, evident successively with Hardy, Bennett, Bridges, and even Galsworthy, is to forget after the funeral. But for thirty years there had been a gradually increasing inclination to reservations regarding the hasty acclamation of his genius in the 'nineties. It is to the credit of Henry James that, while sub-scribing to the general admiration in the early 'nineties, he was particular to underline the term *talent* as descriptive of Kipling's gift. Stevenson, too, felt wounded in "a kind of ambition we all have for our tongue and literature"; he felt that "if I had this man's fertility and courage, it seems to me I could heave a pyramid." Kipling never did heave a pyramid; he never did better than *Kim,* which, in spite of its impressive beginning, settles down to a tale of adventure for schoolboy reading. By 1897 Henry James had lost faith in him—at first he had thought that "he perhaps contained the seeds of an English Balzac," but he saw inevitable degeneration "in the light of one's increas-ingly observing how little of life he can make use of"—and in 1909 Arnold Bennett decided that "he was never great," though "the stories of twenty years ago are touching, if boyish." As a boys' author he may be reclaimed by the next generation, but it seems that his old reputation can never revive, for the scope of his material is only less limited than his capacity for characterisation, and he lacks Stevenson's saving grace of style—his notion of song was that of the baritone at a village cricket club dinner.

But in the 'nineties Kipling was a *furore*, a best-seller, a potent influence and an obvious pattern for imitation. Circumstances conspired to insure his success; he came with the wave of imperialism and pride of empire which followed Randolph Churchill's democratising of the Tory Party, with the popular reaction to romance from the new realism, which was marked as unrespectable by the banning of Zola and as highbrow on its adoption by young men like Crackanthorpe, with the craze of the suburban *bourgeoisie* to read about the picturesque and exciting as an antidote to the uneventful monotony of their own narrow lives. As Le Gallienne remarked, Kipling conveyed the feeling that "we peaceable stay-at-homes are poor milk-and-water creatures, and that there is nothing in the world worth doing save slicing and ' potting ' your fellow-creatures." He also identified himself with India, the one sector of the empire not yet exploited by a novelist, and, as Quiller-Couch observed, "locality" was "playing a strong part in current fiction . . . with Mr. Barrie in the North, and Mr. Hardy in the South; with Mr. Hall Caine in the Isle of Man, Mr. Crockett in Galloway, Miss Barlow in Lisconnell; with Mr. Gilbert Parker in the territory of H. B. C., and Mr. Hornung in Australia," and he should have added, with Rider Haggard in South Africa.

Kipling was not original even in his glorification of "slicing and potting", for Rider Haggard was pre-eminently the novelist of "Blood", and *King Solomon's Mines* appeared a year before *Plain Tales from the Hills*. Haggard, in fact, paved the way for Kipling's reception, and the adulation of Kipling's "genius" by those who allow mere "talent" to Haggard offers an instance of the disciple stealing the prophet's thunder. Both Haggard and Kipling wrote tales of adventures for boys, both lacked skill in drawing character, both wrote more rapidly than was good for them, both possessed in an extraordinary degree the gift of narrative, and both had vivid imaginations, though Haggard's exceeded Kipling's in the ingenuity, variety, and daring of its range. Kipling enjoyed two advantages over Haggard—he specialised in the short story, which was just coming into fashion as an art, and he had a nose for publicity. His *Cleared!* published by Henley after the findings of the Parnell Commission in March 1890, witnessed his instinct for self-advertisement; while Haggard stuck simply to his job of story-telling and entered politics only as a serious advocate of the unpopular cause of agriculture, Kipling became the principal publicist of Henley's Jingoism, so that he, instead of Henley, soon appeared as its chief prophet. A shrewd commercial sense enabled him to gauge the gullibility of the public, and his greatest achievement was his hoaxing a public nourished on Gilbert and Sullivan, a public ripe for sentimental rapture over the songs of Tosti, Fred Weatherly, and Guy d'Hardelot, into mistaking for poetry of genius his talent for jingling doggerel.

Haggard and Kipling wrote books for boys, and boys proved better judges than their elders. In the first fourteen years of the twentieth century, Kipling hardly competed with Haggard as a schoolboy's favourite. To-day Kipling lies in Westminster Abbey, whither a certain Dr. Foxley Norris did not invite the ashes of John Galsworthy; there is a Kipling Society enabling the old boys of *Stalky and Co.* to dine together; there are many survivors of a passing generation who hope to see his continued cultivation as a "classic". Rider Haggard has been dead eleven years longer, and he is no longer the favourite with boys that he was before the war. But no humbug interferes with rational discussion of his merits, among the least of which appears the bare fact that he preceded Kipling in popularising the glories of bloody adventure.

§ 2

The Haggards were an old family of country squires, settled in Hertfordshire from the fifteenth till near the end of the eighteenth century, when the novelist's great-grandfather bought Bradenham Hall, near East Dereham, in Norfolk. William Haggard, son of the first Haggard of Bradenham, was "concerned in banking in Russia" and married a Russian wife named Meybohm, whose eldest son, William Meybohm Rider Haggard, born in 1817, married in 1844 Ella, "elder daughter and co-heiress of

Bazett Doveton, of the Bombay Civil Service," a lady two years his junior, the fruit of which marriage was ten children, of whom Henry Rider Haggard, born 22nd June, 1856, was the eighth. With such a host of youngsters, each within eighteen months or so of the next's age, Bradenham was a boisterous household, and by the time they arrived at school age, the boys were well qualified to withstand the hardships of the new boy.

Nevertheless, Rider Haggard's school career began in disaster, for he was removed from his first school by his indignant father after a master, in a moment of annoyance, had knocked him senseless with his fist. This was at a day school in London, where the Haggards at that time had a town house, soon to be given up from motives of economy. Even in Victorian times, the upbringing of ten children made heavy inroads on a comfortable income, and Squire Haggard at one period thought to save expense by taking the family for their holidays on the Continent. For the same reason, Rider Haggard did not go to a public school; of his five elder brothers, all but the one who chose to be a sailor, went to public schools, two to Winchester, one to Haileybury, the other to Westminster. When Rider's turn came, funds were low, and the squire possibly felt the economy justified as this son showed small prospects of success at school.

For Rider was not a bright boy. When he was seven, he irritated his mother into describing him as "heavy as lead in body and mind," and one of his early school reports provoked his father to roar that he was "only fit to be a greengrocer." So after some terms at Garsington Rectory in Oxfordshire, where the rector took two or three pupils as boarders, he went to Ipswich Grammar School. He described it as "a rough place" in those days, bullying being prevalent, but his hardy upbringing stood him in good stead, and he won respect by having a fight on his first day with an older boy who criticised his hat. His only school distinction was being elected captain of the second football team; as he left before he was seventeen, he did not stay long enough to get into the first.

He spent his holidays in family trips abroad, at a clerical uncle's with one of his brothers, or at Bradenham. His father was "a typical squire of the old sort, a kind of Sir Roger de

Coverley," who "reigned at Bradenham like a king, blowing everybody up and making rows innumerable." If the soup was not to his liking, he would send it back to the cook with the message that she could drink it herself; he would "pull at the bells until feet of connecting wire hung limply down the wall," and inform the answering maid that a lunatic asylum was her proper home. But his popularity was such that nobody minded; it was "only the Squire's way." He read the lessons in church on Sundays, and if on finishing, he thought he had not read the prescribed passage to his satisfaction, he would read it over again. If he fell into argument at table with one of his sons, he would "rise majestically, announce in solemn tones that he refused to be insulted in his own house, and depart, banging the door loudly behind him." His course could then be traced through the house by the succession of banging doors; sometimes he banged his way back again, and would sit down again "in quite a sweet temper, the exercise having relieved his feelings," especially if the offending son had meanwhile banged himself out of the house by another route.

He had a voice like a bull, a legacy inherited by each of his sons, and the noise in the house was "tremendous, because everybody had plenty to say and was fully determined that it should not be hidden from the world." While the hubbub raged, the lady of the house sat at the foot of the table, "like an angel that had lost her way and found herself in pandemonium." Her son revealed her character in his record of her reply to a daughter-in-law's asking how she ever made herself heard above such a perpetual din: "My dear, I whisper! When I whisper they all stop talking, because they wonder what is the matter. Then I get my chance." The anecdote conjures up the picture of that turbulent, healthy household, so like hundreds of others all over England's countryside in the eighteenth and nineteenth centuries —the hearty old squire, looking after his farms, his game preserve, and his trees, riding or driving to the local markets on Wednesdays and Saturdays, grumbling while donning his best clothes to attend the quarter sessions, but enjoying the performance of his duty with dignity, leading the way to Sunday church, riding to hounds, organising his September shoot with the solemnity of a sacred rite, enjoying his port and laying down every year rather more than he drank; the squire's lady, managing her household according to a clockwork routine, forever in and out of child-bed during the first twenty years of her married life, fondly bringing up her numerous brood, dutifully visiting the sick of the parish, presiding at bazaars, and giving tea to the parson, yet finding time to understand sympathetically the problems and troubles, not only of her children, but of all her husband's tenants and dependents. And the children—the boys full of enthusiasm on coming home for the holidays, revelling in horse-play and practical jokes, riding as soon as they were old enough, shooting, fishing, swimming in summer and skating in winter, always in the open air, dog-tired at bedtime, dismal only when counting the days before the return to school; the girls passing from a governess to a polite dame's school before returning to help mama, to learn to be a lady, and to wait till they became the blushing brides of men like their brothers in the services and professions. The sons went out into the world, the daughters left to rear families of their own, and the old couple finished as they began together. And when they were gone to the family vault in the village churchyard, the process began again, with the eldest son succeeding to rear a family as his parents had reared theirs before him.

If Wellington spoke truly that Waterloo was won on the playing fields of Eton, it is a still greater truth that the British Empire was built in the country houses of England's squirearchy. Generation after generation, the sons of squires, equipped with constitutions hardened by an open-air, country life, with a sufficient smattering of scholarship, and with training in the tradition of what was understood by the term "gentleman", ventured into the distant corners of the world, to create and uphold the prestige which came everywhere to be associated with the name of an Englishman and England. And generation after generation, the daughters of squires wore out their youth and looks in bearing large families, whom they successively reared and unselfishly resigned to the service of the country. Dull lives those women lived, according to modern feminist standards, but less dull than the sex-starved wives of emasculated office workers in suburban villas.

Since the squirearchy created the British Empire, Imperialists must find food for discomforting reflection in the extermination of the class. For cases grew increasingly frequent during the twenty years before 1914, when the squire's eldest son, on succeeding to the estate, found his means insufficient to sustain its upkeep, and either delayed the inevitable end by a harrowing policy of ruinous retrenchment or more wisely rid himself of the responsibility by selling out, instead of waiting to be sold up. The last of the squire's sons, robbed before death of their heritage, lie in nameless graves among the foundations of the rebuilt towns and villages of Flanders. The extension of the franchise to the ignorant masses, readily gulled by every opportunist adventurer who came along, compelled the governing body, dependent for existence on the whim of a mob, to pander to cheap popularity with gratuitous benefits in the name of enlightened democracy, entailing an extravagant expenditure, only to be financed by such ruinous taxation that there looms in sight to-day a state of Socialism, produced—not, as the fanatical educationists and welfare workers affect to believe, by a "levelling up"—but by a "levelling down" to a condition in which, there being no more property to tax, and therefore no source of revenue in taxation, every individual in the community must become a subsidised dependent of a bankrupt state. In exterminating the squirearchy, like the aristocracy, by extravagant taxation, the commercial middle-class killed the goose with the golden eggs. The squirearchy used to be the backbone of the nation; to-day the commercial middle-class fairly claims the title, but whatever may be argued in favour of its ossific qualities, it is utterly invertebrate in relation to imperial interests, for the commercial middle-class stays at home in its villas, its appetite for adventure amply satisfied by daily excursions to and from an office, and by picturesque enterprises at second-hand through the columns of the popular press.

The Haggards were a fair sample of a class now obsolete. All the sons entered the services or the professions or went empire-building to the colonies, and succeeded according to their different fortunes and abilities. No sentiment was wasted in their class; the strong triumphed, and the weaker went to the wall. The

Spartan standards of the class find illustration in Rider Haggard's description of his coming to London at the age of eighteen:

"When I was a little lad my elder brothers threw me into the Rhine to teach me to swim. After nearly drowning I learned to swim, and in a sense the same may be said of my London life."

His autobiography is characteristic of a man of his class, straightforward, business-like, matter-of-fact, devoid of posturing garnishings, of psychological argument, of speculative regrets; it is the simple record of reminiscences teeming through the active brain of an habitually busy man, written down as rapidly as the pen could move.

He went to London from Ipswich to the house of a private tutor when he was barely seventeen. At this time he entered the only examination he ever took, the army entrance, and was ploughed in Euclid. Looking back in 1911, he felt glad that he did not pass into the army, as he might by then have been "a retired colonel with nothing to do." At eighteen, he was sent to W. B. Scoones, the well-known crammer, to study for the entrance to the Foreign Office, and he then went into lodgings where he lived uncontrolled by authority. His first lodgings were at the house of a young widow near Westbourne Grove, and perhaps here he took his first ducking in the waters of life, for "they did not turn out respectable," and he was moved to Davies Street, "an excellent situation for a young gentleman about town."

He spent "about a year and a half at Scoones', making many friends, collecting many experiences and some knowledge of the world." Of neither the friends nor the experiences does he give any very precise particulars, but though such omission might be ascribed in most men to the calculated discretion of Humbug, in Haggard it reflects a characteristic innocence of self-importance. Like the heroes of his fiction, he makes no bones about invertebrate theorising; he acted always upon direct motives, which logically derived from duty or necessity. Looking back over the years when writing his autobiography, he must have remembered many sources of passing worry, many personal pleasures and an-

noyances, many revelations of character by friends and acquaintance. But he would have been as astonished, if anybody had
suggested that these memories should be set down for publication,
as if they had proposed that he should indecently expose his person
in public. Yet there was no vestige of prudery in his personality;
he was merely too simple and direct to have even the elementary
instincts of the autobiographer.

Of his student days, he tells how he frequently visited the
spiritualistic *séances* at the house of old Lady Paulet, but except
for one occasion when "two young women of great beauty" were
conjured from the spirit world, he was impressed by little save
the practical jokes played by himself and other young men.
He saw enough to conclude that "the whole business is mis-
chievous and to be discouraged," and "should be left to the expert
and earnest investigator, or become the secret comfort of such
few hearts as can rise now and again beyond the world." For
normal people he felt spiritualism "harmful and unwholesome,"
and having so decided, he characteristically resolved never to
attend a *séance* again, and held to the decision.

He fell in love for the first time in those days with one of "the
three really lovely women" he ever saw. He identifies the other
two as the fifth Duke of Leinster's duchess and a village girl of
Bradenham, but does not name the object of his devotion, though
he remained her friend, his wife afterwards became her friend,
and he was present at her death-bed thirty-five years later.

He never knew if Scoones would have helped him into the
Foreign Office, for he never sat for the examination. His father,
grappling with the liabilities of a large family, "never lost the
chance of finding an opening for one of his sons," and hearing
that Sir Henry Bulwer was appointed lieutenant-governor of
Natal, he asked for a place on his staff for Rider Haggard. Though
he had never set eyes on young Haggard, Sir Henry gave him the
place; the Bulwers of Heydon in Norfolk were old friends of the
Haggard family, and the squirearchy had such confidence in its
caste that a father's advocacy of his son, in such circumstances,
was sufficient recommendation. Enlightened democracy labelled
such proceedings the favouritism of "snobbery" and "influence",
but democracy had no traditions, and professed disbelief and

contempt for what it envied. Sir Henry Bulwer knew the Haggards were good stock, who bred the type of "an officer and a gentleman" to be depended upon to adhere rigidly to duty; dependability was a preferable quality in the imperial service to the self-seeking brilliance of a son of democracy.

Bulwer had no cause for disappointment in his choice of a junior secretary. During the voyage he evidently measured young Haggard as exceptionally capable, normally ambitious, and a glutton for work. He therefore gave him plenty to do, and on arriving at Cape Town, Haggard was "getting on all right, though my position is not an easy one." Finding himself "responsible for everything, and everybody comes and bothers me," he realised that he was doing the work of a private secretary, and though he had not been so officially appointed, he supposed himself virtually holder of that office "as nobody else has appeared."

But Bulwer was an experienced administrator, and knew how to train apt material. Haggard's elder sister, with sisterly frankness, found her brother at this time inclined to be conceited. He was "a tall young fellow, quite six feet, and straight, blue-eyed, brown-haired, fresh-complexioned, and not at all bad-looking." The Zulus called him "Indanda", meaning "one who is tall and pleasant-natured." He was quick to observe and learn whatever interested him, conversed easily, and soon learned to make a speech when necessary. He had an instinct for thoroughness, liking to understand any country or society in which he found himself, and he applied himself as diligently to study South Africa, its peoples and problems, as afterwards to the study of agriculture in East Anglia. Finding himself "getting on all right," he probably acquired the superior air of conscious efficiency frequently found in competent junior officials. With wisdom his chief taught him a tactful lesson, calculated rather to encourage than to damp his zeal, but conveying the warning that the rewards of promotion were only to be won by patient and persistent service. Haggard was kindly told that he would not be private secretary, not because he lacked in competence or assiduity, but because a man senior in age and experience was required for the post. Haggard professed to his people to be "not in the least disappointed", and realising the responsibilities of the post, "would have much wondered if he had made a fellow young as I am private secretary"; he was "very sorry still to be dependent" on his father, but promised his mother to be as "moderate" as he could.

During a year or more as one of the governor's secretaries in Natal, he "copied despatches, received guests," and learned much about buck-hunting and natives. In May, 1876, a powerful Kaffir chief organised a war-dance in honour of the governor's visit to his kraal, and Haggard was moved to write a description of the "splendidly barbaric sight", which he sent to the *Gentleman's Magazine*. He followed this with other contributions, but begged his mother not to "say anything to anybody about my having written things in magazines," possibly fearing that the practice might be frowned upon by his superiors and the subject of jokes among his colleagues.

Those of his superiors who most impressed him were Sir William Butler, afterwards commander of the forces in South Africa and a copious writer on African history, who married Alice Meynell's sister, the painter Elizabeth Thompson, and Sir Theophilus Shepstone. Between Shepstone and Rider Haggard grew an enduring friendship, based on mutual respect and affection, rare in men of different generations, for Shepstone was over fifty years of age. In Haggard the affection began with hero-worship, which Shepstone's character was well calculated to inspire. The son of a missionary, he went out to South Africa at the age of three, and learning to speak many Kaffir dialects like a native, he received an official appointment as government interpreter at the age of eighteen. For twenty years from 1856 to 1876, when he was knighted, he held the post of Secretary for Native Affairs in Natal. "He was a curious, silent man, who had acquired many of the characteristics of the natives amongst whom he lived," he had an "impressive face," and "he observed everything and forgot little." Such a romantic figure was bound to appeal to the creator of Allan Quatermain, to whom Shepstone told stories of his African experiences which "would fill half a volume."

When, at the end of 1876, Shepstone was appointed Special Commissioner to the Transvaal, he took Haggard as a member of his staff, which included also Melmoth Osborn, afterwards Resident in Zululand and the prototype of Alston in *The Witch's Head*, an interpreter named Fynney whose tales of the Zulus supplied material for *Nada the Lily*, and the Swazi hero Umslopogaas, who figures under his own name in *Nada the Lily* and *Allan Quatermain*. Umslopogaas, who must have been over eighty when he died in 1897, was the son of a King of Swaziland, and at one time served in the Nyati Regiment, "the crack corps of the country"; at this time he was "a tall, thin, fierce-faced fellow with a great hole above the left temple, over which the skin pulsated, that he had come by in some battle." The closeness of Haggard's fiction to actual biography in the case of Umslopogaas appears in Haggard's statement that the old warrior used to tell how "he had killed ten men in single combat, of whom the first was a chief called Shive, always making use of a battle-axe." When Haggard's books were famous, and a lady asked him if he was not proud that his name appeared in books read by white men all over the world, Umslopogaas replied with stately dignity, "No, Inkoosikazi, to me it is nothing. Yet I am glad that Indanda has set my name in writings that will not be forgotten, so that, when my people are no more a people, one of them at least may be remembered."

Shepstone's mission, resulting in the annexation of the Transvaal by the British, was momentous in history. After the disaster of Majuba a few years later, the magniloquent Gladstone gave the Transvaal back to the Boers as an independent republic, with the result that, after he had been suitably interred in Westminster Abbey, the British Empire had to engage in a bloody, costly, and ignominious war to win it back again. As Haggard justly points out in his autobiography, the Transvaal cost a million pounds to surrender and two or three hundred millions to reconquer, yet was originally annexed by Shepstone at a total cost of ten thousand pounds, the price of an estate of a thousand acres in an English county. Shepstone was appointed to the commission on account of his unrivalled knowledge of the natives, and his understanding of the natives dictated his decision of annexation. He knew that Cetewayo, the Zulu king, was irritated by the corrupt and unstable conduct of the republic, and meditating an onslaught on the Boers; he knew, on the other hand, that Cetewayo was friendly to the English. Haggard believed, as he asserted in *Cetewayo and His White Neighbours*, that Shepstone saved the Boers from massacre by the Zulus in annexing the Transvaal as a crown colony. Unluckily Sir Bartle Frere, the High Commissioner, ruined Shepstone's diplomacy by going to war with Cetewayo and crippling the Zulu power, so enabling the Boers under Kruger to rebel successfully with the Majuba disaster.

What Justin McCarthy naïvely called " the plain common sense of England" condemned Sir Bartle Frere; he did not say if the same ."plain common sense" demanded the persecution and degradation to which Shepstone was subjected by Gladstone's government after Majuba. What McCarthy did say in one of the most exotic blooms of Humbug ever produced from an historian's hothouse was:

> "There was for a time a great outcry, and many English Liberals, as well as Tories, insisted that the defeat of the English on Majuba Hill ought to have been effaced in blood before England consented to let the Transvaal go. But Mr. Gladstone could not see that the attempt to crush out the independence of a foreign state was so sacrosanct as to justify any policy, however extreme, which might be needed to carry it to complete success. He believed that the policy was wrong in the beginning, and was not to be made right merely by the fact that those against whom it was directed had courage and resolve enough to meet it with a gallant resistance. England had resources enough to extirpate the military defenders, and, indeed, the whole Boer population of the Transvaal if she had thought fit; but Mr. Gladstone was not a statesman who could be brought to believe that the true heart and mind of England would sanction such a course of action."

For such sightless opportunism as Gladstone's, English history is luckily searched in vain until recent times; it never appears to have occurred to any of the pro-Boer sentimentalists, at the date of either Majuba or Mafeking, that the Boers were interloping settlers like ourselves and that South Africa belonged by right to the black races, whose splendid physical and moral well-being

British and Boers alike undermined by the introduction of Christianity and cheap whisky.

Haggard loyally defended his chief; he described the Boer War as "one of Mr. Gladstone's gifts to his country," remarking that the war "cost us twenty thousand more lives and two hundred and fifty millions more of treasure to bring about what was in practice the same state of affairs that Sir Theophilus Shepstone had established over twenty years before without the firing of a single shot." In *Cetewayo and His White Neighbours* he told the whole story from the point of view of those who knew South Africa at first hand in those days; in the handsome dedication of *Nada the Lily*, published in the year before Shepstone's death, he quoted an extract from Cetewayo's message at the time of the annexation, indicating the reason for Shepstone's policy, and roundly declared that "enemies have borne false witness" against him.

On his return from duty on the commission, in June, 1877, Haggard was appointed English Clerk to the Colonial Secretary's Office at a salary of two hundred and fifty pounds a year. But soon afterwards the Master and Registrar of the High Court of the Transvaal died, and after some hesitation on account of his youth, for he was only just twenty-one, the government appointed Haggard to the post, with a salary of four hundred a year. Times were difficult; the handful of English officials at Pretoria lived in daily expectation of massacre either from the assegais of the Zulus or the rifles of the Boers. Probably visitors at such a time presented a source of anxiety, and though Haggard entertained Anthony Trollope, when he called at Pretoria during the tour resulting in his book on *South Africa*, he had no more to say of him than that "Mr. Trollope was a man who concealed a kind heart under a somewhat rough manner, such as does not add to the comfort of colonial travelling." By the end of 1877, conditions had grown so alarming that the English population formed volunteer corps as auxiliaries to the military, and Haggard joined the Pretoria Horse, of which he was soon made adjutant. The hostility of the Boers probably saved his life, for unless the authorities had thought it advisable at the time of Cetewayo's rising to retain the Pretoria Horse for defence of the town against a possible Boer attack, he would have been sent against the Zulus. As it was, though he had some exciting experiences, he saw no actual fighting, for with the British forces strengthened on account of the Zulu War, the Boers decided to bide their time, and wait till the British had been lulled into a sense of false security, when "Sir Garnet Wolseley had sent the last cavalry regiment out of the country." But this was not till the new year of 1881, when Haggard was no longer a member of the Pretoria Horse or the Government service.

After the departure of Shepstone and others of his earliest superiors, he appears to have become restless under their successors, of whose methods he was acidly critical. He suffered also an emotional crisis, which, he confessed, left him "utterly reckless and unsettled." He treated the matter in his autobiography with characteristic reserve, but it seems that he kept up a correspondence with the beautiful girl he had met while at Scoones', and was at length led to consider himself engaged to be married, till "one day the mail cart arrived and all was over." He was, in fact, the hero of such a blighted romance of love as became popular with the novelists of his day, especially in relation to Africa, like the affair of Jack Meredith and Millicent Chyne in Seton Merriman's *With Edged Tools*, of Leonard Outram and Jane Beach in Haggard's own *People of the Mist*, and of Ernest Kershaw and Eva Ceswick in his *Witch's Head*.

He had made a friendship which proved life-long with a youngster of his own age named Arthur H. D. Cochrane, whose native pseudonym of Macumazahn, "he who sleeps with one eye open," he borrowed for Allan Quatermain, and he and Cochrane decided in 1879 to "shake off the dust of Government service and farm ostriches," for which purpose they bought about three thousand acres of land at Newcastle in Natal. On his part he confessed that "it was a mad thing to do," as he had "a high office and was well thought of," and his father received the news with dudgeon, saying he would probably become "a waif and a stray," or, with acid reference to his writing for magazines, "a miserable penny-a-liner." But the decision was for the best as events turned out, for within two years he would "have been thrown out of my employment without compensation, as happened to all the other British officials when Mr. Gladstone surrendered the Transvaal to the Boers after our defeat at Majuba."

Before starting his new career, he took the opportunity of going home for a holiday, and his stay in England was prolonged to eighteen months owing to his engagement and marriage. His bride was the only daughter and heiress of a Major John Margitson of Ditchingham House, Norfolk, an orphan school-friend of one of his sisters; she came of the same squirearchy class as the Haggards, and the match conformed with the conventions of county society, though Miss Margitson, as a lady of property, might have been considered to be " doing not too well for herself" in marrying a younger son. As Haggard emphasised, the word "heiress" in the reference books is "an elastic term", and though the Ditchingham estate may have sustained a family in "something more than comfort" in early Victorian times, its rentals paid for little more than the upkeep of the house and gardens by the time Haggard settled there. The pair became engaged before Christmas, 1879, and hoped to be married by the following April, but the bride was under age and a ward in Chancery, and though this department of the law had been cleansed of some of its cobwebs since the days of Jarndyce *versus* Jarndyce, its machinery still creaked tardily, and demanded such costly lubrication that the Margitson inheritance was depleted by three thousand pounds. The uncertainty of Haggard's plans also contributed to the delay; encumbered by the responsibilities of marriage, he no longer took the same view of reckless optimism towards ostrich farming, and he deferred to the counsels of prudence and his father by seeking to re-enter the colonial service. But Shepstone and his other friends had been transferred from the Transvaal, and the Wolseley government declined to reinstate him, and rejecting a suggestion that he should read for the bar with a view to legal practice in Cape Colony, he at length decided to persevere with the farming venture.

After his marriage in August, he returned to South Africa towards the end of 1880 with his wife and two servants, one of whom, a Norfolk groom, supplied the model for Job in *She*. The Boers had taken up arms in the Transvaal, and uncertain of the advisability of proceeding to Newcastle, Haggard delayed some weeks at Maritzburg, where they stayed with the Shepstones, and where, early in January, 1881, he and his wife dined at Government House with the ill-fated Sir George Colley and his staff. They sat thirteen at table, and within two months Colley and his officers perished at Majuba. Seven years later Haggard and his wife again dined at the same table with Lady Colley, who burst into tears on recognising them, the sole survivors besides herself of the party at their former meeting.

Though expecting soon to be confined with her first child, Haggard's young wife insisted on defying all dangers to make the two-hundred-miles' trek to her new home, over roads so rough that she had to walk most of the way beside their bumping wagon. Their adventures vied for excitement with those of the heroes and heroines of Haggard's own romances. Their farm, Rooipoint, and their house, called Hilldrop, which is described in *Jess* as Mooifontein, was fortunately only a mile and a half from the town of Newcastle, where the presence of British troops was some assurance of safety, but the surrounding countryside was infested with skirmishing Boers, and frequently the sound of firing caused disturbing anxiety during the daily work on the farm. At night they slept with revolvers under their pillows, loaded rifles leaning against the beds, horses ready saddled in the stables, and Kaffirs posted on the hills as sentries to give warning of a possible advance by the Boers. By May, the month of his son's birth, Haggard was "seriously debating clearing out of this part of the world," having decided that "henceforth we can look for no peace or security in South Africa," while the value of his property seriously depreciated in view of the rebel Boers' success. It was a period of pain and despair for British settlers when peace was made after Majuba; Gladstone's effigy was burned in the market-places, troops were resentful almost to mutiny, the natives were stunned and bewildered by the tame submission of the Great Queen's forces, and English people declared in disgust that they were "bloody Englishmen" no more. For six months Haggard and Cochrane toiled on their farm; they had a steam grinding mill, they made bricks for sale in Newcastle, they were the first to rear ostriches in that part of Natal, and among the first to cultivate grass for hay-making. But any doubts about relinquishing the farm were dispelled when Cochrane fell ill, and his health demanded a holiday in England; Haggard left South Africa finally in the autumn of 1881.

§ 3

After some weeks spent with his parents in Bradenham, Haggard took a furnished house at Norwood and entered himself at Lincoln's Inn. During the early months of 1882, he wrote the history of South Africa as he had seen it at first hand in *Cetewayo and His White Neighbours*, and after vainly offering the manuscript to several publishers, he agreed to contribute fifty pounds, "although at the time I could ill afford it," towards the cost of its publication by old Nicholas Trübner, who had published many books "on commission", including *The Cloister and the Hearth*, for Charles Reade. Though the author received encouraging letters from several notabilities to whom he sent copies of the book, including Lord Carnarvon, Colonial Secretary under Disraeli, and Lord Randolph Churchill, only a hundred and fifty-four copies were sold in the year of publication, and Trübner lamented a loss of some thirty-three pounds beyond the fifty-pound advance. Criticism of Mr. Gladstone amounted almost to heresy, and reviewers in the Liberal press damned the book with sarcastic condescension. When Haggard became known as a novelist, Trübner recovered his thirty-three pounds with interest, for Mudie's subscribers, inquiring for other books by the author of *King Solomon's Mines*, were misled by the attractive title of *Cetewayo and His White Neighbours* into expecting it to be a novel, and at the time of the Boer War in 1899, a shilling reprint of the part relating Shepstone's annexation of the Transvaal sold thirty thousand copies. *Cetewayo and His White Neighbours* retains interest only for the student of history, but for the specialist has permanent value as an historical document.

Soon after finishing *Cetewayo*, Haggard began his first novel, *Dawn*. A trait in his own character which contributed to the vital conviction of his romances was his susceptibility to impression by the picturesque and romantic; such incidents as the meeting with Lady Colley years after the Maritzburg dinner possessed for him greater significance than the idiosyncrasies of character and human habit. He believed in "the finger of Fate", having decided that "individual lives and the accidents which influence them are not the petty things they seem to be, but rather a part of some great scheme whereof we know neither the beginning nor the end," and life therefore held for him the intricate interest of a Wilkie Collins novel, in which every detail must be noted as being possibly indicative of important consequences. The incident which inspired the writing of *Dawn* he thus construed as an accident contrived by Fate to determine his career as a romantic novelist. One Sunday in church he and his wife were impressed by the appearance of "a singularly beautiful and pure-faced young lady," and discussing her afterwards, agreed that she seemed a fitting heroine for a romance. Both therefore began to write such a romance, but while his wife tired of the game after writing a few sheets, Haggard persevered with his story, which eventually appeared as *Dawn*. Such were the facts, but though he might never have written *Dawn* if he had not seen the living inspiration of his heroine Angela, his career would otherwise have been little altered. Since his descriptive article on the Zulu war-dance in 1876, he had continued regularly to write magazine articles, and looking to writing as a useful means of supplementing his income while awaiting his call to the bar, he naturally tried his hand at fiction as the most popular and profitable form of expression. But characteristically, with the passage of time, his romantic imagination magnified the consequences of a casual incident, and when *Dawn* was reprinted in 1894, it was dedicated to "that unknown lady, once seen, but unforgotten, the mould and model of Angela, the magic of whose face turned my mind to the making of books."

He wrote three drafts of *Dawn*. The first was unfinished when, late in 1882, he decided from motives of economy to give up the furnished house at Norwood, and live on his wife's estate at Ditchingham House, near Bungay in Norfolk. At Ditchingham he re-wrote the story as "Angela, or There Remaineth a Rest", and offered it vainly to several publishers, including Smith, Elder, whose reader, James Payn, rejected it as lacking dramatic interest —"the interest that comes from an exhibition of the influence of character upon character." Trübner, the publisher of *Cetewayo*, then suggested that he should send the manuscript to his friend, John Cordy Jeaffreson, for his opinion. Jeaffreson, then a man of fifty, was one of the miscellaneous collection of literature's camp-followers, inevitably hovering about the smoking-rooms of literary clubs, diligent in attendance at dinners, luncheons, and other functions promoted in connection with the profession of letters, busy with gossip gleaned from editors and publishers, always *au fait* with the latest literary cliques and petty jealousies, yet all the time gallantly making the most of a mediocre talent to earn, at the expense of exhausting pains and labour, a living meagre even beside that of a small town grocer, who grows fat by handing across his counter the products of other people's creation. The author of biographies, novels, and all sorts of efforts in book-making, Jeaffreson's name is now remembered occasionally only for his two-volume *Book of Recollections*, in which he records valuable memories of contemporary men of letters, especially of Thackeray. Usually it is the men of genuine gifts who find time to show kindness and encouragement to their juniors; the mediocrities are too busy seeking their own advantage, and often too jealous of possible rivalry. But Jeaffreson was an exception, just as his *Book of Recollections* is an exception among Victorian memoirs in escaping their habitual cast of over-powering dullness and pomposity. Without knowing Haggard and with no more than a note of introduction from Trübner, he took the trouble to read the novel in manuscript and write a long letter of advice and encouragement. He agreed with Payn that he would not recommend publication in its present form, though he thought it "small praise to say that Angela's love-story is better than two-thirds of the stories that are published," but warning him against "the notion that novels are dashed off," he counselled him to rewrite the novel, "suppressing much, expanding much, making every chapter a picture by itself, and polishing up every sentence so that each page bears testimony to the power of its producer." When Haggard replied with a letter of grateful thanks, Jeaffreson invited him to dinner, and congratulating him on his youth, generously declared that "I could not have written as good a novel as Angela's story when I was twenty-six."

Haggard took his advice and rewrote the novel. ·One of the principal alterations at Jeaffreson's direction was the substitution of a serene ending with the marriage of Angela and the unsatisfactory Arthur for a tragic *dénouement* with Angela's death. After thirty years' experience as a novelist, Haggard asserted his belief that most library subscribers liked novels to end happily, because "if they seek melancholy, it can be found in ample measure in real life or in the daily papers." From a practical point of view, Jeaffreson's advice was therefore sound, and seven years later Haggard had reason to remember it, for though by then his popularity was established, he had difficulty in convincing his publishers that *Eric Brighteyes* must end in tragedy.

When the novel was rewritten, Jeaffreson introduced Haggard to his own publishers, Hurst and Blackett, successors to the celebrated Henry Colburn (Mr. Bacon of *Pendennis*), who agreed to publish the book at their own expense and risk, paying the author forty pounds on the sale of four hundred copies, and thirty pounds for every subsequent hundred copies. On their objection that the title *Angela* had been used before, the novel was called *Dawn*, and the first edition of five hundred copies in three volumes appeared late in 1883.

From his correspondence with Jeaffreson, it appears that Haggard's models as novelists were James Payn and R. D. Blackmore, a curiously assorted pair, for while Payn was a prolific purveyor of pot-boilers for the libraries, Blackmore was a conscientious craftsman, who, apart from the immensely successful *Lorna Doone*, and the much less popular but still well-known *Maid of Sker*, was finding a comparatively limited vogue. In forty years before his death in 1898, Payn wrote no fewer than a hundred novels, but except *Lost Sir Massingberd*, published as long ago as 1864, none are now read and their titles occur rarely in second-hand booksellers' catalogues. In *Dawn* may be detected some resemblance to the immediately contemporary novels of Blackmore, and Haggard was therefore unconsciously among the literary progeny of Charles Reade, for Blackmore evinced a marked tendency to influence by Reade in *Erema*, *Mary Anerley*, and *Tommy Upmore*. But rather than of Reade or Blackmore, the atmosphere, manner, and construction of *Dawn* seem reminiscent of Mrs. Henry Wood. Arthur Heigham is a hero in the mould of George Godolphin of *The Shadow of Ashlydyat*—brilliant, handsome, with "an intellectual face, a face that gave signs of great mental possibilities, but for all that a little weak about the mouth," to men a "fellow one would like to know," to women of the world "by no means uninteresting, and one who might, according to the circumstances of his life, develop into anything or—nothing in particular." Charlotte Pain, of the same Wood novel, is the same brilliant "bad" lady as Lady Bellamy of *Dawn*, George Caresfoot finds many villainous prototypes in the Wood canon, and the celestial purity of Angela is a commonplace essential in all the suffering beauties of Mrs. Wood's books. The death-bed scene of the adorable Hilda, Angela's mother, is as racking as any of the three or four similar orgies of pathos which Mrs. Wood furnished in almost every one of her novels, and Lady Bellamy's suicide reflects all her striving after crude sensationalism. Occasionally Haggard resorts to Mrs. Wood's irritating trick of breaking off the narrative to address the reader in a confidential aside; having described Angela's feelings for Arthur, he adds:

"'Fine writing!' perhaps the reader will say; but surely none too fine to describe the most beautiful thing in this strange world, the irrevocable gift of a good woman's love!"

And none but Mrs. Wood or an arrant novice could have ended thus naïvely a dramatic scene between the heroine and the villainess:

"She is a fine creature both in mind and body," reflected Lady Bellamy, as she stepped into her carriage. "Really, though I try to hate her, I can find it in my heart to be sorry for her. Indeed, I am not sure that I do not like her; certainly I respect her. But she has come in my path and must be crushed —my own safety demands it. At least, she is worth crushing, and the game is fair, for perhaps she will crush me. I should not be surprised; there is a judgment in those grey eyes of hers—*Qui vivra verra*. Home, William."

But if it reflects many of Mrs. Wood's worst vices, *Dawn* possesses all her virtues—brisk, unflagging narrative, abundant incident, a strong sense of dramatic effect, and splendid fertility of invention. Whatever faults may be found with *Dawn*, it clearly demonstrates the fact that its author had the gift of writing.

Dawn was followed within a year by *The Witch's Head*, which Hurst and Blackett published on similar terms. While the earlier book fell flat, *The Witch's Head* was well reviewed and sufficiently read for the whole edition of five hundred copies to be sold. But the publishers were not disposed to issue a second edition, and having produced three long books for no financial return, *Dawn* having earned nothing, while *The Witch's Head* only reimbursed his outlay on *Cetewayo*, Haggard renounced the notion of making a career as a novelist. He was called to the bar in 1884, and letting Ditchingham, he took a furnished house in West Kensington and began practice in the Probate and Divorce division. Like most beginners at the bar, he was not overwhelmed with work, and a reading of Stevenson's recently published *Treasure Island* suggested the idea of beguiling his spare time in writing a story for boys. In the evenings at home after his days in the Temple, standing at a pedestal writing-table in his dining-room, he wrote *King Solomon's Mines* in "about six weeks".

Haggard was yet another young writer who owed his first step to success to the shrewd judgment of W. E. Henley. He naturally submitted *King Solomon's Mines* firstly to Hurst and Blackett, and after they had rejected it, the manuscript visited so many publishers, that it presented a "battered" appearance on arriving in Henley's hands. Henley showed the story to Andrew Lang, who wrote to Haggard that he found "so much invention and imaginative power and knowledge of African character in your book that I almost prefer it to *Treasure Island*." He promised to find "the best, whereby I mean the coiniest, way to publish it," and though he believed "all boys' magazines pay hopelessly badly," he proposed to see "what Harper's *Boys' Magazine* is able to do." But Lang was unable to secure its serial publication or to interest Longmans in it, and eventually it was the indefatigable Henley who placed it with Cassells's, as he had previously placed *Treasure Island* for Stevenson. Cassells's as a firm seem to have lacked the ability to retain the allegiance of a profitable novelist after having the first call on his services, for they established no more permanent relations with Haggard than with Stevenson; perhaps the reason lay in their being the first of those large-scale publishing concerns, whose manifold activities require numerous departmental heads, who are at a disadvantage by comparison with the smaller individual publisher in establishing personal relations with authors. On being bidden to call on the firm, Haggard interviewed "a business-like editor whose name I never knew," who offered him the choice of two agreements—a sale of the copyright for a hundred pounds, or an advance of fifty pounds on account of royalties at ten per cent of the published price of the book on all copies sold, "reckoning thirteen copies to the twelve." For a book which had cost an inconsiderable fraction of the time and labour expended on the unproductive *Dawn*, the offer seemed so munificent that Haggard was minded at first to accept the hundred pounds, and only a remark by a clerk in the office—one of those incidents which he attributed to the "finger of Fate"—persuaded him to choose the royalty agreement. Henley afterwards reproached him for signing the agreement without first consulting him, as he could have secured better terms, and in his autobiography Haggard, presumably prejudiced like many others by the conventional attitude to the "seraph in chocolate" protest, hardly acknowledged Henley's evident part in launching the book.

Published in a single volume at five shillings in October, 1885, *King Solomon's Mines* enjoyed a much more immediate success than *Treasure Island*, running into a sixth thousand before Christmas. It owed something to finding a path already paved by *Treasure Island*, which had created a public for the story of treasure-hunting adventure, but it owed more to the enthusiastic review by Lang in the *Saturday Review*, an eulogy crowned by the generously sweeping statement, characteristic of Lang, that "we would give many novels, say eight hundred (that is about the yearly harvest), for such a book as *King Solomon's Mines*."

Snobbish critical convention, encouraged by Stevenson's deification after death, has labelled *Treasure Island* as a "classic", while contemptuously denying *King Solomon's Mines* admittance to consideration even as "literature", regarding it merely as a cherished favourite of schoolboys, rubbing covers with the tales of Henty, Marryat, and Fenimore Cooper. But the bare fact, confessed with characteristic innocence of literary pretentiousness by Haggard, that his story was suggested by reading *Treasure Island*, invited a comparison of the two books. The idea is imitated even to the map of the treasure, the route to King Solomon's treasure written in the blood of the Portuguese explorer, Don José da Silvestra, the other in the red ink of the pirate Captain Flint. For his unknown land, Haggard naturally chose the wilds of Central Africa, at that time unexplored, in preference to an unchartered island, since the scene enabled him to draw upon his knowledge of Africa. He began, like Stevenson, by assembling his party of treasure-hunters, but once started, he lost sight of Stevenson's guidance and followed his own star. With Haggard there was no delay in starting the hunt, such as readers of *Young Folks* found a fault in *Treasure Island*. The artist in Stevenson required a circumstantial introduction, showing how it happened that the individual members of the party came to make the venture; Haggard evaded preamble by making Allan Quatermain tell such a traveller's story as he had himself often heard from his friend Fynney, the interpreter. The beginning fore-shadows the sequel; much more happens in *King Solomon's Mines* than in *Treasure Island*. Stevenson always suffered from the handicap of poverty of invention, but Haggard had the unfailing imagination of the born story-teller. In this strength lay his weakness, for his fancy leaps ever faster than his pen, and in his haste to pursue what he sees ahead, he slurs over one scene to be on with the next. Stevenson would have occupied a chapter in describing the horrors of the night in the ice-bound mountain cave, culminating in the terrifying discovery of Don José's corpse? Haggard takes less than two pages, scamping the details and so losing much dramatic effect. The same eagerness to be off with his story prevented him from ever contriving finished studies of character; with possibly the single exception of Umslopogaas in *Allan Quatermain*, not one of his characters lives before the mind's eye even palely beside the vital reality of Long John Silver or Alan Breck. The methods and instincts of Stevenson were those of the complete artist; Haggard's were those simply of a natural story-teller.

Writing to congratulate him on *King Solomon's Mines*, Stevenson noted Haggard's defects; "you should be more careful," he wrote, "you do quite well enough to take more trouble, and some parts of your book are infinitely beneath you." Significantly he criticised the manner of the story's beginning, declaring it "slipshod", and warning him that "what you have still to learn is to take trouble with those parts which do not excite you." Stevenson and Haggard never met; writing from Bournemouth, Stevenson promised to meet him in London, but warned him that "I come rarely to town, and am usually damned sick when I do," and eighteen months later he left England forever. Haggard's brother Bazett, empire-building in the South Seas, became intimate in Samoa with Stevenson, who wrote a letter of congratulation on *Nada the Lily* in 1892, and sent cordial messages in his letters to Lang.

Before the publication of *King Solomon's Mines*, Haggard wrote its sequel, *Allan Quatermain*, during his summer vacation at a farmhouse near Ditchingham, completing it, like its predecessor, in about six weeks. Following the success of *King Solomon's Mines*, Longman's were readily persuaded by Lang to serialise its sequel, and *Allan Quatermain* ran through *Longman's Magazine* from January to August, 1887, the year's delay in publication being doubtless due to the magazine's being already committed to serialising Besant's *Children of Gibeon*. Between finishing *Allan Quatermain* "in the late autumn" and the end of the year 1885, he wrote his story of South African life, *Jess*, working mainly in his chambers at 1 Elm Court, where he attended to pick up occasional briefs, and carrying his manuscript home in the evenings to continue his work after dinner. A month after finishing *Jess*, he began writing *She*, which he completed after six weeks on 18th March, 1886, thus writing three novels in the space of seven months.

Even allowing that Stevenson was frequently a suffering invalid while Haggard normally enjoyed vigorous health, a comparison of their habits of work offers an astonishing contrast. During the whole year of 1885, Stevenson produced only *Dr. Jekyll and Mr. Hyde* and *Olalla*, together less in length than any one of Haggard's novels, and while he began *Kidnapped*, it was not till the following year that he was able to finish it. He had plenty of ideas for beginning stories, but having written a chapter or two, he frequently found himself unable to go on, and wasted weeks in fruitless efforts to concentrate, before turning aside to something else. Haggard, on the other hand, finished the job before thinking about another with machine-like precision. When he sat down to write *She*, he had no clear notion of what he intended to write, except the idea of "an immortal woman inspired by an immortal love." "All the rest," he said, "shaped itself round this figure," and "it came faster than my poor aching hand could set it down." He made no rough draft or synopsis before starting like Anthony Trollope, Arnold Bennett, and most other prolific novelists; he sat down with an idea, and made his pen photograph the workings of his imagination. He obeyed his own instinct in contravention of the advice offered by Jeaffreson and Stevenson, the only two novelists with whom he had discussed his work, both of whom warned him against speed and facility. Of *She* he said with satisfaction that "it was never re-written, and the manuscript carries but few corrections," adding that "it was written at white heat, almost without rest, and that is the best way to compose." He was undoubtedly right as regards romance-writing; Harrison Ainsworth wrote the whole story of Dick Turpin's ride to York in *Rookwood* at a sitting, and Stevenson himself invariably began with a burst of creative energy, writing the first half of *Treasure Island* at a hot pace, and not only writing, but re-writing, *Jekyll and Hyde* in a few weeks.

But Stevenson fairly argued the difference between the prose artist and the story-teller in the article on "My First Book", written for Jerome K. Jerome's paper, *The Idler*, and reprinted in the volume on *The Art of Writing*. He suggested a comparison of the style of *Treasure Island* with the almost contemporary story of *The Merry Men*:

> "One reader may prefer the one style, one the other—'tis an affair of character, perhaps of mood; but no expert can fail to see that the one is much more difficult, and the other much easier to maintain. It seems as though a full-grown experienced man of letters might engage to turn out *Treasure Island* at so many pages a day, and keep his pipe alight."

Possibly piqued at Stevenson's deification as a classic, while the highbrow critics declined to consider his work as "literature", Haggard was irritated into disparaging style. He fairly remarked that the critics were wrong to consider style as more important than the substance of the story, since the substance is "the soul of the matter," while "the style is its outward and visible body". Ignoring the fact that the difference between an ill-written book, and one in a finished style, is the difference between a plain woman ill dressed and a beautiful woman well dressed, he made some trite remarks about style, and asserting that "the greater the simplicity of the language, the better the style," forgot that the simplest word is rarely the first to hand, and that simplicity and clarity are at once the characteristics of a fine style and a painstaking writer.

In Haggard's view "the story is the thing, and every word in the book should be a brick to build its edifice." So much had become a theory among novelists before Haggard's day, since a reviewer had written of Wilkie Collins's *Moonstone* that "not a window is opened, a door shut, or a nose blown, but, depend upon it, the act will have something to do with the end of the book," and it has since become a formula for the modern novel. But the principle finds a different interpretation in the hands of an artist from that of the story-teller. Sir Hugh Walpole in *The Cathedral* provides one of the most finished modern examples of the cohesive novel, in which every incident and utterance contributes to the story, but in his hands incidents are of secondary importance, and designed to illustrate character. Haggard was satisfied that characters should be "definite, even at the cost of a little crudeness;" they were merely the performers or necessary mediums of incident and adventure. The "really needful" qualities of fiction were in his view "adventure—how impossible it matters not at all, provided it is made to appear possible—and imagination, together with a clever use of coincidence and an ordered development of the plot." He not only believed from experience that romances "should be written rapidly", but "if possible, not re-written, since wine of this character loses its bouquet when it is poured from glass to glass."

His theories were justified by popular success. *She*, running as a serial in the *Graphic* before being published as a six-shilling volume by Longman's in December, 1886, more than cemented the success of *King Solomon's Mines*; twenty-five thousand copies were sold within three months, a colossal figure for those days, when the six-shilling novel was an innovation frowned upon by the circulating libraries. Andrew Lang, to whom *She* was dedicated, thought it "the most extraordinary romance I ever read." Walter Besant, then considered a master of popular romance, told Haggard that it placed him "at the head—a long way ahead—of all contemporary imaginative writers," and Edmund Gosse, of all people, declared the latter part of the story "simply unsurpassable", adding, though he was soon to find Stevenson's prose not "above reproach," "may I say, without impertinence, I think the *style* strikes me as a vast improvement upon that of *K.S.M.*?"

The sales of *She* relieved the strict financial economy observed since his marriage, and having corrected the proofs of *Jess* for press, Haggard took a trip to Egypt at the beginning of 1887, with a view to collecting local colour for a novel about Cleopatra, a subject obviously at the back of his mind when he sketched the personality of Ayesha in *She*. Marie Corelli could write a story in a Norwegian setting without having previously visited Norway, but Haggard, like Harrison Ainsworth, believed in visiting the scenes of his stories and observing their atmosphere before writing. Thus in 1888 he visited Iceland in preparation for writing *Eric Brighteyes*, Mexico in 1891 for *Montezuma's Daughter*, Spain in 1904 for *Fair Margaret*, and another visit to Egypt in the latter year produced *The Way of the Spirit*. On his travels, he courted adventure and twice narrowly escaped death —in Egypt escaping from a tomb at Assouan just before falling masonry blocked the exit, and being shipwrecked on a trading steamer returning from Iceland.

On his return to England, he found himself "quite a celebrity", but wasting no time in allowing himself to be lionised, he worked as hard as ever, making hay while the sun shone. In three and a half years between the summer of 1887 and Christmas of 1890, he wrote nine novels, one of which he did not publish, and collaborated in writing a tenth, *The World's Desire*, with Andrew

Lang. *Allan Quatermain* had continued the success of *She*, twenty thousand copies being sold in the month of publication, ten thousand of which were subscribed in London alone, a figure which Longmans believed "more than has ever been subscribed of a 6s. novel before." Haggard was disappointed that *Cleopatra*, which ran serially in the *Illustrated London News* before book publication in 1889, did not enjoy equal success. He wrote it in two months, immediately after his return from Egypt in the summer of 1887, and believed it to be his best work up to that time. He had absorbed much knowledge of Egyptian antiquities, and allowed his enthusiasm for the subject to override his theory that a story should be told simply and directly. He was damped when Lang, having read the manuscript, advised him to

"Put *Cleopatra* away for as long as possible, and then read it as a member of the public. You will find, I think, that between chapters three and eight it is too long, too full of antiquarian detail, and too slow in movement to carry the general public with it . . . The style is very well kept up, but it is not an advantage for a story to be told in an archaic style (this of course is unavoidable). For that reason I would condense a good deal and it could be done."

With his cynically practical appraisal of literary aspirations, Lang saw that Haggard was ambitiously trying to write on a higher plane than he had previously attempted, and probably doubted his ability to succeed, while clearly perceiving that in this book he was falling between the stools of scholarship and popular story-telling. Haggard, however, believed in the book, and backed in his belief by the opinion of his publisher, Charles Longman, he disregarded Lang's advice, arguing that the "cutting out of passages resembles the pulling of bricks from a built wall, since it will be found that every, or nearly every passage, even if it is of a reflective character, is developed or alluded to in some portion of what follows." Respecting Lang's judgment and worried by his criticism, he compromised clumsily by explaining in a prefatory note that "unfortunately it is scarcely possible to write a book of this nature and period without introducing a certain amount of illustrative matter, for by no other means can the long dead past be made to live again before the reader's eyes," and "respectfully suggesting" that "such students as seek a story only . . . should exercise the art of skipping and open this tale at its second book." Reviewers naturally seized upon this advertised weakness as a target for sarcastic barbs, and Haggard "began to feel a certain repletion" of professional critics, when they stupidly disparaged his recreation of Cleopatra because Shakespeare had written a play about her.

Haggard was irritably sensitive to criticism. His first sting from critical whips had followed his acceding, in the flush of the success of *King Solomon's Mines*, to a request from the *Contemporary Review* for an article on "Fiction". This was taken as a pendant to the controversy on the art of fiction waged between Besant, Henry James, and Stevenson, and aroused sneers at the temerity of a novice, who, on the strength of a single success, aired his views in experienced company. Haggard writhed under the imputation, and reflected bitterly that he learned from this experience that it was wise never to "preach about your trade," to "criticise other practitioners of that trade," or to "enter into a controversy with a newspaper," as he did with the *Pall Mall Gazette*. He was so upset that he talked of giving up writing, provoking from Lang the joking rejoinder that "if you jack up Literature, I shall jack up Reading." Lang's criticism of *Cleopatra*, endorsed by the reviewers, again plunged him into despondence, and since Lang was unable to reassure him in this case, Henley did so, saying "it has plenty of faults, but it has an abundance of promise and some excellent—some really excellent—achievement," and adding the assurance that "there is never a sign of exhaustion, but on the contrary no end of proof that you have scarce got into your stride."

He had further cause of depression with his work following the writing of *Cleopatra*. *Colonel Quarich*, *V.C.*, which followed *Jess* as a serious novel in a modern setting against a country background like *Dawn*, was abused privately by Lang as "the worst book that ever was written," though Longman liked it and published it, and its successor, *Nesta Amor*, was actually not offered for publication on Lang's advice. Another sort of vexation committed him to further novels, whether he meant to give up writing in disgust or not. When the first edition of *The Witch's Head* sold out and Hurst and Blackett declined to reprint it, he entered into an agreement with the firm of John Maxwell, Miss Braddon's husband, by which they issued *Dawn* and *The Witch's Head* in a two-shilling edition, paying him a third of the profits, on condition that they should be at liberty to reprint in the same form, and on the same terms, any other novel he might write during the next five years. At the time Haggard had no thought of subsequent complications, being about to take up practice at the bar and give up the idea of writing, but after the success of *King Solomon's Mines* and *She*, Spencer Blackett, "successor to J. and R. Maxwell," demanded the right of reprinting. A lawsuit was eventually avoided only when Haggard agreed to write two novels specially for the firm, but he took a handsome revenge by making a publisher of the hideous old hunks of a villain in *Mr. Meeson's Will*, the first of the two novels supplied, and citing the terms of his own agreement as those under which Mr. Meeson published for the heroine, and which the gallant hero denounced as "sharp practice". The other story written for Spencer Blackett, *Allan's Wife*, which was the first of many pendants to *Allan Quatermain*, and dedicated to his friend Cochrane, the original Macumazahn, ranks among the best of his books; it breathes the grandeur and tragedy of the African veldt in the days of the pioneer settlers, marches in an impressive crescendo of dramatic narrative, and contains a wealth of exciting scenes—the massacre of the Boers by Sususa's Zulus, the duel between Allan and the black giant Bombyane for the life of the little Boer child, the terrified horse galloping with a lion on its back, the attempted murder of Allan by the Baboon-woman, and the battle with the baboons. The description of the moment when Allan, spear in hand, waited the onslaught of the Zulu giant, offers a typical instance of Haggard's faculty of drawing swift impressions of imagined scenes:

"There behind us was the blood-stained laager, and near it lay the piles of dead; round us was rank upon rank of plumed savages, standing in silence to await the issue of the duel, and in the centre stood the grey-haired chief and general, Sususa, in all his war finery, a cloak of leopard skin upon his shoulders. At his feet lay the senseless form of little Tota, to my left squatted Indaba-zimbi, nodding his white lock and muttering something—probably spells; while in front was my giant antagonist, his spear aloft and his plumes wavering in the gentle wind. Then over all, over grassy slope, river and kopje, over the wagons of the laager, the piles of dead, the dense masses of the living, the swooning child, over all shone the bright impartial sun, looking down like the indifferent dye of Heaven upon the loveliness of nature and the cruelty of man. Down by the river grew thorn-trees, and from them floated the sweet scent of the mimosa flower, and came the sound of cooing turtle-doves. I never smell the one or hear the other without the scene flashing into my mind again, complete in its every detail.

"Suddenly, without a sound, Bombyane shook his assegai and rushed straight at me. I saw his huge form come; like a man in a dream, I saw the broad spear flash on high; now he was on me!"

Another fine African story, based on his knowledge of Zulu history, *Maiwa's Revenge*, was written after *Allan's Wife*, though published before it by Longmans in 1888, a small unillustrated shilling volume in boards. He then began to write, in collaboration with Lang, a story about Helen of Troy, evidently suggested as a subject by *Cleopatra*. He wrote about a third of the book, which Lang altered and re-wrote, but Lang then lost the manuscript "for a year or so", during which time Haggard wrote his most carefully written novel since *Dawn*, *Beatrice*. Lang then found the manuscript, which he had pushed between the leaves of a folio volume and forgotten, till he chanced to need the book again for reference, and returned to Haggard, who finished the story without further help from Lang, save suggestions and the occasional verses, including his *Song of the Bow*, some of which were drafted in prose by Haggard. Lang thought the "style *too* Egyptian and all too unfamiliar to B.P." for popular success; he felt it would have been better written in modern English instead of semi-biblical, saga-like style. He objected to the idea of serial publication, believing it "emphatically a book for educated people only," and warned Haggard that as a serial it would "lower your vogue" with newspaper readers. Eventually it ran as a serial in the *New Review*; as a book it appeared in 1890, the same year as *Allan's Wife* and *Beatrice*.

Lang was right in gauging the limited appeal of *The World's Desire*, but it retains devotees to-day among scholars who are not much given to reading fiction. The story is an allegory, illustrating man's eternal search for ideal beauty, the world's desire, and the inevitable thwarting of success in his search by his acceptance of counterfeit beauty. Odysseus is made to renew his wanderings after his reunion with Penelope at the end of Homer's *Odyssey*; forsaken by his patroness Athene, he is sponsored by Aphrodite, who shows him the vision of ideal beauty in the shape of golden Helen, and sends him to Egypt, where Helen lives as a goddess in a temple, awaiting the coming of " the wisest and bravest of men," who shall "sleep at last in the arms of the fairest of women." He resists the allurements of Meriamun, the Pharaoh's Queen, who seeks to play the part of Potiphar's wife, but on the night of his nuptials with Helen, Meriamun practices her magic arts to appear to him in the shape of Helen, and forgetting Aphrodite's warning that he shall know Helen by the Star of Love worn in her bosom, by which star he was to swear fidelity to her, he swears by the human-headed Snake of Evil, and lies with Meriamun. "To Love he turns, in Lust he shall be lost!" In expiation of his crime, at the orders of Aphrodite, he wages war for the Egyptians against his own people, and mortally wounded by the shaft of Telegonus, his own son by Circe, dies in the arms of golden Helen without possessing her. The flaw in the story is that the reader's sympathies are strongly enlisted in favour of Meriamun, a tragedy queen in the mould of Lady Macbeth, whose resolute pursuit of her passions endows her personality with colour, far surpassing the lay figure of Helen and the uninspired heroism of the "crafty" Wanderer. This was Stevenson's feeling about the story when he wrote from Samoa his congratulations to Lang, enclosing a set of humorous verses beginning,

> "Awdawcious Odyshes,
> Your conduc' is vicious,
> Your tale is suspicious
> An' queer."

and continuing,

> "Ye ancient auld blackguard,
> Just see whaur ye're staggered
> From Homer to Haggard
> And Lang!"

Haggard liked *The World's Desire* as well as any of his books, but he thought *Beatrice* "one of the best bits of work I ever did." The modern reader will be puzzled to agree with him; even more than *Dawn, Beatrice* recalls Mrs. Henry Wood, and reveals Haggard frankly as inferior to Mrs. Wood in her own style. The main theme is that of matrimonial complication, which became popular after the Parnell case; a brilliant young man, married to an unsatisfactory wife, falls in love with the noble daughter of a poor country gentleman, who sacrifices herself rather than ruin her lover's parliamentary career with the scandal of a divorce case. The absurdity of its crucial scene alone despoils the story of conviction; the whole of the subsequent happenings depend upon the heroine's sleep-walking into her lover's room, whence, without waking her, the lover carries her in his arms and lays her on her bed in her own room, which she shares with a malicious sister, who is lying awake and watching. Victorian respectability never wrung from any novelist a device more ludicrously crude to evade the offence of sexuality in a drama of sexual emotion.

Haggard was very upset by the reviews of *Beatrice*, and he received cold comfort from his friends. "A deal more popular line than *The World's Desire*" was all Lang would say in its favour, and Jeaffreson thought that "with all its power and dexterity it is not *the book* which will determine your eventual place in the annals of literature." Henley told him that he might attribute adverse criticism partly to envy, "for you can't deny that you've had a damn good innings," and partly to "the inevitable reaction, for I don't know that your admirers have praised you in quite the right way," adding the sound advice to ignore criticism, "do your best, and leave the rest to time." Marie Corelli, a young woman of twenty-six with *A Romance of Two Worlds* and *Thelma* to her name, thought *Beatrice* "beautiful

—full of poetry and deep thought," but Haggard probably took her praise wryly when she added, ingenuously gushing, that "whenever I see a *World* and *Pall Mall Gazette* vulgarly sneering at a work of literature, I conclude that it *must* be good— exceptionally so!"

His next two books, *Eric Brighteyes* and *Nada the Lily*, followed the saga pattern of *The World's Desire*, the former inspired directly by his trip to Iceland, the latter by his intimate knowledge of Zulu territory. Though *Eric Brighteyes* ran into a third edition by 1893, Haggard could hardly have hoped for its success with his greater public, for its style imitates the language of Dasent's *Burnt Njal* and the story aims to be a copy of such a saga. As an imitation of a saga, it is a fine achievement, but as a story, read in relation to Haggard's other work, it reveals a poverty of invention unusual in him; Eric is only a more heroic Wanderer, Gudruda a better Helen, Swanhild a less splendid Meriamun, and Skallagrim the Baresark, the best achievement in the book, is, as Lang said, "a Norse Umslcpogaas". But it held enthralled in 1912 a somewhat precocious boy of nine, who felt a lump in his throat as he breathlessly read of the murder at Middalhof of Gudruda the Fair, and looked on Lancelot Speed's illustration of Gudruda, pinned to her bed, with the sword Whitefire upright between her breasts.

Nada the Lily was Haggard's last book before he left for Mexico to gather material for *Montezuma's Daughter*. When Jeaffreson expressed the opinion that *Beatrice* was not the book Haggard would be remembered by, he added his opinion that Haggard would write such a book "some ten years hence", when "you've come to forty year". But as Haggard remarked in his autobiography, "that wondrous work of fiction which Cordy Jeaffreson anticipated never was and never will be written by me."

"Be it good or be it bad, the best that I can do in the lines of romance and novel-writing is to be found among the first dozen or so of the books that I wrote, say between *King Solomon's Mines* and *Montezuma's Daughter*."

§ 4

While he was in Mexico in 1891, the death of his only son dealt Haggard a blow which left a lasting mark. "Not for many years did I shake off the effects of the shock," he wrote; "indeed I have never done so altogether." Hitherto his religion had followed the conventional lines common to most of his class, but now continual reflection made him a devout Christian believer, faith in the survival of the soul beyond the life of the body becoming necessary to his reason and to endurance of continued existence. If he had not firmly held to this faith, if he had been for a moment shaken by the suspicion that death is the end of everything, "not for any finite earthly life that could be promised me would I endure again from year to year the agony I have suffered on the one count of this bereavement." He had carved on the cross of his boy's grave, "I shall go to him," and implicit confidence in this as a statement of fact sustained him in a sorrow ever present. Some years later, the death of a favourite dog inspired the conviction that, if the human soul survives mortal life, so must the soul of a creature so endowed with personality as a dog, and if a dog survives, so must other animals. Hence he gave up shooting, which had been his principal recreation, as might be expected of one who had hunted big game in his African days; he was not bigoted in his opinions about killing, believing it a matter for personal conscience, but while he still enjoyed going out with a shooting party, he himself never again handled a gun.

The bereavement disastrously affected his health. His nerves gave way, the remainder of his Mexican trip seeming "a kind of nightmare", and he contracted several attacks of influenza one upon the other, severely enfeebling his constitution. Ill health directly affected his work when he found that he could not endure "continual stooping over a desk", compelling him to resort to dictation to a secretary. Many novelists have found dictation a convenient method of work, and even such a stylist as Thackeray resorted to dictation when compelled by illness, but it is a safe bet that every writer of distinction has watched his best work form in his own handwriting. Dictation inevitably encouraged

Haggard's worst fault, carelessness in composition, which became more glaringly apparent in the books following *Montezuma's Daughter*, where a single cursory revision might have removed many blemishes of redundancy, inept expression, and repetition like that, to take an early example, in *The Witch's Head*, where Doll and Ernest go home together, in the last lines of the book hand in hand through the twilight, in almost the identical phrasing used three chapters before.

A further reason for declension in quality seems to have been a carelessness of literary ambition after the shock of his son's death. Previously, in spite of his theory that style was an outward dressing and the story the substance that mattered, he had seduously striven to make each succeeding book better than its predecessor. Though he never came to regret almost with resentment the success of *She*, as Blackmore came to feel towards *Lorna Doone*, the remarks of reviewers that his latest book was "not another *She*" never failed to annoy him. He was worried when Lang was less enthusiastic about *Jess* than *She*, and when Lang agreed with him that "the stuff is the thing", but argued that the "ideal thing" is "the perfection of stuff and the perfection of style," he tried hard in *Cleopatra, Beatrice, Eric Brighteyes*, and *Nada the Lily* to approximate to this standard, and rise above the level of the popular story-teller. When Lang thought to encourage him, he invariably complimented him on improvements in style, but he plunged Haggard into dejection when he criticised structural details of *Eric Brighteyes*.

Yet Lang's criticisms sprang from an earnest desire to see palpable flaws erased from what he genuinely considered an appreciable work of art, for he told Haggard that he regarded *Eric Brighteyes* as "a masterpiece" and "the best thing you have done." Haggard had no high opinion of *Eric*, still preferring *Cleopatra*, and he would probably have sacrificed all Lang's praise of his saga books, if his friend would have shared his own estimation of *Jess* and *Beatrice*, which continued, in defiance of the verdict of the public and critics alike, to hold first place in his affections. Lang sagely recognised that Haggard had no special aptitude for the novel of modern society, while he possessed remarkable talent for adventure stories, and lost few opportunities of telling him how he liked "your *natural* novels better a long way than your modern ones at the best," or how much he preferred "Galazi and Skallagrim to these moderns." Even the publisher Longman, while praising *Beatrice* as the best of his modern novels, preferred him "among the caves of old Kor, or looking back over King Solomon's great road to the old civilisations dead two thousand years ago."

Under stress of illness and depression after his son's death, Haggard bowed to his critics, and the book following *Montezuma's Daughter*, *The People of the Mist*, was the first to be written frankly in imitation of his early successes, without effort at fresh achievement. *The People of the Mist* follows the same pattern as *Allan Quatermain* and *She*; there is a lost race hidden in the heart of Africa, ruled over by a beautiful girl; the hero, Leonard Outram, is a blend of Sir Henry Curtis and Leo Vincey, the heroine is a pale shadow of Ayesha and Nyleptha, the dwarf Otter supplies the comic relief, or Jonsonian "humours", of Umslopogaas and Job. It displays all the flaws of careless writing, which had been superficial blemishes in his previous work, and were to become disfiguring scars in his later books. When the adventurers concoct a plan to deceive the inimical people of the mist, Haggard suddenly remembered that their followers from the slave settlement had to be parties to the plan, and dismissed the difficulty in a sentence: "When their first surprise was past, the Settlement men, who were quick-witted people, entered into the spirit of the plot readily enough." His haste developed a perfunctoriness which became characteristic; he introduces the villainous Portuguese slave-trader, describes him, and adding, "Such was the outward appearance of Pereira, the fountain-head of the slave-trade on this part of the coast, who was believed in his day to be the very worst man in Africa," then breaks off abruptly to begin a new chapter. Haste also blinded him at times to the dramatic potentialities of his plots, as when the dwarf Otter, having been condemned as not being a god and thrown as a sacrifice to the crocodile, is not made to return among his executioners after killing "the Water-Dweller", and strike fear into them, by thus proving himself superhuman as the slayer of the sacred beast.

The People of the Mist was the first of many pot-boilers produced to feed the public created by his early successes, and the ever-popular Allan Quatermain figured in as many subsequent books as Conan Doyle devoted to Sherlock Holmes, or "Sapper" to Bulldog Drummond. When he wrote his autobiography in 1912, he was still writing of Allan in *Child of Storm*, the old hunter appeared as late as 1920 in *The Ancient Allan*, the story of *She* found repetition with almost identical characters under different guises in *Queen Sheba's Ring* of 1910, and the authentic sequel to *She*, *Ayesha, or the Return of She*, appeared in 1905. Whatever illusions he had cherished about his craft as an art were dispelled; he was disgusted when reviewers of *Eric Brighteyes* and *Nada the Lily* disregarded their quality as sagas, and treated them simply as tales of sanguinary adventure, moving Quiller-Couch to describe him as the novelist of Blood. Since the critics assured him that the public wanted more of *She* and *Allan Quatermain*, it should have them, and discarding further effort at creative development, he mechanically manufactured imitations of his popular favourites as a profitable business. Once or twice he ventured again upon a modern subject, as in *Joan Haste* and *Doctor Therne*, though the latter was primarily propaganda against the anti-vaccinationist cranks, but whatever inclination to persevere with the modern analytical novel remaining after the disappointing reception of *Beatrice* was finally dispelled by attacks on the morality of that novel. Haggard showed himself ridiculously sensitive under this sort of criticism, the common sense of Lang and Longman with difficulty restraining him from withdrawing *Beatrice* from circulation, when he received anonymous letters from wives who alleged that their husbands—"one of them a middle-aged clergy-man"—had made advances, after reading *Beatrice*, to ladies of that name, and he heard that another gentleman and lady had reconstructed the sleep-walking scene "with different results from those recorded in the book."

He was persuaded to assuage his qualms of conscience by inserting in subsequent editions of *Beatrice* a preface asserting its innocence of immoral tendencies, but the experience "more or less set me against the writing of novels of modern life." It was characteristic of his intellectual habit and outlook that there never occurred to him the obvious inference that such

baseless charges, courting frivolity in their crassness of Humbug,
reflected a false and unhealthy state of social and intellectual
convention. He was too instinctively saturated in the unimaginative, law-abiding, and conventional phlegm of the
Service caste to feel the vaguest inspiration to rebellion or
reform; when Hardy showed him a review of *Jude the Obscure*,
and remarking, "There's a nice thing to say about a man,"
declared, "Well, I'll never write another novel," he conceived
Hardy's disgust to be directed merely against the malice of
professional critics, not against the sanctimonious hypocrisy and
prurient prudery of popular convention. In his opinion,

> "It is very well to talk about art with a large A, but I have
> always felt that the author of books which go anywhere and
> everywhere has some responsibilities. Therefore I have tried
> to avoid topics that might inflame even minds which are very
> ready to be set on fire."

He defended himself against the charge that his books "breathed
war" by asserting that while he had a horror of war and hoped
never to see his country involved in another, there was "righteous
war", that all war "brings forth many noble actions", and that
there can be no harm in preaching the doctrine of self-defence.
Patriotism he regarded as "the first duty", and declaring that he
would "fight like a wild cat" to repel an invader, believed that he
would not hesitate to use poison to be rid of such an enemy, for
"what is the difference between killing a man with a drug and
killing him with a bomb or by hunger and thirst?" This he
wrote in 1912, so shortly before science included among its benefits
to civilisation the introduction to warfare of poison gas.

He remained utterly aloof from any of the theories and
movements in contemporary art, though in the first years of his
success he mingled freely with literary society. He became a
member of the Savile Club, habitually lunching there on
Saturdays with Lang, Gosse, Walter Besant, Bob Stevenson, and
others, was elected to the Athenæum Club in 1895, and for three
years between 1895 and 1898 served as Chairman of Committee of
the Society of Authors. Besides Lang and Henley, he knew
Hardy and Kipling, and with Gosse he must have been intimate

in the first flush of his popularity between *She* and *Nada the Lily*, for his son was left in the care of Gosse and his wife while Haggard went to Mexico, and died at their house. But in the copious index of the *Life and Letter of Sir Edmund Gosse, C.B.*, by the Hon. Evan Charteris, Haggard's name does not appear. Nor does he figure in the memoirs of many who might be expected to have known him at the Savile and Athenæum in the 'nineties, perhaps because as he said himself, he had ever a tendency to make friends with men older than himself, a habit which contributed to his discomfort in drawing the characters of young men in his books, and brought him sadness in the suffering of repeated bereavements while still in middle life, so that when he began his autobiography in 1911, there remained of his close friends only Lang, Arthur Cochrane, and Charles Longman. In his autobiography, apart from an account of his intimacy with Lang, almost the only information reference to a literary friend is an interesting note on Marjorie Barber, celebrated as the writer of *The Roadmender* under the pseudonym of Michael Fairless, whose sister Agnes married one of his brothers.

During the four years following *She*, he spent much time in London, but after the death of his son, he made his permanent home in Ditchingham. Still under forty years of age, he grew restless at the "humdrum existence in a country parish", feeling that "staring at crops and cultivating flowers" was better suited to a man's declining years, and that writing stories was an insufficient occupation, much as Stevenson felt when he reflected that he ought to have been able to build lighthouses as well as to write novels. In 1893 he declined an invitation, proceeding from people impressed by his knowledge of South African problems, to enter Parliament, but two years later he unsuccessfully contested the Liberal stronghold of East Norfolk in the Conservative interest. He then devoted his energies wholeheartedly to agriculture and local government, remaining for many years chairman of the local bench of magistrates, while his interest in African matters found scope as chairman of the Anglo-African Writers' Club and co-director of a weekly journal called the *African Review*. The writing of fiction became a part-time job, which he practised purely for making money, and sank even lower in his estimation when he allied his pen with his more serious interests. Between September, 1898, and October of the following year, his valuable practical commentary on agriculture, *A Farmer's Year*, compiled from his own journal recording the workings of his Ditchingham estate during 1898, ran serially through *Longman's Magazine*, and its publication in 1899 inspired a commission from Arthur Pearson and the *Daily Express* to tour England, surveying agricultural conditions in the various counties, and write a series of articles which he embodied in the two volumes of *Rural England*, published in 1902. This monumental document led to interviews and correspondence with Asquith, Lord Rosebery, and the Minister of Agriculture, Lord Onslow, and many of Haggard's counsels were adopted and incorporated in Government agricultural policy.

Rural England also led to his appointment in 1905 as Commissioner to the United States to inspect and report on the Salvation Army's labour settlements with a view to possible establishment of similar settlements in British dominions. He was granted three hundred pounds for expenses—not by the Government, but from the Rhodes Trust—and having carried out his task with characteristic thoroughness and considerable additional expense out of his own pocket, he was much aggrieved when, on his return, the Colonial Secretary of the Balfour Government, Alfred Lyttelton, congratulated him on his conscientious report, but lamented that "Arthur won't read it", and finally had a Departmental Committee appointed to "knock the bottom out of it." He was better treated when the Liberals came into power in 1906, Mr. Lloyd George appointing him to a Royal Commission on Coast Erosion and Afforestation, while serving on which, in addition to his regular output of fiction and his duties at Ditchingham, he wrote *Regeneration*, an account of the Salvation Army's achievement, at the request of General Booth, and *Rural Denmark*, a companion and comparative volume with *Rural England*, resulting from a tour of investigation of Denmark's agricultural conditions. His disinterested public work was fairly rewarded with a knighthood in 1912, the same year in which he was appointed one of the six English representatives to the Royal Commission of the Dominions, which took him on a world tour.

During the war he visited the overseas dominions in 1916 on behalf of the Royal Colonial Institute with a view to the post-war settlement of ex-service men, and again in 1918 as a member of the Empire Settlement Committee, after which he received a K.B.E. in 1919.

After his death in London on 14th May, 1925, his old friend and publisher, Charles Longman, took from his safe where, according to Haggard's direction, it had lain under seal since 1913, the manuscript of his autobiography, *The Days of My Life*, which he edited and published in two volumes in 1926. He was helped in this work by Miss Ida Hector, the daughter of the novelist who wrote as Mrs. Alexander, who had remained Haggard's secretary since he began to dictate his novels in the early nineties—doubtless the "I.H." to whom *Joan Haste* was dedicated in 1895.

§ 5

In its successfulness, its decisiveness, above all its direct simplicity, Haggard's life was unlike a literary man's. In his soul were none of the warring elements which play upon imaginative minds to create morbid obsessions amounting to misery, distraction, sometimes almost to madness, and make their victims great. Haggard's imagination was vivid and fertile, but detached, and he lacked the intellectual egotist's instinct, fatal to contentment but essential to creative genius, of introspection. He lived his life according to the conventions of his birth and breeding, dedicating himself diligently to endeavour, duty, and service, and when he died, it could be said with justice that there was a good man gone.

Greatness too rarely springs from goodness, and there is nothing of the first water in Haggard's literary legacy. As he himself recognised, his best work lay between *King Solomon's Mines* and *Montezuma's Daughter*, for the rest was repetition so far as fiction was concerned. Of his excursions into "general literature", *Rural England* remains a useful document in sociological, as *Cetewayo and His White Neighbours* in political history, but his best achievement in this *genre* is *A Farmer's Year*. Haggard was that rare creature in modern England, a practical farmer with brains and imagination, and though scientific development has revolutionised conditions since 1898, the motor, for instance, having changed the entire scheme of dairy farming as it has the technical methods of cultivation, *A Farmer's Year* retains permanent value for its counsel on general methods of cultivation, especially to the farmer of heavy soils. His subsequent volume, *A Gardener's Year*, is a worthy item for a gardening library.

Of his efforts at the serious novel, *Jess* is the best, the others in this style, like *Dawn*, and *Beatrice*, being his only books no longer worthy of shelf-room. For all his romances, even the loosest and least effective, are well worth reading. Fashions change, and for the modern boy, much less naïve than his pre-war predecessor, Haggard is no longer a foremost favourite, but it is safe to say that *King Solomon's Mines* and *She* will find readers as long as there is any taste for tales of romantic adventure, for the *Waverley Novels*, Defoe, and Stevenson. Yet neither can breathe in the same atmosphere of criticism as *Quentin Durward*, *Moll Flanders*, or *Kidnapped*; it is the quality of sheer zest which makes them as irresistible as better books. Haggard could write; that he wrote no better than he did was due to his theory that a story of adventure must be written as rapidly as possible and not revised. Of all his books, his Zulu saga, *Nada the Lily*, best withstands a critical reading; as Lang exclaimed in enthusiasm on reading the manuscript, it is "the epic of a dying people," and his criticism that "it wants relief" only indicates the sustained power of its sombre grandeur. The spirit of tragedy moves with a stately and awful tread from the boyish prophecy of the terrible Chaka to the death of the wretched Dingaan on the Ghost Mountain, and some of the scenes—the dreadful "Ingomboco" of Chaka, the apparition of the Queen of the Heavens before Mopo, Umslopogaas' hunting with the wolves, the duel of Umslopogaas and Jikiza, the fates of Zinita and Nada—bear comparison with the best in romantic literature. In this book Haggard's talent for vivid description is most brilliantly exhibited in variety and quality; an extract from Galazi's narrative to Umslopogaas affords a fair sample and sufficient evidence of Haggard's indisputable literary gift.

"On the floor of the cave lay a she-wolf panting, as though

she had galloped many a mile; she was great and fierce. Near to her was another wolf—he was a dog—old and black, bigger than any I have seen, a very father of wolves, and all his head and flanks were streaked with grey. But this wolf was on his feet. As I watched he drew back nearly to the mouth of the cave, then of a sudden he ran forward and bounded high into the air towards the withered foot of that which hung from the cleft of the rock. His pads struck upon the rock here where it is smooth, and there for a second he seemed to cling, while his great jaws closed with a clash but a spear's breadth beneath the dead man's foot. Then he fell back with a howl of rage, and drew slowly down the cave. Again he ran and leaped, again the great jaws closed, again he fell down howling. Then the she-wolf arose, and they sprang together, striving to pull him down who sat above. But it was all in vain; they could never come nearer than within a spear's breadth of the dead man's foot. And now, Umslopogaas, you know why the rock is smooth and shines. From month to month and year to year the wolves have ravened there, seeking to devour the bones of him who sat above. Night upon night they had leaped thus against the wall of the cave, but never might their clashing jaws close upon his foot."

If Haggard had taken the pains always to write up to this standard, he would rank among the masters of romantic literature. But, with possibly the single exception of *Nada the Lily*, his books unfailingly inspire in the critical reader a feeling of regret that he did not give his work the benefit of careful revision. Delight in the vigour of his narrative and wonder at the fertility of his imagination are tempered by the regret that a Stevenson could not have revised his proofs. When Stevenson wrote congratulations on *King Solomon's Mines* from Bournemouth, remarking that Haggard struck him as "one who gets up steam slowly," while his own case was the reverse—"I always begin well, and often finish languidly or hurriedly,"—he added suggestively, "How about a deed of partnership?" If Stevenson had not gone to Samoa, if he had not quarrelled with Henley and Henley had brought him and Haggard together, if they had collaborated— what a masterpiece of romantic fiction might have resulted!

CHAPTER EIGHT

The Romantics

§ 1

In 1895 a schoolmaster sent Andrew Lang a list of books taken out during one term from the school library. Rider Haggard easily headed the list with 66 takings, Stevenson was as easily second with 48, and Scott third with 33. There followed Conan Doyle with 28, Blackmore 27, "Q." 23, Jules Verne and W. H. G. Kingston 22, Henty, Bulwer Lytton, and Ainsworth 18, and among the rest, Dickens 14, Whyte Melville 13, Henry Kingsley and Mrs. Henry Wood 12, Grant Allen, William Black and Gordon Stables 7, Charles Kingsley 5, Reade and Lewis Carroll 4, Shorthouse 3, George Eliot 2, and Trollope and Disraeli only one each. The list loses much significance from the obvious limitations of the library, for the names of Thackeray, Marryat, and Dumas do not appear, and a host of omissions among contemporary writers occur—Stanley Weyman, Seton Merriman, Hewlett, Kipling, Anthony Hope, Hornung, Guy Boothby, and many more, apart from the great names of Hardy, who, of course, was not sufficiently respectable for a school library, Meredith, whose reputation for unreadableness was not yet discounted by sanctity as a "classic", and Henry James. But it testifies to the supreme popularity of Haggard and Stevenson, while revealing that among contemporary writers, Conan Doyle and Quiller-Couch were enjoying a vogue only inferior to Haggard's.

Born in 1859, Sir Arthur Conan Doyle was three years younger than Rider Haggard, but took to writing about the same time. He came of an artistic family, for both his father and grandfather were artists, and his uncle, Richard Doyle, was the celebrated cartoonist of *Punch*, who illustrated Thackeray's *Newcomes* and published the famous *Adventures of Brown, Jones and Robinson*. Educated at Stonyhurst and in Germany, Conan Doyle took a medical degree at Edinburgh, and worked at Southsea as a general

264

medical practitioner between 1882 and 1890. An athlete and sportsman, he had a taste for adventure, and spent his holidays in travel, accompanying an expedition to the Arctic and visiting the Gold Coast. While still a student, he had contributed to *Chambers's Journal*, and continuing to write for magazines, he made a hit in 1888 when Ward and Lock issued as a shilling shocker the first of his innumerable Sherlock Holmes stories, *A Study in Scarlet*, praised by Lang as "nearer to the true Hugh Conway" than anything since the death of the author of *Called Back*, the famous thriller which had appeared in 1884. The illustrious Sherlock and his famous "methods" were no very original achievement, being borrowed immediately from Emile Gaboriau's *Monsieur Lecocq*, which with its companion volumes, advertised as "the favourite reading of Prince Bismarck," had been issued in shilling translations by the enterprising Vizetelly. But the idea, borrowed from Boswell's *Life of Johnson*, of supplying the infallible detective with a fat-headed foil in his biographer, "my dear Watson", supplied an ideal device for narrating the "problem" story, which has been assiduously copied for forty years, and figures in a huge body of the crime stories, which fill many shelves in every circulating library to-day.

A second Sherlock Holmes novel, *The Sign of Four*, followed in 1889, and its success inspired the editor of the new *Strand Magazine* in 1891 to commission a series of monthly short stories, comprising *The Adventures of Sherlock Holmes*. Whether the *Strand Magazine* established Conan Doyle's success or whether Doyle the magazine's, the popularity of both was assured within a few months. The *Strand* was a shrewd venture by that enterprising young publisher, George Newnes, whose name is inevitably associated with those of Alfred Harmsworth and Arthur Pearson, as the three principal pioneers in catering for the huge ignorant public created by cheap education. Newnes had been first in the field, starting a new class of penny journalism in 1881 with his paper, *Tit-Bits*, which was followed by Harmsworth's *Answers* and *Pearson's Weekly*. Newnes now saw an opening for a sixpenny magazine, which would combine the lighter literary quality of the old-fashioned magazines, like *Cornhill*, and the defunct *Fraser*, with the chatty articles of society gossip, superficial instruction, and romanticised history, the anecdotes of travel, interviews with prominent people, and profuse process illustrations featured in the new style of "family" magazine like *Cassells's*. The *Strand* thus addressed an appeal to the entire middle-class, both the upper quality possessed of sufficient taste to appreciate a good story well written and an informative article by a qualified authority, and the massed bands of the lower order, whose standard of intelligence demanded that the pills of elementary education should be sugar-coated with the condiment of entertainment. With process illustrations of the highest contemporary quality and the best journalism of its order, the *Strand* required only a single sensationally popular feature to secure its introduction to a wide circulation, and this it found in the Sherlock Holmes stories, which proved an attraction so popular that, when the series of twelve *Adventures* was completed, Doyle was commissioned to write a further series, which appeared in book form as *The Memoirs of Sherlock Holmes*.

At the end of the *Memoirs*, Doyle killed Sherlock off. He was heartily sick of his hero, and like Haggard after *She*, wished to consolidate his reputation with work of a higher literary standard. Already he had written three notable historical novels, *Micah Clarke*, a tale of Monmouth's rebellion, *The White Company*, in a mediaeval setting, and *The Refugees*, a story of the Huguenots under Louis Quatorze, in which the historical figures of Madame de Maintenon, the gorgeous Montespan, and Louvois are recreated with some approximation to probability. These were followed in 1896 and 1897 by *The Exploits of Brigadier Gerard*, *Rodney Stone*, and *Uncle Bernac*, a Napoleonic tale in which Brigadier Gerard appears as a young lieutenant. In Gerard, a swashbuckling cavalry officer under Napoleon, whose gallantry and vanity suggest the suspicion that Dumas' D'Artagnan was in his direct line of ancestry, Doyle attempted to create a popular personality as the central figure for a series of historical stories, like Sherlock Holmes for criminal problems. A sequel, *The Adventures of Gerard*, appeared some years later, and a comedy called *Brigadier Gerard* was produced on the London stage in 1906.

But, as with Haggard, popular demand defeated personal inclination, and compelled him to bring Sherlock Holmes to life again in *The Stark Munro Letters*, *The Hound of the Baskervilles*, and *The Return of Sherlock Holmes*. As late as 1918, *His Last Bow* purported to be a final collection of Holmes stories, but the last years of his life before his death in 1930 found him still contributing further adventures of his immortal detective to the *Strand Magazine*. Like Haggard again, Doyle devoted much of his energies to public affairs, and for his services as a surgeon in a field hospital during the Boer War, supported by his popular history of *The Great Boer War* and his pamphlet on the *Cause and Conduct of the War* in defence of the British Government's policy, he received a knighthood in 1902. In later years, he achieved signal public service by his staunch advocacy of the unfortunate Oscar Slater against a tragic miscarriage of justice, and became during and after the war an active and devoted leader of the spiritualists' movement.

As a spiritualist and as the creator of Sherlock Holmes, Conan Doyle lives in contemporary memory. If the detectives of fiction banded themselves into a trade union, including all such popular celebrities as Miss Christie's Poirot, Mr. Bentley's Trent, Miss Sayers's Lord Peter, and Mr. Wills Crofts' Inspector French, they would be bound unanimously to select Sherlock Holmes for their president, as the first master and pioneer of their trade. But his historical romances represent Doyle's best literary work. The same small boy who was enthralled by *Eric Brighteyes* preferred *The White Company* to *Ivanhoe*, though the preference may have been biased by *Ivanhoe*'s being a prescribed holiday task, while Doyle's tale of the adventuring bowmen in the Hundred Years' War was voluntarily chosen from the school library. In any library of historical romance *The White Company* must find an honourable place, as must *Rodney Stone*, a well-constructed story of the prize ring in the days of Beau Brummell, in which a picturesque impression of its period is spoiled only by the reticence required by contemporary humbug.

Doyle was among the first to attempt the revival of the historical romance, which had fallen from favour since its heyday under Harrison Ainsworth and G. P. R. James in the 'forties. Nearly every novelist of note after 1850 had tried at least one costume novel—Thackeray wrote *Esmond* and *The Virginians*,

Dickens *A Tale of Two Cities*, Reade *The Cloister and the Hearth*, George Eliot *Romola*, Trollope *Nina Balatka*—but all had found the departure less profitable than novels in a modern setting, and those who persevered, like Whyte-Melville and Blackmore, achieved generally only minor success. But a renewed interest in historical fiction appeared with Stevenson's *Kidnapped*, about which time such a purely commercial writer as Walter Besant left the modern setting of *Ready-Money Mortiboy* and *All Sorts and Conditions of Men* for the period of the first Jacobite rebellion in *Dorothy Forster* and of the Monmouth rising in *For Faith and Freedom*, a brace of romances in Harrison Ainsworth's style.

Sir Arthur Quiller-Couch, a rather younger man than Haggard and Doyle, having been born in 1863, began writing historical romances with the capitally titled *Dead Man's Rock* in 1887. He began with the advantage of a reputation as a brilliant young man, having secured a fellowship at Oxford and the post of chief book reviewer for the *Speaker*, while his signature of the single mystic letter "Q" attracted curious comment. The "*Duchy Edition*"—so called because he is a Cornishman, who has lived most of his life in Cornwall and written freely of the Cornish countryside and its history—of his tales and romances runs into about thirty volumes, but his early fiction is his best, and he has never improved upon *The Splendid Spur*, a lively story of the Civil War, published in 1889. Not only in material and construction, but in the style of writing, do his earlier compare favourably with his later books, which bear the impress of a certain donnish pretentiousness, as in *Sir John Constantine*, which is a purely academic effort to imitate the manner of the eighteenth-century romance writers, with the digressive verbosity of Sterne impeding a story better handled in the brisk narrative of Defoe. The extent of his recognition as a writer of romance with a polished prose style was testified by his selection, as a young man of thirty-four, for the task of completing Stevenson's unfinished *St. Ives*.

Other writers of distinction to take up historical romance were Sir Gilbert Parker and Maurice Hewlett. Born in Canada in 1862, Parker devoted most of his time to political and public affairs, holding a seat in Parliament for eighteen years, and being

closely associated with imperial interests. His magazine stories
of Canadian life attracted the attention of Henley, with the result
that he was soon well advertised as the story-teller of Canada, as
Kipling was of India. In *The Seats of the Mighty*, published in
1896, he wrote an excellent romance of Canada and its conquest
by Wolfe, though the book for which he may be remembered is
the slighter *When Valmond Came to Pontiac*, the story of a valet in
the service of a Bonaparte, who settled in a Canadian village,
pretended to be a Bonaparte, and came to a tragic end.

Maurice Hewlett was a novelist of altogether higher degree
and achievement, who never enjoyed a just measure of popularity
during his life and has yet to receive fair appreciation of his
merits since his death in 1923. Born at Weybridge in 1861, the
son of a civil servant, he left school at the age of eighteen and
entered his cousin's law business at Gray's Inn with a view to a
partnership after serving his articles. He persevered in his
profession, becoming an expert in antiquarian law, and eventually
succeeding his father as Keeper of Land Revenue Records, but
meanwhile indulged his literary inclinations, contributing
occasional verse, short stories, and articles to the *Academy* and
other literary journals. An inveterate reader, he fell under the
influence of Pater, and spent many of his holidays in Italy,
saturating himself in the art and lore of the Renaissance. He made
a few literary friends, including John Addington Symonds and
Robert Bridges, and published *Earthwork out of Tuscany* in 1895
and *Songs and Meditations* in the following year. Success came to
him suddenly in 1898 when his mediæval romance, *The Forest
Lovers*, which he re-wrote four times in two years of work, was
chosen by the *Academy* as the best book of the year. The most
obvious criticism of *The Forest Lovers* applies equally to most
of his subsequent books—the flowering of the wandering knight's
romantic love affords a theme too frail to support the elaborate
setting of the story. The criticism applies least forcibly to *The
Life and Death of Richard Yea-and-Nay* (1900), a fine tapestry of
Cœur de Lion and the Crusades, and *The Queen's Quair* (1904), one
of the best romances ever written about Mary Queen of Scots,
which was dedicated to Andrew Lang. Hewlett was a scholar and
a poet much more than a story-teller, and his invention rarely

succeeded in creating plot and characters capable of sustaining the ornate tapestries of his backgrounds and the chiselled splendours of a polished style. He wrote carefully, and the poetic imagery of his prose frequently falls into preciosity, as in this passage taken at random from *The Stooping Lady* (1907):

> "A seed of doubt had been sown in the garden-plot of her mind. Like Eve in another garden long ago, she could no longer be as she had been now that she knew herself. Like Eve in that garden of long ago, she ran sheltering into the brake, and made herself an apron of leaves."

But Hewlett was an artist and a stylist, and though he may be best remembered as a poet for his *Song of the Plow*, he brought the dignity of scholarship and style to historical romance, and few who read *The Queen's Quair* will not want to try more of his books.

Perhaps Hewlett will always appeal only to the limited public which appreciates artistry of language, but the books of Stanley J. Weyman must surely always find favour with the readers of historical romance. Weyman had neither the literary style nor the poetic imagination of Hewlett, but he was a gifted story-teller, with a consummate command of plot-construction, a fine sense of the dramatic, and an easy consciousness of period atmosphere. He was older than any of the foregoing writers, being born in Ludlow in 1855, the son of a local solicitor. Educated at Shrewsbury and Christ Church, he was called to the bar in 1881, and for some years practised with small success. His first story, *The House of the Wolf*, an amateur's attempt to reconstruct the temper of France at the epoch of the St. Bartholomew Massacre as it might have been appraised by an intelligent contemporary, appeared serially in the *English Illustrated Magazine* in 1883, but found no publisher willing to risk its issue as a book till 1890. By that time he had begun to contribute short stories to *Cornhill*, and encouraged by James Payn to attempt a full-length novel, he wrote the dullest of all his books, *The New Rector*, an imitation of Trollope, who was a bad master to choose at a time when, as Lang said, everybody seemed to have ceased reading Trollope. *The New Rector* appeared as a serial in *Cornhill* before book publication in 1891, and in the same year he published a much

better book in *The Story of Francis Cludde*, a romance of Bloody
Mary's day, but Weyman first found popularity with *A Gentleman
of France* in 1893. This ever popular cloak and sword story, one
of the best English imitations of Dumas ever written, with a
down-at-heel soldier of fortune, the Sieur de Marsac, playing the
heroic rôle of D'Artagnan in the era of Chicot the Jester, ran
serially throughout 1893 in *Longman's Magazine*, and after a quiet
greeting on book publication, suddenly began to sell, doubtless
owing to Lang's boosting, so rapidly that it was advertised as in
its thirty-fourth thousand at six shillings by February, 1895.

Within a couple of years after this success, Weyman had seven
other books to his name. *Memoirs of a Minister of France* comprised
a collection of magazine stories, and the weakness of *My Lady
Rotha* indicates an earlier composition resuscitated as additional
provender for the appetite greedy for anything by Weyman, but
Under the Red Robe, set in D'Artagnan's own period, and *The Red
Cockade*, a tale of the French Revolution told with a complete
mastery of dramatic situation and rapid narrative, well sustained
the inevitable comparison with Dumas. From 1897 to 1905 he
kept up a fine level of quality with *Shrewsbury*, a story of Fenwick's
plot in 1695, *The Castle Inn* and *Sophia* in a mid-eighteenth century
setting, *Count Hannibal* approximating closely to Dumas' *Marguerite de Valois* in dealing again with the St. Bartholomew
Massacre, *The Long Night* in Geneva at the time of Savoy's attack
in 1602, *The Abbess of Vlaye* in Limousin at Henry of Navarre's
accession, and *Starvecrow Farm* in the Windermere country at
the time Wordsworth, Southey, and De Quincey were living there.
Chippinge (1906), brilliantly recreating the social and political
atmosphere of the Reform Bill epoch, was Weyman's favourite
among his books, though not, as Earle Welby suggests, his first
attempt "to use an English setting and dispense with cloak and
sword," for this he had already done in *The Castle Inn*, *Sophia*,
and *Starvecrow Farm*.

After *The Wild Geese*, a tale of Irish country society in the first
years of George I., appearing in 1908, Weyman published nothing
for ten years. He must have made an ample income from his
books, and he lived quietly in rural retirement at Ruthin, in
Denbigh, where he was chairman of the local magistrates' bench

He may have felt that he had written himself out, that he had no new ideas, and that, since he did not need money, there was no point in repeating his former stories in a different dressing. For, while his invention never failed him in the contrivance of plot and dramatic situation, the most striking weakness in his books is the stereotyped sameness of his characters. His heroines are always proud beauties of spirit, who are won in spite of themselves from frank dislike to love of the hero, and his heroes as invariably are mature men of the world, with unenviable reputations and grim demeanour—Count Hannibal, Sir Hervey Coke of *Sophia*, Anthony Clyne of *Starvecrow Farm*, the Vidame de Bezers of *The House of the Wolf*, Sir George Soane of *The Castle Inn*, all are as like as portraits by Kneller.

On the other hand, he may have ceased to write out of disgust with the critics. Earle Welby claimed that "the higher gifts which enabled him . . . to reproduce the atmosphere of a period, not simple nor obviously romantic, were perceptible chiefly by readers who were not much attracted by the picturesque simplicities of his earlier tales." But these discerning readers were apparently unnumbered among the reviewers, who had Weyman ticketed and docketed as the author of *A Gentleman of France*, and greeted each new book of his as "another rattling good story" in "Mr. Weyman's well-known style." To Weyman, seriously striving to recreate the atmosphere of a period, such fatuous appraisement must have been galling. Because he did not ostentatiously parade his learning like Quiller-Couch, nor weave a tapestry too heavily elaborate for the structure of his story like Hewlett, the average critic lacked the knowledge of history to realise the profundity of scholarship and ease of artistry, which enabled Weyman to be so familiar with his period that he could concentrate on the dramatic vitality of his story, without pausing to invoke extraneous effects of atmosphere. The critics, in fact, were unprepared to concede that he was so much an artist and a scholar that he could write good history while telling a good story. He wrote no prefaces or explanatory notes to indicate the extent of his learning, but a searching scrutiny of any of his books reveals intimate detailed knowledge in a single sentence or allusion. In *The Castle Inn*, Lady Dunborough exclaims of

Julia: "She is a shameless baggage if ever there was one; and ruddled to the eyes, as I can see from here. I hope the white may kill her!" The allusion is to the death of the contemporary Lady Coventry, one of the beautiful Gunning sisters, from poisoning through the use of white paint on her face and neck. In the same book, when Sir George Soane refuses to duel after dark, saying "I will be neither Lord Byron nor his victim," he alludes to the killing of Chaworth by the fifth Lord Byron in 1765, two years before the date of the story's setting. Though English critics lacked competence justly to assess Weyman's merits, the municipality of Geneva made him a presentation in recognition of the historical accuracy of *The Long Night*.

The book which broke his ten years' silence, *The Great House*, published in 1918, is a pendant to *Chippinge*, reconstructing the political and social scene of England at the time of Peel's repeal of the Corn Laws. Evidently written with care, this romance follows a more analytical and thoughtful bent than its predecessors, and in Mary Audley he achieved a living woman of character and charm, whose naturalness shames the artificial females portrayed by many of the famous novelists who wrote during the period of the story. But still Weyman was regarded as a mere entertaining romancer by obtuse reviewers, who failed utterly to recognise the warning historical parallel between the story of commercial boom and slump after Waterloo in *Ovington's Bank* and the similar post-war situation of 1922, the year of the book's publication. In 1925 he returned to the vein of *A Gentleman of France* with *The Traveller in the Fur Cloak*, a breathlessly dramatic story of secret service in Central Europe after Wagram in 1809, and in *Queen's Folly* reproduced Jane Austen's atmosphere in a study of social life at the time of Nelson's naval victories, while *The Lively Peggy*, published a few months after his death in 1928, treats of Devon seafaring men and country society at the same period.

Weyman left a rich legacy of historical romance, which challenges comparison with the output of any other English historical novelist after Scott. Odd books by other novelists may be preferred to obvious comparisons among his works; Blackmore's *Springhaven* looms larger than *The Lively Peggy*,

Sir Hugh Walpole's *Herries Saga* towers high in size and stature above the modest achievement of *Starvecrow Farm*, *Our Mr. Dormer* of R. H. Mottram has some advantages over *Ovington's Bank*. But no historical novelist from Harrison Ainsworth down to living contemporaries has written a body of books, over a period of thirty-five years, so consistent in the quality of their entertainment and workmanship.

§ 2

A novelist whose name is always associated with Weyman's is Hugh Stowell Scott, who wrote under the pseudonym of Henry Seton Merriman. Born in 1862, Merriman published his first novel, *Young Mistley*, in two volumes with Bentley in 1888, but he afterwards withdrew from publication this novel and its three successors (*The Phantom Future*, two volumes, 1888; *Suspense*, three volumes, 1890; and *Prisoners and Captives*, three volumes, 1891), believing them "crude and immature", and since he could not prevent their re-printing in America, he re-wrote them, though "conscious of a hundred defects which the most careful revision cannot eliminate." All four, together with *Dross*—a novel which, after serial publication, he declined to issue as a book because this also fell below his standard of self-criticism—were added to the collected edition of his works in 1932, and their reader, on finding them emphatically readable and remarkably fresh after fifty years from the time of composition, will realise that Merriman was a fastidious worker.

Like Andrew Lang, he desired at his early death in 1903 that no biography should be written of him; he objected strongly to advertisement and self-advertisement, holding strictly aloof from interviewers, and as he never moved in literary society nor made any intimate literary friends except the equally reticent and retiring Weyman, little is known of his life, save that he was for some years an underwriter at Lloyd's and spent much time in travelling about Europe. He believed that a writer should be known to the public only by his books, and while the popularity of his novels during his lifetime defied the theory of Wilde, Frank Harris, and Bernard Shaw that self-advertisement assures success, the absence of posthumous interest in the personality of their creator has undoubtedly militated against a just appraisement of his novels. When Congreve told Voltaire that he wished to be visited, not as a writer, but as a private gentleman, Voltaire replied that if Congreve had been merely a private gentleman, he would not have troubled him with a visit; no man, who has claimed the public attention for work of his creation, can reasonably expect that the curiosity he has himself aroused shall not extend to his work's creator. True criticism must always be constructive; the critic who seeks simply to destroy, injures the object of his criticism immeasurably less than he insults his own intelligence; the true critic approaches his task in a spirit of appreciation, seeking to understand the intentions of the creative artist and to sympathise with the motives of his inspiration, thus virtually attempting to view the creation as its creator conceived it in imagination and so enabling himself to measure the extent of success in achieving the conception. Hence biography supplies, if not an essential, certainly an illuminating complement to criticism, and the creative artist who screens his personality from scrutiny cannot grumble if his critics fail to assess fairly the merits of his works.

Lacking information concerning Merriman's habits of thought and study, it is impossible to trace the intellectual development leading to the writing of *Young Mistley*, but obviously his influences were French, and he had gone direct to Flaubert, Maupassant, and de Goncourt, without passing, like George Moore, through a phase of devotion to the naturalism of Zola. With all its looseness of construction and such clumsiness, characteristic of the beginner, as the introduction of the story's protagonists in hurried and undramatic procession through the opening chapters, like the members of a touring cricket team at a royal presentation, *Young Mistley* shows a striving for cohesion, for rejection of all elements superfluous to the plot, which amounted almost to innovation as early as 1888.

This cohesion, simplicity and shapeliness of design, which has become the first principle of the modern novel, was clearly Merriman's primary objective, and his success in its achievement marks him as a pioneer in the novel's transition from Victorian shapelessness to modern conformity. Like Weyman, he suffered

in subsequent consideration from his success, for the rising
generation, contemporary with Wells, Bennett, and Galsworthy,
taking their cue from the highbrow dilettantes of the *Yellow
Book*, could not conceive that anything approaching art could
achieve wide popularity in the 'nineties. At Merriman's death,
Lang confessed:

> "The great popularity of the regretted author has never
> been quite explicable to me. I have read several of his books
> with eagerness, not because they actually interested me, but
> because they made me feel that they were just going to begin
> to be interesting. They did not keep their promise, to my
> taste . . ."

Lang's taste demanded "more claymores"; in a review of
Barlasch of the Guard, he declared the "long passages of moralising"
to be "excrescences", and thought that "Mr. Seton Merriman's
preachments are drawbacks to his interesting romance."

Lang failed to realise that Merriman's design was to apply
to popular romance the principles of psychology and refinement
advocated and practised by Henry James and W. D. Howells—
or, if he did realise it, he deplored it as he deplored most other
serious endeavours for the progressive reform of the novel.
In *Flotsam*, which ran serially, probably to Lang's disgust, in
Longman's Magazine through the first eight months of 1896, the
whole story illustrates a psychological conception, showing how
a strain of weakness in the brilliantly gifted Harry Wylam created
tragedy for himself and sorrow and suffering for all around him.
The Sowers, published in the same year as *Flotsam*, contains no
scenes of violence save the attempted shooting of Steinmetz by
De Chauxville and the peasantry's attack on the castle, yet every
chapter holds a dramatic situation, and the story moves in a
swelling crescendo towards impending tragedy. Merriman
derived his effects from the skilful play of character upon
character, the incidents of his narratives being the inevitable
results of the coming into contact and conflicting interests of
individuals, and the drama of *The Sowers* derives entirely from
the mutual reactions of Prince Paul, the Russian aristocrat
secretly working for the welfare of his serfs, his beautiful wife

with a secret in her past, the unscrupulously intriguing De Chauxville, and his antithesis in Steinmetz, the sage old diplomat.

Obviously Merriman aimed his appeal at readers of higher intelligence than the wider public of Rider Haggard, and no fewer than six of his novels appeared between 1891 and 1902 as serials in *Cornhill*, a magazine now definitely confining its circulation to the cultured classes. *The Sowers*, which ran to twenty editions in four years, was his most popular and remains the most widely read of his novels, but *With Edged Tools* in 1894 first established him in the front rank of popularity. This brilliantly constructed story well illustrates Merriman's blending of romance with the realism of the analytical novel; half the scenes are set in London drawing-rooms, half in the wilds of Central Africa, Haggard's own happy hunting-ground, and instead of buried treasure or lost tribes, Merriman invented the mysterious herb simiacine, productive of an amazing strength-giving drug, and found only on a remote African plateau. So realistic was the story that several readers wrote asking if they could take up shares in the Simiacine Company formed by Oscard, Durnovo, and Jack Meredith. The character of Victor Durnovo, the slave-trafficking, ruthless adventurer, together with the journey up the river and the camp at Msala, are worthy of Conrad, and Haggard might have envied Durnovo's horrible death in gibbering terror of the sleeping sickness.

Though James Payn, with a low opinion of public intelligence born of long experience as popular novelist and magazine editor, warned him that British insularity disliked stories in foreign settings, all Merriman's best books have part of their action in countries which he knew well from his travels. *The Grey Lady* is enacted mostly in Majorca, *Roden's Corner* in Holland, *The Vultures* in Poland, *The Isle of Unrest* is probably the best English novel about Corsica, and *In Kedar's Tents* and *The Velvet Glove* are set in Spain. Stanley Weyman shared some of his travels, dedicating to his memory *The Abbess of Vlaye* because he had visited the scenes of the story with Merriman, and S. G. Tallentyre, who collaborated with Merriman in the book of essays and sketches, *From Wisdom Court* (1893), and *The Money Spinner* (1896), related how

"His greatest delight was to merge himself completely in the life and interests of the country he was visiting—to stay at the mean *venta* or the *auberge* where the tourist was never seen—to sit in the local cafés of an evening and listen to local politics and gossip; to read for the time nothing but the native newpapers, and no literature but the literature, past and present, of the land where he was sojourning."

The intimate knowledge thus derived enabled him, not only to endow his books with local colour and atmosphere, but to create such living characters, so strikingly vital that they were obviously drawn from observation, as Captain Cable and Kosmaroff in *The Vultures*, Evasio Mon and the Sarrions, father and son, in *The Velvet Glove*, von Holzen in *Roden's Corner*, and finest of all Concepcion Vara, the sort of Andalusian Sam Weller of *In Kedar's Tents*.

Merriman's familiarity with foreign languages affected his literary style, and while he followed Flaubert and Maupassant in striving for cohesive shapeliness of structure, it cannot be said that he shared their fastidious choice of the appropriate word. His language is continental, being almost literally translatable into French or Spanish; it is simple and direct, without elaborate trappings, but assumes a lack of distinction, of flexibility and force, from the unbroken monotony of its unpretentious quality. He has a marked tendency to begin sentences with a conjunctive "and" or "for", to say "this man" instead of "he", to finish a speculation with a figurative Gallic shrug, "Who shall say?" or "Who knows?" That he wrote with fluent facility is evident from his output of eighteen full-length novels, besides short stories and collaborations, in fifteen years; he followed Trollope's practice of planning his novels, with a synopsis of every chapter, before starting to write, and his manuscripts are said to contain few alterations or erasures.

His most carefully written books are among his last—*The Velvet Glove*, a tale of Carlist Spain, *The Vultures* in Poland under the Czar Alexander II., and *Barlasch of the Guard*, a vivid picture of a middle-class Dantzig household at the time of Napoleon's march on Moscow—and these three, with *The Sowers*, *With Edged Tools*, and *In Kedar's Tents*, comprise the best of Merriman. His greatest attractions are skilful delineation of character and strength of story. Some of his principals lack originality; he was fond of the strong, silent English hero, and Cartoner, Prince Paul, Oscard, Marcos Sarrion, and Jem Agar are stamped with the same die; more than once he resorts to the stale antithesis of the shallow, fickle beauty and the steadfast woman of the world, like Etta and Maggie in *The Sowers*, Millicent and Jocelyn in *With Edged Tools*, and Maria and Miriam in *Flotsam*. But none of his people are ever colourless or unconvincing, and Concepcion Vara, the gallant Spanish scallywag, and old Barlasch, unsurpassed as a study of the common soldier till Zweig's *Sergeant Grischa*, wear the insignia of greatness.

Sir Anthony Hope Hawkins (1863-1933), who wrote under the name of Anthony Hope, provides another instance of a novelist whose success denied him fair consideration by the critics. The son of a London clergyman, he won a scholarship at Marlborough and an exhibition at Balliol, took a double first at Oxford and was President of the Union at a time when Archbishop Lang, Lord Cecil of Chelwood, Gilbert Murray, Sir Michael Sadler, and Quiller-Couch were contemporaries, and having been called to the bar in 1887, for a time devilled for Asquith. Like Haggard, he beguiled his leisure in waiting for briefs by writing, and in 1890 published at his own expense his first novel, *A Man of Mark*. The story is a political skit somewhat after the manner of W. H. Mallock, the flippant satire of which was pompously pronounced by the *Spectator* to be cynicism "nothing less than repulsive" and "not far off deserving the epithet of immoral." His second book, *Father Stafford*, though seriously treating the tragedy of a priest's falling in love, was also rebuked by the *Spectator* for cynicism and betraying "the prevailing tendencies of modern English fiction" in the year of the publication of *Tess* by the iniquitous Hardy.

Though only two hundred copies of *Father Stafford* were sold in the year of publication, and in addition to his work in the courts, he unsuccessfully contested a parliamentary seat as a Radical, he continued to write, and published three novels in eighteen months, *Mr. Witt's Widow*, *A Change of Air*, and *Half-a-Hero*. *Mr. Witt's Widow*, an amusing satire on fashionable society, had been out for fifteen months when Andrew Lang stumbled upon it, and remarking that he did not remember having seen any reviews of it, pronounced it "an extremely clever and capable novel" and thought the author "a little like" W. E. Norris, the popular society novelist of the day, with "a touch of Trollope." Lang's notice came out appropriately on the eve of the publication of *Half-a-Hero*, a political novel on the Parnell theme, which drew from Henley's *National Observer* an appreciation which applies to most of Hope's books: "Mr. Hope has humour, character, insight, the sense of fitness; he writes clean English; he is often witty; he is nearly always agreeably intelligent; so that you read him for himself as well as for his story." The sales of his novels continued slight, but the praise of Lang and Henley, allied with the amusing *Dolly Dialogues* which Hope began to contribute to the *Westminster Gazette*, attracted the notice of the shrewd Bristol publisher, Arrowsmith, who had started his "Bristol Library" of shilling shockers with Hugh Conway's *Called Back* in 1884, and his later series of three-and-sixpenny fiction with the equally successful *Three Men in a Boat* of Jerome K. Jerome. He offered Hope a royalty of twopence in the shilling for either a shilling or a three-and-sixpenny book, and Hope sent him *The Prisoner of Zenda*, the first draft of which, before revision, he wrote in a month.

Arrowsmith published *The Prisoner of Zenda* in the spring of 1894 as No. 18 of his three-and-sixpenny series, which included, besides *Three Men in a Boat*, two early books by Eden Phillpotts, *The End of a Life* and *A Tiger's Cub*, Grant Allen's *Recalled to Life*, and George and Weedon Grossmith's *Diary of a Nobody*. Its success was assured when Andrew Lang described it at the Royal Academy banquet as "the type of story he loved"; the immensity of Lang's influence was such that probably nobody else ever created a vogue for an author with an after-dinner speech till a late Prime Minister achieved as much for Mary Webb. Most of the critics, except Le Gallienne and the *Yellow Book* circle, followed Lang and Henley, and the book was the great success of the season, seven thousand copies being sold in the first six weeks after publication.

No account is necessary of the romance of Rudolf Rassendyll, the gallant red-haired English gentleman who is persuaded to impersonate temporarily the unsatisfactory King of Ruritania, a state somewhere between Germany and the Balkans, and falls in love with the King's affianced bride. Nearly everybody who has ever subscribed to a circulating library has read the story, or if they have not, they have seen the stage play, originally produced by George Alexander, or one of the several films featuring Messrs. Henry Ainley and Gerald Ames, Lewis Stone, and Ronald Colman. By the time of Hope's death, over half a million copies had been sold in England alone—probably more than twice as many in America—and the sales still continue. "Ruritanian" has become the appropriate descriptive adjective for romances of imaginary kingdoms such as those so popular in post-war musical comedy. Probably the name of Anthony Hope will be always remembered simply as the author of *The Prisoner of Zenda*, like Blackmore for *Lorna Doone*, Thomas Hughes for *Tom Brown's Schooldays*, Lewis Carroll for *Alice in Wonderland*, and James Payn for *Lost Sir Massingberd*.

Yet Hope wrote many books after *The Prisoner of Zenda*—many that aimed at much higher achievement and cost him more pains and labour. Within three months of the appearance of *The Prisoner of Zenda*, he resigned his practice at the bar to devote himself entirely to writing—a step which he sometimes regretted in later years. For he was never able to escape from *The Prisoner of Zenda*. Just as the public expected more of *She* from Haggard, more *Lorna Doones* from Blackmore, so it demanded Ruritania everlastingly from Hope, and was disappointed when it did not get it. When, in the summer of 1894, he published *The Indiscretion of the Duchess* and *The God in the Car*, Quiller-Couch's review in the *Speaker* represented the sort of review he was to receive for the rest of his life; it talked of "a touch of Dumas" and "more than a touch of Sterne," it found a chapter of *The God in the Car* comparable with a similar chapter in *The Ordeal of Richard Feverel*, both novels were "most entertaining books by one of the writers for whose next book one searches eagerly in the publishers' lists," but—though "the telling of *The Indiscretion of the Duchess* is "firmer, surer, more accomplished, . . . story for story, it falls a trifle short of *The Prisoner of Zenda*."

He tried hard to escape from Ruritania. *The God in the Car* is a serious character study of an empire-builder, in whom contemporaries recognised an obvious likeness to Cecil Rhodes, though Rhodes himself, on reading the book, remarked shortly, "I'm not such a brute as that." In *The Chronicles of Count Antonio* (1895) he followed Conan Doyle in attempting mediaeval romance, and in 1898 achieved a much better historical romance in *Simon Dale*, drawing an idealised portrait of Nell Gwyn which despoils her of her charm of vulgarity. *Phroso* (1897) is what Arnold Bennett called a "fantasia", a satirical treatment of improbable people behaving improbably under a semblance of reality, which sustained Hope's reputation for wit and humour created by the *Dolly Dialogues*. Having adopted writing as a means of livelihood, he would have been foolhardy to resist the demand for more Ruritania, and the advisability of a sequel to *The Prisoner of Zenda* was proved when he sold the serial rights of *Rupert of Hentzau* for nine hundred pounds. The story of Rassendyll's return to Ruritania to fight the battles of his lady against the gay scallywag Rupert, whose character obviously derives from the popular legend of the historical Rupert as the dashing young victor of cavalry skirmishes in the Civil War, was followed breathlessly by thousands through its serial course in the *Pall Mall Magazine*, like Lang, who publicly confessed that he pined to know "whether Rudolf set up as a king for good and all," but feared that the story would not "end well."

With much skill Hope sought to compromise with his Ruritanian popularity by combining his styles. In *The Heart of Princess Osra* (1896) he set the scene in Ruritania of the eighteenth century, but the stories of the beautiful Elphberg princess's flirtations and courtships are told with the flippancy of the *Dolly Dialogues*. In *The King's Mirror* (1899) he created another Ruritania, but it was only a background for a character study of a young king, on the lines of the empire-building hero of *The God in the Car*, showing his progress from boyhood, through loves and intrigues and struggles between duty and inclination, to maturity and a political marriage. Some sound critics acclaimed *The King's Mirror* as his best book, though most, as Hope complained, would "not *follow* the writer, I mean, try to see what he was at: they always want him to have been at something else." Most of them, finding themselves in Ruritanian surroundings, hoped for more cloak-and-sword stuff like the adventures of Rassendyll and Rupert, and felt aggrieved when they received instead a brilliantly conceived study in the making of a monarch, the imagined autobiography of a young king, who was probably suggested by Louis XIV. Lang was probably exasperated by its "preachments":

> "I feel that I give involuntarily a darker colour to my life than the truth warrants. When we sit down and reflect we are apt to become the prey of a curious delusion; pain seems to us the only reality, pleasure a phantasm or a dream. Yet such reality as pain his pleasure shares, and we are in no closer touch with eternal truth when we have headaches (or heartaches) than when we are free from these afflictions. I wonder sometimes whether a false idea of dignity does not mislead us. Would we all pose as martyrs? It is nonsense; for most of us life is a tolerable enough business—if we would not think too much about it. We need not pride ourselves on our griefs; it seems as though joy were the higher state because it is the less self-conscious and rests in fuller harmony with the great order that encircles us."

But Lang must have recognised some scenes of fine drama, like the death of old Prince von Hammerfeldt, the statesman and mentor who perhaps owed a little to Mazarin, a little to Metternich, and more to Bismarck and Baron Stockmar:

> "An old man struggling hard for breath; gasps now quicker, now slower, a few words half-formed, choked, unintelligible; eyes that were full of an impotent desire to speak; these came first. Then the doctors gathered round, looked, whispered, went away. I rose and walked twice across the room; coming back I stood and looked at him. Still he knew me. Suddenly his hand moved towards me. I bent my head till my ear was within three inches of his lips; I could hear nothing. I saw a doctor standing by, watch in hand; he was timing the breath that grew slower and slower. 'Will he speak?' I asked in a whisper; a shake of the head answered me. I looked again into his eyes; now he seemed to speak to me. My face grew hot and

red, but I did not speak to him. Yet I stroked his hand, and there was a gleam of understanding in his eyes. A moment later his eyes closed; the gasps became slower and slower. I raised my head and looked across at the doctor. His watch had a gold front protecting the glass; he shut the front on the face with a click."

The King's Mirror was followed in 1900 by another ambitious novel, *Quisanté*, the study of an opportunist adventurer in English politics, whose conception was generally reckoned to have been suggested by Disraeli's career. The tale of his tragedy, and the tragedy of the noble woman he married, represents perhaps Hope's highest achievement; certainly he wrote nothing better afterwards, and none of his books more lucidly reflects the command of language which was Hope's major gift and charm.

The charm of the unscrupulous Quisanté fascinates the reader as it fascinated Lady May Gaston:

"That strange, intolerable, vulgar, attractive, intermittently inspired creature, who presented himself at life's roulette-table, not less various in his own person than were the varying turns he courted, unaccountable as chance, baffling as fate, changeable as luck. Indeed he was like life itself, a thing you loved and hated, grew weary of and embraced, shrank from and pursued. To see him then was in a way to look on at life, to be in contact with him was to feel the throb of its movement. In her midnight musings the man seemed somehow to cease to be odious because he ceased to be individual, to be no longer incomprehensible because he was no longer apart, because he became to her less himself and more the expression and impersonation of an instinct that in her own blood ran riot and held festivity."

Lady May is as good as Quisanté himself, and her sacrifice of herself and her feeling for the decent and worthy Marchmont to the fascination of the brilliant cad, though conscious of his failings and repelled by his vulgarities, affords a subtle study of feminine psychology.

In *The Intrusions of Peggy* (1902) Hope returned to the vein of light social satire, in which he had already scored his greatest success with the *Dolly Dialogues*. These dialogues between Dolly,

Lady Mickleham, a "bright young thing" of the 'nineties, and the man she has jilted were considered as "clever" in their day as the works of Mr. Noel Coward and Mr. Michael Arlen in the nineteen-twenties; they were praised by Meredith, and retain the curiosity to-day of a period piece.

> "'Besides, it's awfully *bourgeois* to go to the theatre with one's husband.'
>
> '*Bourgeois*,' I observed, 'is an epithet which the riff-raff apply to what is respectable, and the aristocracy to what is decent.'
>
> ' But it's not a nice thing to be, all the same,' said Dolly, who is impervious to the most penetrating remark.
>
> ' You're in no danger of it,' I hastened to assure her.
>
> ' How would you describe me, then?' she asked leaning forward, with a smile.
>
> 'I should describe you, Lady Mickleham,' I replied discreetly, ' as being a little lower than the angels.'
>
> Dolly's smile was almost a laugh as she asked—' How much lower, please, Mr. Carter?'
>
> ' Just by the depth of your dimples,' said I thoughtlessly.
>
> Dolly became immensely grave.
>
> ' I thought,' said she, ' that we never mentioned them now, Mr. Carter.'
>
> ' Did we ever?' I asked innocently.
>
> 'I seemed to remember once: do you recollect being in very low spirits one evening at Monte?'"

The success of the dialogues naturally suggested the potentialities of a playwright, and Hope enjoyed several successes on the stage, though several of his novels were adapted for the theatre by other hands.

In the ten years following *The Prisoner of Zenda* in 1894, Hope published sixteen books, besides writing several plays, and his earnings for the period totalled seventy thousand pounds. In addition he was lionised in London society and much courted by fashionable hostesses. The strain of these strenuous years told its tale, and at forty-two he found that he had virtually written himself out. After *Sophy of Kravonia* (1906), a first-rate romance of an adventuress who rises from the situation of a domestic

servant to become queen of a Ruritanian state, obviously
suggested by the career of the Empress Catherine I. of Russia,
Hope published only six novels during the remaining twenty-
seven years of his life. These were all stories of social and
domestic life, except *A Young Man's Year* (1915), in which he drew
upon his own recollections of early days at the bar and in the
theatre for the romance of a young barrister's struggles through
vicissitudes to success. *Mrs. Maxon Protests* (1911), like the earlier
Double Harness, deals with matrimonial problems and preaches
the practical, perhaps cynical, philosophy that contentment and
happiness depend on compromise.

During the war he worked hard on pamphlets in counter-
action against German propaganda, and received a knighthood.
He was "tickled" when he heard a young critic's remark that, if
he was to receive a knighthood, it should have been from Queen
Victoria, but when Haggard died, he wistfully envied that fertile
romancer's retention of his inventive faculty through forty
years. Hope's books in his fruitful years reveal all the equipment
of the accomplished novelist—vivid imagination, shrewd observation, skill in devising plot and character, the sense of drama, an
easy, cultured, and flexible style. Yet when commercial success
had removed the immediate need for pot-boiling and he might
have been expected to produce at leisure the polished work of
maturity, the well of his creative gift unaccountably dried up.
It seems simply that the vital germ of genius was lacking, and
he is to be remembered gratefully as a competent, delightfully
readable craftsman, who produced, besides the famous romances
of Ruritania, two such satisfying novels as *The King's Mirror* and
Quisanté.

§ 3

Ruritania found many imitators, the ten years following
The Prisoner of Zenda witnessing the creation of a whole continent
of imaginary states. Sir William Magnay (1855-1917), a
Hampshire baronet, wrote a good story called *The Red Chancellor*,
telling the adventures of an Englishman in a state somewhere in
east central Europe, ruled over by an intriguing chancellor
endowed with the personality of a Richelieu. Another story of

Magnay's, *The Master-Spirit*, tells of how Paul Gastineau, a barrister as brilliant and unscrupulous as Quisanté, being crippled in a railway accident, allows himself to be thought dead and becomes the secret mentor of a young barrister, helping him to a great career till his *protégé* becomes the favourite suitor of the society beauty whom Gastineau himself had hoped to marry.

Novodnia, on the lower Danube, was the scene of *The Garden of Lies*, an able romance which made the mark of Justus Miles Forman as a popular storyteller. If that voluminous romancer, William Le Queux, never invented an imaginary state, many of his secret-service stories had a Ruritanian colour, and Mr. E. Phillips Oppenheim, who began his prolific output of popular stories in the 'nineties, added at least one item to the imaginary map of Europe by setting most of the action of *The Black Watcher* in Bergeland. Memory does not recall if any Ruritania figured in the works of C. N. and A. M. Williamson, who wrote probably the first romance of motor-car travel in *The Princess Passes*, and whose husband-and-wife collaboration inevitably calls to mind two other pairs of collaborators, Alice and Claude Askew and Agnes and Egerton Castle. The Castles wrote some historical romances—one was called *Incomparable Bellairs*; the Askews specialised in sensational tales of society. Their books are now even more utterly lost in the basements of second-hand book-sellers than those of such minor writers of a former generation as Florence Marryatt, Percy Fitzgerald, and George Augustus Sala, but their sevenpenny editions offered entertainment on every railway station boasting a bookstall in 1914.

One of the best writers of popular romance who created a Ruritania was Guy Boothby (1867-1905), who wrote a tale of adventure and intrigue in an imaginary South American republic called *A Maker of Nations*, an able story combining something of Merriman's manner—his Spielman is a cosmopolitan in the mould of Merriman's Steinmetz and Paul Deulin—with the more obvious debt to *The Prisoner of Zenda*. Boothby was an Australian, who personally courted adventure in his unfortunately short life, penetrating the Australian bush to cross the continent from north to south in 1891 and travelling widely in the East. In seven years between 1894 and 1901 he published no fewer than twenty-three books, many of which enjoyed great popularity and maintained big sales in the old sevenpenny reprints till the war in 1914. His best known books were *A Bid for Fortune* and *Dr. Nikola*, which had several sequels like *Dr. Nikola's Experiment* and *Farewell Nikola*, all relating the daring adventures of a megalomaniac scientist thirsting for knowledge and power, and incorporating much of Boothby's intimate knowledge of the East. *The Kidnapped President* was another romance of an imaginary South American republic, but his best Ruritanian essay was *The Fascination of the King*, the story of a white man who made himself the sovereign of a state in the Malay peninsular—a fiction suggested by fact, as an adventurer named de Mayrena actually established himself as king of a province in Annam during the late 'eighties, and was for some time recognised by the French government.

Boothby wrote a good story in a bald, clipped style, which has the merits of simplicity and swiftness, but a much better writer was E. W. Hornung (1866-1921), who provides one of the most inexplicable omissions from the *Dictionary of National Biography*. On leaving Uppingham, he spent three years in Australia, but returned to take up a journalistic career and published his first novel, *A Bride from the Bush*, in 1890. He wrote several Australian stories, one of the most successful of which, *Stingaree*, he adapted for the stage, and competently attempted the romance with a problem in books like *Peccavi* (1900), but his name is inevitably associated, like Conan Doyle's with Sherlock Holmes, with his creation of Raffles, the debonair gentleman-burglar whose adventures are related in *The Amateur Cracksman*, *The Black Mask*, *Mr. Justice Raffles*, and *A Thief in the Night*.

When Hornung died, Anthony Hope wondered if he had ever realised "what a low scoundrel his Raffles was." A scoundrel he was, and a cad, too, not only in his graceless habit of accepting country-house hospitality to steal the valuables of fellow-guests, but in his luring of his friend and biographer into the career of an accomplice. But Raffles was not low; he never invites contempt, like Casanova or Cellini or Mr. Meyerstein's *Terence Duke*, but remains ever the most winning of rascals, such as have wrought havoc with the hearts of women since the beginning of time, though Raffles has nothing of the bounder about him like most men successful with women, but, on the contrary, possesses the graces of a prince of good fellows, ever welcomed with a glad hand in club or tavern. We are sad at the wanton sacrifice of his brilliant gifts, sadder still when he becomes an outcast from society as a result of his crimes, causing his exile from his rooms in the Albany and his cricketing triumphs at Lord's—when he has to resort to disguises and live, hunted, as a pretended invalid or in lodgings on Ham Common. With his subtlety and resource, what a bowler he must have been! Never does he lose our sympathy and admiration, for he has the irresistible charm of genius, and when he commits his meanest crime by deluding poor Bunny into helping him to rob the house of his former fiancée, the reader echoes the feelings expressed by Bunny in deciding that, even though he had been tricked into the sacrifice of love and honour, he could not desert his friend.

"It was Raffles I loved. It was not the dark life we led together, still less its base rewards; it was the man himself, his gaiety, his humour, his dazzling audacity, his incomparable courage and resource."

Like Sherlock Holmes, Raffles was killed and brought to life again; his second death, on a field of battle in the Boer War, was so fitting that Hornung did not again revive him, but resorted in later books to his biographer's reminiscences of earlier exploits.

CHAPTER NINE

Best Sellers: Hall Caine and Others

§ 1

SYMONS'S definition of symbolism, "a representation which does not aim at being a reproduction," could easily be distorted into Haggard's working axiom that impossibility does not matter, "provided it is made to appear possible." George Moore's pro-Zola campaign in the 'eighties, and the trend of Hardy's work, suggested an imminent adoption of realism in fiction, but the banning of Zola placed realism definitely beyond the pale of respectability, and while the success of *Esther Waters* in 1894 raised its stock, the market fell again with the reception of *Jude the Obscure* in 1896. In the 'nineties, realistic fiction was written only by young and new writers, by Hubert Crackanthorpe in his brilliant and important books of short stories, *Wreckage* and *Sentimental Studies*, by Somerset Maugham in *Liza of Lambeth*, and by Arthur Morrison in *Tales of Mean Streets*. Besides Hardy, Gissing was almost alone among the older writers, and his novels were not best-sellers. The older generation, and the majority of their juniors, made a compromise on the lines of Haggard's theory of romance—they approached reality and real problems, but escaped into improbability to avoid offence.

Of these novelists Hall Caine was the most phenomenally successful. Ford Madox Hueffer wrote of George Eliot that, "taking herself with an enormous seriousness, she dilated upon sin and its results, and so found the easy success of the popular preacher who deals in horror." The description fits Hall Caine like a glove; he was a master of melodrama with a moral. He saw that the public fed greedily on the sorrows and horrors which Lang lamented to see the daily delight of sensational newspapers; he saw that Hardy, like Reade before him, was execrated for treating such sorrows and horrors with the sympathy of a constructive artist, revealing, not the bare narrative of facts as in a press report, but the sequence of causes leading to tragedies. But he also saw that respectability forgave much in the interests of morality; topics unmentionable in ordinary conversation might be treated freely from a pulpit with a biblical text. He realised the affinity of the novel of moral purpose to the biblical parable, and knowing the popular partiality for taking the medicine of instruction in pills coated with the sugar of entertainment, saw how he might win the public of the sensational newspapers by serving up horrors with morals.

He began with George Eliot as his model, for he relates his despair on reading aloud a chapter of his first novel after the Rainbow scene in *Silas Marner*; certainly he took himself as seriously. He was born on the 14th May, 1853, the eldest son of a Manxman settled at Liverpool "in a humble way of life." Much of his boyhood was spent with his uncle and grandmother at their farmstead in the Isle of Man, and in the opening chapter of *My Story*, he sketches the peasant life of the island, because "it records in its homely way the birth of what the public has been pleased to call the Manx novelist." It supplies the atmosphere of most of his novels; few of the peasants could read or write, their religion was the narrowest Methodism strongly flavoured with the superstition of old wives' tales, family feuds were rife and the craze for litigation was such that two brothers would "'put the law' on each other about a coil of rope," "drink was the besetting evil," and it was the custom for courting to be done in the kitchen at night after the elder members of the family had gone to bed, the result being a generous crop of bastards, though a mother of a family might legitimatise her child if she married its father "within a year or two," and hid her baby under her petticoat while she stood before the officiating cleric.

A delicate, under-sized boy, Caine went to school "for the most part" at Liverpool, and read everything he could lay hands on, "without guidance of any kind," at the city's free library. He early developed the "scribbling itch", writing mostly "histories whereof facts were not always the principal factors," and he found a schoolfellow of the same tastes in W. E. Tirebuck (1854-1900), whose *Dorrie* (1891), describing life in the squalid surroundings he himself knew in Liverpool, was praised by Lang and has fallen with others of his later novels, like *Miss Grace of All Souls* and *'Twixt God and Mammon*, into undeserved neglect, for Tirebuck, if uncouth of structure and style, wrote with a crude power well suited to the gloom of his backgrounds. Leaving school early, Caine was articled to an architect, but "at the first hint of one of the nervous attacks which even then beset me," he ran away from the office to the Isle of Man, where for a year he earned his keep as a schoolmaster and contributed gratuitous articles on Christian Socialism to the local press. Returning to the Liverpool architect, he wrote articles in imitation of Ruskin for the *Builder* and the *Building News*, paid his first visit to London at the invitation of the editor of the *Builder*, changed his job to become the clerk to a builder, and made some literary friends locally, among them William Watson. The publication of Rossetti's *Poems* in 1870 had inspired him with passionate admiration, which found fruit after eight years in a lecture on Rossetti at the Liverpool Free Library. The lecture being printed, he sent a copy to Rossetti, who wrote him a letter of thanks and asked him to call on him when in London.

In common courtesy Rossetti could have done little less, but to the little provincial clerk, full of literary aspirations and bravely struggling to educate himself in an adverse environment, the celebrity's friendly gesture seemed an overwhelming gift of grace. He expressed his gratitude so fervently that Rossetti wrote again, and to Caine's delight, who did not know that the poet was a drug victim and found a distraction from moods of morbid brooding in writing to the unknown admirer who so ardently appreciated his letters, the correspondence continued. It was a year before the clerk could find an opportunity of going to London, but in the autumn of 1880, he called on his way to a fortnight's holiday on the south coast, and impressed Rossetti favourably enough to be invited to stay the night on his way home from his holiday. Whether he was prompted by the drug addict's desire to insure secrecy, since Hall Caine that night discovered his bondage to chloral, or by the feeling that this little admirer would alleviate his loneliness without intruding upon his desire for solitude, Rossetti suggested that, if he decided to settle in London, Caine should live with him. The young clerk laughed at what seemed "the remotest contingency," but the suggestion naturally remained in his mind, as a dazzling possibility, on his return to the Liverpool office.

My Story tells how Caine's health broke down during the following year, and he decided to give up his clerkship and "to sink or swim in an effort to live by my pen." He admits that he had no literary connections "safe for sixpence," and found it "amusing to me to remember" that, when he announced his intentions to Rossetti, "it was he—he who had predicted such certain success for me—that was thrown into a state of the greatest alarm." It seems fair to suppose that the clerk would not have thrown up his modest livelihood for the bare chance of picking up some journalistic work, unless he had been sure that the poet would feel in honour bound to offer an asylum, and that he persevered confidently with his project when Rossetti evinced dismay at the possibility of being forced into fulfilment of his rash invitation. Anyhow, the events fell out as well as Caine could have hoped; as soon as Rossetti found that the young man had thrown up his job, and was installed in a Cumberland cottage, prepared to subsist "on oatmeal porridge and barley bread," he resigned himself to the consequences of his rashness and invited Caine to live with him.

Rossetti was in poor health and low spirits; in the letter saying that he was "getting the rooms cleared out" for Caine's reception, he confessed to worry over "having become perfectly deaf on the right side of his head." He was in need of somebody on whom he could depend, for attendance to practical necessities of daily routine and for companionship when he wanted it. A man like Watts-Dunton, who wanted to be his male nurse and guardian as he was afterwards Swinburne's, was a nuisance about the house, interfering with his privacy and habits, but Hall Caine, so much his junior, a social inferior, dependent on his hospitality, a hero-worshipper, prepared to listen in awe to his utterances, to defer to his whims, and to learn as an adoring pupil, might be the domestic attendant exactly suited to his needs.

The task of attending a drug victim during his last months of life was fraught with anxieties and sadness, but it did not last long. Caine came to Rossetti's house in August, 1881, and

Rossetti died in the following April. Immediately after his benefactor's death, with true journalistic opportunism, Hall Caine published his *Recollections of Rossetti*, creating a pleasant fluttering in the drawing-rooms by the revelations of Rossetti's sufferings under the fell habit of chloral; Miss Violet Hunt vividly remembers Watts-Dunton's vexation when Caine forestalled him in "fingering the bloom off Gabriel." The little ex-clerk also established his first remunerative journalistic connection by making copy out of one of Rossetti's friends, William Bell Scott, an article on whom he sent to the *Liverpool Mercury*, which promptly invited him to join its staff as an "outside contributor" at a hundred pounds a year. *My Story* naïvely reflects upon this "extraordinary proposal", and how "in the sequel it proved both the generosity and the practical wisdom of the man who made it," but it is not surprising that a provincial newspaper was willing to secure so cheaply first call on the services of the cuckoo in the nest of the Pre-Raphaelites, who had first-rate "news" value. Nor is it remarkable that, "after the first six months of our informal relation"—after, in fact, the revelations about Rossetti—the *Liverpool Mercury*, having "not anticipated that you would do so much for the paper," increased his "honorarium" to a hundred and fifty pounds.

He became "our London correspondent" of the Liverpool paper, reviewing books, attending theatrical first nights, and making a speciality of obituary notices. He lived in two rooms at Clement's Inn, acquiring "some knowledge of life" and "a genuine love of humanity." He picked up further odds and ends of work, writing occasional reviews for the *Academy* and *Athenæum*, and acquiring some reading from a publisher, and after two years decided to try his hand at fiction. His account of his beginning illustrates the method which served throughout his career.

"When I began to think of a theme I found four or five subjects clamouring for acceptance. There was the story of the Prodigal Son, which afterwards became 'The Deemster'; the story of Jacob and Esau, which in the same way turned into 'The Bondman'; the story of Samuel and Eli, which after a fashion moulded itself finally into 'The Scapegoat'; as well as half-a-dozen other stories, chiefly Bibli~al, which have since been written, or are still on the forehead of the time to come."

For the plot of his first novel, *The Shadow of a Crime* (1885), he took a legend of Cumberland, his mother's county, on which he grafted a piece of lore taken from Blackstone at second-hand, and endowed the hero with the consciousness that "God's hand was upon him." He sold the book to Chatto and Windus for seventy-five pounds, and "fared only a little better" with *A Son of Hagar* in the following year, but *The Deemster*, his first Manx story, though he received by it only "one hundred and fifty pounds in all," laid the foundation of his success, partly owing to its stage production by Wilson Barrett.

In the dramatisation of *The Deemster* appeared the first distinctive sign, apart from his capitalisation of Rossetti, of the commercial shrewdness which enabled the little Liverpool clerk to die worth a quarter of a million sterling, the richest author in the history of English letters. He saw how hack dramatists seized upon the plots of novels for stage purposes, and like Charles Reade before him, decided to exploit this profitable field on his own account. He chose Wilson Barrett, a fine actor with a fine presence, as the most popular player of melodrama, and secured his promise to produce a stage version of his novel. To render it difficult for Barrett to back out of his bargain, he dedicated the novel to him in laudatory terms, and finally on the eve of production, "insisted on coupling Barrett's name" with his as part-author of the adaptation. To what extent Barrett collaborated, Caine found it "unnecessary to say," except to acknowledge his debt to the actor's "knowledge of the 'ropes' of the theatre," but Caine shrewdly foresaw that the association of Barrett's name—which, though not yet famous for *The Sign of the Cross*, had appeared in successful collaboration with Henry Arthur Jones's—would insure respectful consideration from dramatic critics.

The Deemster was not a remarkable success on the stage, but it provided good publicity for *The Bondman*, which was published by Heinemann in 1890 on royalty terms and began the accumulation of its author's la ge fortune. *The Scapegoat*, relating the trials and troubles of Israel Ben Oliel and sentimentalising the Hebrew's ostracism, followed in 1891, and presumably inspired an invitation from the Russo-Jewish authorities to visit the scenes of Jewish persecution in Poland, the first of much travelling to provide useful publicity for his books. He became noted as the most able publicist of his own work in his time. If he did not invent, he was among the first to practise, the fashion of sending advance copies of books to celebrities for the purpose of obtaining quotable praise for publishers' advertisements. The lists of quotations advertising *The Bondman* and *The Scapegoat* were headed by the applause of Mr. Gladstone, who had been Hall Caine's hero since early Liverpool days, when he found his architect-employer was a distant relative of Gladstone's.

Caine kept his name regularly before the public by writing to the press, and he became active in the interests of the Authors' Society, visiting Canada to conclude an agreement on Canadian copyright in 1895. In *Who's Who* he claimed to have "had a good deal to do, 1894, with breakdown of three-volume novel," and no doubt he did figure prominently at the official obsequies of the old-fashioned guinea-and-a-half format, which had fought a losing battle for ten years against the increasing imitation of Henry Vizetelly's original six-shilling venture. After the publication of *The Manxman* in 1894 and his accession to affluence, he established himself at Greeba Castle on the Isle of Man— thereby achieving permanent advertisement as the author who lived in a castle—gained election to the House of Keys, and secured identification as the national Manx novelist, a sort of local Walter Scott. He became one of the sights to be seen by holiday-makers, who bought his books along with a touring-map on arrival at Douglas, as they buy *Lorna Doone* and Whyte-Melville's *Katerfelto* in North Devon and the works of Words-worth and Sir Hugh Walpole at the Lakes. Local guides showed impressed tourists actual scenes described in the novels, and there were not wanting local romancers of picturesque imagination who professed to have been personally acquainted with the prototypes of Caine's characters, one native of Ballure actually making a lucrative business in selling photographs of himself as the original of Pete Quilliam in *The Manxman*.

Arnold Bennett remarked in 1908 that "it was the commercial genius of Mr. Hall Caine that invented the idea of publishing important novels during the 'off' season." Caine did not produce much—he lacked invention, the same set of characters repeatedly reappearing to struggle with slightly dissimilar awful destinies—and there was an interval of at least two or three years between all his novels after *The Scapegoat*, but he engineered the production of each with an eye to every possible means of publicity and profit. The theatre was purely a medium for publicity in his hands, for his dramatic talent consisted in dressing the crudest melodrama with what William Archer called "sanctimonious claptrap"; he made a practice of producing a stage adaptation of a novel a few months after its book publication, so stimulating the book sales just as they were beginning to flag after the end of their season. In several cases he used more than one version of the same book; *The Manxman* was first adapted in collaboration with Barrett, then Barrett twice produced a version of his own, in 1908 Caine collaborated with Louis N. Parker in a version called *Pete*, and two years later produced a fourth version unassisted called *The Bishop's Son*, while both *The Christian* and *The Eternal City* enjoyed at least two different adaptations. His shrewdness extended to his choice of actors, for if Barrett was the master of melodrama in the 'nineties, Tree, who produced *The Eternal City* at His Majesty's in 1902, was supreme in the same field for fifteen years before the European War. With the advent of the film industry, Caine was quick to recognise its commercial value, and Miss Pauline Frederick's appearance in *The Eternal City* about the middle of the war years was the most elaborate achievement of Hollywood up to that time.

During the war, Caine was active in public service. As editor of *King Albert's Book*, which was sold in aid of the Belgian relief fund and included contributions from all the leading writers of the day, from Galsworthy, Bennett, and Hardy, to Marie Corelli, Baroness Orczy, and Ella Wheeler Wilcox, he received the Order of Leopold for the work. He was in the forefront of other similar schemes of patriotic work, did much propaganda in America, and received one of the many knighthoods awarded at the end of the war. His vogue began to fade with the rise of the post-war generation, which bitter experience had robbed of too many illusions for sentimentalism to be patiently received. Probably his shrewd commercial instinct realised that his harvest was over, for he soon abandoned the effort to sustain his sequence of novels —an effort obviously doomed to failure, for the fount of his scant invention had finally dried up. *The Master of Man*, a serial in *Nash's Magazine* before book publication in 1921, was merely a variation of the theme of *The Manxman*, and *The Woman of Knockaloe* a sermon in extravagant sentimentality on the falling in love between a Manx woman and a German prisoner of war.

Even in his heyday, Hall Caine was never taken seriously by the intelligent public; Ford Madox Hueffer spoke of the publisher's "purple blush of shame" for "having poured innumerable copies of Mr. Caine's work upon the world," and when, in 1909, Arnold Bennett protested against the banning of books by Mudie on moral grounds, he quoted a correspondent who pointed out that Mudie had no more right to sit in judgment on the moral welfare of subscribers than subscribers to complain of the general tommy-rot issued by Mudie, but "if Mudie came along with a pistol and two volumes of Hall Caine, and said to me, ' Look here, I'll make you have these,' then perhaps I might begin to murmur gently." But for twenty years, he was the biggest seller among popular novelists, and his amazing career provides an illuminating comment on the spacious days preceding 1914.

Hall Caine was not a humbug; the turgid mixture of narrow Nonconformity and picturesque superstition treacling his novels was the crude religion in which he had been bred, and its faithful reflection represents his nearest approximation to art.   His talents were those of the sensational newspaper reporter, his appeal was that of the press report of a murder trial—he exaggerated everything in terms of melodrama and sentimentality.   All his novels were tarred with the same glutinous mixture; his public always knew what it was getting. His most characteristic books were those laid in the setting of the Isle of Man, where his knowledge of his background screened his poverty of characterisation; he was less comfortable when he ventured into other fields.   In *The Eternal City*, for instance, he elected to write about Rome, where he spent several winters in his first years of affluence, evidently intending a romance on the mediaeval story of Rienzi set in the age after Garibaldi. Apparently he read Bulwer's *Rienzi* beforehand, for his principal characters are cast in the same mould, Bruno Rocco is an almost literal copy of Cecco del Vecchio, Roma is Nina Raselli without her nobility and natural womanliness, and Rossi appears a lacklustre Rienzi, mouthing to modern audiences trite revolutionary doctrines which read like mediaeval survivals.

The Manxman was his most celebrated and probably the most successful of his novels. It begins with Caine's usual preamble about the parentage of his characters: Thomas, the elder son of old Deemster Christian, was disinherited for defying his father to marry a peasant girl; the wicked younger son had a bastard by another peasant girl, but married respectably and inherited the family estate. Pete Quilliam, the bastard, brought up a peasant, plights his troth with pretty Kate Cregeen before going to seek his fortune in South Africa, leaving his girl to the care of his cousin and boyhood friend, Philip Christian, son of Thomas. Philip falls in love with Kate and she with him, and when Pete is reported dead, he seduces her—or rather, she seduces him, for he is an insufferable prig incapable of initiative. Philip has been brought up by a maiden aunt, who holds perpetually before him the danger of marrying beneath him and incurring the sad fate of his father, so he is very sorry for himself after the seduction. But Pete, of course, is not dead, but returns home with worldly wealth sufficient to warrant matrimony, and Philip, who is a brilliantly successful young man and about to become Deemster, allows him to marry his mistress. The agony is then piled on with the morbid gloating on which Caine's huge public glutted its greedy sadistic appetite. "The more Kate realised that she was in the position of a bad woman, the more she struggled to be a good one ;" the hapless Pete dotes on her and on the baby which he believes his, but is, of course, the prig's, for Caine's women are always quick to conceive—Bessie Collister, in *The Master of Man*, only forgot her moral carriage on one occasion, and so apparently did Kate. After an orgy of anguish, Kate asks Philip to take her away from her husband, which the prig feels it his duty to do, though "the honour in which he had tried to stand erect as in a suit of armour was stripped away," and "he was an abandoned hulk, with anchorage gone and no hand at the helm—broken, blind, rolling to destruction."

It is not surprising that Kate eventually fled from the protection of "the hulk", who must have been poor company, but it is odd that she should have been able to live with a personage so distinguished as the Deemster as his housekeeper, without exciting gossip and incurring discovery of her identity. Such improbabilities were overlooked for the delight of wallowing in anguish. Kate is absent for six months without a penny in her pocket; she is an ignorant peasant girl, with no asset save physical beauty, but though she "descended to the depths of poverty and privations," she had not "lived a life of shame." We are not told the means of her subsistence, but we must not be allowed to suppose that she took the only obvious course in those days of Victorian respectability, for Kate had to retain the reader's sympathy, and respectability forbade sympathy with females of Magdalene's profession. After many chapters of maudlin pathos over Pete's pretence to the outside world that his defaulting wife had gone on a holiday, the end is reached, as in all Caine's homilies, in the righteous expiation of the errant hero, who renounces his honours, avows his perfidy, and goes forth, his arm about the melting partner of his guilt, "like a man trans-figured."

> "The extreme pallor of his cheeks was gone, his step was firm, and his face was radiant. It was the common remark that never before had he looked so strong, so buoyant, so noble. This was the hour of his triumph, not that within the walls: this, when his sin was confessed, when conscience had no power to appal him, when the world and the pride of the world were beneath his feet, and he was going forth from a prison cell, hand in hand with the fallen woman by his side, to face the future with their bankrupt lives."

The rest of his novels follow the same pattern, except that there is frequently some blood and murder to enhance the sum of horror. In all there is the same concentrated monotony of morbid gloom, sentimentality, and sanctimony, unrelieved by the vaguest suggestion of a smile, for Hall Caine lacked the faintest spark of humour, a defect which materially contributed to his success, for a sense of humour would have mitigated the sublime belief in his own powers and the value of his work which verged on megalomania. The difficulty of stomaching the absurdities of his stories is intensified by his style, which his admirers conceived to have the simplicity of Biblical English.

> "Grannie saw nothing of Philip that night. He went home tingling with pleasure, and yet overwhelmed with shame. Sometimes he told himself that he was no better than a Judas, and sometimes that Pete might never come back. The second thought rose oftenest. It crossed his mind like a ghostly gleam. He half wished to believe it. When he counted up the odds against Pete's return, his pulse beat quick. Then he hated himself. He was in torment. But under his distracted heart there was a little chick of frightened joy, like a young cuckoo hatched in a wagtail's nest."

It is even worse when he embarks on his notion of fine writing:

> "The winter was cold and the ground was white, but two roses of love still grew in the garden of God. The frost could not freeze the two roses of love, for they were warmed by the air of heaven; the sun could not scorch the two roses of love, for they were watered from the wells of life. Two roses of love on a single stem; two roses of love in two fond young hearts, two roses of love and joy!"

The *Yellow Book* made play with the cautious "curtain" to the scene in *The Manxman* where the prig "knew that hell was in his heart. . . . The moon had come up in her whiteness behind, and all was quiet and solemn around. Philip fell back and turned away his face." The reviewer in the *Yellow Book* likewise fell back and turned away his face; though he had negotiated only 41 of the book's 439 pages, "it was the final, the crushing, blow," and he gave the volume to his valet. The *Yellow Book* reviewer wrote in October, 1895, but while we salute the little Liverpool clerk's achievement of a castle of his own, a huge public for his lucubrations, and a huge fortune from his pen's hectic perspiration, the verdict on his novels must still remain the same:

> "Their artificial simplicity, their clumsiness, their heaviness, their dreary counterfeit of a kind of common humour, their laborious strivings for a kind of shoddy pathos, their ignorance, their vulgarity, their pretentiousness, and withal their un-mitigated insipidity—these are the qualities, no doubt, that make them popular with the middle classes, that endear them to the Great Heart of the People, but they are too much for the likes o' me. I don't mind vulgarity when I can get it with a dash of spice, as in the writings of Mr. Ally Sloper, or with a swagger, as in the writings of Mr. Frank Harris. I don't mind insipidity when I can get it with a touch of cosmopolitan culture, as in the writings of Mr. Karl Baedeker. But vulgarity and insipidity mingled, as in the writings of Mr. Hall Caine, are more than my weak flesh can bear."

§ 2

In the first years of the twentieth century, as Mr. Grant Richards notes from knowledge of actual sales, "Hall Caine and Marie Corelli had the largest figures after their names." Marie Corelli (1855-1924) was somewhat unjustly satirised as Caine's female *Fidus Achates* in popular fiction, a legend originating in Lang's gibe at *The Master Christian* (1900) as the "apocalypse which combines the titles of Mr. Zangwill's *The Master* and Mr. Caine's *The Christian*, as if one should call a book *The Bride of Ivanhoe*." By the choice of this title and *God's Good Man* (1904), following Caine's novel, she fostered the charge that she imitated or emulated Hall Caine, but while she shared his exaggeration, sentimentality, and religiosity, her only other similarities lay in catering for the same huge public, and the megalomania which assessed her facility and trashy talent as inspired genius. Her work falls into the same category as Caine's in having been written for the same public, in wearing the motley of absurdity, and in enjoying the cheap and ephemeral popularity of a patent medicine, but she was a better writer than

Caine, because her education rendered her incapable of the same ingenuous crudity.

She was the daughter of Charles Mackay, a well-known Victorian journalist who attained popular celebrity as author of the songs, "Cheer, Boys, Cheer," and "There's a Good Time Coming," by an English lady who became his second wife, but her egotism played upon her romantic imagination to surround her birth with mystery, and she described herself as Mackay's adopted daughter, "of mingled Italian and Scotch (Highland) parentage." Her sole Italian attribute was her pseudonym, which she adopted, according to the convention that music is as native to Italy as dancing to Russia, when her father designed her for a musical career. Her first writings appeared in 1883 under this name in Clement Scott's magazine, *The Theatre*, and included characteristically extravagant eulogies of Wagner, the violinists Joachim and Sarasate, and the 'cellist Hollman, with "his big friend." In *Who's Who* she related in those terms of egregious vanity which made her a target for jest:

> "A curious psychical experience occurring to herself personally, caused her to write her first book, *A Romance of Two Worlds*, published in 1886. It was an instant success, and from that time she devoted herself entirely to literature. She has never, however, abandoned her love of music, and is a proficient on the piano and mandolin."

A Romance of Two Worlds, a fantastic tale elaborating the theory of "the Electric Origin of the Universe," with a spiritual descendant of Cagliostro, professing descent from the New Testament "wise men of the east," for hero, struck a loud chord of appeal to women of the upper and middle classes, who were trying to reconcile the unsettling doctrines of science with the conventional platitudes of the churches. It reveals Marie Corelli as an apt pupil of Ouida, to whose career, in the garish tinsel of its pretentiousness, its dramatised vanity, and the pathos of its absurdity, her own bore marked features of resemblance. She had at first a similar taste in titles, her next three novels being *Vendetta*, *Thelma*, and *Ardath*, but in her passionate sincerity as a novelist of purpose, she imitated Charles Reade and Wilkie

Collins in their use of preface and appendix, pointing the moral and documenting the facts on which the fiction was based. As early as 1887, she added in a new edition of *A Romance of Two Worlds*, not only a preface asserting the basis of her faith to be that "sacred little book," the New Testament, but an appendix of letters from readers thanking her for "the wonderful change your book has wrought in my life," and so forth. Like Hall Caine, she was innocent of any sense of humour, and accepting the most ridiculous protestations as tributes to her achievements, she speedily developed an obsession that she was a missionary of divine inspiration, and lost all sense of proportion in the swelling exuberance of her extravagance. In her fifth novel, *Wormwood* (1891), a lurid diatribe against the absinthe habit, suggesting in its extravagance a country spinster's hysterical nightmare after reading Zola's *L'Assommoir*, she ascribed "the open atheism, heartlessness, flippancy, and flagrant immorality of the whole modern French school of thought" to "the reckless absinthe-mania, which pervades all classes, rich and poor alike." Naïvely she asked her readers to "refrain from setting down my hero's opinions on men and things to *me* personally," and forestalled any possible aspersions on her maidenly respectability by declaring that "for the description of the low-class *bal masqué* in Paris I am in a great measure indebted to a very respectable-looking English tourist," whose conversation she overheard on a steamer. She was as unconscious of the possible inaccuracy of such second-hand information, as of the real artist's instinct to write of nothing outside his own experience and observation; she boasted, for instance, of having written the ecstatic descriptions of Norwegian scenery in *Thelma* without having herself previously visited Norway, regarding the feat as evidence of her vivid imagination and unaware that such accomplishment forms an indispensable item in the equipment of every descriptive reporter in Fleet Street.

Over Hall Caine she possessed the advantages of a superior fluency of language, greater fertility, wider invention, ready facility, and of coming closer to the realities of life, as in *The Sorrows of Satan*, where there emerges amongst the hysterical confusion of melodrama and false values some genuine satire on the vices of the society, and in *The Master Christian*, which possessed the sincere motive reflected in its dedication "to all those Churches who quarrel in the Name of Christ." But as the ridiculous vanity of her prefaces alienated sympathy from such courage as she showed in her gesture of contempt for criticism, when prohibiting the issue of review copies of *The Sorrows of Satan*, so the shrieking hysteria of treatment overwhelmed the slight merits of her novels.

"Shaken by tearless sobs of mortal agony, I gazed distractedly upon that maiden image of sweet wisdom and repose; the loose gold hair, unbound to its full rippling length, caught flickers from the sunlight through the window-pane— the fringed white eyelids, fast closed in eternal sleep, were delicately indented as though some angel's fingertips had pressed them down caressingly—the waxen hands were folded meekly across the bosom, where a knot of virgin lilies wept out fragrance in lieu of tears. Dead—dead! Why had Death taken her?—why had God wanted her—God, who has so many saints—why could He not have spared her to the earth which has so few? Dead!—and with her had died my last hope of good—my last chance of rescue! And I buried my head again among the odorous funeral flowers and wept as I had never wept before—as I shall never have sufficient heart or conscience in me to weep again!"

This passage from *Wormwood* is not an isolated example of overstrained effect in a dramatic crisis; it fairly sounds the shrill note of hysteria in which the general tone of her narratives is pitched. Arnold Bennett's witticism that "if Joseph Conrad is one Pole, Marie Corelli is surely the other," epitomises the critical derision which heralded the advent of all her novels, yet she shared with Hall Caine the biggest sales among novelists for two decades. That even the devastating weapons of ridicule failed to dissipate her popularity provides the most damning comment on the taste of the Edwardian reading public. Her vogue, like Hall Caine's, petered out in the war years, when she suffered prosecution for food-hoarding, which, in the overwrought days of war-time prejudice, brought upon her much undeserved odium, for in private life she was a generous little rotundity of good nature, who conferred many benefits on Stratford-on-Avon, where she lived for the last twenty-three years of her life, flattering her vanity with the thought that her residence must be a shrine for tourists second only to Anne Hathaway's cottage.

§ 3

The novels of Mrs. Humphry Ward (1851-1920) occasioned only less stupendous sales and critical derision than the novels of Hall Caine and Marie Corelli. The publication in 1908 of *The Testing of Diana Mallory* drew from Arnold Bennett a gem among his "Jacob Tonson" articles in the *New Age*.

"Mrs. Humphry Ward's novels are praiseworthy as being sincerely and skilfully done, but they are not works of art. They are probably the best stuff now being swallowed by the uneducated public; and they deal with the governing classes; and when you have said that you have said all. Nothing truly serious can happen in them. It is all make-believe. No real danger of the truth about life! . . . Mrs. Humphry Ward has never got nearer to life than, for instance, 'Rita' has got —nor so near! Gladstone, a thoroughly bad judge of literature, made her reputation, and not on a post-card, either! Gladstone had no sense of humour—at any rate when he ventured into literature. Nor has Mrs. Humphry Ward."

Mrs. Ward was a painfully earnest woman. She was born the grand-daughter of Thomas Arnold of Rugby, the niece of Matthew Arnold, and she never recovered. She wore blue stockings almost from babyhood, going early to the Ambleside school of Miss Anne Clough, an early feminist and first head of Newnham, where she daily absorbed the atmosphere till lately breathed by Wordsworth, and at fourteen she would feel faint with gladness at the news of her father's reversion from Roman Catholicism and make notes in her diary on hearing "a droll sermon on Convictional Sin." She found her appropriate atmosphere when her father became an Oxford don in 1865, for she ever exuded the camphorated culture of the Banbury Road. At fourteen, she seemed seventeen, and hung eagerly on the jewelled words of Jowett and Mark Pattison when having lunch or tea with them, and Mandell Creighton, and that Bywater who edited the *Poetics*. When she was eighteen, she met George Eliot and "realised at last that I was in the presence of a great writer," but "not a great *talker*." The same year she had a story rejected by Smith, Elder, and thanked them for doing so, as it was "a juvenile production" and "I should probably have been ashamed of it by and by," but her "joy and pride were unbounded" when she had another story accepted by the *Churchman's Companion*, a journal edited by Miss Charlotte M. Yonge. At twenty she wrote "a little essay", apostrophising the delights of "A Morning in the Bodleian", which "became to me a living and inspiring presence"; she must have been among the first of those diligent, earnest females who crowd the Old Reading Room to pore over books which they might buy from a bookseller for sixpence, and consequently limit the activities of genuine research to the comparative peace of the Long Vacation.

At twenty-one she married the Brasenose don whose name she was to endow with celebrity, and in the intervals between bearing three children, she contributed to the *Saturday Review* and fraternised with the notables of the Oxford society, which was shocked by Pater's "paganizing tendencies" and fluttered by his Morris wallpapers and blue china. She was "all on fire for women's education," became first secretary of Somerville Hall, and invited Millicent Garrett Fawcett to lecture at Oxford, though her own ideas were insufficiently advanced to venture on the revolutionary advocacy of female suffrage. She also met Ernest Renan, who influenced her probably more than her researches for articles contributed to the *Dictionary of Christian Biography*, to which she ascribes her interest in the roots of religion—the "*sources—testimony*" which existed before generations of divines had obscured its message in twisted skeins of different interpretations and dogma. One of her sisters married Leonard Huxley, and she was thus brought into close touch with the most formidable enemy of the superstitious elements in church ritual.

When John Morley became editor of *Macmillan's Magazine* in 1883, he invited Mrs. Ward to be the "Sainte-Beuve" of the magazine, and for two years she contributed critical articles.

Her first novel, *Miss Bretherton*, suggested by lovely Mary Anderson's recent success on the stage, appeared in 1884, and won her a letter of encouragement from Henry James. A year later came her translation of Amiel's *Journal Intime*, the philosophy of which she incorporated in the character of Langham in *Robert Elsmere*, her most famous book, published in 1888. *Robert Elsmere*, like most of Mrs. Ward's subsequent novels, may be reckoned a novel of moral purpose, but it is rather a thesis thinly larded with fiction. The characters are vehicles of various views on contemporary religious controversy; Mrs. Ward subsequently declared that many of the characters were drawn from her acquaintance, but they rather embodied the ideas of their proto-types, the Squire representing the scholarly scepticism of Mark Pattison, Henry Grey the idealistic philosophy of Thomas Hill Green, and so on, with Elsmere the advocate of Mrs. Ward's considered view of Christianity, largely adopted from her uncle Matthew Arnold's *Literature and Dogma*, rejecting all the superstitious and miraculous and relying on the facts of historical "testimony". It was a tract for the times, when the upper and middle classes were uneasily seeking to reconcile the subversive doctrines of the scientists with the conglomeration of romance and didacticism imbibed from the churches. Marie Corelli's *Romance of Two Worlds* was seized upon by the vast body of shallow-minded women, such as Rider Haggard found attending *séances* when he came to London in the 'seventies; *Robert Elsmere*, learned with the lore of the intellectuals of Mrs. Ward's intimate acquaintance, commanded the attention of the cultured, as well as the credulous, class, as a summary of topical controversy. It raised a storm of conflicting criticism; Pater praised it in the *Guardian*, but its great advertisement came from Gladstone's article on "*Robert Elsmere* and the Battle of Belief" in the *Nineteenth Century*, championing the cause of "orthodoxy". Seven editions of *Robert Elsmere* in three volumes were sold in four months; in the following year and a half the sales of a six-shilling edition approached fifty thousand.

Four years elapsed before her third novel, *The History of David Grieve*, but from 1892 till her death in 1920, she produced over twenty novels. It is idle to suggest a selection of her best books; those who digest one will find equal satisfaction in any of the others, for Mrs. Ward was a painstaking and conscientious worker, who gave always of her best. But her best was hardly good enough to sustain permanent interest, because her characters are always primarily the puppets of a theory rather than human beings. Theories are as ephemeral as feminine fashions in clothes, and few novelists of her time so immediately produce the impression of having dated as Mrs. Ward. *David Grieve* attempts a psychological study of a working man's problems with the detached knowledge of a welfare worker; *Marcella* more convincingly shows the earnest young woman of culture grappling with sociological problems, and its sequel, *Sir George Tressady*, conveys the warning that women of charm cannot take part in practical affairs without incurring the risk of emotional complications; *Daphne* is an indictment of American divorce laws; *Delia Blanchflower* illustrates the Anti-Suffragist persuasion ardently championed by Mrs. Ward in the years preceding the European War. All the controversies, movements, and theories discussed are now historical curiosities, but if Mrs. Ward had made them the background to human dramas of living people, instead of the major interest to which the characters were subordinate as vehicles of illustration, her books would still have the quality of historical novels instead of the incidental interest of historical documents.

In obvious dismay at being catechised for fear of giving offence, Henry James endeavoured to explain to Mrs. Ward, when asked for his opinion on the proofs of *Eleanor*, the flaw in her equipment as a novelist. Since the orbit of the story is the "consciousness" of the heroine, he said, "make the consciousness full, rich, universally prehensile and *stick* to it—don't shift— and don't shift *arbitrarily* . . . go behind *her* . . . miles and miles; don't go behind the others, or the subject—*i.e.* the unity of impression—goes to smash." Mrs. Ward was incapable of "going behind", of absorbing herself in her characters and allowing them to develop the story; always her own personality was uppermost and her characters mere toys for her manipulation, like the figures of a puppet show. In *Helbeck of Bannisdale* she came nearest to success, when handling the theme of love between

a rigid Roman Catholic and a girl brought up in the agnosticism
of science to hate "bigoted people who believed in ridiculous
things"; it is the most concentrated drama she ever accomplished,
and the tragedy of the heroine's morbid longing for faith is well
worked out, but the hero is typical of her characters in being
merely an institution personified. But even in *Helbeck*, the
heroine loses humanity in her unrelieved preoccupation with her
lack of faith; her tears and self-torment irritate impatience.

> "She did not answer. She simply looked at him, while
> the tears rose softly in her clear eyes. The question seemed to
> hurt her. Yet there was neither petulance nor evasion. She
> was Laura, and not Laura—the pale spirit of herself. One
> might have fancied her clothed already in the heavenly super-
> sensual body, with the pure heart pulsing visibly through the
> spirit frame."

She shares the exasperating quality of all Mrs. Ward's women,
which inspired Arnold Bennett to write of "those harrowing
dolls":

> "I have invented a destiny for Mrs. Humphry Ward's
> heroines. It is terrible, and just. They ought to be caught,
> with their lawful male protectors, in the siege of a great city
> by a foreign army. Their lawful male protectors ought,
> before sallying forth on a forlorn hope, to provide them with a
> revolver as a last refuge from a brutal and licentious soldiery.
> And when things come to a crisis, in order to be concluded in
> our next, the revolvers ought to prove to be unloaded."

Mrs. Ward was intimate with the inner circle of political
life, and future generations may find an historical interest in
Lady Rose's Daughter (1903) and *The Marriage of William Ashe*
(1905)—the latter a version in modern dress of Lady Caroline
Lamb's unhappy career—as period portraits of contemporary
society. Like Rhoda Broughton, who remarked ironically that
"I began my career as Zola, and finish it as Charlotte M. Yonge,"
Mrs. Ward found that the march of time sped beyond the horizon
of her intellectual outlook. The woman's movement over-
stepped the conventions of her dutiful upbringing, and she

accepted the condition of a reactionary by figuring as an Anti-Suffragist. The churches, of course, did not advance, remaining listlessly embedded in the ruts of obsolete tradition, but when she wrote a sequel to *Robert Elsmere* in *The Case of Richard Meynell* in 1911, she was no longer the rebel bluestocking who had broken a lance with Gladstone. She had decided, as she declared in *A Writer's Recollections*, that "these great national structures that we call churches are too precious for iconoclast handling, if any other method is possible. The strong assertion of individual liberty within them, as opposed to the attempt to break them down from without:—that seems to me now the hopeful course." So Richard Meynell is shown as a Modernist young parson, asserting his right to humanise the doctrines and services of his church in defiance of its purblind and ineffectual rulers. This novel reveals that, after twenty-three years, Mrs. Ward was as far as ever from understanding Henry James's remarks on the novelist's art, while her intellectual force remained unimpaired and she finished as earnest as she began.

§ 4

Andrew Lang told Mrs. Humphry Ward that *Robert Elsmere* was not "his sort", and as he was a personal friend, avoided discussing her novels. For him, no doubt, they belonged to the same unhealthy category as *The Story of an African Farm*, the publication of which, in 1883, was the first small voice of the feminist movement to remind middle-class male complacency that women possessed certain intellectual, as well as merely domestic and procreative faculties, and that George Eliot, in the time of their mothers, had not scrupled to flout the conventions. One utterance by the girl, Lyndall, was alone sufficient to suggest discomfort:

"The woman who does woman's work needs a many-sided, multiform culture; the heights and depths of human life must not be beyond the reach of her vision; she must have knowledge of men and things in many states, a wide catholicity of sympathy, the strength that springs from knowledge, and the magnanimity which springs from strength. We bear the world, and we make it. The souls of little children are marvellously delicate and tender things, and keep for ever the shadow that falls on them, and that is the mother's, or at best a woman's. There was never a great man who had not a great mother—it is hardly an exaggeration. The first six years of our life make us; all that is added later is veneer; and yet some say, if a woman can cook a dinner or dress herself well she has culture enough."

The book is a little masterpiece of sombre beauty; it is full of disquisitions and long soliloquies, yet these never irritate or pall, like the detached preachings of Mrs. Ward, because they issue naturally from the characters and narrative. The daily life on the lonely ostrich farm unfolds in a living picture, with all the minor characters exquisitely etched, and the tragedy of Lyndall and the boy Waldo moves to its crisis the more impressively against the picturesque rusticity of its setting. The charge of improbability, that the introspection and advanced ideas are incompatible with the simple environment, is obviously unfair and unimaginative; the author herself might have been Lyndall, and knew the life she was describing, while she reveals in the realistic portrayal of the background how the circumstances of their life induced the intellectual development of the characters.

The author's pseudonym of "Ralph Iron" for a time concealed the identity of Olive Schreiner (1862-1920), who was an example of talent flowering early and failing to repeat the brilliance of its first bloom, for she never wrote another book worthy of surviving the season of its publication. *Dreams* is a volume of parables, told simply like fairy tales for a child, and Lang missed nothing by declining to read *Trooper Peter Halket of Mashonaland*, which is a partisan pamphlet, thinly draped with fiction, against Cecil Rhodes and imperialism in South Africa, revealing that Miss Schreiner retained her earnestness but had lost sight of her art.

Miss Schreiner is assured of a permanent place in literature by virtue of one book, but few others of the many other women writers who enjoyed popularity in the 'nineties call for even passing notice. Mrs. Pearl Craigie, the lady whose personal charm captivated George Moore, made a great hit with a public schooled by Wilde to admiration of the epigram when she published her first book, *Some Emotions and a Moral*, in 1891 under the pseudonym of "John Oliver Hobbes." But her facile wit in this book and the later *The Gods, Some Mortals and Lord Wickenham* seems to have dated sadly, and *Robert Orange* in 1902 is a corollary on Moore's *Evelyn Innes*, with a male politician instead of a female opera-singer. Madame Sarah Grand created a sensation with *The Heavenly Twins* in 1893—after only sixty-four of the book's 679 pages, one of the heroines leaves her husband immediately after the wedding, on discovering that he was "not at all a proper person for a young girl to associate with," suggesting the revolutionary notion that women should demand in their husbands the same purity expected in themselves—but this inordinately long novel has all the tedious dogmatism of Mrs. Humphry Ward, with a prolixity and diffuseness reducing to despair the most patient perseverance. Though W. L. Courtney in 1904 expressed the view that fiction was too much in the hands of women, the women novelists of those days compare humbly and meanly with the rich feminine talent of the nineteen-twenties; there are no names to vie with those of Stella Benson, Sheila Kaye-Smith, Ethel Colburn Mayne, Mary Webb, Rose Macaulay, "Henry Handel Richardson", Winifred Holtby, Dorothy Whipple, Rosamond Lehmann, Clemence Dane, Ethel Mannin, Storm Jameson. Miss Netta Syrett was writing in both periods; so, too, were Mrs. Alfred Sidgwick and Miss Beatrice Harraden, and the latter scored a big success in 1893 with *Ships That Pass in the Night*. Does any one now read the novels of Charles Kingsley's daughter, "Lucas Malet"? She wrung the withers of pathos with *The Wages of Sin* in 1891, and ten years later *The History of Sir Richard Calmady* was the fashionable novel of its season. Mrs. Margaret L. Woods wrote a good historical novel about Swift, *Esther Vanhomrigh*, in 1891, but her circus story of three years later, *The Vagabonds*, looks pale and wan beside Lady Eleanor Smith's *Red Wagon*, and a comparison between the two illustrates the artistic handicap of prudery's conventions.

Frankly, Mrs. Humphry Ward was as good as any contemporary writers of her own sex, except George Egerton and Miss May Sinclair. Australian born, the lady who became Mrs. Golding Bright by her third marriage later devoted herself to writing plays, but in the 'nineties her *Keynotes* and *Discords* entitled her to be reckoned the female counterpart of Hubert Crackanthorpe as a pioneer of the modern short story. *Keynotes* appeared with a cover design by Beardsley, in 1893, the year before the *Yellow Book*, to which George Egerton contributed a couple of stories, and its publisher, Lane, made it the first of his "Keynotes Series", which included Arthur Machen's *The Great God Pan*, M. P. Shiel's *Prince Zaleski*, Grant Allen's *The Woman Who Did*, H. D. Lowry's *Women's Tragedies*, Harland's *Grey Roses*, and Ella D'Arcy's *Monochromes*. Some stories in *Discords* (1894), like "Wedlock", tend to the harsh realism of Crackanthorpe, a style in which George Egerton, as Le Gallienne noted, excelled less than in the "dream" story, but "Gone Under", "Her Share", and "The Regeneration of Two" have the same haunting charm and fatality as the stories in *Keynotes*. Le Gallienne hoped that George Egerton might be "saved from being a mere realist and woman's-righter," but she was too fine an artist to be in danger; she was "advanced", but her treatment of the divorced woman in "A Little Grey Glove" instances the instinctive artistic integrity which prevented her from allowing dogma to interfere with dramatic values. In her subjective narrative, her simplicity and dreaminess, she seems in the lineal ancestry of Mr. A. E. Coppard, and repeated re-reading only enhances the impression of freshness and exquisite finish. If the test of greatness is whether a work seems to have "dated", then *Keynotes* is a great book of short stories.

It seems incredible that Miss May Sinclair began her career in the 'nineties, for her reputation is largely post-war. Her first novel, *Audrey Craven*, appeared in 1896; her second, *Mr. and Mrs. Nevill Tyson*, a dramatic study of married life moving to disaster against a background of a hunting shire, striking in its reality and honesty of treatment for that time, foreshadowed the close preoccupation with woman's sexual emotions, which became a salient feature of Miss Sinclair's work and success as a psychological novelist. Miss Sinclair ripened slowly, and so the more surely and strongly, to maturity; her first success came in 1904 with *The Divine Fire*, a powerful study of a poetic genius against the background of contemporary literary society, but though it stands out in a class by itself among novels by women in its decade, it is marked by a tendency to rhetoric and "preaching", expressive of the author's militant idealism and spleen against artificial convention. The mellowness, sombre power, and sensitive understanding of passion, which marks the books entitling her to estimation among the important novelists of her generation, first appeared impressively in *The Three Sisters* (1914), a brilliant study of contrast between the characters of a country clergyman's three daughters, in an atmosphere of sex suppression and parochial narrowness. Gwenda Carteret is a woman splendidly alive, such as none of her sex had drawn since George Eliot, and the story poignantly unveils feminine sexual emotion with a fidelity and frankness impossible twenty years before, significantly indicating that the citadel of Humbug was tottering on the eve of war in 1914. The Brontë atmosphere of the vicarage in *The Three Sisters* is obviously apparent, and while in *The Tree of Heaven* (1917) Miss Sinclair drew a vivid portrait of a family, which stands apart from other work as a document of a period, her later work in *Mary Olivier, Ann Severn and the Fieldings, Arnold Waterlow,* and *The Rector of Wyck,* identifies her as the nearest approach among modern novelists to a combination of the different genius in Charlotte and Emily Brontë.

§ 5

Ironically, in spite of all the earnest women writers, the most sensational novel advocating advanced feminist views in the 'nineties was written by a man. Grant Allen was born in Canada, of mingled Scots and Irish parentage, in 1848, and went to school in France and at Birmingham before winning a Merton scholarship at Oxford. He read classics, though his interests were in science, and he became an ardent disciple of Herbert Spencer. He supplemented slender means by coaching till he obtained a professorship at a Government college in Jamaica, where he remained three years. Returning to England in 1876, he published at his own expense a book on *Psychological Aesthetics,* which sold only three hundred copies, but won him a commission from Leslie Stephen to write articles on popular science for

Cornhill. In 1879 he became a leader-writer on the *Daily News*, and the same year published his second book, *The Colour Sense*, "an essay in comparative psychology", which earned praise from Herbert Spencer, Charles Darwin, and A. R. Wallace, but less than thirty pounds for the author in ten years, moving Allen to write bitterly, "As it took me only eighteen months, and involved little more than five or six thousand references, this result may be regarded as very fair pay for an educated man's time and labour, and should warrant the reproach of thoughtless critics for deserting the noble pursuit of science in favour of fiction and filthy lucre."

Necessity and accident drove him into writing fiction. Writing an article on the improbability of a man's being able to recognise a ghost even if he saw one, he used the form of narrative for the better illustration of his argument, which the editor of the magazine *Belgravia* liked so well that Allen regularly contributed scientific stories under the pseudonym of "J. Arbuthnot Wilson." When James Payn took over *Cornhill* from Stephen, he wrote to Allen in his own name, saying he would require no more scientific articles, but by the same post he sent a letter to "J. Arbuthnot Wilson", inviting such stories as he was writing for *Belgravia*. A selection of these stories appeared as *Strange Stories* in 1884, more than ten years before the first book of H. G. Wells, who made his name as a writer of popular novels on scientific, or quasi-scientific subjects. Allen continued to write serious books and articles on evolution and natural history, but need of money increased his output of fiction, which appeared under various pseudonyms, as he believed that critics would sneer at serious scientific work coming from a writer of light fiction. His first novel, *Philistia*, appeared in 1884, as by "Cecil Power"; it is one of the earliest novels in advocacy of Socialism—for Allen was a Socialist and an early member of the Fabian Society.

Soon he despaired of his ambition to make a reputation as a serious scientific writer, and resigning himself to making "a comfortable living by hackwork" for his wife and son, cheerfully put his own name to everything he wrote—novels, magazine stories, short biographies, scientific essays, travel books, philosophy, and a verse translation of the *Attis* of Catullus. In his autobiography, Mr. Wells frankly acknowledges "a certain mental indebtedness" to Grant Allen, and remarks that his scientific books were "too original to be fair popularization and too unsubstantiated to be taken seriously by serious specialists." His fiction, with the single exception of *The Woman Who Did*, maintained a consistent level of competent mediocrity, which testifies his character as a conscientious worker, for he wrote too much and too fast to achieve the polish of quality; in the last ten years before his death in 1899, he produced between forty and fifty books!

But in *The Woman Who Did*, published by John Lane in 1895, Allen wrote "for the first time in my life wholly and solely to satisfy my own taste and my own conscience." His views in all directions were startlingly advanced for his time, and though tolerant of opinions differing from his own, he did not hesitate to state his convictions plainly. He denied that he was an agnostic, since an agnostic merely declines either to acknowledge or deny the possible existence of the supernatural; the agnostic says, "I do not know", but Allen went beyond agnosticism to atheism, saying, "There is nothing to be known." Bigots of fanatical faith, seeing sin and blasphemy in such an avowal, must have been disappointed to find in Allen a practical Christian far above the average virtue of churchgoers; he was a man of gentle and lovable temperament, who lived a worthy, hard-working life, and apparently never injured a fellow being by word or deed. His nephew, Mr. Grant Richards, tells how, after Churton Collins's damaging attack on Gosse, he was fearful of meeting Collins, since he was both his friend and Gosse's; he declined to take sides with either, and preferred to avoid them, rather than wound either of them, or take refuge in disingenuous agreement with the one who happened to be temporarily in his company. When he died, everybody spoke of him with regret and affection; he inspired neither envy nor enmity, and those of his casual acquaintance, like Mr. Wells, felt liking and respect, while those who knew him intimately, such as Mr. Grant Richards and his biographer, Edward Clodd, were moved to deep regard. He was sensitive and sincere, and as Mr. Wells says, "social injustice and sexual limitation bothered his mind." Therefore, he wrote from his heart, in *The Woman Who Did*, the tragic story of the independent young feminist who falls in love, refuses to commit "treason to her sex" by accepting the "assertion of man's supremacy over woman" implied by marriage, insists on loving in "terms of perfect freedom", and becomes an unmarried mother.

The Woman Who Did is not a work of art. No doubt Allen wrote hurriedly, as was his habit, but even had he taken more pains, there is nothing in any of his work to suggest that he had the imaginative insight to clothe the bones of his heroine with the flesh and blood of conviction. He was a novelist by necessity, not by nature; like Mrs. Humphry Ward, he was concerned rather with illustrating an idea than with story and character, and his novel is what Andrew Lang might fairly have called a treatise. But it is a remarkable book in relation to its day, and will retain the interest of a literary curiosity on that account. Its message is still in advance of our own enlightened times, so the sensation created forty-four years ago may be imagined! So many publishers refused the book that Allen was only deterred from destroying it when E. B. W. Nicholson, realising its eventual curiosity as a revolutionary document, proposed to house the manuscript in the Bodleian; eventually Mr. Grant Richards persuaded Lane to publish it.

Probably with his tongue in his cheek, for Allen did not lack humour, he sent a copy to Gladstone, who told Anthony Hope that he was puzzled with his letter of thanks, but "I sent him my best wishes, adding that they would be very different from what he probably wished for himself." The book roused a storm of righteous wrath; even Mr. Wells "slated" it, as he unashamedly confesses in his autobiography, for, though he was to treat a kindred theme in *Ann Veronica* fourteen years later, he was "the more infuriated because I was so nearly in agreement with Grant Allen's ideas, that this hasty, headlong, incompetent book seemed like a treason to a great cause." But *The Woman Who Did* did anticipate *Ann Veronica* by fourteen years, and since *Ann Veronica* in 1909 was "banned by libraries and preached against by earnest clergymen," the courage of Allen's venture in the 'nineties receives emphasis. Naturally the book sold; more than twenty editions—or impressions—appeared in the year of publication. And it did good, for though its tilt at the most cherished institution of Christian civilisation could produce no direct result, the mere fact of its succeeding in discussing such a subject flouted the conventions of Humbug, and established a precedent for freedom of expression.

At a glance, the conjunction of William J. Locke with Grant Allen seems a *non sequitur*, for they belonged to different generations and possessed few similarities in talent or the trend of their careers. But they shared an unusual quality as individuals, in being generally liked on account of their gentleness of disposition and charm of personality, and Locke's first novel, *At the Gate of Samaria*, appeared in the same year as *The Woman Who Did*, and its main theme argued in favour of female emancipation.

William John Locke was born at Demerara, British Guiana, on 20th March, 1863, of English parents. A year after his birth, his father, a banker of Barbados, moved to Trinidad, where Locke was educated at Queen's College till he won an exhibition at St. John's, Cambridge, in 1881. Taking an honours degree in mathematics in 1884, he became a schoolmaster, and moved in 1890 from the Oxford Military College at Cowley to Clifton College. He remained at Clifton for less than a year, for there he developed the tubercular trouble which afflicted him for the rest of his life, and the situation of Clifton being inimical to his complaint, he obtained the post of modern languages master at Glenalmond, which he held till 1897, when he became secretary of the Royal Institute of British Architects. He disliked schoolmastering, and the second paragraph of *The Morals of Marcus Ordeyne*, written in 1904, reads like autobiography:

"To-day is the seventh anniversary of my release from captivity. I will note it every year in my diary with a sigh of unutterable thanksgiving. For seven long blessed years have I been free from the degrading influences of Jones Minor and the First Book of Euclid. Some men find the modern English boy stimulating, and the old Egyptian humorous. Such are the born schoolmasters, and schoolmasters, like poets, *nascuntur non fiunt*. What I was born passes my ingenuity to fathom. Certainly not a schoolmaster—and my many years of apprenticeship did not make me one. They only turned me into an automaton, feared by myself, bantered by my colleagues, and sometimes good-humouredly by the boys."

Ever the most unassuming of men, he talked little of himself, and since few of the memoir-writers seem to have met him in his early years, his literary beginnings remain to be disinterred. There is an obvious reason for the obscurity of his early contributions to magazines; he wrote under the pseudonym of "J. Locke Williams", and when he became known under his own name, none thought of any connection with the literary schoolmaster who used to send his manuscripts from Glenalmond. Probably most of his school holidays were spent abroad, partly for his health's sake, partly from inclination, for he had a love and understanding of the French and their countryside rare among English writers.

Though not of the *Yellow Book* circle, he was a friend of its editor, Henry Harland, who probably introduced him to Lane, the publisher of all his books except *Septimus*, issued by John Murray in 1909. At Lane's death, Locke wrote to the *Times*, as one of the few authors "who can sit as I do now at this moment of writing, and see a few feet away a line of thirty volumes under the same publisher's imprint," to pay tribute to "the most loyal of friends, the most wise of counsellors, and the most honourable of partners in what, after all, is the work of a lifetime." When he became an established best-seller, Locke received many tempting offers, but turned them down without hesitation. He was under no legal pledge to Lane, but remained with him from gratitude in contented loyalty, because, as he once remarked to his wife, "John Lane stuck to me before these others wanted me."

His first novel, *At the Gate of Samaria*, is a study of the "new woman". Clytie Davenant, a vivid young creature rebelling against the narrowness of humdrum provincial respectability at "Durdleham", with an elderly churchwarden father and two staid elder sisters, escapes on coming into an income of a hundred a year to study art in London. Her assertion of independence finds illustration in her outburst at the suggestion that she should try to reform her street-arab model:

"He is human . . . That's why I cultivate him. Delightfully human! Refreshing! As for reforming him . . . I'm not a Sunday-school teacher. I have nothing to do with the submerged tenth; let the good respectable folks who have submerged them raise them with their polite and respectable hands. I am an artist—a student of life—what you will. Each one to his trade."

A year later, in *Sir George Tressady*, Mrs. Humphry Ward attempted to show how women hazard interference with their work in extra-domestic affairs from emotional complications, but her success was superficial, since she designed her heroine as if woman was purely intellectual, undefiled by sensual instincts. Locke penetrated deeper—to the crux of feminine psychology; he attempted to show frankly how a woman, however fortified with intellectual independence, readily succumbs to admiration and animal passion. Clytie is on terms of sentimental friendship with a Bohemian scientist, when a big game-hunting explorer is attracted and sweeps her off her feet.

" Unlike a man, a woman cannot live by sense alone. Senti-ment invariably plays its part. This in Clytie's case was fed by the glamour of Thornton's heroic history, so different from that of ordinary men, whose lives, compared with his, seemed tame and colourless. The glow of her personality bathed magically all his actions, all his words. In his superb manhood he stood before her eyes as the incarnation of physical force, the victorious protest against the shams of art, culture, and other pale shades of our morbid civilisation. When she was lifted high with him in his triumph, sense and sentiment were fused together and she was wholly at his mercy. Thornton had come into her life at the most delicately critical moment of a woman's career, when the current of her nature, checked at the turning-point between friendship and love, struggles tumultuously for some other channel into which to empty itself."

There are flaws in the development of the story; if it is allowed that Clytie was too wrapped in herself to recognise the scientist Kent's love, even when he virtually tells her after hearing of her engagement, it is hard to realise why Kent had made no avowal long before then, and there is pathos in the last chapter, where

O.G.F.   X

Locke makes a concession to respectability by allowing Kent and
Clytie to live for two years under the same roof on platonic
terms, though they have already exchanged kisses of passion,
until the death of the husband admits their lawful union. But
the character of Clytie is original and psychologically convincing,
and th look clearly indicates Locke's great gift of telling a story
and enlisting sympathy with his characters; he writes to
illustrate emphatic sociological and ethical views, but weaves
them into his story with an artist's skill. Almost the only
occasion when he digresses into such detached preaching as
Mrs. Ward's occurs in the last chapter, when Clytie's separation
from her husband inspires a reflection characteristic of Locke's
life-long tender sympathy with unhappiness.

> "Perhaps when enlightenment sheds a fuller ray upon our
> civilisation we shall make radical changes in our marriage laws,
> for they are based upon the sad old fallacy that human conduct
> and human emotion are indifferently susceptible of regulation.
> As yet we can universalise only of material things; security of
> property, full stomachs, and warm backs for the poor. The
> fact of broken lives and torn hearts we can recognise only
> in particular instances, as they come within each man's indi-
> vidual sphere. The universality of spiritual, moral, and emo-
> tional suffering is as yet far from being a national conception.
> When this is attained we may hope for social conditions happier
> than those under which we struggle at present."

Though not published as a book till 1903, *The Demagogue
and Lady Phayre* evidently appeared in a magazine before 1897,
and was probably written before *At the Gate of Samaria*, for it
reveals less skill in psychological development. It tells of the
mutual attraction between a society woman and a man of the
people, ending with the refined woman's revulsion on encountering the man's drunken slut of a wife. The characters lack
conviction, and the wife is much of a *dea ex machina*; the story
would have gathered point and power if the woman's refinement
had been shown to suffer gradual revulsion from the man's own
personal crudity.

At the Gate of Samaria enjoyed little success, not being reprinted
till Locke's burst into popularity in 1905, and he tried a different

style in *Derelicts* (1897), which suggests the same close study of Flaubert and Maupassant, as was at the same time occupying such different novelists as George Moore and Arnold Bennett. A young solicitor, emerging from penal servitude for embezzlement, finds every hand turned against him; his fruitless efforts to obtain work reflect sharp satire on righteous respectability. The good offices of the heroine obtain for him an engagement in a touring musical comedy company, but just as he is making good, his colleagues discover that he has been in prison, and he has to leave. After a vain effort to farm in South Africa, he returns to write novels which do not sell, and become a bookseller's assistant. The heroine provides food for further satire on the institution of marriage; supposing herself a widow, she marries a clerical dignitary, who, on accidentally discovering that her first husband is alive, put her from him in horror, though he genuinely loves her and she is a perfectly satisfactory wife—hence she is a bigamist and social outcast, because the letter of the law holds her to be still officially tied to a man by whom she was deserted years before. The title of *Derelicts* suggests affinity to the *Yellow Book* group, and the story's unrelieved preoccupation with the sad and seamy side of life resembles Crackanthorpe's manner. Except the heroine, whose innocence verges upon inanity, the characters are skilfully drawn; such deft sketches as the two minor derelicts—Noakes, the little consumptive writer of blood-and-thunder stories, and Annie Stevens, the chorus girl who falls to prostitution and finds regeneration in the Salvation Army—are rare in Locke's later books, in which he rarely took pains over his lesser characters.

A short novel, *A Study in Shadows* (1898), presents interesting possibilities by starting with the sex craving of women living in the arid atmosphere of a Geneva *pension*, but peters out into a trite love story. *Idols* (1899) invites comparison in construction and narrative power with the social problem novels of Merriman and Anthony Hope. Two friends from boyhood love Irene Merriam, who idolises the one she marries, and secure in her wifely devotion, keeps up a close friendship with his friend Colman, who drifts into a secret marriage with the daughter of a wealthy Jewish money-lender. The moneylender is murdered, and suspicion points to Colman, whose wife can supply the evidence of an alibi, since he was with her at the time of the murder. But the Jewess loses her inheritance if she marries a Gentile, and declines to speak; as Colman quixotically keeps her secret, he is in danger of conviction when Irene saves him by giving false evidence that he spent the night with her. Secretly tired of her, her husband chooses to accept her false confession as fact, and divorces her; she comes to idolise Colman, and counting on the Jewess to keep their secret as he kept it, Colman bigamously marries Irene, whose second idol is shattered when she discovers his deception. Apart from the wild improbability of Irene's false witness, the story develops naturally in accord with the four principal characters, and the narrative is lucid, powerful, and dramatic. *Idols* won high praise from many critics, it was the first of Locke's books to run into a second edition in the year of its publication, and its success encouraged Lane to reprint *Derelicts*.

In the five years following, Locke consolidated the reputation created by *Idols* with three novels of similar style, *The White Dove*, *The Usurper*, and *Where Love Is*, and two one-act plays which secured London production. But in 1905 he captured with *The Morals of Marcus Ordeyne* the huge library public for which he catered successfully during the rest of his life, and this book, and its successor, *The Beloved Vagabond*, will always be conjured to memory by Locke's name. The story took the form of what the 'nineties called extravaganza, what Arnold Bennett termed fantasia—it treated improbabilities realistically. Sir Marcus Ordeyne, an unworldly and pedantic scholar, a vague caricature of Marcus Aurelius in modern dress, escapes from drudgery as a schoolmaster on unexpectedly inheriting a baronetcy with a fortune. He finds on the Victoria Embankment a young girl, who has eloped from a harem in Alexandretta and been deserted by her lover, and adopts her, to the horror of respectable society, which suspects the worst. The first half of the book is taken up with anecdotes of the girl's artless charm, as she gradually entwines her protector's heart, blending romance and sentiment with the wistful whimsicality, which became recognised as

Locke's intrinsic characteristic. The beautiful girl, who, with all her innocence and charm, never quite disarms the reader's suspicion of her being a minx, elopes with her protector's close friend; deserted by him, she returns, has a baby which dies, and having passed from a girl to a woman, bestows on "Seer Marcous" a love enduring, wifely, and maternal.

Like all Locke's subsequent work, the tale is told lightly, flippantly, with a joyous whimsicality, and the fluent ease of a writer who was always a scholar of taste and refinement. To-day it seems superficially a pretty story of improbable romance; read in relation to the year 1905, it appears a remarkably clever gibe at respectable convention. Much of the naughtiness is impishly delicious, and the harem education of the girl lends itself to smart satire. She has the harem view that a girl's sole destiny is marriage, and Sir Marcus asks her governess to "kindly instil into Carlotta's mind the fact that no young English woman ever thinks about marriage until she is actually engaged, and then her thoughts do not go beyond the wedding." Sitting in Hyde Park, watching society's parade, she asks, "Seer Marcous, is this the marriage market?"—and insists that "they come here to sell the young girls to men who want wives," for she has read it in a book of Thackeray's given to her by her governess. And young maids and old doubtless felt a wicked thrill at the *double entendre* of Carlotta's remark, on being told that some people have grey hairs at twenty, that it would be "dreadful" if she had them, as "no one would care to have me."

The circulating libraries must have scratched their heads; humour not being their strong point, they were not sure whether *The Morals of Marcus* was subtly and insidiously wicked, or whether their decently be-skirted legs were being shrewdly and impudently pulled. So they compromised; they did not ban the book, but a well-known university bookseller, then manager of a seaside town's branch of one of the largest libraries, remembers that he was instructed by London headquarters to keep it on the top shelf—it was there for sale on specific demand, but would not be seen by casual browsers about the shop. The sensation of its season, like Mr. Arlen's *The Green Hat* some twenty years later, it sold like wildfire; Locke became a best-seller—all his previous books, including the ten-year-old *At the Gate of Samaria*, began a series of regular reprintings.

Locke remained a best-seller to the end of his life. *The Morals of Marcus Ordeyne* was followed by the equally popular and celebrated *The Beloved Vagabond*, a humorous venture into picturesque romance with a roystering, gay and gallant scallywag of a whimsical hero in Berzelias Nibbidad Paragot, whose character Herbert Tree interpreted on the stage in 1908. Paragot might have stepped out of the pages of Anatole France; he owns spiritual kinship to Jérôme Coignard in *La Rôtisserie de la Reine Pedauque*, for the English translation of which, published by Lane, Locke wrote an enthusiastic introduction. His love and understanding of the French grew more and more apparent in his later writings, and he came almost to be identified as the novelist of Provence as Kipling of India or Hall Caine of the Isle of Man; such books as *The Town of Tombarel*, welcomed by the greater English and American public as merely the latest Locke, won enthusiastic praise from French *hommes de lettres*.

His success enabled him to resign his secretaryship of the R.I.B.A. in 1907, and devote himself entirely to novel-writing and enjoyment of the good things of life. He had a connoisseur's taste in many things—he read old French and the classics, he loved music and painting, good food and wine—"especially wine," said Anthony Hope, "in which he had learning as well as taste; I liked to hear him talk of it." He loved life too well for diligence as a worker, lingering in idle observation with his quizzical smile, before breaking late away to his writing-table. Hence, as he required a book a year to sustain his popularity and income, much of his later work bears witness to haste. But his repetition of themes and characters he had used before is due less to this cause than to commercial instinct and personal inclination. Prodigally generous of hospitality—his dinner parties on the Riviera were as famous for the richness and originality of their menus and the quality of the old wine, as for the celebrities to be met there and the famous musicians who entertained their fellow guests after dinner—he lived expensively, and the necessity for keeping up his income compelled his giving to his public what it expected of him. "Seer Marcous" and the Vagabond had won his public, and they repeatedly appeared in different guise to keep the public. His heroes are always eccentrics of one model or the other—as Septimus, Simon de Gex, Ephraim Quixtus, are the mould of Marcus, so are the heroes of *The Great Pandolfo*, *The Mountebank*, and *The House of Baltazar* in direct descent from Paragot. How completely he succeeded in maintaining his popularity finds evidence in his having been retained by Hearst's publications for the American rights of all serials and short stories from 1911 to 1928.

But Locke used these characters from inclination, because they were fanciful embodiments of his own personality. He was instinctively a sentimental romantic, and he caricatured himself as Marcus Ordeyne, just as, when he went over to France and sat sipping his wine in crowded cafés, he saw himself in imagination rampaging eccentrically about township and boulevard like Paragot. Consequently, there is much autobiography in his novels. In *Septimus* (1909), he saw himself as the little scholarly eccentric, hopelessly and unselfishly loving an unattainable brilliant woman; in *Simon the Jester* (1910), he saw himself as the brilliant eccentric who at last, after both have passed through trouble and illness, finds happiness with the seemingly unattainable brilliant woman; in *The Glory of Clementina Wing* (1911) he is again the scholarly eccentric, drawn gradually to the same brilliant woman by their common interest, first in a boyish nephew, then in their adopted daughter. As Marcus Ordeyne, the solitary bachelor, he played fancifully on his longing for the upbringing of a daughter; when he married in 1911, his wife adopted a little girl, who bore the same name of Sheila as the child in *The Glory of Clementina Wing*, and whom he idealised in many of his later books, notably in *Stella Maris* (1913). The brilliant, independent type of woman of personality, like Clementina Wing, Zora of *Septimus*, and Lola of *Simon the Jester*, represented Locke's ideal; while he saw himself in the character of the eccentric parent, like Marcus to Carlotta, in relation to subsequent representations of his adopted daughter, he drew from his conception of himself the likeness of the lovable unworldly eccentrics gladly depending on the sense and devotion of a woman of personality—as Quixtus depended on Clementina, so Locke looked with implicit confidence to his wife,

During the war, he worked untiringly in public service. He edited an anthology on the same lines as Hall Caine's *King Albert's Book* for the Belgian Relief Fund, and like Hall Caine, received the Order of Leopold. He was chairman of a war emergency committee, including Miss May Sinclair and F. Anstey, appointed by the Society of Authors for the relief of distressed writers, and he and his wife gave their house, Corner Hall at Hemel Hempstead, as a hospital for wounded soldiers. From his experience among private soldiers enjoying his hospitality, he derived the material for one of the best of his later books, *The Rough Road* (1918), which is the saga of "Doggie" Trevor, an ineffectual little man cast in the mould of Septimus, who succeeds in "doing his bit" and finding romance, in spite of the inferiority complex and general contempt which has handicapped him from birth.

His health compelled his living out of England for the last nine years of his life—at Cannes, in the villa "perched on the top of a cliff", described in *The Coming of Amos*. He died in Paris from a complication arising from the tubercular trouble, which had haunted him for forty years.[1] Like Grant Allen, he was a gentle, lovable man, whose death brought tributes of affectionate regard from all sides. "In person he was lean, eager, pince-nez'd," wrote Sir John Squire, "a courteous and affectionate man with no enemies." His long and sustained popularity inspired ungenerous critics to undervalue the unfailing competence of his regular output, but as Anthony Hope wistfully remarked, "I got my success before he got his, but he kept his much longer than I have kept mine," and his most merciless critics must allow to Locke a peculiar charm of writing, which enabled him to retain his attractions with their bloom of freshness unfaded for more than twenty years. In Anthony Hope's words, he is "always pleasant to read, 'a scholar and a gentleman', with, moreover, a pretty humour; a little too much sentiment, but better too much than too little for our trade (as even the greatest bear their witness)."

[1] *The Dictionary of National Biography* states that "several novels from his pen were published posthumously," but actually there was only one, *The Shorn Lamb*. For much personal information additional to, and corrective of, the *D.N.B.* article, the present writer is gratefully indebted to the novelist's widow, Mrs. Aimée Maxwell Locke.

CHAPTER TEN

Arnold Bennett: The Card of Genius

§ 1

WHEN "George Paston", the cousin of John Addington Symonds, lamented in 1896 "the decadence of the novel since Thackeray and George Eliot," Arnold Bennett retorted that "in future years the present would be regarded as a golden age of fiction." The decadence began some ten years after Thackeray's death, for during the 'sixties, Reade and Wilkie Collins were giving their best, and good novels came also from Dickens, the Kingsleys, Trollope, Meredith. But during the 'seventies, Reade, Trollope and Collins had finished their best work, and the best of the popular novelists was William Black, of whose books Meredith not unjustly remarked that "there is nothing in them but fishing and sunsets." Worse followed in the 'eighties, when the best quality in demand at the libraries was represented by W. E. Norris and Rhoda Broughton. Meredith, Hardy, and Henry James were producing work of genius, but they were appreciated only by the cultured minority; neither Meredith nor James was ever popular, and Hardy never achieved remarkable sales. The decadence was dictated by the public, whose taste, as witnessed by the furniture and feminine dress of the period, was the crudest since the age of Boadicea, when women believed bodies to be beautified by tattooing. Other novelists, besides Meredith, Hardy, and James, might have produced better work but, as Grant Allen observed in the introduction to *The British Barbarians*, the professional novelist "in order to write . . . must first eat"; hence, by the commercial law of exchange, in return for his bread-and-butter, he had to supply the milk-and-water required by the public.

If, by "the present", Bennett meant the 'nineties, he was wrong, for that decade, as had been sufficiently indicated in the preceding chapters, was a period of regeneration and revolt by a muzzled minority, an epoch of transition, when the foundations beneath the effigies of the idolatrous gods of the decadence began first to crumble. But Bennett meant not to be taken literally; the "golden age of fiction" was to be his own age, with himself a liberal purveyor of the ore. To say that again he was wrong is to assume the mantle of prophecy, but obvious indications suggest that, on Bennett's death in 1931, the stage was set for the dawn of the golden age of fiction. At the time of writing, the crippling shackles of Humbug imprisoning expression in the 'eighties have been shaken off, and the tendency, precipitated during the war years, to look on life with clear and honest contemplation, unwarped by the prejudice of hypocrisy, has steadily extended its growth. The defeated forces of Humbug are still abroad; there are visible signs of timid efforts to reorganise their scattered remnants. It remains to be seen whether progress or reaction will triumph, whether the nineteen-forties will be the golden age, not only of fiction, but of enlightenment and culture, or whether the history of the eighteen-forties will be even more disastrously repeated—whether, as then, the forces of regeneration will fatally hesitate, lose their way, and fall captive to the massed bands of the Philistines, so inducing a process of retrogression, by which English civilisation, beginning with a repetition of Victorianism, will gradually retreat by the way it came.

When Bennett came to London in the 'nineties, he found novelists struggling under a seemingly hopeless handicap; when he died, writers enjoyed more complete freedom of expression than at any period since the seventeenth century, when culture was a privilege of aristocracy. To this progressive change, he and Galsworthy and Mr. H. G. Wells, alongside Mr. Shaw in the theatre, contributed more than any of their contemporaries; these three were the first great novelists since Charles Reade who succeeded, like Thackeray and Dickens, in capturing the franchise of the general reading public. In so doing, they educated the popular taste, raising it from the sticky mud of late-Victorian ignorance, and prepared the way for the succeeding generation of Walpoles, Lawrences, and Mackenzies, who have further blazed the trail for the rising generation of writers.

Mr. Wells was born in the year before Bennett and Galsworthy; of lower middle-class parentage, he progressed from a chemist's apprentice to a schoolmaster before Henley accepted as a serial for the *New Review* his first novel, *The Time Machine*, a fantastic projection of history into the remote future, in 1895. In this book and such successors as *The Invisible Man*, *The War of the Worlds*, and *When the Sleeper Wakes*, he utilised the fantastic romance of Jules Verne as a medium for social satire and the advocacy of progressive scientific and socialist theory. These books stand in relation to Mr. Wells's work like his "fantasias" to Bennett's; they were written rapidly as journalism for money. He had apparently in mind the same plan as Bennett followed throughout his career—so long as he needed money, he would feed the popular appetite with fantasias, while finding time to concentrate on more carefully-written books, which would go to the building of his reputation as a novelist. The first of these carefully-written books was *Love and Mr. Lewisham* (1900), in which he drew upon personal experience for the story of a serious-minded young man of the city clerk class, converted to socialism, and persevering in pursuit of ambition according to a self-imposed self-discipline, till he falls in love and sacrifices his theories and hopes in marriage. This book reveals realistic creation of atmosphere and careful development of character, allied with the talent for social satire and theorising already manifested in his fantasias, and as a notable signpost in the trend of the developing realistic novel, marked its author as a probably master in the art of creative fiction.

But in the year of the publication of *Love and Mr. Lewisham*, Mr. Wells arranged with W. L. Courtney to publish in the *Fortnightly Review* a series of papers prophesying likely developments in the new century, called *Anticipations*. He undertook the work as commercial journalism appropriate to the author of *The Time Machine*, but he reveals in his *Experiment in Autobiography* (1934) how he realised that he had lighted on "a new thing in general thought," and became his own first disciple. He saw that "this sort of thing could not remain simply journalistic," that he was "carrying on the curves instead of the tangents of history," that his imaginative flights, controlled by his scientific knowledge and logical reasoning, might supply indications for the development of "rationalized social political and economic effort." Thenceforth Mr. Wells became primarily a prophet, engaged in "writing the human prospectus"; he was only secondarily a novelist, using fiction as a popular dressing for the elaboration of his theories, with the same impulse, though with vastly different equipment, as Mrs. Humphry Ward.

He wrote at least three other books possessing permanent value in the history of the novel's artistic development. *Kipps* (1905) is the humorous saga, affording fine scope for social satire, of a draper's assistant, who comes into money and consequently ventures into higher walks of life, with results so discomforting that he is glad to go back to his old environment. *Tono-Bungay* (1909) is the tale of a chemist's assistant, who, with his Uncle Ponderevo, "flashed athwart the empty heavens" to fortune on the back of a patent medicine; here again satire receives full play, with modern commercial advertising its principal butt, and the characters of the autobiographical hero's uncle and aunt, which Mr. Wells calls "caricature-individualities", have the skill of Dickens in the cartoonist's exaggeration to intensify the high-lights of personality. But the gem of Mr. Wells's fiction— perhaps individual preference based on affectionate prejudice— is *The History of Mr. Polly* (1910). Mr. Wells relates in his auto-biography how, about the time of writing *Mr. Polly*, he realised that he might be falling into an intellectual groove by remaining longer in an environment where he had been settled for several years, and thereupon sold his house at Sandgate. *Mr. Polly* is a satire on suburban lives wasted in petty respectability. By nature he was a romantic; struggling in the depths of his being "crawled a persuasion that over and above the things that are jolly and ' bits of all right', there was beauty, there was delight," which he manifested in boyhood by sneaking out on moonless winter nights to stare at the stars and reading tales of hunters and explorers. As a draper's assistant, his romantic self finds air on Sunday excursions about the countryside, in reading, and finally in flirtation with a schoolgirl of the upper-classes over the school wall. But he drifts into an unsatisfactory marriage, and for fifteen years endures the drab existence of a respectable small-town shopkeeper, till, during a bout of indigestion, he makes an abortive attempt to commit suicide, and then runs away to seek adventure like the hero of Borrow's *Lavengro*.

Mr. Wells has expounded how he arrived at his theory of the novel after many discussions with Henry James. He fairly argues that the possibilities of the novel are not exhausted by James's "novel of completely consistent characterization arranged beautifully in a story painted deep and round and solid," and that the realistic portraiture of character is rather the province of biography than fiction. He allows that there may be such a thing as the ideal realistic novel, beside which his "so-called novels" are "artless self-revelatory stuff", but asks if that great ideal has ever been realised—"or can it ever be realised?" The question is surely that of every destructive materialist—are any ideals in this materialistic world capable of attainment? Why should not the artistic ideal of the realistic novel be as attainable as Mr. Wells's ideal of "a planned world"? If the supreme masterpiece of realistic fiction yet remains unwritten, creditable efforts have been made towards its achievement—by Galsworthy in *The Forsyte Saga*, by Bennett in *The Old Wives' Tale*, by Mr. Wells himself in *Tono-Bungay* and *Mr. Polly*.

When Mr. Wells wrote *Anticipations*, and saw in it the keystone to the arch of his creative imaginings, which logically develops to *The Shape of Things to Come* (1933), he preferred to work for his sociological ideal rather than the artistic ideal—he chose to be a prophet rather than an artist, a thinker rather than a novelist. As Henry James objected, in most of Mr. Wells's novels, the reader is more conscious of the writer's personality than the personalities of his characters. He does not "go behind", any more than Mrs. Humphry Ward. Like Mrs. Ward, he uses the novel as a vehicle for illustrating theories; his characters are always secondary in importance to his ideas. He freely admits that he sketches "scenes and individuals, often quite crudely," and resorts "even to conventional types and symbols, in order to get on to the discussion of relationships." If by "relationships", he meant the throwing into relief of one character by its reactions upon another, revealed in the action of the story, he would still be writing as a realistic novelist, but his relationships usually mean assemblies of conflicting types for the discussion of theories. Wells and Shaw are booked for history as two of the great constructive thinkers of their day, but Mr. Wells has used the novel, as Mr. Shaw the drama, as a popular means of preaching his theories. The means finds vindication in its result; if Mr. Wells had presented his doctrines in the conventional form of the sociological treatise, he would have reached a public of hundreds, but by assuming the guise of fiction, he has been read by hundreds of thousands.

But if the means thus finds justification according to the ethics of the journalist and publicist, it as certainly invites condemnation according to the ethics of art. Andrew Lang was right in regarding the novel as a form of entertainment; he was wrong only in supposing that entertainment was confined to light romance, and could not extend to the serious problems of practical life. A reader of average intellectual attainments may be equally entertained by a tale of romantic adventure, like Stevenson's *Treasure Island*, and by a story of emotional complications, like Galsworthy's *Man of Property*. But it depends upon the standard of his intellectual development whether he can equally enjoy Mr. Wells's doctrinal disquisitions dressed as fiction. The man of culture, who, had Mr. Wells written treatises, would have read him as he reads Carlyle or Huxley or Mill, appreciates art in a novel, and feels irritation when Mr. Wells holds up his story, leaving his characters suspended in the air, to expound his personal views, just as he feels irritation when listening to a Wagner opera on the radio and a B.B.C. pundit beguiles the interval between the acts with a discussion of the composer's aims in writing the opera. If it is allowed that the realistic portrayal of character belongs to the art of biography, it may be equally fairly argued that the self-revelation of Mr. Wells's fiction belongs to the art of autobiography.

Mr. Wells was one of the great minds of his generation, but he has contributed nothing more important than *Mr. Polly* to the novelist's art. Arnold Bennett was not a great mind, but he has left a few novels which rank among the most remarkable of his generation, and he succeeded in getting them read by the public, to which Meredith was merely a name and Henry James probably not even a name.

§ 2

Arnold Bennett was a great little man. Like Hall Caine, he was a provincial clerk, self-educated and naïvely self-centred, who taught himself to write, and made a fortune by shrewd commercial sense. But there the likeness to Hall Caine ends, for Bennett was a man of remarkable gifts and personality, with a creative fertility as amazing as his capacity for work. Mr. Wells, who knew him well for thirty-four years, has described him vividly as a "card", like Denry Machin in Bennett's novel:

> "He was as objective about himself and as amused about himself as about anything else in the world. He improved a certain swing in his movements to a grave deliberate swagger; he enriched his gestures. He brushed up his abundant whitening hair to a delightful cockscomb. The stammer he had never been able to conquer was utilised for a conversational method of pauses and explosions. He invented a sort of preliminary noise like the neigh of a penny trumpet. He dressed to the conception of an opulent and important presence. He wore a fob. He made his entry into a club or a restaurant an event. It pleased his vanity no doubt, but why should pleasing one's vanity by evoking an effusive reception in a room or restaurant be any different from pleasing one's palate with a wine? It was done with a humour all his own. Deep within him the invincible Card rejoiced. He knew just how far to carry his mannerisms so that they never bored. They delighted most people and offended none."

This is the Bennett whom all his surviving acquaintance remember, and the legend is arising that Denry Machin was a self-portrait, and Bennett himself an agreeable but amusing grotesque, for ever congratulating himself on his amazing success, because it provided the wherewithal to foot it with the "nobs" at such palaces of plutocracy as he described in *The Grand Babylon Hotel* and *Imperial Palace*, with the naïve self-satisfaction of little Sid Jenkin in *Lord Raingo*. This would have been all very well if Bennett, like Denry Machin, had made a fortune by opportunism in commercial speculation, but it does not explain how the provincial clerk came to be one of the most prolific and gifted novelists of his day. Bennett was something more than a card, or if he was a card, there was much more behind. It is to be suspected that Mr. Wells's vivid sketch is one of his "caricature-individualities"—that he did not "go behind" to the essence of the man. The essential Bennett, the extraordinarily alive little man who, by sedulous industry, persistent application, and steadfast tenacity of purpose, rose from the station of a solicitor's clerk to become one of the great men of letters of his day, appears with astonishing self-revelation in his *Journals*, published after his death under the editorship of Mr. Newman Flower, and comprising the most candid admission to the workshop of a writer's mind since the *Autobiography* of Anthony Trollope.

Enoch Arnold Bennett was born at Hanley on 27th May, 1867; the name Enoch is suggestive of the narrow Methodist atmosphere with which he endowed the scene of his boyhood in many novels. Like the hero of *Clayhanger*, he was educated at the local grammar school,[1] and on leaving school, he entered his father's office as a clerk. His father was a solicitor, not a printer, like Darius Clayhanger; from the few glimpses in the *Journals*, Enoch Bennett Senior seems to have been affectionately idealised in Osmond Orgreave, while Darius is drawn from Arnold Bennett's grandfather, who once, after a boyish escapade of his son's, knelt down and prayed before thrashing him with a pair of braces "till neither of them could very well stand." If his father adjured Bennett in Orgreave's philosophy to "play with the same intentness as you work," to "live to the uttermost instant and to the last flicker of energy," the future novelist certainly adopted the parental direction as the guiding principle of his life.

In *The Truth About an Author* (1902), Bennett reveals that in boyhood he had the same passion for water-colour painting and schemes of house decoration as Edwin Clayhanger; painting

[1] *Who's Who*, presumably checked by Bennett himself, and Mr. Newman Flower in the foreword to *The Journals of Arnold Bennett*, say at Newcastle Middle School; Mr. J. B. Simons, in *Arnold Bennett and His Novels*, says at Ashton -under-Lyne Grammar School.

remained a cherished hobby throughout his life, though his talent was such that Mr. Wells once told him he painted "like Royalty". He evinced no literary inclinations; besides Long-fellow's *Hiawatha* and "the enforced and tedious Shakespeare of schools," he read nothing except Ouida, who inspired him like George Moore, "with that taste for liaisons under pink lamp-shades which I shall always have," though, unlike Moore, his humour forced him to confess that "a puritanical ancestry and upbringing" prevented its personal indulgence. He never "wanted to write, until the extrinsic advantages of writing had presented themselves to me," and he first recognised these advantages when a local newspaper offered a guinea apiece for short stories worth printing. The story was rejected, but he then wrote a serial in imitation of Zola's *L'Assommoir*, which he had read in Vizetelly's edition, and though this also was rejected, the editor of the newspaper, in which his father was financially interested, told him that he was "marked out for the literary vocation," and invited him to contribute weekly gossip para-graphs without remuneration.

Apparently he passed the London University matriculation examination, but having reached the age of twenty-one without tackling his law examinations, he decided to "escape from an intellectual and artistic environment which had long been excessively irksome to me," and like the hero of *A Man from the North*, obtained a job in London as a solicitor's shorthand clerk. "Some achievement of literature certainly lay in the abyss of my desires, but I allowed it to remain there, vague and almost un-noticed." For two years he was busily occupied in "making a meal off London." He never lost his zest and naïve wonder in life; at every fresh achievement, at every new experience, he paused to marvel exultantly that he should be the hero of his sensations, just as Sid Jenkin in *Lord Raingo* exulted: "I've worked on the coalface and gone 'ome black and 'ad me bath in me kitchen, and now 'ere I am 'aving a bite with a millionaire, and I'm in the War Cabinet and 'e isn't. What about it?" Just as Raingo found it "impossible to be offended by Sid's crudity," so Mr. Wells and everybody else found it impossible to feel derision at Bennett's—not crudity, but rather naïvety—for there was a charm about his pleasure in his own situation—the glow of his pleasure spread its warmth to those in his company, who felt as they feel on witnessing the spontaneous pleasure of a child in receiving the gift of a toy it genuinely likes. And the reason that the apparent egotism failed to offend was because it sprang from humility; Bennett never forgot his humble beginnings, his first blind gropings for the bauble of his destiny, and consequently never failed to reflect on his good fortune in the achievement of each new triumph.

His escape from the smoky repressive atmosphere of the Five Towns and his coming to the hub of the universe was his first triumph, and it took two years for him to overcome the flush of exultation. Many times he must have sallied forth from his lodgings of an evening, like the hero of *A Man from the North*, swelling his chest as he surveyed the lights of Piccadilly, pausing before entering a theatre to muster an air of careless custom for the benefit of the commissionaire, blushing, tongue-tied, and turning hurriedly away when a woman accosted him, and then cursing himself all the way home for not having seized the opportunity of adventure by speaking to the girl. His respectable upbringing and the instinct of self-preservation saved him, like George Moore, from transitory amours.

A fellow clerk, probably the prototype of Aked in *A Man from the North*, inspired him with a craze for book-collecting; he haunted Hodgson's sale-room, buying huge calf-bound volumes for the splendour of ornate bindings as bargains, with no intention of reading them. He first realised the advantage of being a "card", when he found that he had impressed the managing clerk with a conviction of his exceptional brilliance, "solely from the habit of buying books printed mainly in languages which neither myself nor my acquaintances could read." Thereupon he cultivated "the invaluable, despicable, disingenuous faculty of seeming to know much more than one does know;" he assumed the pose of an authority, and afterwards carried the pose "into newspaper offices and the very arcana of literary culture," without ever incurring disaster. He exaggerated when declaring that "in the whole of my life I have not devoted one day to the systematic study of literature," for his *Journals* reveal a vast amount of miscellaneous reading, but it is true that he never attempted a complete mastery of any subject, being content with skipping and skimming all manner of books to acquire a universal smattering. Characteristically he took advantage of a special offer by the publishers of Bohn's Libraries to purchase a selection of one hundred of the six hundred volumes; admiring the "long beautiful row" of books, he "cut several of them and looked through Juvenal, Suetonius, and da Vinci," and noting that a passage in Beaumont and Fletcher's *Philaster* must be based on a passage in Juvenal's Sixth Satire, duly stored the fact in his memory for future illustration of his erudition. Very likely he never looked at Juvenal or Suetonius again—he knew enough of them to seem to know all about them. The provincial clerk justly praised the culture of enlightened democracy; you had only to be a card to be credited with a scholarship equal to Andrew Lang's.

The revelation of the managing clerk's admiration revived his literary ambition. He changed his lodgings to Chelsea, and made some artistic friends, who were readily impressed by his pretended erudition and accepted him "as a fellow-idealist". He learned a new scale of values when he showed one of the artists as a treasure "a *rarissime* illustrated copy of *Manon Lescaut*," and the artist pronounced it one of the ugliest books he had ever seen. He earned his first money from writing in 1891, when, following the thousand-pound prize story competition won by Grant Allen's *What's Bred in the Bone*, *Tit-Bits* offered twenty guineas for "the best humorous condensation" of Allen's serial in two thousand words. Bennett was afraid that his friends would not consider such an undertaking "art", but when they assured him that "caricature was a perfectly legitimate form of art," he ventured, and won the prize.

Thereupon he embarked on what he calls "the humiliating part" of his career. Honesty is the keynote of all Bennett's writing, and a corner stone of its success; in *The Truth About an Author* he scornfully explodes the rubbish written by hacks on "How to become an Author", and advertised by correspondence schools, about the "glorious freedom" of the free-lance journalist.

"The free-lance is a tramp touting for odd jobs; a pedlar crying stuff which is bought usually in default of better; a

producer endeavouring to supply a market of whose conditions
he is in ignorance more or less complete; a commercial
traveller liable constantly to the insolence of an elegant West
End draper's 'buyer.' His attitude is in essence a fawning
attitude; it must be so; he is the poor relation, the doff-hat,
the ready for anything. He picks up the crumbs that fall from
the table of the 'staff'—the salaried, jealous, intriguing staff
—or he sits down, honoured, when the staff has finished. He
never goes to bed; he dares not; if he did, a crumb would fall.
His experience is as degrading as a competitive examination,
and only less degrading than that of the black-and-white
artist who trudges Fleet Street with a portfolio under his
arm."

Bennett pursued this career of degradation, which has broken the
spirit of many men better than the editorial pocket-potentates
on whom they dance attendance, through the early and middle
'nineties; he began with *Tit-Bits* articles on subjects such as
"How a bill of costs is drawn up," progressed to short stories for
halfpenny evening papers, and thence to "political skits in
narrative" for the more austere penny papers, so rising from
"a concocter of 'bits' articles to be the scorpion-sting of cabinet
ministers!" He nursed the sores of rejected manuscripts in his
secret bosom—"mere vanity," he said, "always did and always
will prevent me from acknowledging a reverse at the moment;
not till I have retrieved my position can I refer to a discomfiture."
Another trick of the card!—by hiding his failures and talking
only of his successes, he impressed his friends as a prodigy of
effortless brilliance.

He learned much in these years. He found that most of the
editorial staffs in Fleet Street are rarely well fitted for their jobs,
their principal aptitude being for picking the brains of those
innocent enough to let them be picked, just as he found, on
getting a staff job himself, that there was "almost nothing"
in sub-editorial technique and "the arcana of journalism partake
of the nature of an imposture," as may be said of "all professional
arcana." He read a good deal, especially in French fiction; from
this time "Turgenev, the brothers de Goncourt, and de Maupassant were my gods." Moreover, he learned to write. With so

much work rejected, he reckoned he earned at the rate of barely threepence an hour, but he persevered in writing everything with "a nice regard for English"—"I would lavish a night on a few paragraphs; and years of this penal servitude left me with a dexterity in the handling of sentences that still surprises the possessor of it."

In 1893 a weekly paper called *Woman* applied for an assistant-editor. Bennett had never written for a ladies' paper, but he applied, submitting a list of the papers to which he had contributed, with some specimens of his work. He was dismayed when he received the appointment, for the salary was only one hundred and fifty pounds a year, and he was getting two hundred as a clerk. But the time was only one whole day and three half-days a week, leaving him plenty of leisure for his own work, so he became sub-editor of *Woman* and wrote smart paragraphs over the signature of Gwendolen. Here again he learnt much which contributed to his novelist's equipment—"about frocks, household management, and the secret nature of women," and he never lost the habit of glancing "first at a woman's skirt and her shoes." He was sub-editor for three years; in 1896 his chief resigned to go to a better billet, and Bennett became editor.

Meanwhile, in July 1895, a story called "A Letter Home", by Enoch Arnold Bennett, appeared in the *Yellow Book*. With Maupassant in mind, he "took incredible pains to be realistic, stylistic, and all the other *istics*," and for the first time "knew by the glow within" that he had "accomplished a good thing." He sent it first to the editor of a popular weekly, who rejected it —"he liked the plot, but the style was below his standard." The *Yellow Book* then accepted it, and when that issue came to be reviewed by the literary weeklies, Bennett saw himself praised in print for the first time. The praise, united with the plaudits of his artist friends, inspired him to write a novel; he has described the gusto with which he began, how he lost confidence as soon as "the fundamental brain-work began," how he realised that he could not "become Flaubert by taking thought," how he persevered and "drove forward like a sinking steamer in a heavy sea." The novel took nearly a year to write; when it was finished, he feared that it was "not well-knit", and if not hysterical, "at any rate strained in tone," but felt that it might impress "many respectable people," and comforted himself that the worst of it seemed better than his well-praised *Yellow Book* story. His good luck held, for the novel suffered no rejections; he sent it to Lane, the publisher of the *Yellow Book*, who made him an offer, on the advice of his youthful reader, John Buchan, within a fortnight of receiving the manuscript. It was not a handsome offer—a five per cent royalty on a three-and-sixpenny edition—but, as Bennett reflected, "many a first book has cost its author a hundred pounds," and he got a new hat out of his!

On 27th April, 1896, shortly before finishing his novel, he began to keep a journal. He does not say why: there is no introduction describing his motives. The first entry, descriptive of scenes observed during the day, suggests a notebook of ideas, such as Charles Reade kept, for subsequent conversion into fiction. But, if it began no more ambitiously, Bennett had hardly started his second entry before he realised that he might follow the example of his idol de Goncourt by keeping a record of his intellectual development, alongside a diary of his daily doings. In January, 1897, he remarked, referring to the de Goncourts' declaration that they wrote "for posterity", that he would not "care a bilberry for posterity". Nor did he so far as his novels were concerned; he worked frankly for money and fame. But his *Journals* were intended for posterity, or as a possible insurance against a want in his old age; if he proved a failure, he might still live for posterity as a Pepys; if he enjoyed only ephemeral success, the publication might be a source of income in his declining years; if as he anticipated, he became a great novelist, his *Journals* would have the value of de Goncourt's. The idea also appealed to his sense of economy, for, by using a few trifling minutes each day, he would accumulate in a few years the material of a full-length book, equal in length and labour to the solid work of a whole year of life.

The first three years of the *Journal* illustrates the latter half of *The Truth About an Author*; the process of self-education continued. Mr. J. B. Priestley—who, perhaps because he went to one but not to the other, occasionally allows virtues to universities, though he derides public schools—has expressed the irrelevant opinion that, if Bennett had shared his privilege in attending one of "our older universities", he might have "relaxed into genial idling", instead of which he was unable to "relax from the awful standard of the London Matriculation" and to "take knowledge easily and lightly". Bennett had idled, if not genially, at least congenially, during his first two years; he must have idled, apparently less congenially, during some five years previously at his father's office, since he was only a short-hand clerk at twenty-one. He was twenty-four when he won his *Tit-Bits* prize and settled seriously to the idea of writing; he had read little or nothing at that time. He had no time for "genial idling", if he was to have an outside chance of success as a writer.

In his self-education, he did not swat at books like a matriculation student. He went out and enjoyed himself, for to the end of his life he enjoyed himself if he was learning anything new. When, as a celebrity in 1911, he made his first trip to America, he spent his first day at sea in a tour of the liner, discovering "vast parts of the ship whose existence I had not imaginatively preconceived," and on the second day he contrived that the chief steward should take him on a tour of inspection, during which he noted how they boiled eggs and mixed dough in the kitchens; nothing was too trivial for notice, for it all contributed to his stock-in-trade as a novelist. The staff job on *Woman* put him "in the swim"; he received press tickets for concerts and theatres. Entering imposing places for the first time, he felt like Denry Machin on his first visit to the Sports Club at Hillport, but it is a safe bet that, at his first important dinner, he was careful to observe which knives and forks his neighbours used.

> "I had not attended many first nights before I discovered that the handful of theatrical critics whose articles it is possible to read without fatigue, made a point of never leaving their stalls. They were nobody's old chap, and nobody's old pal. I copied their behaviour."

For five or six years, between 1893 and 1899, he wrote dramatic criticism, first for *Woman*, subsequently for two other papers. He worked prodigiously as a reviewer, obtaining regular work from Lewis Hind, the editor of the *Academy*, on the strength of the weekly book *causerie* he wrote for *Woman*. He felt that he had a natural aptitude for criticism—"Whenever I read a work of imagination, I am instantly filled with ideas concerning it; I form definite views about its merit or demerit, and having formed them, I hold those views with strong conviction." He is probably the only reviewer who has written honestly about his own methods of reviewing. He confessed how continual practice taught him the art of tearing the guts out of the average book in ten or twenty minutes. "In the case of nine books out of ten, to read them through would not be a work of supererogation—it would be a sinful waste of time on the part of a professional reviewer." He pointed out—as all editors and reviewers know, though Humbug prevents editors from recognising and reviewers from admitting—that it is "economically impossible for the reviewer . . . to read every book through;" the work is too meanly paid. Bennett made a rule "never to work for less than ten shillings an hour on piece-work. If an editor commissioned an article, he received from me as much fundamental brain-power and as much time as the article demanded—up to the limit of his pay in terms of hours at ten shillings apiece." He applied the principles of ordinary business to journalism, and as his literary reputation increased, he proportionately raised the price of his time. After 1900 he twice undertook regular work as a reviewer: for four years, 1908 to 1911, he wrote weekly articles under the pseudonym of "Jacob Tonson" for the *New Age*, a selection of which, in the volume called *Books and Persons* (1917), supplies such a useful literary log of its period as Le Gallienne's *Retrospective Reviews* of the early 'nineties, and in the last years of his life, he appeared as the weekly literary pundit of the *Evening Standard*, when he was the most quoted critic of the day.

For some reason, though Lane accepted his first novel in May, 1896, he did not publish it till February, 1898; originally called "In the Shadow", it appeared as *A Man from the North*, having been advertised as No. 5 of "Lane's Library" of three-and-sixpenny novels, by "E. A. Bennett", in the last number of the *Yellow Book* for April, 1897. Apart from its autobiographical interest in describing the descent upon London of its Five Towns hero and his beginnings in literature, *A Man from the North* is not a remarkable book; though Mr. Priestley believed the reading of all his minor books necessary to an appreciation of Bennett, he did not mention this first book in his *London Mercury* article. It was written "under the sweet influences of the de Goncourts, Turgenev, Flaubert, and de Maupassant," especially of Maupassant, and Bennett afterwards noted that he might have been suspected of plagiarising in some parts from *Bel-Ami*, though he was not conscious of having imitated. Mr. Priestley, who united in the common conspiracy of condescension to Bennett as a card, seems to regard this French influence as unfortunate, being apparently unaware that the same influence affected nearly every considerable novelist of the time, from Henry James to Conrad and Galsworthy; on one page he praises the French influence for saving Bennett from falling into "the disgraceful slovenliness that spoils so much of Mr. Wells's later work," on the next he condemns Bennett for "following the wrong masters" in striving for a "technique", which "really meant nothing more than a suppression of the narrator and a deliberate simplicity and unity in the narrative, the action, the background." Clearly Mr. Priestley wants to eat his cake and keep it; the "slovenliness" he dislikes in Mr. Wells's later work is mainly due to the non-suppression of the narrator. In *A Man from the North* the theme is the frustration of a serious young man's ambition; he lacks the moral strength to decide what he wants and take it, and finally resigns himself hopelessly to the drab outlook of suburban domesticity. If the result seems unsatisfactory, it is largely because the hero is an unsatisfactory young man. The minor characters are all well drawn, especially the women, the young Adeline and the waitress, Miss Roberts; the clerk Jenkins was drawn from life, and probably the other characters were at least "composite portraits" of people known personally to Bennett.

The sales of the novel brought Bennett one pound above the cost of having the manuscript typewritten; the reviews were conventional. Soon after finishing *A Man from the North*, he began "a study of parental authority" which eventually became *Anna of the Five Towns*, but though thus begun in 1896, it was not published till 1902. He was too busy with his growing journalistic activities to concentrate on the novel, and his second book was the first of his several "self-help" manuals, *Journalism for Women*, published by Lane about the same time as *A Man from the North*. He reflected wryly on the different receptions of the two books, the novel, "a serious and laborious work," waiting nearly two years for publication, while this piece of hack work, "thrown off in about eight weeks, is to be printed and published in less than a month," with a royalty of fifteen per cent.

During 1897 he made the acquaintance of Mr. Eden Phillpotts, the first and one of the closest of his literary friendships. His friend's example awakened him to the possibility of writing popular fiction to pay the way of more serious work, and in the autumn of 1898, he "decided very seriously to take up fiction for a livelihood."

"To write popular fiction is offensive to me, but it is far more agreeable than being tied daily to an office and editing a lady's paper; and perhaps it is less ignoble and less of a strain on the conscience. To edit a lady's paper, even a relatively advanced one, is to foster conventionality and hinder progress regularly once a week. Moreover I think that fiction will pay better, and in order to be happy I must have a fair supply of money."

He "put aside indefinitely" his serious novel, and decided to give a full year's trial "to writing the sort of fiction that sells itself." He decided to follow Mr. Phillpotts's suggestion that he should write a short story every month, and he was impressed on finding that Mr. Phillpotts could write a serial of seventy-thousand words in a month. Following his resolution, he recorded that during the last quarter of 1898 he "produced about twice as much work as in any previous similar period," including "two thirds of a serial story, four or five short stories, a lot of reviews for the *Academy*, and all my usual stuff for *Woman* and *Hearth and Home*."

He finished his first sensational serial, *For Love and Life*, in three months, and decided that, having "got fairly into" the business, he "could comfortably write 2,500 words in half a day." Tillotsons' Syndicate offered him sixty pounds for it, which was the price he had himself expected, but he asked eighty, and obtained seventy-five. He then elected to try writing for the stage, and his third book, *Polite Farces* (1899), contained one-act curtain-raisers, one of which secured him an interview with Cyril Maude, who invited him to write a full-length play for his consideration, whereupon, as he tells in *The Truth About an Author*, he collaborated with Arthur Hooley in *The Chancellor*. By the end of the year, he had earned nearly six hundred pounds, and feeling that his prospects in making a living from fiction were justified, he consulted his father about resigning the editorship of *Woman*. In 1898 he had become obsessed with the idea of living in the country, like Mr. Phillpotts, and when he looked up a "list of our foremost writers" and found "they nearly all lived in the country," country life became an essential to his literary equipment. Possibly his father promised some financial guarantee; at least his cost of living was to be much reduced, since it was arranged that his parents and an unmarried sister should live with him. His residence had to be "on a certain main-line at a certain minimum distance from London," and having secured a house at Hockliffe in Bedfordshire, he resigned from *Woman* in September, 1900.

§ 3

During the year 1900, Bennett achieved such an amount of work as he produced annually for the rest of his life. Besides *The Chancellor*, he collaborated with Eden Phillpotts in an adaptation of the latter's novel, *Children of the Mist*, and had a curtain-riser, *The Postmistress*, produced by Cyril Maude. He wrote half a dozen short stories and 196 articles; he made a selection of his articles in the *Academy*, published in 1901 as *Fame and Fiction*; he acted as publisher's reader to Pearson's, a job which he disliked and soon relinquished, as he relates in *The Truth About an Author*; he completed the first draft and began the final writing of *Anna of the Five Towns*, and he wrote another serial for Tillotson's in *The Grand Babylon Hotel*.

Along with *The Card*, *The Grand Babylon Hotel* is reckoned by conventional critics the most characteristic of Bennett's books; just as Denry Machin is a naïve self-portrait, so they say *The*

Grand Babylon Hotel reflects Bennett's unageing childish delight in the expensive palaces of the rich, a peculiarity which they deprecate, in the complacent superiority of their conscious gentility, as a harmlessly amusing eccentricity of the parvenu provincial, a characteristic of the card. Sufficiently aware of Bennett's genius to feel uncomfortable in his condescension, Mr. Priestley borrowed the undiscerning biographer's device of supposing his subject to have had Dr. Jekyll's ability to assume the guise of Hyde, and credited Bennett with three individualities, the second of whom is the card who wrote "the Grand Babylon Hotel Cycle" of fantasias.

It is rather alarming to note in the bibliography of Mr. Priestley's works that he is the author of a monograph on Meredith; if he found it necessary to credit Bennett with three individualities, he must have made Meredith seem like a roomful of people. For Bennett was not a complex character, like Meredith or Thackeray or Joseph Conrad; he was simple and direct, and he intensified his simplicity by writing of himself with exceptional honesty. Perhaps it is only fair to Mr. Priestley to note that, at the time of his essay on Bennett, the *Journals* were not available. But *The Truth About an Author* was available, though Mr. Priestley does not refer to it; perhaps he overlooked it, as many do, supposing it to be from its title merely one of Bennett's several self-help handbooks. *The Truth About an Author* was published anonymously as a serial in the *Academy* before book publication in 1903; the paper was a struggling sixpenny weekly, and when Bennett suggested to the editor that its circulation might be stimulated by a sensational serial, Lewis Hind replied, "Yes, I know, and I should like you to write your literary autobiography for us!" Bennett tackled the task with zest; the book is not only a commentary of shrewd wisdom on various departments of the writing trade—editing, reviewing, the writing of novels, serials, plays, and dramatic criticism—but vividly records his own apprenticeship as a writer. It is Bennett's own statement of the making of his literary personality; it ends with his retirement to live at Hockliffe, when he finally devoted himself to writing fiction as a livelihood. His literary character was then finally formed for better or worse, at the age of thirty-three; thenceforward, he followed for thirty years the self-devised system by which he made himself into a money-making writing machine.

The keynote of *The Truth About an Author* is zest; Bennett tells his own scoops as a card as eagerly as Denry Machin's. So he approached everything in life, anticipating novelty in every experience. Mr. Priestley justly recognises him as "essentially a Romantic", for life to Bennett was a great adventure; when he got up in the morning, each day presented a prospect of enchanting mystery, for who knew what new experience he might encounter, what fresh astonishing item might be added to his stock of knowledge. Zest was the keynote of Arnold Bennett; he was never bored, because he never drifted aimlessly into doing anything—never "idled genially" or otherwise—for he had every moment of his waking existence planned, and consequently a motive and an object for everything he did.

Why is *The Grand Babylon Hotel* still read after thirty-five years of steady popularity? It is a sensational novel of the most feathery lightness; Bennett wrote it as such, in fifteen days of work. Somebody took him to the Savoy Hotel, a rare experience in those days; he sat amongst the "nobs"—probably he discovered by casual questioning of the hall porter that the hotel "counted that day wasted on which it did not entertain, at the lowest, a German prince or the Maharajah of some Indian State"; his humour inspired the thought of how the imperturbability of a waiter might be ruffled if somebody asked for "a steak and Bass"; noticing how waiters served the "nobs" without any apparent consciousness of their importance, and speculating on the possibilities of their private characters, he suddenly saw the dramatic potentialities of making the ambassadorial head-waiter, the omnipotent chef, and the immaculate receptionist, into a trio of grand-scale crooks. He worked on the idea, as on everything, with zest; it is such a theme as William Le Queux treated dozens of times, yet Le Queux wrote nothing like it, because he had neither Bennett's zest nor his genius. Bennett was not two, three, or more individualities; he was simply a man of genius, with absorbing zest in his work. Because he needed money, he had to write light fiction and self-help manuals, but he never fell into the error of despising such work. On his own initiative he had chosen this way of making money, and he gave of his best to supply the highest-priced article; it was as much an achievement to hold a big public breathless with sensation as to satisfy his self-criticism of his art—it was only a difference of values. Mr. Priestley rightly declines to "condemn" any of Bennett's minor work, for everything he did bears the mark of the artist; he wrote nothing much more trivial than *Lilian* (1922), which carries no more ballast than the average serial in an illustrated magazine, but its technique has the effortlessness of mastery—the effect is the same as Kreisler playing the intermezzo from *Cavalleria Rusticana*, which any street musician can readily murder. As he said himself when reading one of his early Tillotson's serials, *The Gates of Wrath*, "its smartness and clarity prevent me from being quite honestly ashamed of it."

Bennett contented himself at Hockliffe only about a year before he decided to live in Paris. Gentility smiles again—to the little provincial Paris was the Mecca of high art and original sin. But Bennett never did anything without a reason. Unluckily a hiatus occurs in his *Journal* before his going to Paris, and the motives of the move are open to conjecture. Since he looked to French fiction for his masters, he probably wanted to saturate himself in French influences and atmosphere with a view to making himself essentially an English Maupassant; probably too, he decided that country life at Hockliffe was not conducive to inspiration of ideas. He needed the stimulus of continually seeing something new, and throughout his life he was continually moving about, rarely sleeping a score of nights successively in the same bed. He never acquired, or attempted to acquire, the faculty of Stevenson and Lang for writing while travelling— he was then too busily occupied in seeing the sights—but he wrote as comfortably in a hotel bedroom as in his own study.

For several years he wrote on an average from two hundred to three hundred thousand words a year; he earned a good living, but it was hard-earned money at the rate of two or three guineas a thousand words. He described 1907 as a record year, when he wrote 375,000 words and earned thirty-two thousand francs, which may be reckoned as double his income of six hundred pounds in 1900. In 1908, during which he wrote *Buried Alive* and three quarters of *The Old Wives' Tale*, he said he had "never worked so hard as this year," and "have not earned less for several years." But his amazing perseverance and application won its reward at the end of that year with the publication of *The Old Wives' Tale*, and in 1912 his income was sixteen thousand pounds. He did not relax to bask in the sunshine of success; he went about freely to social functions, but he went on producing his annual three hundred thousand words with clockwork precision.

He returned to England to live in 1913, taking a "new-old" house at Thorpe-le-Soken in Essex, whence during the war he travelled up to town, like his own Lord Raingo, to attend at the Ministry of Information, where, under Lord Beaverbrook, he was director of British propaganda in France. Even during the war, when he made himself useful in public service in every possible way, he contrived to keep up an average of about two hundred thousand words of his "own stuff", besides propaganda writing. The only difference that affluence brought to his life lay in more expensive pleasures; he kept a yacht, entertained lavishly, travelled always *au prince*, played at casino tables, ate and drank of the best in the most splendid and exclusive of hotels and restaurants. Always he enjoyed life; in 1907, when reading Taine's letters,

"The portrait of the man gradually grew clear to me, and inspired me with ideals similar to his own; the doing simply of the work which one believes to be best, and to neglect of all gross and vain considerations. Why should I worry after fame and money, knowing as I do that these will not increase my happiness?"

The answer was simply that he loved life too much to devote himself to the contemplative serenity of a creative artist absorbed entirely in his work for his own sake; he had not lingered long in the rural retreat he coveted as a London journalist. Carrying out with astonishing tenacity the programme he planned when deciding to devote himself to fiction, he trained himself to habits incapable of being broken. He never willingly wasted a moment of life; if he was at work, pen in hand, he must be out and about, seeing and learning about life, taking his pleasures as energetically as he worked.

Obviously such a disciplined mechanism was an intolerable proposition to live with, and it is not surprising that Bennett's marriage ended in separation. In *The Glimpse* (1909), when the husband, having discovered his wife in a flirtation with his close friend, protests that "I've always done the decent thing by you," she bursts out: "Never! You never did the decent thing by me! You never thought of any soul on this earth except yourself. . . . You never really thought of anything but your work." And he replies, "with a short condescending laugh," "Well, work is work!" Bennett married his French wife, Marguerite Soulié, in July, 1907, some eighteen months before writing *The Glimpse*, and Mrs. Bennett herself, in *Arnold Bennett* (1925), observes how hard it is "for an artist's wife to have but second place in her husband's heart," and how, realising it, "she will train herself to find out the secret reasons of his apparent or real neglect of her." Remarking that he was not only not cold-hearted, but an unusually affectionate man, Mr. Wells thinks that "his sexual life did not flood into his general life," that "his personality never, so to speak, fused with a woman's," and adds his belief that there was "some early scar that robbed him of the easy self-forgetfulness" of a lover.

That there was a scar appears in the first volume of the *Journals*. In June 1906 he became engaged to be married to Miss Eleanora Green, sister of the French novelist, Julian Green, but she had "a definite 'Melisande' quality", and the engagement was broken off after seven weeks. But even supposing he had married Miss Green instead of Mlle Soulié, the result could have been hardly different. Mr. Wells truly says of him that "there were pleasures in love but they had their place among other pleasures." Bennett would allow nothing to monopolise more than its duly allotted meed of his daily attention. Moreover, it seems likely that he preserved a native provincial caution towards women; on coming to London as a young man, he observed the same "instinct for self-preservation" which saved George Moore from sex entanglements. Probably he himself experienced his hero's hesitant feelings towards the original of Adeline in *A Man from the North*, always holding back from committing himself to a full expression of his emotions, in fear that this might prove not to be the woman of his destiny. The hero of *The Glimpse*, having avowed his love, finds himself "solitary and secure" with his lady "in the tiny flat, under the shaded lamp, and she the image of modest acquiescence," but his "unconquerable conventional pride surged up and took control," and he reflects, as he holds her in his arms, "No. . . . You aren't going to have any complications in your life; you aren't going to be at the mercy of accidents; you aren't going to do anything silly." So, he says, "I left her immaculate," and the next day set the necessary machinery in action to possess her lawfully. This seems true Bennett; he scrupulously avoided any possible complications which might intrude upon his settled scheme of work.

It seems that a *liaison au français*, such as his Lord Raingo enjoyed with Delphine, would admirably have suited Bennett's sexual requirements. He was naturally affectionate and kind, and he needed a woman's affection and kindness—but at the right time and place, when his work permitted. After his separation from his wife, he incurred a complication, at the age of fifty-eight, when he became the lover of Miss Dorothy Cheston, who became the mother of his daughter and assumed the name of Bennett by deed-poll. In her book on *Arnold Bennett* (1935), Miss Cheston Bennett expresses the belief that, with her, Bennett achieved such a "fusion" as Mr. Wells describes—a fusion "resultant on a mutually subjective contact of the two persons, the result perhaps of mutual perception of the other's subjective being," but if so, it found no expression in the few works remaining for him to write in the six years between her entry into his life and his death on 27th March, 1931, unless it is in *Accident* (1929), where he reflects on old Mr. Lucass's passion for "his marvellous hag-beauty" of a wife, "a passion which age could not chill":

"The passion had gloriously survived his wife's slow transition from beauty to her ugliness, her maladies, her nerves, her tantrums, her tyrannies, her senseless preoccupation with such trifles as trunks, her eternal knitting, her injustices, her infernal tongue, her ruthless disregard (as on that morning) for the

O.G.F.   Z

infirmity of his years, her fiendish obstinacy in having her
own way. And it had survived his physical decay. He ought
to have been as cold as a fish, as indifferent as a mummy!
And here he was behaving like a lusty youth! The thing was
magnificent, enheartening, inspiring."

Perhaps this expressed wistful regret that his own life had lacked
such long-enduring passion.

The quality of passion is likewise lacking in his novels.
Miss Cheston Bennett, in her prefatory note to the *Journals*,
expresses the view that his work, like his personal taste and
temperament, contained the paradox that, " while it was definitely
robust, with gusto for detail and for material effect, the inner
spirit of the author, directed always towards beauty and a kind
of perfecting of material existence, was intensely shy and averse
to the profanation, the ' vulgarisation', of unreserved expression."
What she diagnosed as shyness seems to have been his provincial
caution—the card's instinctive reluctance to give himself away—
and the notion of his being averse to unreserved expression fits
into his character as revealed neither in his novels nor in his
Journals, for Bennett was at once too fine an artist and too
instinctive a journalist to refrain from using any important
personal experience in his work. With a fine sense of his abilities,
he generally avoided the portrayal of passion, but as if resenting
the admission of a limitation, he attempted to draw a woman of
passion in the character of Hilda Lessways, one of the few
unconvincing women to be found in his novels.

For Mr. Wells delivers scant justice in dismissing Bennett's
women as "for the most part good hard Staffordshire ware."
Wary of women so far as they were likely to intrude too intimately upon his peace of mind, Bennett penetrated deeply into the
psychology of the sex from a vantage point of detachment.
On the staff of *Woman*, he learned much from the contributors,
all of whom were women; on becoming editor, he employed a
female secretary in the days when few women were engaged in
business. He learned to notice such phenomena, usually un-
observed by men though obvious to the intelligent woman, as the
need for women with turned-up noses to dress simply, especially
avoiding "frocks that attract attention". In June, 1898, he

noted his belief that "no serious attempt had yet been made by a man to present essential femininity," and that, while woman may have drawn woman "with justice and accuracy for her own sex," yet "a woman is too close to woman to observe her with aloofness and yet with perfect insight—as we should do if we had the insight." He set himself the task of observing and appreciating women; he watched women on omnibuses, noting the mannerisms of "the well-dressed well-bred unattended woman of twenty to thirty-five," and how, in spite of their easy assurance, their faces reflected that women's emancipation "has yet penetrated but slightly into the ranks of the middle-class," and that they were "unacquainted with the realities of existence." He noted that only the "cold, questioning stare" betrayed the effect of her profession on the character of a well-preserved prostitute, and how common girls of the chorus type detected "instantly and furtively" the light woman for what she was. He was fascinated by the pale wistfulness of a barmaid's face, pressed against the glass separating the corridor from a theatre's auditorium, as she watched the triumph of a famous dancer; he realised the potential truth of the Helen of Troy legend when he saw the beautiful Miriam Clements on the stage—"the sight of her gave me an understanding sympathy with the man who ' goes mad ' about a woman, dishonours himself to possess her, and continues to worship her." Bennett made himself a connoisseur of women, and viewed them with the connoisseur's detachment, assessing their merits as the hero of *The Glimpse* admired his wife's grace of movement and her way of wearing her clothes.

The origin of Bennett's greatest novel, *The Old Wives' Tale*, is well known; he was moved to commiseration by the sight of a poor, grotesque, old woman being laughed at in a restaurant, and reflecting how she had been "once young, slim, perhaps beautiful; certainly free from these ridiculous mannerisms," he conceived the making of "a heart-rending novel out of the history of a woman such as she." He admitted "the example and challenge" of Maupassant's *Une Vie*, and aimed to "go one better" than Maupassant by describing "the life-history of two women instead of only one." Of the two daughters of Mr. Baines, the Bursley draper, Constance is certainly "good, hard Staffordshire

ware;" capable and complacent, she fulfils her duty successively
as daughter, wife and mother, but her colourless solidity,
conforming with the colourless solidity of her narrow provincial
background, represents her triumph, for she emerges a living
personification of her type—the type which peopled the lower
middle-class created by the Industrial Revolution. Her husband,
Samuel Povey, the honest little tradesman who, after a life of
humdrum routine, "embraced a cause, lost it, and died of it," is
equally a life-like conception: he and Constance and their
surroundings, etched with Zola's particularity of minute detail,
entitle Bennett to recognition as a great representative novelist
of the lower middle-class.

It is difficult to decide whether Constance or her sister Sophia
reflects the greater credit in naturalistic portraiture. Constance
lives before the reader's eyes in spite of the unbroken monotony
of her life; Sophia, endowed with the richness of beauty and
wilful impetuosity, which leads to her elopement with a handsome wastrel, has dramatic atmosphere to enliven the development of her personality. But the process by which the brilliant,
vital girl becomes the hard, business-like landlady of a French
pension presents a masterly study in psychology; the scene where
she steals the banknotes from her sleeping lover, an act "characteristic of her enterprise and of her fundamental prudence,"
illustrates Bennett's strength in artistic unity, his skill in contriving the mutual development of plot and character, the incident
deriving power not simply from its dramatic value as a crisis in
the narrative, but from significance in relation to its consequences.

As he had drawn in Constance Povey an imaginative study
of the ordinary provincial woman of the lower middle-class, in
Clayhanger (1910) he wrote the biography of such a man as he
had seen in dozens during his youth in the Five Towns, rising
gradually on the swelling tide of Victorian prosperity from the
lower to the upper middle-class. Mr. Priestley thinks that, as he
conceived *The Old Wives' Tale* backwards from the old woman
in the restaurant, so *Clayhanger* developed from "a mental picture
of a seemingly commonplace married couple, middle-aged,
middle-class, prosperous, contented, apparently prosaic." But
while he was writing *Clayhanger*, Bennett read Galsworthy's

Man of Property, which impressed him as "a really distinguished, passionate, truly universal book," with "the only large fault . . . that the end is not an end," and he conceived the idea of ending *Clayhanger* likewise inconclusively, to be completed in a trilogy. So *Hilda Lessways* (1911) runs parallel with the story of *Clayhanger*, explaining in a full-length study of Hilda how she came to marry another man on the eve of her union with Edwin Clayhanger, and the third volume, *These Twain* (1916), relates the tale of the middle-aged couple's married life. The two sequels have never received the same praise as *Clayhanger*, a fact undoubtedly due to the absence of complete conviction in Hilda's character. In *Hilda Lessways*, she figures as the new woman asserting her individuality and encountering the inevitable emotional complications which Mrs. Humphry Ward and William J. Locke differently attempted to illustrate in *Sir George Tressady* and *At the Gate of Samaria*:

> "She was disconcerted, if not panic-struck, by the violence of his first kiss; but her consternation was delectable to her.
> And amid her fright and her joy, and the wonder of her extreme suprise and the preoccupation of being whirled down the river, she calmly reflected somewhere in her brain: 'The door is not locked. Supposing someone were to come in and see us!' And she reflected also, in an ecstasy of relief: 'My life will be quite simple now. I shall have nothing to worry about. And I can help him.' For during a year past she had never ceased to ask herself what she must do to arrange her life; her conscience had never ceased to tell her that she ought not to be content to remain in the narrow ideas of her mother, and that though she preferred marriage she ought to act independently of the hope of it. Throughout her long stay in Preston Street she had continually said: 'After this—what? This cannot last for ever. When it comes to an end what am I to do to satisfy my conscience?' And she had thought vaguely of magnificent activities and purposes—she knew not what . . . The problem existed no more. Her life was arranged. And now, far more sincerely than in the King's Road twenty minutes earlier, she regarded the career of a spinster with horror and with scorn."

The moody, wayward girl of *Clayhanger* and *Hilda Lessways* appears in *These Twain* as a beautiful, alluring, and elusive woman; the change is due to her having come through the testing fire of vicissitudes to the goal of love and happiness. Bennett conceived the change as a natural psychological development like that of Sophia in *The Old Wives' Tale*, but in Hilda's case he did not reveal the process of development—she is left, at the end of *Hilda Lessways*, in love with Edwin and about to bear another man's child, and reappears again after an interval of ten years in the last part of *Clayhanger*. This flaw extends the sense of Hilda's elusiveness to the reader, who consequently never attains to the same sympathy with her as with Edwin, so that both sequels fail to give the same satisfaction as *Clayhanger*. Nevertheless, the trilogy of *The Clayhanger Family* not only ranks with *The Old Wives' Tale* as Bennett's supreme achievement, but commands its place in literary history as the representative novel of the late-Victorian lower middle-class, as Galsworthy's *Forsyte Saga* is the representative novel of the upper middle-class.

The Old Wives' Tale made Bennett's fame and fortune; in Sir John Squire's words, "it put him immediately in a class to which nobody except his most intimate friends knew that he aspired." Apart from the Clayhanger books, he only once afterwards wrote a novel in the same superlative class—the grim satire on avarice, *Riceyman Steps* (1923), in which the miserly Clerkenwell bookseller and the trim little widow he marries are brought by his greed for money to death from insufficient nourishment. It is fashionable, therefore, to assume that Bennett left three books by which to estimate his quality as a major novelist, and the rest of his voluminous works belong to the pulp dump of ephemeral fiction. But he wrote at least three novels before *The Old Wives' Tale* which command shelf room in any representative library of modern fiction. *Anna of the Five Towns* (1902) was his first serious novel after *A Man from the North*, and while it exhibits an enormous advance on its predecessor, its slow beginning weighs heavily with the excessively meticulous care of the earnest novice. In all his books Bennett followed Zola in his minute attention to detail, but the eighth chapter of this book, containing a careful description of an earthenware factory, provides a rare instance in Bennett's work of including material extraneous to the development of the story—evidently he had made a tour of a pottery business, and as a journalist, he felt the material too good to waste. The story quickens from the school treat in the ninth chapter, and Anna's gradual emancipation from the dominion of her miserly father, against the grey background of Methodist Revivalism in the growing pottery town, provides a foretaste of the power for painting the sombre tints of lower middle-class life which found fullest expression in *The Old Wives' Tale* and *Clayhanger*.

Bennett is accused of harping too continually on the note of disillusion, because so few of his characters ever feel emotions of genuine passion. But in the drab lives of the lower middle-class he painted, passion has no place, save as a nameless vice, like alcoholism or prostitution, menacing the sanctuary of respectability. Most women of her class married like Anna, who allowed love to go out of her life with poor Willie Price, and settled serenely to make the best of marriage with the rising young business man whom she liked and respected. In *Leonora* (1903), Bennett visualised revolt in a woman after twenty years of such a marriage. A beautiful, elegant woman of forty—the type which Bennett, as a connoisseur, most admired—the respectable wife of a pottery manufacturer, dreams sadly, like the working girls of her husband's factory, "of an existence more distinguished than her own; an existence brilliant and tender, where dalliance and high endeavour, virtue and the flavour of sin, eternal appetite and eternal satisfaction, were incredibly united."

"Even now, on her fortieth birthday, she still believed in the possibility of a conscious state of positive and continued happiness, and regretted that she should have missed it . . . the field of her mind's eye seemed to be entirely filled by an image of the woman of forty as imagined by herself at the age of twenty. And she was that woman now! But she did not feel like forty; at thirty she had not felt thirty; she could only accept the almanac and the rules of arithmetic. The interminable years of her marriage rolled back, and she was eighteen again, ingenuous and trustful, convinced that her versatile husband was unique among his sex. The fading of a short-lived and factitious passion, the descent of the unique male to the ordinary level of males, the births of her three girls and their rearing and training: all these things seemed as trifles to her, mere excrescences and depressions in a vast tableland of her monotonous and placid career. She had had no career. Her strength of will, of courage, of love, had never been taxed; only her patience."

The story of how Leonora finds romance at forty is finely conceived, but Bennett deferred to respectable convention in the means of helping his heroine to the consummation of her love. The library public of 1903 had progressed far enough to recognise that a respectably married woman could still feel sexual emotion after twenty years of marriage, but it could not countenance that the mother of grown-up daughters should throw her cap over the windmill of convention. So the husband had to be killed off out of the way, and a period of fifteen months allowed to elapse in decent mourning before respectability blessed Leonora's morally illicit love in a second marriage.

Bennett's third important novel before *The Old Wives' Tale*, *Whom God Hath Joined* (1906), deals with marriage, divorce, and the cruelty of scandal. In the brothers, Mark and Lawrence Ridware, Bennett seems to have visualised something of himself; Mark, the artist, who has broken away from the Five Towns and is successfully pursuing ambition, is Bennett as he actually was— Lawrence, the lawyer's clerk, is Bennett as he might have been if he had stayed in the Five Towns and married. The story is of two divorces, and in both cases the innocent parties suffer most. Lawrence has drifted apart, through continual bickering, from his wife, who takes a lover; when he discovers her infidelity, he feels the greater spleen from his sense of insult added to injury. In the other case, Lawrence's employer, the successful solicitor Fearns, is discovered by his daughter in a casual amour with her governess. The atmosphere of the divorce court, with all its callousness and crudity, is conveyed with all Bennett's meticulous attention to detail, and the lash of his satire is as keen as Galsworthy's in *In Chancery* and *Over the River*.

"All the hidden shames were exposed to view, a feast for avid eyes. The animal in every individual could lick its chops and thrill with pleasure. All the animals could exchange candid glances and concede that they were animals. And the supreme satisfaction for the males was that the females were present, the females who had tempted and who had yielded and who had rolled voluptuously in the very mud. And they were obliged to listen, in their prim tight frocks, to the things which they had done dishevelled, and they were obliged to answer and to confess and to blush, and to utter dreadful things with a simper. The alluring quality of this wholesale debauch of exciting suggestiveness could never fail until desire failed. As an entertainment it was unique, appealing to the most vital instinct of the widest possible public."

After it is made to seem that Lawrence, by sensitively declining to assert his marital rites on a woman without love, had driven his wife to take a lover, the secret of his illegitimate birth is dragged out to prove a quibble of legal formality; in the other case, the daughter breaks down under the stress of giving evidence against her father, and the suit is withdrawn. The whole story presents a grim picture of the hatreds and misery fostered by the cruelty of formal conventions; its intensity of feeling reflects Bennett's own mental anguish, for the book was written at the time of his broken engagement to Miss Green.

Of Bennett's lighter books, *The Card* (1911), published in America as *Denry the Audacious*, is a magnificent frolic, from the first chapter, in which the solicitor's clerk starts his career as a card by inserting his name in the list of invitations to the grand municipal ball, where he creates a sensation by dancing with the great lady of the place, to the last, when he becomes the youngest mayor his town has ever known. Mr. Wells thinks *The Card* was Bennett's "self-explanation", and it is an extravaganza on the theme of his own philosophy of "seeming to know more than he really knew." *The Card* is light fiction, to be identified, as one of his fellow councillors says of Denry, "with the great cause of cheering us all up," but it is a work of genius in its line—one of the greatest light novels of the present century. Its sequel, *The Regent* (1913), where Bennett used his intimate knowledge of theatrical life for the scene of Denry's activities in the greater world outside the Five Towns, is hardly so good, but every book by Bennett offers first-rate entertainment. Bennett was a genius, and everything to which he turned his hand bears the unmistakable stamp of his quality. Slick and smart in the mastery of his craft, he always succeeds brilliantly in what he sets out to achieve; if many of his books attain to a level no higher than light entertainment, it is because they aspired to nothing more; they are to be criticised in their own class, where they brilliantly withstand comparison with all their kind.

CHAPTER ELEVEN

Galsworthy and the Forsytes

§ 1

"INDEPENDENCE is the state best worth having in life, and such as believe they can achieve it in their later tales by servitude to fashion in their youthful efforts are doomed, I fear, to the drinking of bitter waters." So wrote John Galsworthy in the foreword to *Caravan*, the collection of his short stories published in 1925. Arnold Bennett may be taken as a case in vindication of the truth of this assertion, for having begun with the idea of making money from "fiction that sells itself", to purchase comfortable leisure in which to write the work of his choice, he remained to the end of his life enslaved to his own popularity, and actually produced very much more top-class work in the earlier than in the latter half of his writing career. John Galsworthy and Joseph Conrad were notable instances of novelists who followed Henry James's example in disdaining the dictates of popular taste and writing according to conscience. Conrad paid the penalty by waiting till the last few years of his life for recognition in a wider sphere than the fireside circle of genuine culture, after a long career of bitter disappointment and anxiety under threatening clouds of poverty. To Galsworthy, on the other hand, success came without any protracted and embittering delay, and he never needed money from his work. Cynics have grounds for the sneer that he could well afford to disregard the demands of popular fancy, and though they must confess that his fortunate situation in no way detracted from a great record of conscientious endeavour and magnificent achievement, there is a tendency among the romantically minded to belittle Galsworthy because he suffered none of the painful but picturesque vicissitudes commonly the lot of literary genius. So the conspiracy of disfavour, which seems inevitably attendant upon a great writer's death in recent years, has widespread tentacles in

Galsworthy's case, for while there is this tendency to irrational snobbery in the romantically minded, the forces of respectability have never forgiven one of their legitimate sons for his crime of intellectual patricide.

Galsworthy belonged to the social class least likely and least inclined to produce artists. The Forsytes of his novels, representative satirically of the upper middle-class, were drawn in close individual likeness to prototypes in his own family. Old Jolyon Forsyte, "in whom a desperate honesty welled up at times, would allude to his ancestors as: ' Yeomen—I suppose very small beer'." The Galsworthys were Devonshire yeomen for many generations, rooted in the same farm of the same village, like the Voiseys in *A Man of Devon*, and the visit of Soames Forsyte to the parish where "his roots lay", described in *Swan Song*, probably followed such a visit by John Galsworthy to Wembury, near Plymouth, where he found a large field still called " Great Galsworthy" as Soames found " Great Forsyte". " Superior Dosset" Forsyte, "not at all what is called a Jerry-builder", migrated from Devon to London in the eighteen-thirties to make a fortune out of house property; so likewise did Galsworthy's grandfather. His sons were the originals of the old Forsytes, and the eldest, the prototype of Old Jolyon, was Galsworthy's father. Old Jolyon and his generation were thus born of the new middle-class appearing in the early years of Victoria's reign, and Galsworthy's father married into a family superior of standing to his own, for the Bartleets of Worcestershire were landed gentry and Galsworthy's maternal grandfather was a needle manufacturer of Redditch in the days when big business was still in the hands of privilege. Blanche Bailey Bartleet, whose character figures in *The Freelands* as that of Frances Fleeming Freeland, married John Galsworthy, solicitor and director of companies, in 1862, and their son, the novelist, was born on 14th August, 1867 at Kingston Hill, whence, on such a summer's day as when Old Jolyon died, the Grand Stand at Epsom could be seen far away, as from Robin Hill, the site of the house built for Soames by Bosinney, in which Young Jolyon and Irene lived their married life.

Galsworthy was "a quite normal, not at all unusual type of boy," who "read voraciously books of history and adventure and made himself short-sighted by doing this generally face down-wards on the floor." At nine, he went to a preparatory school at Bournemouth, to which he was taken by his father's confidential clerk, the original of old Gradman, who likewise escorted Soames when he was a "shaver". In due time, he proceeded to Harrow, where his career followed the same even tenor of normality; he was a sound but not outstandingly brilliant scholar, adequate at games, a good disciplinarian as a monitor, ruling rather by his prestige and being generally liked than by severity, and finished as captain of football, first string at gymnastics, and a notable athlete. He therefore went up to New College, Oxford, in 1886, with the credentials of a "blood", and being "a little intoxicated on the novels of Whyte-Melville," probably followed a very similar course to that attributed to Young Jolyon in "A Sad Affair" of *On Forsyte 'Change.* He belonged to most of the best clubs, including Vincent's, the Grid., and the O.U.D.S., of which he was an interested member, his favourite study was *Ruff's Guide to the Turf,* and as a strained heart prevented his sustaining his school reputation as a footballer and athlete, he was mainly associated with the hunting set. He led "the conventional life of the well-to-do, not very intellectual undergraduate," enjoyed the reputation of being "the best-dressed man in College," and possessed "a certain nonchalance and languor of manner which, to those who did not know him, gave the impression of superior-ity." He took a second-class honours degree in law, and a year after leaving Oxford, gained his call to the bar in 1890; he made some pretence to begin practising, but acquired only that intimate knowledge of legal procedure which enabled him to make it the butt of incisive satire in his books.

Whether on account of an unfortunate love-affair, or merely because his father, seeing that he had dutifully fulfilled the parental wish that he should qualify for the law, decided, like Old Jolyon, that his son was "an amiable chap", he was allowed to seek widening experience in travel; he went on trips to Vancouver and Russia, as well as making a protracted tour to the South Seas, Australia, and South Africa, in company with E. L. Sanderson, the friend who figures prominently in the correspondence of Conrad and Edward Garnett, as well as

Galsworthy. He hoped to call at Samoa and see Stevenson, but though he did not carry out this plan, he made the acquaintance of Joseph Conrad, who was first mate of the ship which carried him from Adelaide to Cape Town. The *Reminiscences of Conrad* in *Castles in Spain* (1927) reveal that Galsworthy was duly impressed by the sailor—when Conrad asked him to his cabin on his last evening aboard, "I remember feeling that he outweighed for me all the other experiences of that voyage"—but it was "of life, not literature", that they talked, though Galsworthy carried a copy of "that fascinating little book, *The Story of an African Farm*" in his pocket. He kept up the acquaintance, and after 1895 stayed frequently with Conrad, who was "indefatigably good to me while my own puppy's eyes were opening to literature"; then they "burned together many midnight candles, much tobacco," discussing each other's work and the art of fiction as practised by Turgeniev and Henry James.

Soon after his return from this voyage in 1893 came Galsworthy's inspiration to write. In 1891 his first cousin, Arthur Galsworthy, had married Ada Cooper, the daughter of a Norwich doctor; in *The Man of Property*, Irene, daughter of Professor Heron, is persuaded into marriage with Soames by his persistence and her unhappy home life, and whether or not Ada Galsworthy was likewise persuaded the result was the same— she learned the tragedy of a loveless marriage to a sensitive woman. Through his sisters, who were her confidantes and ardent partisans, like June Forsyte to Irene, Galsworthy became a sympathiser in her case, pity and sympathy changed to love, and in the autumn of 1895 they became lovers. The story of fact, as related by Mr. H. V. Marrot in his *Life and Letters of John Galsworthy*, here differs somewhat from the fiction of Irene's history. Both disliked the clandestine conduct of their love and would have welcomed its open proclamation, but Galsworthy's father was "a Victorian of the Victorians", to whom divorce represented social damnation, and since Galsworthy felt for his father the deep affection of Young Jolyon for Old Jolyon, and Ada Galsworthy that ascribed to Irene in *The Indian Summer of a Forsyte*, they decided to forgo inclination for the sake of the old man's peace of mind. For no less than nine years, they snatched such lovers' meetings as Irene and Bosinney, sitting together in the Park, seeking to screen their feelings in company at dinners, dances, the theatre; Galsworthy himself knew the awful longing, the anguish in loving a woman legally compelled to live with another man, the agony at the thought of a woman as "property", which he described in Bosinney of *The Man of Property*. Not till December, 1904 were they released from their secret life by the death of old John Galsworthy; then they went away together to the house at Manaton, near Moretonhampstead, where later they made their country home for many years. There they were shadowed, as Irene and Jolyon were shadowed by Mr. Polteed's employees; on their return to London, they were served with divorce papers, like Irene and Jolyon; like Irene and Jolyon again, they went abroad and were married as soon as the decree *nisi* became absolute.

And thenceforward their lives together were much like Irene's and Jolyon's. Little Jon Forsyte "had never heard his father or his mother speak in an angry voice, either to each other, himself, or anybody else; " from the vast evidence of Mr. Marrot's book and the portraits of Galsworthy by his sister, Mrs. Reynolds, by Herr Leon Schalit, Mr. Herman Ould, and the many friends who wrote of him after his death, it seems that everybody noted this same rare habit in Galsworthy and his wife which Jon observed in his parents. That single sentence carries a wealth of meaning, implying a perfection of happiness, a complete accord, a sympathy and understanding occurring so rarely between man and woman that few have encountered such cases or can imagine their existence. John and Ada Galsworthy found happiness after a long and harrowing test of saddened years, which left them both a legacy of instinctive sympathy with suffering, a burning passion against injustice and oppression, and a sensitive, imaginative consideration for the feelings of their fellow creatures.

In Mr. Marrot's apt phrase, Galsworthy's "was no sensational career; it was rather a progress as well ordered as his own nature." The great adventure of his life was this devotion to a woman, which the world saw announced in the divorce reports as Galsworthy *v.* Galsworthy and Galsworthy; probably the sensational press made salacious play with the evidence of Mr. Polteed's employees, and sex-starved suburbans licked their lips in savouring at second-hand the illicit sweets of "sin". Of Galsworthy more truly than most writers, it may be said that his biography lies in his books, for he wrote always from his heart, with the spontaneous inspiration of a genuine artist. As a man, he belonged to the traditional public-school type described in the short story, "The Man Who Kept His Form", and to the casual observer he presented many of the impressions attributed to Miles Ruding:

> "He was not exactly popular—being reserved, far from showy—but he had no 'side' and never either patronised or abused his juniors . . . He never fell off in 'trials' at the end of a term, and was always playing as hard at the finish of a match as at the start. One would have said he had an exacting conscience, but he was certainly the last person to mention such a thing. He never showed his feeling, yet he never seemed trying to hide them . . . He was greatly respected without seeming to care; an independent, self-dependent bird, who would have cut a greater dash if he hadn't been so, as it were, uncreative . . ."

In appearance, he was neat, clean, finished, with an air of distinction, a self-contained erectness; with his intellectual head, his firm mouth and chin, he looked like the successful barrister of fiction. To the huntresses of literary lions he must have been a perpetual source of disappointment; his manners and bearing corresponded in correctness to his spotless linen—he represented the traditional type of Englishman, very out of fashion in the nineteen-twenties.

I once went to a literary dinner, at which he was the principal speaker, purposely to meet Galsworthy—it was rather more than three years before his death—in November, 1929. He followed at least one after-dinner speaker of no ordinary calibre in the late Lord Moynihan, but he held the attention of his audience with an ease I have never seen equalled by a professional politician. He made no effort at rhetoric, but read his address clearly and expressively from a type-written script; he was an author addressing fellow practitioners of his craft on a subject of professional interest, and he read them an essay which was a polished gem of a master's workmanship. He sat on the chairman's right, with left and right an array of lords and ladies and best-selling novelists; aged twenty-five and the author of one book, I shared a distant small table with a literary colonel, a nondescript lady of almost any age, who spoke only when spoken to and probably wrote stories by passionate sheikhs to support an invalid mother, and an elderly lady of life-long literary traditions who contributed to the *Yellow Book*.

I did not meet Galsworthy. Richard Hughes's *High Wind in Jamaica* had been a recent publishing success, and I missed a golden chance when Mr. R. H. Mottram, attracted by my beard, asked if I was Hughes, with a view to presenting me to Galsworthy. I need not have emulated Bennett's Denry Machin to have secured an introduction through Mr. Mottram, but I merely denied identity with Richard Hughes. Galsworthy escaped early and unobtrusively from the scrum of lionising admirers and autograph collectors, and I followed him out. I stood aside for him to take his coat from the attendant before I took mine; I could have nudged his arm, remarked about the weather—any fool could have opened a conversation. Vanity perhaps deterred me; probably if he asked my name, he would forget it as soon as it was given, and go away remembering me vaguely for a day or two among the brood of cackling hens, who cadged his autograph to show to envious fellow Forsytes. So I watched him leave, neat and erect, carrying his coat over his arm, an elderly man of careless distinction, looking like dozens of others to be seen any night on the pavements of Pall Mall. Yet I wanted to know him more than any other man of letters of his generation; I would rather have known Galsworthy than Bennett, or D. H. Lawrence, or Conrad. Usually writers produce an effect of disappointment when met in the flesh, but somehow I don't think Galsworthy would have produced that effect. For Humbug is the armour in which most artists fortify the bodies of their personalities—not usually sanctimonious Humbug, but the even more irritating pseudo-artistic variety—and Galsworthy was instinctively hostile to Humbug.

Quoting the saying that "no man is a hero to his valet-dechambre," his sister, Mrs. Reynolds, in her *Memories of John Galsworthy*, declares that by contrast "it was most especially to the members of his own family and household that J. G. endeared himself." It might be added that few men, however hailed as heroes by the outside world, seem remarkable to their family circle, and Mrs. Reynolds's tribute gathers force in coming from a sister, than whose eyes none can look with more judicious critical detachment. Her picture of him finds ample verification from the massed evidence of Mr. Marrot's book; it paints a man of essential nobility, of great human as well as artistic conscience, who religiously observed a sense of duty to his fellow creatures while unassumingly producing some of the greatest literary work of his time. Fortune favoured him with ready success besides furnishing the means to keep him forever from want; he was probably the most popular of all genuinely inspired novelists since the European War, universities showered honorary degrees on him, he received several foreign orders and the Nobel Prize for literature, he refused a knighthood during the broadcast issue of 1918. But if he never knew the embittering influence of penury and the depressing want for recognition, success only mellowed his personality.

"Whatever other cares or business might be weighing on his mind, he never let one feel that he was hurried, but gave his time and attention with a beautiful leisureliness that brought a special comfort of its own."

Not only to his own family and friends did he manifest this generosity of patience; none appealed to him in vain, and a letter from Galsworthy was not a secretary's typewritten formality—it was in his own hand, and Mr. Marrot's book reveals the astonishing amount of time he lavished on writing to all sorts of appellants to the bounty of his pocket and his intellect. But even in regard to his own character, he forestalled his biographer in his novels, for Young Jolyon, with his whimsical irony, his self-consciousness, his quizzical detachment, must come very close to self-likeness.

For though the man himself had the reserve of his traditional caste and a natural modesty, which prevented self-revelation or even the involuntary expression of emotion in personal contact, in his art he gave himself unreservedly. The natural integrity of the man compelled complete honesty in the artist, and because he never wrote a line which did not spring from conviction, a study of his books reveals the intellect and personality of their author. But there has been no attempt on the part of surviving relatives to shelter behind this plea; few novelists in history have had the documents of their lives so frankly exposed within a few years after death. There has been none of the pompous suppression, none of the pretentious possessiveness of small-minded relatives ridiculously pretending that a man of genius belongs only to his family, as was the case with most of the Victorians. Galsworthy's good fortune in his career continued after death, and it is evidence of his wife's sympathy and understanding of a man who hated and despised Humbug that, though the full divulgence of his history necessitated the exposure of intimate details relating to herself, she did not hesitate to place the materials in the hands of a biographer. Consequently Mr. Marrot's book bears no relation to the worthless and disingenuous volumes of Victorian "lives and letters"; it may be argued that he made a heavy and unwieldly volume, containing much that might have been omitted without detracting from the clarity of the portrait, but future biographers and critics will bear him a debt of fervent gratitude for preserving in print much correspondence which, in the course of years, may become distantly scattered or irretrievably lost. His book will remain the basis of future biographies of Galsworthy, and meantime supplies a rich source of illuminating commentary and reference in relation to the novels.

§ 2

Some months before love was declared between them—in the spring of 1895—Ada Galsworthy remarked, "Why don't you write? You're just the person."

"I received her remark with the smile of one who knows better. If one has been brought up at an English Public School and University, is addicted to sport and travel, has a small independent income, and is a briefless barrister, one will not take literature seriously; but one may like to please her of whom one is fond. I began. In two years I wrote nine tales. They had every fault. Kiplingesque, crudely expressed, extravagant in theme, deficient in feeling, devoid of philosophy, with the exception of one or two perhaps, they had no temperament."

On the advice of Conrad, his only literary friend, he sent the short stories to Conrad's publisher, T. Fisher Unwin, who published them, at the author's expense, as *From the Four Winds*, by "John Sinjohn," in 1897. He then wrote a short novel, *Jocelyn*, the story of a married man's love for a girl, who renounces him in thinking that their love has caused his wife to commit suicide, but finally discovers her error. On Conrad's advice, he asked a small royalty for this book, but Fisher Unwin wanted to publish again on commission, and Galsworthy took his manuscript to Gerald Duckworth, who agreed to publish at his own risk. Neither book attracted much attention; reviewers saw likenesses in *From the Four Winds* to Kipling, Bret Harte, Crackanthorpe, and Miss Flora Annie Steel, while the *Saturday Review* traced the influence of Henry James in *Jocelyn*. But through Conrad, his work came to the notice of Edward Garnett and Ford Madox Hueffer, who wrote letters of encouragement, and Garnett soon fulfilled the function of critical adviser and mentor as he did to Conrad.

"About this time," wrote Galsworthy, "I began to read the Russian Turgenev (in English) and the Frenchman de Maupassant in French." These were the first writers who gave him æsthetic excitement and an insight into proportion of theme and economy of words. Under these influences, he wrote *Villa Rubein* (1900); "it was more genuine, more atmospheric, better balanced, but still it was not ' written'". In the following year appeared *A Man of Devon*, including, besides the title story, "The Salvation of a Forsyte," "The Silence," and "A Knight," the last of which earned fifteen pounds by publication in a magazine. So "in 1902 after seven years and four books I was still some seventy-five pounds out of pocket, to say nothing of incidental expenses, and had made no name."

The Island Pharisees (1903) was twice re-written, on Garnett's advice; he made about fifty pounds out of it, but it "underwent a thorough Spring-cleaning" before being reprinted in 1908, while he re-wrote *Villa Rubein* and the four tales of *A Man of Devon* for reprinting in 1909. He laboured long and hard over *The Man of Property*, which he again revised, making Bosinney's death accidental instead of suicide, when Garnett objected rightly that suicide by Bosinney would be psychologically false. *The Man of Property* made Galsworthy's name and fame as a novelist in the same year, 1906, as he achieved the first of his many stage successes with the production of *The Silver Box* at the Court Theatre. From his apprenticeship to writing, he deduced the moral that "to begin too young is a mistake".

> "Live first, write afterwards. I had seen, unself-consciously, a good deal of life before I began to write, but even at twenty-eight I began too young. The spiritually stressful years of my life came between then and 1904. That is why *The Island Pharisees* and *The Man of Property* had, in crescendo, so much more depth than the earlier books."

A great work of creative imagination must contain a measure of self-revelation; hence the truth of Galsworthy's argument, since there must be marked personality to be revealed. And the reason that *The Island Pharisees* fell so far short of *The Man of Property* is that it reveals only the author's intellectual ideas, while the latter book sprang from emotional conviction. The "spiritually stressful years" established Galsworthy's character, and imbued him with the sensitive and imaginative understanding of emotional stress which enabled him to become the most universally human novelist of his time. So Dr. H. A. L. Fisher marked the change in him when, having never seen him since they were at Oxford together, he met him again at a performance of *Justice* in 1910: "The cynicism of youth, which was probably quite superficial, had completely fallen away," and "one was sensible only of a quiet depth of character and of a fervent interest in humanitarian causes."

Of his four early books, published under the pseudonym "John Sinjohn", *Villa Rubein* is an interesting Galsworthian relic.

It is the love story of a painter who is rebuffed by his sweetheart's family on account of his lack of worldly goods and conventional ideas. The tale itself is faulty in construction, but the theme is prophetic of Galsworthy's subsequent development. Christian's family are the forerunners of the Forsytes, and, in old Nicholas Treffry, the author achieved the first of that wonderful series of late Victorian portraits which are such a delight in his books.

"There was something at once vast and unobtrusive about his personality. He wore a loose brown velvet jacket, and waistcoat, cut to show a soft frilled shirt and narrow black ribbon tie; a thin gold chain was looped round his neck and fastened to his fob. His heavy cheeks had folds in them like those of a bloodhound's face. He wore big, drooping, yellow-grey moustaches, which he had a habit of sucking, and a goatee beard. He had long loose ears that might almost have been said to flap. On his head there was a soft black hat, large in the brim and low in the crown. His grey eyes, heavy-lidded, twinkled under their bushy brows with a queer, kind cynicism. As a young man he had sown many a wild oat; but he had also worked and made money in business; he had, in fact, burned the candle at both ends; but he had never been unready to do his fellows a good turn. He had a passion for driving, and his reckless method of pursuing this art had caused him to be nicknamed: ' The notorious Treffry '."

The Island Pharisees was his first novel under his own name, and artistically still a failure. It depicts the process of disillusion in a man of the privileged classes, who spends his time in observing life and the social scale, and conducting introspective operations on himself and his acquaintance with the aid of the knowledge thus acquired. Plotless, loosely limned, without life or lustre, the book is the immature effort of a novice, giving no indication of the masterpiece which was to follow only two years later.

The Man of Property was begun in June, 1903, and finished two and a half years later. The plot was based on his own experience —a sensitive wife was to tire of an insensitive husband and seek solace in a grand passion. Irene Forsyte was the personification of feminine beauty; Soames, her husband, the man of property, to whom possession, the desire for possession, and the pleasure in possessing, represented life; while Bosinney, the lover, was not only the conventional artist, the embodiment of all that a woman of Irene's character would desire in a man, but a dramatic foil to Soames. There is nothing original about the rudiments of the plot. In the hands of an ordinary writer, it would resolve itself into one of the countless best-sellers which are the joy of the publisher and the public. But in the hands of the maturing genius, of a consummate artist who was writing from the conviction of his soul, it was resolved into an epoch-making literary event. Unlike the popular writer, Galsworthy did not make Soames a villain of the deepest dye, nor of Bosinney a beautiful Bobadil of a hero. Soames is both the hero and the villain of the piece; he is the central figure about whom the rest of the characters revolve, not in the autobiographical or picaresque fashion, but by a process which has become the approved manner of modern fiction.

Nor was he content with the precise portrayal of his principals. He created a whole family of Forsytes, an unique achievement in the history of fiction. In the case of each, the hand of the dramatist is apparent. He carefully deputes the parts which his characters are to play and turns each one out a finished article. The fastidious Swithin, the shrewd Jolyon, the finicking James, tempestuous June, George the sportsman, all are indelibly stamped upon the reader's imagination by deft dexterity of phrase.

"Close to the window, where he could get more than his fair share of fresh air, the other twin, James—like the bulky Swithin, over six feet in height, but very lean, as though destined from his birth to strike a balance and maintain an average, brooded over the scene with his permanent stoop; his grey eyes had an air of fixed absorption in some secret worry, broken at intervals by a rapid, shifting scrutiny of surrounding facts; his cheeks, thinned by two parallel folds, and a long, clean-shaven upper lip, were framed within Dundreary whiskers. In his hands he turned and turned a piece of china."

We are admitted into the interior lives of the Forsytes, we live and feel with them, and all the time we do not realise that we are being made to think and feel as their author pleases. Galsworthy's satire, a mighty weapon in his armoury, is almost always tempered with a sardonic humour. He is never exuberant nor exaggerated; there is an evenness about his narrative of facts which corresponds to the evenness, the inexorable inevitability of the lives he is describing. He does not preach patently, like Wells, nor does he lose himself in his plot or characters, like Bennett; he leaves his people to explain his lessons to the reader. He is the most real of realists, the perfector of the invention of which Zola was the patentee and George Moore the doubting and doubtful apostle.

Less profound, but more popular, was *The Country House* (1907). Its treatment is almost identical with that of *The Man of Property*, less austere, perhaps, less cruel, but equally convincing. It is a masterpiece of delicate irony. The Pendyces are the spiritual cousins of the Forsytes, though they would be the first to deny even the most remote relationship. They are more intellectual, possessed of more visible virtue, less virile, but similarly bitten by the adder of social convention. Their household god, however, is not so much property as tradition.

Horace Pendyce, in whom the typical country squire is pilloried, is one of the most finished masterpieces in the Galsworthian gallery. Greater still is the Rev. Hussell Barter, a character which is a cruel lampoon on the Church, for which the author was to make some amends a dozen years later in Edward Pierson in *Saint's Progress*. He is drawn from the old type of country cleric, the type which shot and drank port with the squire, whose tolerance told him that "the poor chap can't help his profession", and instilled the fear of God into the common herd, who regarded their spiritual guide, not as God's servant, but as His human personification. His attitude towards the liaison between the squire's son and a married woman, towards his own wife in childbed, towards prayer and his profession, all are described with a neatness, a delicate irony, an unobtrusive attention to detail rarely encountered in any writer. The portrait of Hussell Barter is an exquisite etching, executed with an ecstasy of gusto. Mrs. Pendyce is so true to life that, were it not for the sympathy with which her creator surrounds her, one might suppose that only a woman could have conceived her. She is, to use a word of her own, "delicious".

"At the foot of the breakfast table sat Mrs. Pendyce behind a silver urn that emitted a gentle steam. Her hands worked without ceasing among the cups, and while they worked her lips worked too in spasmodic utterances that never had any reference to herself. Pushed a little to her left and entirely neglected, lay a piece of dry toast on a small white plate. Twice she took it up, buttered a bit of it, and put it down again. Once she rested, and her eyes, which fell on Mrs. Bellew, seemed to say: 'How very charming you look, my dear!' Then, taking up the sugar-tongs, she began again."

Paramor, the lawyer, would be Dickensian were he less immaculate, and Charles Pendyce may still be seen any fine day in the neighbourhood of Pall Mall for—damme—do not he and his kind always live there, close to their clubs?

The spaniel John, however, is a product peculiar to Galsworthy. Surely no other novelist has ever understood dogs quite so well. The dog Balthazar, young Jolyon's *protégé* and old Jolyon's companion, the moonlight-coloured Miranda, the Hilary Dallisons' lady bulldog, the mandarin Ting-a-ling in *The White Monkey*, and its successor in Fleur Mont's affections, the Dandie Dinmont, are all treated with more than the care bestowed by many authors on leading human characters. Which is, after all, proof positive of an extraordinary understanding of the canine species, for dogs have more Christian qualities than most humans.

The plot of *The Country House* is facile and flexible. Everything hinges on George Pendyce's affair with Helen Bellew. Again Galsworthy chose a theme which has been done to death by almost every gimcrack juggler with the romantic novel. It is as though he wished to make manifest his superiority over his contemporaries by meeting them on their own ground with their own weapons. Superficially, the treatment is completely conventional. The story has such an even tenor, it is so easy to negotiate, that one does not notice the ground covered. Galsworthy is like a highly-powered Rolls-Royce limousine; when you journey with him, you move so smoothly that you do not realise the rapid rate at which you are travelling.

In the average novel, the characters are subservient to the plot, but clean contrary is the case with the creator of *The Country House*, for the story serves simply to illustrate the individuals. Perhaps it is on this account that certain critics have condemned the author as a sociologist and a doctrinaire, but it is here that the realist supervenes and the romanticist retires. Galsworthy was not a purveyor of pretty stories. He applied the lessons learned from Ibsen to the novel just as he did to the drama. He subjugated the scheme of the novel, and made it dance at his direction to his own tune. The Pendyces, Hussell Barter, and the spaniel John are alive to us by means of the plot of *The Country House*. They are incipiently sketched for us, but they develop themselves by their thoughts and actions throughout the length and breadth of the story. By the time you arrive at the end of the tale, if you were introduced to Mr. Barter at afternoon tea, if you saw General Pendyce in the Royal Automobile Club, if you went to Mr. Paramor to draft your will, if you met Horace Pendyce at a September shoot, you would recognise each without a moment's hesitation, and feel that you had known them very well at a more or less distant date.

In *Fraternity*, which appeared two years later, the tone is more sombre, the satire as pungent but less penetrating in quality, and the characterisation less classical. From the point of view of construction, it is less successful than either of its immediate predecessors, mainly on account of its lack of utter unity. The interest is not concentrated, and there is no sort of close connection between the various individuals and scenes or action. Social contrast was to be reflected more realistically and far more admirably in *The White Monkey*. Most of the minor characters are plausible, though not particularly impressive, but the elaborate, if slightly exaggerated, Sylvanus Stone, and the little newsvendor, "name of Creed," who had once been a butler, belong as essentially to Galsworthy as Micawber and Mr. Jingle to Dickens. Bianca, the woman of Leonardo da Vinci, suffers from the absence of vigour in outline, but has sympathy and fragrance, and Hilary Dallison is a triumph compared with Shelton in

The Island Pharisees. The tragedy of their married life is terribly manifest, the reader being purged with pity to a degree that would have delighted Aristotle himself. They are defeated by their refined sense of humour. They are both perfunctorily proud. The scene of their conjugal chamber where their natural are vanquished by their intellectual selves might easily, if treated with less discriminating directness and delicacy, have developed into farce, but so stark and staccato is the realistic touch that the effect is one of infinite pathos verging on real tragedy. He finds her waiting for him one night when he returns home:

"' Has the wind gone round? My room is cold.'

"' Yes, north-east. Stay here.'

"Her hand touched his; that warm and restless clasp was agitating.

"' It's good of you to ask me; but we'd better not begin what we can't keep up.'

"' Stay here,' said Hilary again, kneeling down beside her chair.

"And suddenly he began to kiss her face and neck. He felt her answering kisses; for a moment they were clasped together in a fierce embrace. Then, as though by mutual consent, their arms relaxed; their eyes grew furtive, like the eyes of children who have egged each other on to steal, and on their lips appeared the faintest of faint smiles. It was as though those lips were saying: ' Yes, but we are not quite animals! '"

"Hilary got up and sat down on his bed. Bianca stayed in the chair, looking straight before her, utterly inert, her head thrown back, her white throat gleaming, on her lips and in her eyes that flickering smile. Not a word more, nor a look, passed between them.

"Then rising, without noise, she passed behind him and went out."

As he had done with the upper middle-class in *The Man of Property*, with the landed gentry in *The Country House*, so Galsworthy attempted to do with the aristocracy in *The Patrician*. Once more he took a comparatively hackneyed plot for his purpose, the married woman living apart from her husband, suitably toned to meet the situation required. Where George Pendyce's troubles are founded upon petty convention, however, Miltoun's cup of bitterness is brimmed with higher reputation. The result is infinitely more sentimental and far less patent to sardonic satire, on which grounds, doubtless, one unkind contemporary declared that the book might have been written by Mrs. Humphry Ward. Another critic who, hailing the author as "our first English writer", likened it to "a beautiful frieze on marble", was nearer the mark. It is an achievement, its execution is perfect, but it is coldly lacking in virility. Perhaps the author was in awe of the delicate situation in which he had placed himself and his creatures, perhaps it is the extreme correctness of its setting— possibly the most poignant satire in the book—perhaps for once he let the plot run away with him. One of the most romantic and least realistic of his works, were it less sincere and more artificial, it might almost have been modelled on Disraeli.

In *The Dark Flower*, Galsworthy essayed an exhibition of the effect of love upon an artistic temperament. Here we find him writing prose as well as ever, charming us with philosophy and fancy, intriguing us by technique and turn of phrase. But we miss the crystallised characterisation, the compact plot, the inimitable satire, the sociological subjective. Disconnected and discursive, the book reveals a backsliding in craftsmanship. Mark Lennan, the subject of this amorous biography, neither convinces nor captures our affections. In the flower of his youth, he is only caddish and priggish in his affair with his tutor's wife. In the maturity of his summer, when he finds the object of his great love in a young married woman, he appears, not as the artist, but the man of property. Again he is a cad, and he is still a cad when, in middle life, he plays with the immature affections of his old school-friend's daughter, and finally assumes himself the victim of his own virtue by retiring beyond the tentacles of temptation behind the skirts of his colourless wife. We are spared the vision of his winter, which could only be that of a senile and liquorish curmudgeon.

In *The Freelands*, Galsworthy found an outlet for what Arnold Bennett once called his "extraordinary passionate cruelty towards the oppressors as distinguished from the oppressed" by turning his attention to the land. Here there is abundant scope for sociological dictum and doughty satire. As in *The Country House*, the legal profession is subjected to a ridicule as discriminating as it is deserved, the flamboyance of youth is admirably assimilated, and in Felix Freeland is found another figure of hovering scepticism, alternating between desired optimism and instinctive pessimism. But the climax, which should be devastating, misses fire. The fuse has burned itself out, almost as though it has been incorrectly timed. The tragedy of Tryst is strained, we have lost sympathy with Sheila and Derek, we are impatient with Nedda, we find in Tod a candidate for mental treatment, and Kirsteen so bizarre as to be a bore.

When we plunge into *Beyond*, we experience a shock like leaping into a cold bath, for we are back with the great Galsworthy, the dramatic realist who impresses with infinite distinction, sympathy, and power. Gyp and her father, Fiorsen, Count Rosek, Bryan Summerhay, Hotspur the horse, Pettance and Betty, all are masterpieces minutely perfect. The tale is rightly designated a narrative, for the plan is distorted and by no means faultless in form, but as a tale, it is an epic, echoing with sonorous grandeur, vibrant with vigour and subtleties, a *tableau vivant* of human vanities and circumstance.

Searching sidelights on the war are to be found among Galsworthy's short stories, but *Saint's Progress* alone of his novels has its action in the war period. Even so, it is not a novel of the war; it cannot be classed as war literature. The problem of the war baby is exploited as an excuse for satire and raillery, sincere sympathy being lavished upon the unmarried mother. But the story is incidental to, illustrative of, the main object, which is the progress of the saint. The latter is the only convincing character in the story, but the fact that he does convince is an auspicious achievement, since he is an institution personified, being emblematic of the literal doctrine of the church. We are shown his inability to grasp the problems of the war, much less grapple with them, his apparently wilful obtuseness, his firm futility. When one of his daughters is about to be parted from her lover, perhaps for the last time, and the husband of the other is at death's door:

"He went to the bare narrow little room he had occupied ever since his wife died; and, taking off his boots, walked up and down, with a feeling of almost crushing loneliness. Both his daughters in such trouble, and he of no use to them! It was as if Life were pushing him utterly aside! He felt confused, helpless, bewildered. Surely if Gratian loved George, she had not left God's side, whatever she might say. Then, conscious of the profound heresy of this thought, he stood still at the open window.

"Earthly love—heavenly love; was there any analogy between them?

"From the Square Gardens the indifferent whisper of the leaves answered; and a newsvendor at the far end, bawling his nightly tale of murder."

It is a sad picture, this illustration of a moribund institution, the more so because we are made to sympathise with his short-comings and respect him for his blind, useless belief. That we sympathise with Pierson provides a tribute to Galsworthy's genius in drawing character, for we can feel only contempt for an institution which fails in its function from sheer lack of intellectual vitality.

Galsworthy reckoned the happiest day of his writing life to have been a July Sunday in Devon during 1918, "when it suddenly came to me that I could go on with my Forsytes, and complete their history in two more volumes with a link between." That summer he had published *Five Tales*, including—besides *A Stoic*, that inimitable portrait of old Sylvanus Heythorp, the hearty old boy who cheated his creditors by enjoying such a dinner as his soul loved, which became the celebrated play, *Old English*— *Indian Summer of a Forsyte*, the story of Old Jolyon's idyll with Irene and his death, and the praise this story won from such friends as Conrad, Thomas Hardy, and William Archer, probably inspired the idea of further Forsyte chronicles. By January, 1921, when he had just finished *To Let*, he had decided that "*The Forsyte Saga*, when published in one volume containing *The Man of Property*, *Indian Summer of a Forsyte*, *In Chancery*, *Awakening*, and *To Let*, will be my passport, however difficult it may be to get it viséd, for the shores of permanence."

The succeeding seventeen years have revealed that all Galsworthy's novels will possess permanent interest. He alone of all novelists since the death of Dickens commands attention from all sections of the reading public—from the ultra-highbrow intelligentsia, who belittle Galsworthy as they belittle Thackeray and Dickens, while professing to exalt above them as novelists such as Peacock and Pater and George Moore, and equally from the confiding females who ask the circulating library attendants for "a nice book"—as a national novelist in the grand tradition of Fielding, Thackeray, Dickens. *Fraternity* and *The Freelands* may find no more readers than *Bleak House* and *Little Dorrit*, *Saint's Progress* and *The Patrician* may remain mere names to many of the tolerably well-read like *Philip* and *Lovel the Widower*, but *The Country House* will hold a place like *Nicholas Nickleby* and *The Newcomes*, and there is no doubt that *The Forsyte Saga* will stand forever among the handful of masterpieces which includes *Tom Jones*, *Vanity Fair*, and *Pickwick*. Mr. Marrot describes the publication of *The Forsyte Saga* in 1922—the first of the "omnibus" volumes which have become a feature of post-war publishing, and a novelist's device to achieve the massive dignity of the Victorian novel while still conforming with the limitations of the short modern novel—as "the last of the turning-points in Galsworthy's career".

"For sixteen years his name had been a household word amongst the intelligent and advanced; but it was not till this (at that time unprecedented) publishing achievement brought home to the great public the majesty and the intimate achievement of the Saga that he became in any real sense a popular writer. His eminence was already unquestioned both at home and abroad . . . but it was only now, as a direct result of the one-volume *Saga*, that he became a 'best-seller'."

In a matter of months a hundred thousand copies were sold both in England and America; during the bookselling boom of 1929, copies of the first English edition, though the first issue must have numbered ten thousand, were catalogued at twenty-five pounds. Thenceforward Galsworthy held a world-wide reputation and an undisputed supremacy such as no English writer had achieved since Dickens.

In Chancery (1920) takes its name from the legal condition of Soames and Irene at the outset of the story in 1900; for fourteen years, since she left him after Bosinney's death, they have lived apart, but as neither has sought divorce, they remain man and wife in the eyes of the law. Soames now feels an urgent need for a son and heir to inherit his property; he has an eye on Annette, the pretty daughter of a French restaurant-proprietress, but recoiling from the scandal of the divorce necessary to obtain legal possession of her, he seeks reconciliation with Irene, who feels nausea at the idea. She seeks advice from no-longer-Young Jolyon, her trustee under Old Jolyon's will, love develops between the widower of fifty and the beautiful woman of thirty-eight, they are driven together by Soames's pursuit of Irene, and finally Soames "takes steps". Following divorce, Irene marries Jolyon and Soames his Annette, and there is a flutter "on Forsyte 'Change" at Timothy's in the Bayswater Road when Irene gives birth to a son much too soon after marriage. Such is the main theme, but there is much besides. Soames has many other worries; his brother-in-law Montague Dartie, the prize bounder, exceeds "the limit" by going off with his wife's pearls and a Spanish dancer; declining to plead cruelty or adultery for her children's sake, Winifred Dartie sues for restitution of conjugal rights as a prelude to divorce; her son Val Dartie falls in love with Jolyon's daughter Holly. Above all, there is old James Forsyte, approaching second childhood and worrying because "nobody tells me anything", a continual source of trouble to Soames because "James mustn't be told" anything of the woes besetting his family. When Winifred informs her mother of Dartie's return, they agree it's "no good fussing" and Emily undertakes to tell James, but then they "see the disaster in the corridor".

"There, attracted by light from a room never lighted, James was standing with his dun-coloured camel-haired shawl folded about him, so that his arms were not free and his silvered head looked cut off from his fashionably trousered legs as if by an expanse of desert. He stood, inimitably stork-like, with an expression as if he saw before him a frog too large to swallow.

"'What's all this?' he said. 'Tell your father? You never tell me anything.'

"The moment found Emily without reply. It was Winifred who went up to him, and laying one hand on each of his swathed helpless arms, said:

"'Monty's not gone bankrupt, Father. He's only come back.'

"They all three expected something serious to happen, and were glad she had kept that grip of his arms, but they did not know the depth of root in that shadowy old Forsyte. Something wry occurred about his shaven mouth and chin, something scratchy between those long silvery whiskers. Then he said with a sort of dignity: 'He'll be the death of me. I knew how it would be.'

"'You mustn't worry, Father,' said Winifred calmly. 'I mean to make him behave.'

"'Ah,' said James. 'Here, take this thing off, I'm hot.' They unwound the shawl. He turned, and walked firmly to the dining-room."

James, of *In Chancery*, ranks among the greatest minor characters in all fiction; perhaps Galsworthy's greatest triumph in imaginative psychology appears in the gradual progress of the ageing Soames in the later books towards the likeness of his father. *In Chancery* is a great book—much greater than *The Man of Property* because greater in scale of design. The several themes blend in wonderful adroitness, each illustrating and intensifying another, and few novels in modern times compare in perfect mastery of construction. It is the first of Galsworthy's novels revealing in full magnificence the maturity of his genius; all his subsequent books possess the same play of exquisite irony, the same illuminative power of narrative, flexibility of phrase, skill in construction and characterisation, the same uncanny faculty of observation.

Linked to *In Chancery* by *Awakening*, an idyllic study of the childhood of Irene's son, *To Let* (1922) shows the Forsytes in the first years after the war. All the eldest generation are dead, except Timothy, who lives in his bedroom, taking "nice exercise between his bed and the window in the morning, not to risk a change of air", and so sedulously guarded by Cook and Smither that he does not know there has been a war. The story has the unity of *The Man of Property*; it is the tale of ill-fated love between Fleur, the daughter of Soames, and Jon, son of Jolyon and Irene. Fleur, true daughter of the man of property, fighting tenaciously to win possession of her lover in defiance of all opposition, presents the type of the immediate post-war girl, and her portrait in this book and the subsequent trilogy ranks among the finest in Galsworthy's gallery. The old feud proves too strong for the young lovers, though the struggle causes the death of no-longer-Young Jolyon, and with Jon seeking forgetfulness abroad with Irene and Fleur marrying the heir to a title, the Saga ends, with Bosinney's fateful house at Robin Hill "to let".

"' To Let '—the Forsyte age and way of life, when a man owned his soul, his investments, and his woman without check or question. And now the State had, or would have, his investments, his woman had herself, and God knew who had his soul. ' To Let '—that sane and simple creed!"

In the preface to *The Forsyte Saga*, Galsworthy wrote:

"Looking back on the Victorian era, whose ripeness, decline, and ' fall-off ' is in some sort pictured in *The Forsyte Saga*, we see now that we have but jumped out of a frying-pan into a fire. It would be difficult to substantiate a claim that the state of England was better in 1913 than it was in 1886, when the Forsytes assembled at Old Jolyon's to celebrate the engagement of June to Philip Bosinney. And in 1920, when again the clan gathered to bless the marriage of Fleur with Michael Mont, the state of England is as surely too molten and bankrupt as in the eighties it was too congealed and low-percented."

His remaining books mirrored the contemporary "molten and bankrupt" period of the nineteen-twenties, a period subsequent to the scope of this present book, which seeks to leave literature as it looked on the bookstalls of 1914. Producing his novels at regular intervals of two years, Galsworthy completed two more trilogies before his death on 31st January, 1933. *A Modern Comedy* comprises the second Forsyte trilogy, *The White Monkey* (1924), *The Silver Spoon* (1926), and *Swan Song* (1928), all dealing with the fortunes of Fleur and Soames, who dies fighting to save his most valued property, his collection of pictures, from a fire ignited by the carelessness of his beloved daughter in her anguish of thwarted love, and by his death assures Fleur's safety from the danger of throwing her cap over the windmill. These books find vent for mellow social satire; in the first, Fleur's husband, a type of the post-war young man as Fleur represents the post-war young woman, begins his career of "doing his bit" to fulfil the politician's promise of "a country fit for heroes to live in", while Fleur plays with fire in flirtation with his best friend, and their matrimonial problems find contrast with those of the little consumptive packer, who sells balloons after losing his job through "snooping" books, and his wife, who precipitates a crisis by earning money for their emigration as an artist's model. The second shows young Mont's further endeavours, as an M.P. and champion of the land, while Soames is harrowed by the implication of his daughter in a society scandal, and the third re-introduces Jon Forsyte to renew Fleur's ill-starred passion, ending with Soames's splendid exit from earthly tribulation. These books introduce another great character in Mont's father, the "tittupping" baronet who supplies a foil to Soames, and he led Galsworthy to the creation of a new family, the Cherrells, who provide the *dramatis personæ* of his last trilogy, *End of the Chapter*, comprising *Maid in Waiting* (1931), *Flowering Wilderness* (1932), and *Over the River* (1933), which tell the story of Dinny Cherrell, another type of the modern girl, born of the dying aristocratic class.

§ 3

Before *The Forsyte Saga* established him above the range of the critics' pop-guns—Mr. Marrot fairly remarks that, after *In Chancery*, Galsworthy was "securely ' taped ' by the critics, and to the end of the chapter they went on saying the same things about him"—Galsworthy was accused of being obsessed by a social economy, of writing with his obsession as his object, of being unable to focus his powers of observation on the human character owing to the myopia arising from the mists of his obsession. He was declared narrow in his sympathies, incapable of artistry on account of his incessant craving for justice and reason, a slave to types instead of individuals. The objection strangely echoes Lang's old complaint that psychology should be confined to treatises and fiction to the romantic fields of a never-never land.

That Galsworthy closely studied sociology provided the substance, not the chinks, of his armour. He approached the science of life, as he approached the art of the novel, as a serious student earnestly striving to acquire mastery of his subject. And the success of both studies enabled him to achieve a measure of perfection in the realistic novel unapproached by his precise contemporaries and immediate predecessors. Twenty years before Galsworthy began, George Moore, crude and uncouth, sensed the possibilities of the novel as a mirror of life, but failed in any very considerable achievement on account of his third-rate talent, his overweening vanity, and his lack of sincere sympathy with humanity. Stevenson, an instinctive artist, clearly visualised the same possibilities, but force of circumstances defeated his pursuit of his convictions. Henry James, the great teacher of the novelist's art, lost himself in theory and allowed the fascination of psychology to obscure his humanity of outlook. Writers like Mrs. Humphry Ward and H. G. Wells fairly offered themselves to the charge of obsession with a social economy, using fiction as a medium for their sermons and treatises. Arnold Bennett partially succeeded, but he valued his mastery of the art of fiction as the trick of a card, and lacked the profound knowledge of life and faculty of universal sympathy necessary for the highest achievement.

Galsworthy alone attained to the fullest expression of the theories of the art of fiction which haunted the consciences of nearly all writers between 1887 and 1914. He attained to his achievement because he strove always conscientiously after the truest artistic expression, while approaching the problems of humanity with imaginative sympathy. In the preface to *The Forsyte Saga*, he denies that he attempted "a scientific study of a period", but "rather an intimate incarnation of the disturbance that Beauty effects in the lives of men".

"The figure of Irene, never, as the reader may possibly have noticed, present, except through the senses of other characters, is a concretion of disturbing Beauty impinging on a possessive world."

The devastating effect of Beauty the forces of Respectability affected to ignore; they deprecated any manifestation of appreciating Beauty, as they deprecated a man's confession that he kept a mistress—it was a departure from convention, of which it was not good form to speak. Beauty intruded uncomfortably on their consciousness, like a vice to be avoided; they craved it, yet feared the craving, and the strong-minded avoided its indulgence while the weak furtively dallied with makeshifts. *The Man of Property* interpreted this craving, and by treating Soames sympathetically, making him an object of pity instead of execration, Galsworthy won the huge franchise of thousands of people of property who secretly knew the same problems.

In 1906 *The Man of Property* was a revolutionary book, for it not merely advocated the liberty of the individual woman to live her own life, like such books as *The Woman Who Did*, but introduced speculation on a woman's reactions to sexual commerce. Shrewdly Bennett expressed the opinion that "the erotic parts —and there are plenty of them—were done under the influence of George Moore". No evidence forthcoming from Galsworthy's biography suggests that he ever felt Moore's influence, but he served his apprenticeship under the same influences as Moore. In the work of Galsworthy, the aims after which Moore strove clumsily and incapably, found fruition; they were the same aims to which every serious novelist of the time aspired, but were mostly hindered by fashionable Humbug from attempting.

Though *The Man of Property* ventured upon an erotic subject, its treatment presented no possible grounds for offence. By presenting Irene only through the senses of the other characters, Galsworthy evaded the perils of frankness. Nine years later, *The Rainbow* of D. H. Lawrence, also dealing with a woman's sexual reactions, was banned, because Lawrence treated his woman subjectively instead of objectively. *The Man of Property* dealt a trenchant blow at the foundations of Respectability and Humbug by asserting the right to freedom of artistic expression in relation to the natural facts of life, but the old gods had not yet finally fallen when Lawrence ventured to speak more plainly. The war finally swept them away, along with many other traditions of Forsyteism, and *The Rainbow* was marketed in a cheap edition in the nineteen-twenties.

The modern Englishman displays a tendency to brag of his freedom, when echoing his grandfather's satisfaction with "enlightened democracy" in derisive contrast with the tyrannous dictatorships prevalent elsewhere in Europe. Truly he pays in all sorts of taxation more heavily for his privileges than any of the vassals of history. The popular press brags even more loudly of its freedom, though every intelligent person realises that he reads in any particular paper only so much as its proprietor deems reasonably good for him to know—and in another paper he may find that its proprietor has other views on his amelioration. Books are the only comparatively unfettered mediums of expression. Some publishers have their foibles and personal prejudices, but all are eager and willing to publish anything likely to be profitable, regardless of political, sectarian, or social bias, and there are many prepared to risk slight profit for the privilege of publishing genuinely inspired books of limited appeal. Never in the history of fiction have there been so many competent novelists and novels as in the period since 1918, when the old gods of Respectability, Prudery, and Humbug were overthrown; either the past nineteen years have been "the golden age of fiction" which Bennett foresaw, or they were the prelude to the golden age. However that may be, the moral emerges in warning, as wholesomely as from a late-Victorian novel: let English writers and readers zealously cherish the freedom so long and hardly fought for and won—let there be no return to the irritant vexation of the 'nineties or the arid sterility of the 'eighties. The old gods are fallen, and may they never be reinstated in abominable idolatry!

THE END

LIST OF ACKNOWLEDGMENTS

A BOOKSELLER'S catalogue would be required to enumerate the volumes incidentally mentioned, or even discussed in some detail, in the foregoing pages. The following list is intended to indicate only the sources from which illustrative quotations in the text have been taken, and the respective owners of copyright in the sources quoted are requested to accept the writer's grateful acknowledgment of his indebtedness to the works here listed.

ALLEN, GRANT—*The British Barbarians* (London, John Lane, 1895); *The Woman Who Did* (London, John Lane, 1895).
(See also CLODD, EDWARD.)

ATHERTON, GERTRUDE—*Adventures of a Novelist* (London, Cape, 1932).

BENNETT, ARNOLD—*Accident* (London, Cassell, 1929); *Books and Persons* (London, Chatto, 1917); *Denry the Audacious* (*The Card*) (New York, Dutton, 1911); *Hilda Lessways* (London, Methuen, 1911); *Journals*, Edited by Newman Flower (London, new ed., Cassell, 1932-33); *Leonora* (London, Chatto, 1912); *The Regent* (London, Methuen, 1913); *The Truth About an Author* (London, Methuen, new ed., 1928); *Whom God Hath Joined* (London, Nutt, 1906).
(See also BENNETT, D. C. and M., PRIESTLEY, and SIMONS).

BLUNT, WILFRED SCAWEN—*My Diaries* (London, Secker, 1932).

BENNETT, DOROTHY CHESTON—*Arnold Bennett* (London, Cape, 1935).

BENNETT, MARGUERITE—*Arnold Bennett* (London, Philpot, 1925).

CAINE, SIR HALL—*My Story* (London, Heinemann, 1908); *The Manxman* (London, Heinemann, 1894); *The Prodigal Son* (London, Heinemann, 1904).

CHRISTIE, O. F.—*The Transition to Democracy, 1867-1914* (London, Routledge, 1934).

CLODD, EDWARD—*Grant Allen: A Memoir* (London, Grant Richards, 1900); *Memories* (London, Watts, 1926).

COLLINS, JOHN CHURTON—*Ephemera Critica* (London, Constable, 1901).

COLLINS, WILKIE—*The Woman in White.*

COLVIN, SIDNEY—*The Colvins and Their Friends,* by E. V. Lucas (London, Methuen, 1928); *Robert Louis Stevenson: Letters to His Family and Friends* (London, Methuen, 2 vols., 1899); *Memories and Notes* (London, Arnold, 1921).

CORELLI, MARIE—*Wormwood* (London, Bentley, 1891).

CORNFORD, L. COPE—*W. E. Henley* (London, Constable, 1913).

DISRAELI, BENJAMIN—*Sybil.*

FREEMAN, JOHN—*A Portrait of George Moore in a Study of His Work* (London, Werner Laurie, 1922).

GALSWORTHY, JOHN—*Caravan* (London, Heinemann, 1925); *Castles in Spain* (London, Heinemann, 1927); *The Country House* (London, Heinemann, new ed., 1926); *The Forsyte Saga* (London, Heinemann, 1922); *Fraternity* (London, Heinemann, new ed., 1925); *Saint's Progress* (London, Heinemann, 1919); *Villa Rubein* (London, Duckworth, new ed., 1920).
(See also MARROT and REYNOLDS.)

GISSING, GEORGE—*The Letters of George Gissing to Members of his Family,* Ed. Algernon and Ellen Gissing (London, Constable, 1927).

GORDON, G. S.—Article on Andrew Lang in *Dictionary of National Biography* (Oxford University Press).

GOSSE, SIR EDMUND—*Life and Letters of Sir Edmund Gosse, C.B.,* by the Hon. Evan Charteris, K.C. (London, Heinemann, 1931); *Silhouettes* (London, Heinemann, 1925).

GRIBBLE, FRANCIS—*Seen in Passing* (London, Benn, 1929).

HAGGARD, SIR H. RIDER—*Allan's Wife* (London, Longmans, new ed., 1909); *Dawn* (London, Longmans, new ed., 1894); *The Days of My Life,* Ed. C. J. Longman (London, Longmans, 2 vols., 1926); *Nada the Lily* (London, Longmans, 1892); *The People of the Mist* (London, Longmans, 1894).

HARRIS, FRANK—*On Bernard Shaw* (London, Gollancz, 1931).

HENLEY, WILLIAM ERNEST—*Views and Reviews* (London, Macmillan, 1921).
(See also CORNFORD.)

HEWLETT, MAURICE—*The Letters of Maurice Hewlett,* Ed. Laurence Binyon (London, Methuen, 1926); *The Stooping Lady* (London, Macmillan, 1907).

HOLMES, SIR RICHARD, K.C.V.O.—*Edward VII.: His Life and Times* (London, Amalgamated Press, 1910).

HONE, JOSEPH—*The Life of George Moore* (London, Gollancz, 1936).

HOPE, ANTHONY—*The Dolly Dialogues* (London, Westminster Gazette, 1896); *The King's Mirror* (London, Methuen, 1899); *Quisanté* (London, Nelson, cheap ed., n.d.). (See also MALLET.)

HORNUNG, E. W.—*A Thief in the Night* (London, Harrap, 1926).

HUEFFER, FORD MADOX—*The Critical Attitude* (London, Duckworth, 1911).

JAMES, HENRY—*The Letters of Henry James*, Ed. Percy Lubbock (London, Macmillan, 2 vols., 1920).

LANG, ANDREW—*Adventures Among Books* (London, Longmans, 1905); *At the Sign of the Ship*, monthly papers in *Longman's Magazine*, vols. vii. to xlvi. (London, Longmans, 1886-1905); *Essays in Little* (London, Henry, 1891). (See also CLODD, *Memories*, and GORDON.)

LE GALLIENNE, RICHARD—*Rudyard Kipling: A Criticism* (London, John Lane, 1900); *George Meredith: Some Characteristics* (London, John Lane, 6th ed., 1905); *Retrospective Reviews: A Literary Log* (London, John Lane, 2 vols., 1896).

LOCKE, WILLIAM J.—*At the Gate of Samaria* (London, John Lane, 1895); *The Coming of Amos* (London, John Lane, 1924); *The Morals of Marcus Ordeyne* (London, John Lane, 1905).

" LONDON MERCURY "—*Editorial Notes*, by Sir John Squire, v.d.

" LONGMAN'S MAGAZINE "—Volumes I. to XLVI. (London, Longmans, 1882-1905).

LUCAS, E. V.—*The Colvins and Their Friends* (London, Methuen, 1928).

MALLET, SIR CHARLES—*Anthony Hope and His Books* (London, Hutchinson, n.d.).

MARROT, H. V.—*The Life and Letters of John Galsworthy* (London, Heinemann, 1935).

MAY, J. LEWIS—*John Lane and the Nineties* (London, John Lane, 1936).

McCARTHY, JUSTIN—*A Short History of Our Own Times* (London, Chatto, 1915).

MEREDITH, GEORGE—*Letters of George Meredith*, Ed. by his son (London, Constable, 2 vols., 1912).

MERRIMAN, HENRY SETON—*The Slave of the Lamp* (London, John Murray, 1919). (This, the first volume of the Collected Works, contains a Biographical Note, signed E. F. S. and S. G. T.)

MITCHELL, SUSAN L.—*George Moore* (New York, Dodd, Mead, 1916).

MOORE, GEORGE—*Celibates* (London, Walter Scott, 1895); *A Drama in Muslin* (London, Walter Scott, n.d.); *Evelyn Innes* (London, Fisher Unwin, 1898); *Impressions and Opinions* (London, Werner Laurie, 1913); *Spring Days* (London, Vizetelly, 1888); *Vain Fortune* (London, Walter Scott, 1895). Other works by George Moore quoted, including *Confessions of a Young Man* and the trilogy of *Hail and Farewell*, are now obtainable in the Ebury Edition of his works (London, Heinemann).
(See also FREEMAN, HONE, MITCHELL, WOLFE.)

PRIESTLEY, J. B.—*Figures in Modern Literature* (London, John Lane, new ed., 1928).

QUILLER-COUCH, SIR ARTHUR—*Adventures in Criticism* (Cambridge University Press, new ed., 1926).

REYNOLDS, M. E.—*Memories of John Galsworthy* (London, Robert Hale, 1936).

RICHARDS, GRANT—*Author Hunting* (London, Hamish Hamilton, 1934); *Memories of a Misspent Youth* (London, Heinemann, 1932).

ROTHENSTEIN, SIR WILLIAM—*Men and Memories* (London, Faber, 1931).

SCHREINER, OLIVE—*The Story of an African Farm*, by Ralph Iron (Olive Schreiner) (London, Chapman and Hall, new ed., 1892).

SIMONS, J. B.—*Arnold Bennett and His Novels* (Oxford, Blackwell, 1936).

STEUART, JOHN A.—*Letters to Living Authors* (London, Sampson Low, 1890); *Robert Louis Stevenson: Man and Writer* (London, Sampson Low, 2 vols., 1924).

STEVENSON, ROBERT LOUIS—*The Art of Writing* (London, Chatto, 1905); *Essays Literary and Critical* (London, Heinemann—Tusitala Edition); *Familiar Studies of Men and Books* (London, Chatto, 1920); *Memories and Portraits* (London, Chatto, 1895); *Plays* (London, Heinemann—Tusitala Edition—contains prefatory note by Lloyd Osbourne); *The Stories of Robert Louis Stevenson* (London, Gollancz, 1928); *Weir of Hermiston* (London, Chatto, 1896); *Vailima Letters* (London, Methuen, 1901); *Virginibus Puerisque* (London, Chatto, 1888).
(See also COLVIN and STEUART.)

SYMONDS, JOHN ADDINGTON—*Letters and Papers*, Ed. Horatio F. Brown (London, John Murray, 1923).

TOMLINSON, H. M.—*All Our Yesterdays* (London, Heinemann, 1930).

WARD, MRS. HUMPHRY—*Helbeck of Bannisdale* (London, Smith, Elder, 1898); *A Writer's Recollections* (London, Collins, 1918); *The Life of Mrs. Humphry Ward*, by her daughter, Janet Penrose Trevelyan (London, Constable, 1923).

WELLS, H. G.—*Experiment in Autobiography* (London, Gollancz and the Cresset Press, 2 vols., 1934); *The History of Mr. Polly* (London, Nelson, 1910).

WEYMAN, STANLEY J.—Collected Edition (London, John Murray).

"WHO'S WHO"—Volumes for 1905 and 1927 (London, A. and C. Black).

WOLFE, HUMBERT.—*George Moore* (London, Thornton Butterworth, new ed., 1933).

"YELLOW BOOK, THE"—13 vols., April, 1894, to April, 1897 (London, John Lane).

N.B.—For kind permission to make the more extensive quotations from the works of George Moore, the author is gratefully indebted to Messrs. Field Roscoe & Co.; for Stevenson, to Mr. Lloyd Osbourne; for Andrew Lang and Rider Haggard to Messrs. Longmans Green and Co.; for John Galsworthy, to Mrs. Galsworthy.

INDEX